THE UNHOLY ALLIANCE

THE UNHOLY ALLIANCE

C. GREGG SINGER

ARLINGTON HOUSE·PUBLISHERS
NEW ROCHELLE, N. Y.

Library of Congress Cataloging in Publication Data

Singer, Charles Gregg, 1910-
    The unholy alliance.

    Bibliography: p.
    Includes index.
    1. National Council of the Churches of Christ in the United States of America. 2. Federal Council of the Churches of Christ in America. I. Title.
BX6.N2S56   262'.001   75-11478
ISBN 0-87000-327-5

Contents

Preface

In spite of the fact that the twentieth century has witnessed a vast increase of interest in ecclesiastical history on the part of American historians, no history of either the Federal or the National Council of Churches has been written except by a few apologists of the ecumenical movement. This failure is all the more remarkable because of the controversial character of the Federal Council and its successor, the National Council, which was formed late in 1951 for the purpose of making the ecumenical movement a more effective instrument for the realization of the movement's goals in this country.

Only two ecclesiastical leaders arose to the defense of the Federal Council of Churches and no one has yet risen to accept a similar challenge in behalf of its beleaguered successor in the field of ecumenical leadership. The National Council has many enemies who, in an almost endless succession of attacks, have taken it to task in books and church periodicals. This has led to a serious split in one major denomination, the Presbyterian Church in the United States, and has caused a large-scale disaffection in many other denominations to such an extent that the Council itself is facing a serious financial situation, which has its parallel in several of the member denominations.

This book is written in the belief that the history of both Councils and their leadership in the ecumenical movement should receive a thorough investigation through the use of all the available *primary* material. It is not my intent to be sensational and to give added currency to the many rumors and allegations that have been hurled against both of the Councils. Nor is it my intention to misuse the evidence to paint a picture of sinister conspiracy by the leadership of the Federal and National Councils where there is no evidence that any existed. But neither is it my purpose to overlook and bury the evidence that has come to my attention in regard to the liberal and radical activities of the Councils. It is regrettable that some critics of the National Council have allowed their zeal for the Gospel of Jesus Christ to betray their historical training and accept rumor rather than fact. On the other hand, it is equally regrettable that defenders of the ecumenical movement have stubbornly refused to acknowledge Communist infiltration when it plainly exists. Their zeal for their cause has unnecessarily subjected the Federal and National Councils to a growing public distrust, both within the constituent denominations and by the American public.

For this reason I have consciously and carefully confined my research, for the most part, to the primary sources, namely, the publications of the Councils themselves, for the purpose of letting their leaders speak. On occasion it has been necessary also to use the findings of congressional committees created for the express purpose of investigating Communist activity in this country and armed with the necessary authority for carrying out their assigned duties.

Salisbury, North Carolina
August 1974

8

Acknowledgments

No author can produce a book of this length without the help of many others and this work is no exception. I am deeply indebted to the staffs of the Duke University Library and the Divinity School Library; to the constant and cheerful cooperation of the Reverend Kenneth Foreman, director of the Presbyterian Historical Foundation at Montreat, North Carolina, and his excellent staff. I am also greatly indebted to Gail Stewart, my student secretary at Catawba College, who spent hours in typing this work. Above all, I am indebted to my wife, Marjorie, for her untiring efforts in spending hours in typing and doing research, without whose help this book would not have been finished.

9

1

The Background
of the
National Council of Churches

Although the National Council of Churches was formed from the older Federal Council of Churches of Christ, the origins of this twentieth-century ecumenical movement trace to the theological and ecclesiastical developments that took place in this country during the nineteenth century. In a very real sense, the ecumenical developments of our own day, the National Council of Churches, and the current discussion involving COCU are the expression of the religious and intellectual currents that engulfed many of the larger denominations during the latter half of the previous century.

In fact, the failure to understand the theological background of the ecumenical movement has led many loyal Christians to embrace it as a legitimate and even necessary expression of the unity that all believers have in Christ, and the leaders of the efforts to bring an outward expression of unity to Christendom have not been slow to misuse this biblical emphasis on the inward unity of the Christian church to paint a picture of denominationalism as sin. In like manner, the failure of many Christians to understand the true purposes lying behind the formation of the Federal and National Councils of Churches has made it possible for them to be cajoled into supporting an organic unity and union of the various churches for purposes that are, for the most part, not only contrary to the Gospel, but actually treasonable in nature to the historic message of the Christian church and even to the nation and the American heritage.

The Federal Council of Churches of Christ and its successor, the National Council, have their origin, then, in the ecumenical impulse that characterized much of the ecclesiastical activity of the nation after 1865. But this ecclesiastical activity, in turn, was dominated by the theological currents that appeared in this country before 1860 and that achieved new status and influence after 1865. These theological currents, which became so prominent in the life of the American churches after 1865 or so, were inspired by the arrival of the German idealism of Immanuel Kant and G. W. F. Hegel and English Romanticism. Their effects on American theology were soon evident. The first was seen in the emergence of a new type of Unitarian thought that, true to its transcendental contacts, was pantheistic rather than deistic and was more radical in its departure from historic Christian orthodoxy. Older Unitarian leaders looked with horror on these new developments, and Ralph Waldo Emerson was forced to surrender his pulpit because of his open adherence to this more radical theology.

Transcendentalism furnished the inspiration for most, if not all, of the reform movements that swept the nation after 1830. It had its most immediate and probably greatest impact in the abolitionist movement, which emerged after 1830.[1] Although transcendentalism lost its philosophical impetus after 1865, its zeal for reform lingered and found a new home and support in the evolutionary theories of the postwar era. The socialism and communism inherent in abolitionism gained a new footing in the American mind and by the 1880s were gaining a wider support from both the discontented elements in society and the theological liberals who were espousing the social gospel and offering it as the panacea for every social ill.

If transcendentalism had a profound impact on the social,

1. C. Gregg Singer, *A Theological Interpretation of American History* (Nutley, N.J., 1964), pp. 74-76.

economic, and political aspects of American life, it had an equally important influence on American theology. This newer and more radical form of Unitarianism renewed the attack on evangelical Christianity in general and Calvinism in particular. Their hostility to Calvinism was epitomized in "The One-Hoss Shay" by Oliver Wendell Holmes. Unitarianism not only gained a new lease on life and on the New England mind, but even indirectly influenced those churches where immunity seemed assured. This is seen in the drift away from historic Calvinism and in the rise of the New England theology and of the New School thought in American Presbyterianism and the resulting split of that denomination between the Old and New Schools in 1837. On an even greater scale this retreat from Calvinism toward an Arminian theology took place in nearly all of the denominations, but was most marked in Congregationalism. There can be no doubt that transcendentalism had a permanent influence on nearly all of the established denominations; it also gave rise to new cults, which reflected even greater departures from the historic Christian faith.[2]

Involving the denial of man's total depravity, the departure from Calvinism brought with it an optimistic view of human nature. This optimism promoted not only the belief that man must and can cooperate with God in the achievement of his eternal redemption, but also its corollary that man in the same manner can achieve a millennial existence on earth. This fondness for millennialism brought with it an addiction to reform, which swept the nation in the three decades before 1860. Arminians, Unitarians, and devotees of the cults joined hands in the quest for utopia under the banners of millennialism. Although for most of them the crusade for abolition was the dominant interest before 1860, peace, prohibition, and other causes rallied their loyalty to lesser degrees.

Even as the period from 1860 to 1876 is a kind of watershed in the constitutional and political life of the nation, even so was it a Great Divide in its theological and ecclesiastical history. The very forces that brought the great change in our political development also produced an even more important change of direction in the life of most of the American denominations.

With the realization of their goal for the abolition of slavery, the crusaders found themselves in a peculiar psychological condition. Their major dream was now realized, but their zeal for reform was undiminished and was demanding new outlets of expression in the social, economic, and political life of the nation.

2. See Alice Felt Tyler, *Freedom's Ferment, passim,* esp. pp. 68-85.

In the new conditions that faced the American people after 1865 the crusaders found a new challenge for their political philosophy.

The reconstruction of the South, as over against Johnson's program of restoration, offered the first challenge to the radicals for the application of their radicalism to a whole region. But beyond that the reconstruction of the South provided the radicals with the key to the reconstruction of the whole nation after their basic concepts.[3] The war had given them their golden opportunity to bring about a major revision of American life for which the reconstruction of the South was to be the prelude. It was their goal to recast all of American society in terms of a secularized philosophy. Radical reconstruction was, therefore, directed against not only the South, but the whole American constitutional and political tradition as well. It was undergirded and inspired by the theological liberalism and radicalism of the transcendentalist era and its principal aim was to replace the American Constitution and Republic with a democratic philosophy and form of government founded on egalitarian principles. The assault on the South, as it was carried out under the congressional Plan of Reconstruction, was designed to be the prelude to the reconstruction of the whole nation according to this radical formula.[4]

The failure of the radicals to accomplish their ultimate purpose was caused by the results of the contested election of 1876, which broke the backbone of the radical strength in the South. This defeat caused Northern radicals to turn their attention to the North as the scene of new crusades, as outlets for their undiminished zeal in the cause of reform.

This new direction was reinforced by the new theological currents that also had emerged from the war period. Political radicalism received a powerful stimulus from the postwar theological liberalism that flourished after 1870 and became the inspiration for the social gospel. The social gospel had its roots in the earlier movement known as the New England theology, but it received a new character as a result of the impact of Darwinism on American thought after 1870.

Darwinism was hailed by the theological liberals as an important ally for their whole position, but they quickly saw that its most important role would be in the area of what had become known as

3. Singer, *op. cit.*, pp. 88-91.

4. *Ibid.* The radical Republicans had mixed motives in their plan for reconstructing the South and not all of them were theological radicals. But, at the same time, it is also true that theological and political radicalism furnished the ideological inspiration for much of this program.

the social gospel. Its promise of inevitable progress appealed to those who were determined to throw off the shackles of a conservative orthodoxy, which insisted that men were sinners by nature and could not be redeemed apart from the grace bestowed upon them by the sovereign God. Darwinism was used to throw doubt and ridicule not only on the historicity of Genesis, but also on the evangelical doctrines of God, man, sin, and redemption. They viewed it as an invaluable aid and tool for the destruction of evangelical Christianity and the substitution of the social gospel, which while using the old biblical terminology would give to it a whole new substance and meaning. In short, the theological belief in the possibility of progress of the race, physically, mentally, and morally found new scientific support in the evolutionary theory. The earlier reforming impetus found in abolitionsim and related movements had lacked such a scientific appeal to justify its expectations and promises and had relied upon the unstable romantic impulses supplied by German idealism.

By 1870 the American mind was quite receptive to the new intellectual currents emanating from Europe. Darwinism gave a new motivation to the zeal for social reform; at the same time, for many churchmen it had discredited the bibical account of creation to such an extent that that biblical doctrine was no longer such a formidable obstacle to the realization of the liberal dreams.

The specter of the sovereign God of Calvinism had for many scholars been removed. With the aid of evolution man could now exert his own sovereignty in the realization of his destiny on earth and in the means that he would choose to achieve that destiny. Man was now sovereign and he would refashion his society according to the basic implications of this principle.

If this principle gained credence in the secular world of thought and scientific endeavor, it also got hold of the thinking of many evangelical groups; Christian theology, even among evangelicals, was modified to bend with the winds of the new scientific naturalism, posing as humanism and democracy. Once again democracy sought to rewrite theology in terms of the sovereignty of man; many theological leaders were demanding a god who would cooperate with democracy and rejecting the God to whom they must submit.

Darwinism and the rise of the democratic theology provided the fertile soil out of which would come the demand for Christian social action, and an appropriate theology for the necessary reinterpretation of the biblical message. Inherent in this insistence was the tacit assumption that theological differences, which had long divided the Protestant churches, were no longer of any vital importance. The need for a common social action must take precedence over historical doctrinal differences, which were no longer relevant to the world of the late nineteenth century. This tendency to minimize the importance of doctrine for the achievement of an outward unity in the church was clearly visible in the successful efforts to bring about a reunion of the Old School and New School Presbyterian churches in 1869. Their separation in 1837 over strictly doctrinal issues was the result of the Arminian drift of the church. But in 1869 reunion took place, with these basic theological divisions still unsettled, as Lefferts Loetscher has freely admitted.[5] The distinctive Calvinistic emphasis of Old School Presbyterianism was muted by an Arminian outlook, which would soon become the vehicle by which those who sought a social gospel would also work for a union of evangelical churches for the achievement of their goals for society. This same tendency was evident in the Congregational, Northern Baptist, and Methodist churches to varying degrees during the decades after 1870. Thus the rise of the social gospel in this country paralleled the appearance of a common theology that ignored denominational barriers and differing theological traditions.[6] These twin developments in turn made some kind of ecclesiastical unity not only desirable but probable. Unity was likely only when the Protestant churches would renounce their heritage of the Reformation and advance theologically in this age of science. Leading advocates of the social gospel and theological liberals soon began to act upon the suggestions of C. A. Briggs. In 1889 Dr. Henry Van Dyke urged the revision of the Westminster Confession of Faith on the grounds that it did not explain with sufficient clarity what the church truly believed concerning the sovereignty of God and the role of man in redemption. Van Dyke called upon the Presbyterian church to modify its historic belief in the doctrine of election as it was set forth in the Westminster standards (the Confession, the Larger and Shorter catechisms) in the interests of evangelical unity.[7]

5. See his *Broadening Church: A Study of Theological Issues in the Presbyterian Church Since 1869* (Philadelphia, 1954), esp. pp. 28-37.

6. One of the leading spokesmen for this ideal of Christian unity was Dr. Charles A. Briggs of Union Seminary in New York. In an article in the *Presbyterian Review* (8)[1887]: 445 ff., he stated very clearly that subscription to elaborate creeds such as the Westminster Confession and the Lutheran Augsburg Confession was a great barrier to the reunion of Christendom. This subjection to creeds was the great sin of the Lutherans and Presbyterians and his disdain for creedal formulations is clearly seen in his statement that the differences separating Lutherans, Calvinists, and Arminians had nothing to do with the essentials of Protestantism.

7. Henry J. Van Dyke, "God's Infinite Love to Men," *Presbyterian*, October 5, 1889.

Although the movement for a revision of the Westminster Confession of Faith failed to achieve its goal before 1903, a similar movement met with greater success in those evangelical churches that were less creedal in their outlook. In Northern Baptist circles, as well as in the Methodist and Congregational churches, there was a definite trend away from the historic principles of Reformation theology toward what might well be called a common denominator of doctrine, which practically denied such doctrines as foreordination and election and the substitutionary atonement of Christ upon the cross. In general, the theological development under way took a more optimistic view of human sin and the condition of man than was warranted by the Scriptures; its view of the work of Christ upon the cross was equally foreign to the biblical position. The culmination of this early attempt to produce an ecumenical theology came with the work of Walter Rauschenbusch, particularly his *A Theology for the Social Gospel* (1917).

The Movement for Christian Unity in The Nineteenth Century

The effort to produce a form of Christian unity suitable for the movement, however, did not wait for the appearance of the theological exposition of its thinking. In fact, the first efforts toward a form of Christian unity, if not union, originated with evangelicals who were seeking greater strength for various missionary and evangelistic efforts which they held in common and in which they felt they could and should cooperate.

The American branch of the Evangelical Alliance, formed in 1867, was one of the earliest expressions (if not the earliest) of evangelical unity for the sake of a stronger witness for the Gospel. Like its parent, the Evangelical Union of Great Britain, its basic purpose was unity against infidelity and for the promotion of true religious freedom. The American branch adopted nine articles for the parent organization. These affirmed the divine inspiration of the Scriptures, the doctrine of the Trinity, the utter depravity of mankind, the atoning work of Christ the Son as the only hope for redemption, the immortality of the soul, the resurrection of the body and the everlasting punishment of unbelievers. The tone of these articles and of the conferences of this organization was decidedly evangelical, although it is also true that these formulations represented an ecumenical theology that, in the opinion of many observers, greatly weakened their usefulness in defending the evangelical faith against infidelity.

In 1873 during the sessions of the sixth general conference, steps were taken to form an alliance of Reformed Churches over the world, churches that held to a Presbyterian system of government. The result was the appearance of The Alliance of the Reformed Churches Throughout the World Holding the Presbyterian System. Its first general council was held in Edinburgh in 1877 and the second met in Philadelphia in 1880. However, even in this organization a movement began to appear looking toward what was called a simplification of doctrine, even though there was no visible demand for the organization to embrace the social gospel. However, Josiah Strong (1847-1916), a Congregational minister who served as its secretary for twelve years, had such a purpose in mind for the alliance. He wanted closer cooperation between the major denominations to make their witness in the social order more effective. However, when this alliance failed to provide the ecumenical foundations he desired, he resigned from his post in 1898 to work for the formation of a distinctly ecumenical movement much wider in its appeal and scope than the Presbyterian Alliance. From then on he played an important role in the founding of the Federal Council of Churches in 1908.

The Events Leading to the Formation of the Federal Council, 1900-1908

During the last quarter of the nineteenth century, in both evangelical and liberal circles in American Christendom, developments were under way that were creating an atmosphere favorable for forming a national council of Protestant churches of some kind. Not only had the theological foundations for such an organization emerged, but the various alliances and groups of organized Christians that had become characteristic of the religious scene in this country had pointed the way toward the formation of an ecclesiastical council designed to move in areas for which the individual denominations felt themselves ill equipped.

With this impetus supplied by the developments of the nineteenth century, architects of the new ecclesiology by 1900 turned to the practical task of forging a national organization out of existing groups and movements.[8] Although the Federal Council of Churches

8. Ecumenical groups of an evangelical nature included: the Student Volunteer Movement formed at Mount Hermon in 1886 under the influence of Dwight L. Moody, the American Bible Society (1816), the American Sunday School Union (1824), and the Young Men's Christian Association (1851) and the Young People's

of Christ was officially organized in December 1908, this action was the result of five preliminary steps, which are well described by Elias B. Sanford, the honorary secretary of the organization from its beginning.[9]

The first of these was a series of conferences looking to the formation of local and state federations. These were held during the 1890s. The available evidence suggests that the sponsors of this ecumenical movement placed a great deal of importance on these local meetings in order to create an impression and image that their work was the result of local and popular pressure for a new type of ecclesiastical cooperation. The Federal Council must not be imposed from the top down on local communities, but emerge from local and state federations. In this effort the sponsors of the Federal Council met with some success in New York City, Hartford, New Haven, Syracuse, Pittsburgh, Cleveland, and Chicago.

The second step was the calling of a conference to meet in Philadelphia early in 1901 for the purpose of forming the National Federation of Churches. The second annual conference of this federation meeting in Washington early in 1902 constituted the third step in the formation of the Federal Council. This conference took the fourth step when it created a committee on correspondence. This committee was probably the most active ingredient in the actual formation of the Federal Council. With Dr. Sanford as its secretary, the committee on correspondence traveled extensively over the United States, visiting local federations and theological seminaries. Its work looked to the meeting of the Inter-Church Conference on Federation, which was held in New York late in 1905. The meeting of this conference was the fifth of the preliminary steps. This conference made the formal proposal for the formation of a federal council at a conference to meet in 1908.

This Inter-Church Conference of 1905 laid the foundations for the Federal Council in formulating and accepting a constitution for it known as the Plan of Federation.[10] Its preamble declared the time had come to manifest more fully the essential oneness of the Christian churches of America in Jesus Christ as their Lord and

Society. The first attempts at Christian unity for social reform seem to have been the Women's Christian Temperance Union (1874) and the Anti-Saloon League (1893).

9. Elias B. Sanford, *Origin and History of the Federal Council of Churches of Christ in America* (Hartford, 1916).

10. The plan is set forth in detail in Elias B. Sanford, *Church Federation* (New York, 1906), pp. 33-36.

Savior and to promote spiritual fellowship, service, and cooperation among them.

After clearly asserting that the Federal Council should not have authority over the constituent bodies, but be able only to recommend a course of action in matters of common interest to the member churches, the Plan of Federation set forth the terms of membership. Each church was to have four representatives, plus an additional representative for every 50,000 members. An action taken by the Federal Council was to be by the general vote of its members. But if one third of the members present should request it, the vote was to be taken by the bodies represented, with the members of each body voting separately; such action was to require the vote, not only of a majority of the members voting, but also of the bodies represented.

The officers were to be a president, and one vice president from each of the constituent bodies, a corresponding secretary, a recording secretary, a treasurer, and an executive committee that should perform the duties usually assigned to such officers. The executive committee was to consist of seven ministers and seven laymen, together with the president and all the vice-presidents, the two secretaries and the treasurer. This committee was to have the authority to attend to all business of the Federal Council between meetings of the Council, and to fill any vacancies. Other Christian bodies could be admitted into the Council on their request, if it should be approved by two thirds of the members voting at a session of the Council and by two thirds of the churches represented, with the representatives of each church voting separately.

The last provision is of special interest. It would seem at first glance that this provision for a two-thirds vote of the individuals present and of the churches present should have been a sufficient safeguard. But it should also be noted that apart from the use of the word *Christian*, there was no other stipulation as to the creedal qualifications of a church applying for membership.

The Plan of Federation could be altered by a majority vote of the members present, followed by a majority vote of the representatives of the churches present, each body voting separately.

The Federal Council of Churches was officially launched at a conference held in Philadelphia in 1908. Thirty-three Protestant denominations were represented. Its major, but not only, purpose was to ratify the work of the Inter-Church Conference of 1905. That this is the case is abundantly evident from the testimony of the leaders of the movement: "When the Inter-Church Conference on Federation adjourned not only were the Protestant forces of the United States officially united as never before, but a definite program of action had been placed in the hands of the committee authorized to carry forward the work made necessary by the adoption of the plan of federation, report to be made to the Federal Council of 1908."[11] The conference also decided that four other offices should be created in strategic centers over the country. But this seems to have been largely ignored.

The meeting of 1908 was in a sense anticlimactic, so far as the reality of this new ecumenical venture is concerned. It officially adopted the Plan of Federation of 1905 as the constitution of the Federal Council. This first meeting also decided to seek close co-operation with the Religious Education Association and the National Education Association. This last decision is serious and must be very difficult to explain for many contemporary supporters of the National Council, for in 1908 the Federal Council was quite interested in se-curing religious instruction in the public schools of the nation. After deciding to make New York the headquarters of the organi-zation and selecting Bishop E. R. Hendrix of the Methodist Episcopal Church (South) as its first president, the conference then proceeded to its most important business of this first session, the creation of the Committee on the Church and Modern Industry, which pre-pared the first pronouncement of the Federal Council of Churches.[12] This paper, popularly known as the Social Creed of the Churches, patently indicates the direction the newly formed council would take in its thinking and the direction in which it would attempt to lead the constituent denominations.

In a very real sense this meeting of 1905 was prophetic of what was to come, once the Federal Council became a reality. In the first place there is no doubt that organic unity of the Protestant churches was the real goal of that small group that brought about the conference in 1905. Sanford made it quite clear that in the early discussions leading to the series of conferences resulting in the for-mation of the Federal Council there was a strong desire for organic unity. This desire was the dominant note in an address that Dr. Philip Schaff had given in 1893 in Chicago. Calling schism a sin, he

11. *Ibid.*, p. 225.

12. The Social Creed of the Churches makes up article nine of this statement and its first form was written by Dr. Harry F. Ward. It is essentially the Methodist Social Creed. Ward wrote it for the use of the Methodist Federation for Social Ser-vice, of which he was the secretary, and it was adopted by the Methodist General Conference in 1912.

said: "Where the sin of schism has abounded the grace of future reunion will much more abound."[13]

Schaff, however, was an evangelical in his outlook and it is most unlikely that he envisioned the creation of a federation of churches to be a political and social force in American life.

But that such a goal was in the thinking of the leaders of the movement cannot be doubted. Washington Gladden had said that the woe of the world was because the church had rejected all that was central and constructive in Christianity, and that the teachings of Jesus provided not only the goal but also the motive power for realizing the world-ideal after which men were groping. In the meeting of 1905 several speakers had emphasized the need of abolishing the distinction between the secular and the sacred as a prelude to social action.

The conference on interchurch relations of 1905 had actually revealed the fundamental purpose of this ecumenical gathering in bringing political issues before its attention. Particularly was it concerned with the problem of the misrule of Leopold II of Belgium in the Congo.[14] This report of one of its commissions in regard to the Congo was not an isolated event. Other commissions became involved with the temperance and immigration issues on the home front. Thus even before it was formally organized, it was crystal clear that the Federal Council of Churches was to be an ecclesiastical pressure group in national and international political, social, and economic affairs.

Article one declared that "this federal council places upon record its profound belief that the complex problems of modern industry can be interpreted and solved only by the teachings of the New Testament and that Jesus Christ is the final authority in the social as in the individual life."[15] To defend the Council against possible charges of making innovations in the witness of the church, the article then insisted: "The interest of the Church in men is either recent or artificial. No challenge of newly posted sentries can exclude it from the ground where are struggle, privation and need. It has its credentials and knows the watchword."

After insisting that the church then confronted the most significant crisis and the greatest opportunity in its long career, article three asserted the belief of those who had brought the Council into being:

13. Sanford, *Origin and History of the Federal Council*, p. 96.

14. *Ibid.*, pp. 226 ff.

15. The complete text of this statement is in Sanford, *Origin and History of the Federal Council*, pp. 494-98, All quotations from it will come from this source.

22

"We believe, not for its own sake but in the interest of the kingdom of God, the church must not merely acquiesce in the movements outside of it which make for human welfare, but must demonstrate not by proclamation but by deeds its primacy among all the forces which seek to lift the plane and better considerations of human life."[16] The declaration admitted the complex nature of modern industrial life and gave its blessings to labor unions and the growing spirit of conciliation in settling trade disputes. It then declared that "the church must meet social bewilderment by ethical lucidity, and by gentle and resolute testimony to the truth must assert for the whole Gospel, its prerogative as the test of the rightness of both individual and collective conduct everywhere."

Article nine, the Social Creed as such, proclaimed the following economic and social goals for American Society:

> We deem it the duty of all Christian people to concern themselves directly with certain practical industrial problems. To us it seems that the churches must stand—
>
> For equal rights and complete justice for all men in all stations of life.
>
> For the right of all men to the opportunity for self maintenance, a right ever to be wisely and strongly safeguarded against encroachment of every kind.
>
> For the right of workers to some protection against the hardships often resulting from the swift crises of industrial change.
>
> For the principle of conciliation and arbitration in industrial dissension.
>
> For the protection of the worker from dangerous machinery, occupational disease, injuries and mortality.
>
> For the abolition of child labor.
>
> For such regulations of the conditions of toil for women as shall safeguard the physical and moral health of the community.[17]
>
> For the suppression of the "sweating system."
>
> For the gradual and reasonable reduction of the hours of labor to the lowest practical point, and for that degree of leisure for all which is a condition of the highest human life.
>
> For a release from employment one day in seven.
>
> For a living wage as a minimum in every industry, and for the highest wage that each industry can afford.
>
> For the most equitable division of the products of industry that can ultimately be devised.
>
> For the abatement of poverty.

16. *Ibid.*

17. This stands in sharp contrast to the support which many groups and churches in the National Council have given in recent years to the Women's Liberation Movement.

This document clearly reveals the "Christian socialism" of Walter Rauschenbusch, who was a member of the conference that created the Federal Council. It was subjected to revision in 1912 and again in 1932. Although the document's proposals seem mild in the light of contemporary social and economic legislation, they contain the seed of a strict governmental regulation of all of life in the name of the Gospel, and a socialism that was and is essentially communistic. Their theological basis was the social gospel of Rauschenbusch, George Herron, and Harry F. Ward. Rauschenbusch was keenly aware of the necessity of a policy of deception in introducing his brand of Christian Socialism into the churches of this country. He thus gave it a name that was designed to make it seem evangelical in character and not revolutionary at the same time. Calling for the Christianization of the social order for the realization of the kingdom of God, Rauschenbusch avoided demanding the government ownership of the railroads and other public utilities. He simply called for governmental controls of various kinds, confident that such a program would eventually bring the kind of socialism he wanted. He was willing to uphold a policy of gradualism in his program of social and democratic revolution.

Underlying this attempt to give to the program a Christian veneer, Ward, Rauschenbusch, and their colleagues adopted a theology quite different from that found in the Scriptures. In the first place, it must be noted that the first article insists that the complex problems of modern industry can be solved only in the light of the teachings of the New Testament. This was quite in keeping with their liberal approach to the Scriptures, an approach that placed little or no importance on the Old Testament as such. But the Jesus Christ who was their final authority in the social as well as the individual life is not the Jesus Christ of the New Testament. Their Christ was a great teacher; but even more, he was filled with a great social passion that was most truly reflected in this social creed.

This document further reflects the shift of concern among the leaders of the ecumenical movement from individual to social redemption, the loss of interest in the problem of human sin and its effects upon men, and a new zeal for the salvation of society from its various evils. But it was a kind of salvation that stopped short of the grave and had no answer to the deepest question that confronts mankind: "If a man die, shall he live again?" These architects of this new gospel were prone to forget that the very social evils against which they were waging war were the expression of the sin in the human heart, with which they were less and less concerned. For them human nature was essentially good, and evil in society could and should be attributed to environmental factors.

Underlying this document was a subtle shift of thinking from a biblical frame of reference to a democratic concept of God, man, and society, a concept that transferred the sovereignty of God to man himself or to such agencies as he might erect to exercise it for him. The Social Creed of 1908 seemingly was willing to confer it upon the government of the United States. And this federal government would be the agency by which the kingdom of God would come to earth, at least on the American earth.

This democratic philosophy is further reflected in the significant omission of any reference to those duties that men owe to their fellow men as unto God. The God whose sovereignty has been denied to Him is in no position to demand the fulfillment of duties from His former subjects. Men now owe duties to society or to the state, not to God. The biblical emphasis upon duties was replaced in this document with an emphasis upon human rights, an emphasis that is a basic ingredient of the democratic philosophy, but that can survive only in a Christian frame of reference. Human rights that do not arise from the duties men owe to God are without any foundation and will soon evaporate as secular political thought brings with it the idolization of the sovereign state.

Thus the grandeur of this superstructure of a humanly designed and achieved kingdom of God rested upon the quicksands of its own humanistic origins. Its inherent weakness could not long be concealed by its external ornamentation with biblical phraseology. Rauschenbusch and his colleagues in their use of biblical concepts poured into them a very different content. This was notably true in their reiteration of the idea of the kingdom of God. For them it was not the final triumph of the heavenly kingdom foreseen by the prophets of the Old Testament and foretold by Christ in the Gospels. Rather, it was the triumph of a socialistic society based on a socialistic ethic that looked for the salvation of society in this world, a salvation not from sin but from sin's effects—war, injustice, poverty, exploitation, even diseases. It was to be a humanly achieved heaven on earth. This message did not deny the existence of a future heavenly state for men. But it did insist that all men of goodwill who would enter into the task of ushering in this heaven on earth would merit the enjoyment of the eternal heaven promised in the Scriptures to believers in Christ as their Savior from sin.

The Reception of The Federal Council

At the close of the 1908 conference Dr. S. J. Nichols gave an address that revealed the almost hysterical joy of those in attendance who were witnessing the birth of this ecumenical endeavor.

> The song of the bird is in the trees, and the flowers are blooming: the frozen drift is slowly yielding to genial spirit in the air—its crystals are being dissolved until they join in little rivulets, the laughing brook in the valley that goes on to join the river. Soon where it lay, the grass will be green and the violets and the anemones bloom. So bigotry is being dissolved.[18]

Staunch supporters of the ecumenical movement were no less enthusiastic in their appraisal of the developments at the 1908 conference, if somewhat less florid in their language. A Lutheran editor declared rhapsodically: "The Federal Council is witness to the consciousness in Protestantism that below all the surface differences there is a common platform of evangelical faith where they can meet and cooperate as brethren in Christ. . . . There are lines of cleavage, but below them there is one body in Christ."[19]

The *Reformed Review* of the Reformed Church in the United States had much more to say about the emergence of such a council of churches. Declaring that it was an historic assembly, it solidly endorsed the work of the conference of 1908: "Whatever the immediate or distant results may be, the Protestant Churches of the United States have entered into new relations toward each other and have shown, in a concrete way, a unity of spirit in reference to the spiritual, moral, and social problems of the age."[20] Yet this same periodical, apparently aware of possible or actual criticism of the new organization arising within the denomination, carefully pointed out just what the Federal Council was not as well as what it was or could be. It emphasized very clearly that the Council could have no authority over the member churches, could not draw up a common creed, and could not devise a form of unity. This reassurance was for those in this and other denominations who viewed the formation of this Council with suspicion and even with the fear that it might attempt to become a kind of superchurch: "It has no authority to

18. Quoted in *Literary Digest* 38 (January 2, 1909): 19.

19. *Reformed Review* 56 (1909): 108.

20. Sanford, *op. cit.*, p. 203.

draw up a common creed or form of government or of worship, or in any way to limit the full authority of the Christian bodies adhering to it."[21]

In view of the later zeal of the Reformed Church in the United States for both organic union and reformulation of its creed away from its Reformation heritage, one can only wonder at the insistence of the editor of the *Reformed Review* that organic union was not the purpose of this new council of churches: "The watchword of the Council was federation, not organic union." This journal defended the legitimacy of denominationalism and declared that denominations were necessary for the proclamation of the Gospel. The editor went so far as to declare that denominations have their basis not only in past controversies, but also in the constitution of human nature itself, a word of wisdom that is as true now as it was then.

Other periodicals of the religious press were varied in their reaction to the formation of the Council. The *Standard*, a Baptist paper in Chicago, was favorable while the *Christian Advocate* (New York), an influential Methodist publication, heralded the Philadelphia meeting as a great convocation. The *Presbyterian Banner* (Pittsburgh) declared that the formation of the Federal Council of Churches was the result not of a sudden impulse, but of the fact that leaders in all the churches "have gradually awakened to the necessity of united action on the mission field, at home and abroad."[22] The *Christian Observer* gave a somewhat guarded endorsement, feeling that a body of unity would be a distinct advantage, but in its next issue it commended the study of the Social Creed to all branches of the church.[23] On the other hand, *the Presbyterian*, probably the most influential of all Presbyterian journals in the North, gave a rather unfavorable assessment of the new venture. Except for the *Christian Observer*, Presbyterian journals in the South gave it either little attention or none at all.

One of the most strongest criticisms of the Federal Council came from the *Presbyterian Standard*, published in Charlotte, North Carolina, and one of the most conservative Presbyterian voices in the country at that time.

> The elaborate relation of the church to all classes of people who go to make up our multiform and complex social status by the recent Fed-

21. *Ibid.*, p. 109.
22. December 10, 1908, p. 7.
23. *Christian Observer*, January 6, 1909, p. 3; January 13, 1909, p. 7.

eration Council . . . comes to us with the ring of a degree of ignorance about both what the church recognizes and is doing, at least in this latitude. . . . There has been no necessity in the past and there is none now for multiplied and bewildering man-made machinery to renovate corrupt society and save a dying world.[24]

The *Standard* offered a remedy for the situation which the ecumenical movement was trying to correct, preaching the Gospel in its fullness and with vigor.

This same paper, in a later issue, pressed its criticism of the Federal Council with an insight that very few, if any, other journals mentioned. It too stood strong against the desire of some leaders of the movement, notably Robert E. Speer, to eliminate all denominational differences, including theological differences, in the foreign mission endeavor: "It is strange if zeal for foreign missions renders one indifferent to the whole range of what we call nonessential truths."[25]

Other denominational journals voiced some disagreement with the aims of the Federal Council, largely in the social and economic areas of our national life. On the other hand, the greatest enthusiasms for the Council came from those denominations that were leaders of the ecumenical movement and that were most enamored of the social gospel. It was to be expected that the Disciples of Christ would give a hearty welcome to the new organization and that the columns of the *Christian Century* would loudly endorse it and be lavish in its praises.

Widespread criticism of the Federal Council from conservatives within the denominations was infrequent until after 1920, when the Council became involved in radical movements of various kinds on a wider scale than it had been during the years from 1908 to 1917.

The Federal Council, 1908-1920

The enthusiasm with which the Council was launched and which greeted the work of the 1908 conference was not self-sustaining or sufficient in itself to nurture the newly formed organization. The promises included in the rhetoric of the conferences of 1905 and 1908 now had to be translated into ecumenical practice in the life of the nation. The time had come for hard work. The leaders chosen in 1912, notably Bishop E. R. Hendrix, the first president of the

24. *Presbyterian Standard*, January 6, 1909, pp. 2, 3.

25. *Ibid.*, January 13, 1909, p. 3.

28

Council, Elias Sanford, honorary secretary, and the Reverend Charles MacFarland, the first corresponding secretary, launched its career in developing ecumenical cooperation.

Bishop William M. Bell, in his opening address to the first Quadrennial Session of the Council held at Chicago in 1912, presented to it the task before the churches. He reflected both the optimism of the 1908 conference and the sense of urgency and opportunity that made such a council necessary:

> We are confronted with the immediate necessity of an unprecedented adjustment. It is felt in intellectual activities and social service. Everywhere institutions are being tried and religion is called upon for new pronouncements and new justifications in relation to every kind of organization. These questions come all along the line, and our hospitality to them will be an index of wisdom and will reflect the statesmanlike view of our generation. . . .
>
> The church is open, as never before to this appeal, and this great Federal Council is the exemplification of the fact that American Christianity is on the move with the larger ideal in behalf of humanity, and in the name of Christ. This new agency which we have created in the Federal Council of the Churches stands to the age, perhaps to serve it as we shall empower it to serve, perhaps to serve it as we may agree to allow it to serve. . . .[26]

Perhaps consciously, perhaps unconsciously, Bishop Bell, in this address, laid down the fundamental issues and questions that would constitute the chief concerns of the Federal Council through its forty-two years of history and that would be bequeathed to its successor, the National Council of Churches. In regard to the Council's social outlook and challenge, he said:

> In business we are to give adequate touch and leadership. One of these days we are to have an American business life sanctified and purified. It is no Utopian dream. It will be business, not for colossal individual realization, but business for human ministry and the elevation of all mankind. . . .
>
> Unless we build toward the skies and build above the mold America shall have failed and failed signally and fatally. . . .[27]

But this whole dream was scuttled by the definition that Bishop Francis J. McConnell gave to the religious task of the newly formed council in his opening address. He took the churches to task for their

26. Charles S. MacFarland, ed., *Christian Unity at Work*, p. 27.
27. *Ibid.*, p. 28.

differing interpretations of the Scriptures and then virtually denied the idea of absolute truth. In so doing he clearly stated what he felt to be the intellectual task and challenge to the Council as a necessary part of its social leadership:

> In the next place, the work of the federated movement of the churches is bringing a very remarkable intellectual gain. There is a certain kind of mocking question asked the church, "What is truth?" The Presbyterian Church says it is one thing, the Congregational another, the Episcopalian another and the Methodist another. We are coming to see very clearly in these days that we cannot define truth in abstract terms. We are coming to see, from the Christian standpoint, that truth is true living. That is the absolute end in itself; everything else is instrumental.[28]

The theological liberalism that brought the Council into being is here clearly evident. The ecumenical leadership, while protesting at the time that it had no intention of destroying the denominations as such, was actually laying the foundation for their destruction by denying that there is absolute biblical truth, or absolute truth of any kind. The existing character of its position is unquestionably clear in the statement, "We are coming to see, from the Christian standpoint, that truth is true living." But how can a Christian know what true living is if there is no standard in the light of which he is to evaluate his true living? Indeed, what is true living? This kind of fallacious thinking, which characterized the first session of the Council, has haunted the Council's pronouncements from that day until it became the National Council of Churches. The National Council has continued the tradition. This instrumentalism, this ecclesiastical adaptation of the philosophy of John Dewey would prove to be as catastrophic for the life of the churches as it would be for American education.

The basic contradiction in this position appeared in the bishop's address:

> We shrink from drawing that conclusion, sometimes, that organizations are instruments, that rituals are instruments, that church organizations are instruments, but we are coming fast to agree on that. One man likes one kind of instrument and another another, but we are all working for the same purpose. Every representative here tonight will say that he is trying to bring in the kingdom of God and make man like

28. *Ibid.,* p. 29.

Christ. We are trying to make men live a good life. One man can work better with one instrument than another man. We can make a better impression upon the intellectual world if we insist upon that, the good of life is the end, and that everything else that leads up to it is the instrument. . . . The creed is an instrument and is to be judged by its effectiveness as an instrument.[29]

Here in bold outline is the future of the Federal Council portrayed. Here is set forth in unmistakably clear terms the basic relativism that would be its guide. Yet the leaders of the movement seemed not to realize that this relativism, born of the instrumentalism guiding them, would ultimately destroy their own liberal assumptions as to the desirability, and even the meaning, of the "kingdom of God." If the creed is merely an instrument and its usefulness to be measured by its effectiveness, then the whole program would be in great jeopardy. Such glowing liberal concepts as righteousness and social progress would ultimately become relative in meaning for the liberals of later decades, who would be the intellectual and theological successors of the formulators of the Social Creed of 1908 and these first affirmations of the Federal Council.

Perhaps the antitheological and antiintellectual character of the new organization was no more clearly expressed than in the third of the opening addresses, given by Dean Shailer Mathews of the University of Chicago, who was elected by this same conference to be second president of the Federal Council:

The Federal Council of Churches of Christ in America embraces thirty different denominations seeking unity. The Council of Nicaea also sought unity. It too tried to bring peace into society and the state and sought it in its theological definition. This representation of 17,000,000 Protestant Christians comes to discuss how they can best carry on its cooperative work for the good of mankind. If the Council of Nicaea, instead of wasting weeks over the discussion of a word, had organized a mission society to go into Germany what a different story history would have told.[30]

Dean Shailer Mathews and Bishop McConnell obviously chose unity at any cost, above doctrinal truth, certainly. The Council of Nicaea (A.D. 325) had been called by the Emperor Constantine to settle the Arian heresy rampant in the Eastern Church. Arianism denied the doctrine of the Trinity by denying the complete deity

29. *Ibid.*, pp. 28-29.
30. *Ibid* p. 34.

of Jesus Christ. It asserted that Christ possessed a nature only *similar* to that of God, not complete deity.

Apparently these efforts to clarify the understanding of the church in regard to this vital doctrine of the Trinity were a waste of time in the eyes of these twentieth century critics who would have us believe that the whole course of history would have been changed if those ecclesiastical leaders would have simply sent missionaries to Germany to preach. But to preach what? To preach an uncertain faith in a message that wavered on whether Jesus Christ was truly God? Was it such a waste of time to decide this fundamental issue which lies at the heart of the Gospel? The fallacies in this argument are so apparent that it is hardly necessary to explore them in any depth. To say that the whole course of history would have been different is logically impossible. How can anyone know what would have happened in the event that "if" in history had taken place?

But had the church failed to reach agreements on the doctrine of the deity of Jesus Christ, we may in the light of the Scriptures safely affirm that there would have been no Gospel to preach; a missionary activity in Germany on the basis of a defective Gospel, or without any Gospel, would have been utterly in vain. The lofty optimism that the newly formed Federal Council would result in great intellectual gain for the churches of this country and for American society is hard to understand in view of the antiintellectual character of the theological outlook of these leaders. Although the leadership of the Federal Council made valiant efforts to maintain the facade of an organization resulting from a grass-roots demand, the facts point to a contrary conclusion; the meeting of 1912 was quite conscious that it was not the product of a popular demand for unity at the top of the ecclesiastical pyramid and that it lacked grass-roots support.

Actually the session of 1912 paid a great deal of attention to the necessity of creating both local and state federations. By the end of that year the Federal Council could claim twenty-one state bodies, thirty-five county and district federations in six states, thirty-nine partial or tentative federations in twenty-three states and the District of Columbia, and ninety-nine federations in twenty-seven states and Honolulu.[31] Between 1908 and 1913 eighty-nine local federations had been formed with twenty-five additional denominations represented in them, denominations that were not constituent members

31. Charles MacFarland, *Christian Unity in the Making*, pp. 66-68.

of the Federal Council.[32] However, these statistics do not tell the true story for most of these local federations were short-lived and existed on inadequate budgets.

There was a great deal of confusion within the leadership of the Federal Council itself. Some leaders felt that these local federations should be composed of churches belonging to denominations within the Federal Council while others were quite willing to include churches not part of the Council.[33] There is also evidence that in certain cases at least, some of the Council's officers drew up constitutions for these local federations.

In this area the early efforts of the Federal Council to strengthen its base of operations were quite disappointing. The movement had to run a continual barrage of criticism because of its economic, social, and theological outlook; by the end of 1911 Charles Mac-Farland had reached a number of conclusions, the most important of which was that the state and local federations could not be forced to make their respective constituencies identical with that of the Federal Council. He also felt that they should be free to draw up their own constitutions and not be forced to accept the model proposed by the Federal Council. In place of the emphasis on local councils and federations, MacFarland urged a new policy of bringing denominational agencies into cooperation, particularly in such areas as social service, international peace, race relations, and evangelism.

While MacFarland gave little place to evangelism in his own comments at the quadrennial sessions of 1912, evangelism was not overshadowed by the call to social service. The committee on evangelism made a report reaffirming that the supreme mission of the church is always to proclaim Christ as the Savior of sinful men.

> That supreme mission clearly stated is to proclaim Christ as the Savior of sinful men, the author of that new life, which beginning with a new heart, shall make all things new through a new view of God, a new thought of men, a new perception as to human life on earth, a new conception of human life beyond the grave, and a new force controlling each believer, the life which is his with Christ in God.[34]

On the surface this definition of the mission of the church would

32. Ross W. Sanderson, *Church Cooperation in the United States* (Hartford, 1960), p. 80. However, of the 103 local federations existing in 1913, only twelve had been organized before 1908.

33. *Ibid.*, p. 82.

34. Charles MacFarland, *Christian Unity at Work* (New York, 1913), p. 145.

seem to be biblical and satisfactory. But while it undoubtedly has an evangelical tone, it is also less than biblical in some aspects. In the first place, while Christ is proclaimed to be the Savior of men from sin, the destiny of the unbeliever is not mentioned. Neither is the nature of Christ's atoning work. Several theologians who were less than biblical in their outlook could accept this statement. The weakness of this approach to evangelism is clearly demonstrated in other parts of the report of this commission. The Gospel is regarded as mainly the cure for social discontent. While the desire to save individual souls in evident, it is very difficult to escape the conclusion that at this quadrennial session evangelism was looked upon as the handmaid of social reform. And for the realization of this goal the committee on evangelism commended to this 1912 session of the Federal Council the creation of a commission for evangelism.[35] Even evangelism must primarily serve the cause of social reform.

That this conclusion is warranted is also quite obvious from the disproportionate length of time given to the reports of the commission concerned with the social concerns of the Federal Council. Much of the time and attention of the quadrennial session of 1912 was on the consideration of reports dealing with the church and social service, and the church and the new internationalism. This commission investigated the Bethlehem steel strike and issued a large body of literature dealing with the church and labor, the church and modern industry, and other related problems.[36]

Even more optimistic was the report of the commission on peace and arbitration, appointed early in 1912 by the executive council of the Federal Council and modeled after the Commission on Church and Social Service. This committee worked to support the ratification of treaties of arbitration in conjunction with the Carnegie Endowment for International Peace. Under the able and aggressive leadership of its secretary, Charles S. MacFarland, it gained great influence both in the Federal Council and in the nation at large. In its report to the session it urged the formation of a church peace society in America and issued its own statement of faith in regard to peace.

We believe that the time has come when civilization must make the choice between two ways for the future; the way of statesmanship or the way of the battleship; the old way of settling disputes by force or the new way of settling them by justice. . . . In our time a

35. *Ibid.*, p. 155.
36. Ibid., pp. 171-72.

34

great throng of noble men, prophets, statesmen, teachers, poets, yes, businessmen have seen the vision of the new way, the way of the Lord, the way of brotherhood, justice and good will. They are demanding that we choose international tribunals, arbitration treaties and such judicial methods as Christian men practice among themselves. The choice must be made soon, and once for all, or militarism will gain the day. . . .[37]

This commission gave its reply to this demand by urging the creation of a permanent court of international justice proposed by the third Hague Conference. But before the Federal Council would meet again in a quadrennial session, the guns would be booming on the western front and the nations of Europe would be engaged in a deadly war that would soon involve the United States. The peace stand of this organization would be subjected to a strain so great that many who supported peace in 1912 would yield to the cries to fight "the war to end all wars" and "to save the world for democracy."

But the addresses of 1912 as well as the reports of the committees and commissions breathed a spirit of optimism, which was almost totally unrelated to the diplomatic forces that were bringing Europe to the mightiest conflict yet known in human history. This optimism was born of a view of human nature that savored much more of the humanism of the Renaissance and the evolutionary theories of Darwin and others than of the biblical doctrine of total depravity. It is quite evident that the Federal Council in the first four years of its history had been heavily influenced and penetrated by the democratic philosophy that was engulfing the nation. Thus Dean Shailer Mathews, in an address before the Religious Education Association, could say: "The theology of democracy has yet to be written. Whereas, Calvin spoke of God's election of man, the democrat speaks of man's election of God. The democratic spirit of the age is demanding that the church abandon sovereignty as the controlling concept of its theology and leaven itself with democracy."[38]

Mathews, the second president of the council, was calling upon the theologians of the day and the member churches to renounce their heritage of the Reformation, the doctrine of the sovereignty of God, and make common cause with the democratic philosophy that was derived from humanistic and pagan philosophies and that had nothing in common with historic Christianity. Increasingly

37. Ibid., pp. 204-5.

38. Quoted in Edgar Bundy, *Collectivism in the Churches*, pp. 27-28 from the *Journal of Religious Education* (1910): 84.

after 1912 these churches were subjected to pressures for easing their creedal statements and loyalty to their heritage and replacing their historic doctrinal positions with a humanistic philosophy sufficiently tinctured with biblical statements to trap the unwary into believing that the program of the Federal Council was actually scriptural in its thrust and the ecumenical movement was only a joint effort for the preaching, teaching, and practical application of their historic faith. A theology that stood in the way of the advance of the social gospel and the march of democracy must give way to one that would accommodate itself to the world of man.

However much Shailer Mathews might call for a democratization of theology, many observers both in Europe and in this country were becoming convinced that democracy itself was on trial for its very life because of the imperialism and militarism of Germany. The pacifism and the call for social amelioration that played such a large part in the deliberations of the 1912 quadrennial sessions seem out of place. President Woodrow Wilson, however, was able to push through some parts of his own moderate program of reform, but after 1915 he was increasingly concerned with the events in Europe and the possible involvement of this country in the great carnage taking place over there.

2

The Federal Council of Churches, World War 1 and the League of Nations

During the four-year interval between the first quadrennial of 1912 and the second of 1916, even though the specter of war hung low on the European horizon, the Federal Council was entering a period of development in its organization and growth. Taking advantage of the Men and Religious Forward Movement, which had gained much popular support over the country from September 1911 to May 1912, the administrative committee of the Federal Council appointed a commission on state and local federations in 1912. Dr. Alfred Williams Anthony was its executive secretary and its purpose was to develop grass-roots support for the ecumenical movement. In 1913 a second commission was created, known as the Commission on Interdenominational Cooperation. The effort to expand and develop grass-roots strength, however, was plagued by a perplexing problem, for which no real solution had yet been found. How much authority should the Federal Council exert over these emerging local federations? Should the ecumenical endeavor be a closely knit organization with the Federal Council assuming the authoritative leadership or should these local federations keep their local autonomy and merely cooperate with the Federal Council? This very important question did not receive any clear-cut answer in the discussions at 1913 and it remained to haunt future quadrennials.[1]

In spite of its inability to settle this question, the Federal Council did enter upon a period of expansion after 1915, largely because of the work of Dr. Roy B. Guild and Fred B. Smith, the latter having been named chairman of a special committee on federated movements in January 1915. In its report in March 1915 the Council recommended the appointment of a new and enlarged committee on federated movements, the first of which was to be concerned with the task of "organizing, inspiring and standardizing local and state federations." It declared that no community with two or more churches should be without a federation and that the whole country needed federation. The second major feature of this report called for bringing various Christian organizations into a closer fraternal relationship with each other and with the Federal Council.[2] This second proposal was an obvious effort to bring the foreign missionary societies of various kinds, domestic associations such as the YMCA and the YWCA, and home missionary groups like the American Sunday School Union into a closer working agreement with the Federal Council. This last goal was not achieved until the formation of the National Council of Churches, and even then it was not fully realized.

In an effort to create a favorable attitude for the creation of the proposed commission on federated movements, a conference on interchurch activities was held in Atlantic City, New Jersey, in 1915 with some sixteen groups of various kinds in attendance. This conference favored the proposed commission and President Shailer Mathews of the Federal Council appointed the commission the same year. Fred B. Smith was chairman. At its first meeting in September, with thirty-two members present, it elected Dr. Guild as secretary and James A. Whitmore as field secretary. This new commission soon began to inaugurate conferences on its own initiative to aid the growth of local federations.

The business of creating grass-roots strength for the Federal Coun-

1. See Ross W. Sanderson, *Church Cooperation in the United States* (Hartford, 1960), for a valuable discussion of the details of the question, especially pages 91-95.

2. *Federal Council Report for 1915*, pp. 53-54.

cil was not only tedious and time-consuming, but also quite complex. While there was much enthusiasm for this program, the reports of the various committees and conferences concerned with it fail to reveal that the grass-roots strength was as numerous or as vigorous as the leadership expected.[3]

The committees concerned with federation were by no means the only activity of the Federal Council between the meetings of its first and second quadrennials. Its commission on peace and arbitration was in active cooperation with the Church Peace Union and the World Alliance for Promoting International Friendship through the Churches. The Church Peace Union had been established at a meeting at the home of Andrew Carnegie in 1914 with an endowment of two million dollars to sustain its work. Its board of trustees was composed of some of the outstanding ministers of the day, but its Christian character was seriously jeopardized by the inclusion of those whose presence greatly weakened the claim of the Federal Council that it was concerned with Christian activity and with cooperation among the churches. The Church Peace Union was actually founded in February 1914, before the war began, but amid those tensions that had been plaguing Europe since 1905 and that would bring on a general war before the year was over.

Notwithstanding the threats of war, the optimism of those working was apparently undiminished. They planned for peace and what would be done with the funds of the union once arbitration had been firmly established as the means for maintaining international peace.[4] Further to insure the triumph of their plans for world peace, the union instituted an essay contest dealing with war, its causes, and plans for peace. Interestingly, among the prizewinners of 1914 were Gaius Glenn Atkins, who wrote *The Causes of War;* Reinhold Niebuhr, then a student at Yale School of Religion, for *Patriotism and Altruism;* and Paul Blanchard who took as his topic, *Industrial Patriotism.*[5]

Early in February 1915 the Church Peace Union issued a message to the churches in which it declared that Christianity had not failed the nations, but rather the nations had failed Christianity. Calling

3. The amount of time and energy devoted to this one task is amazing but tedious to recite. In *Church Cooperation in the United States* Ross Sanderson presents these conferences and meetings in detail.

4. Sidney L. Gulick and Charles S. MacFarland, *The Church and International Relations,* vol 3 (New York, 1917), p. 4.

5. *Ibid.,* p. 11.

on the ministers of all churches to avoid partisanship and its ally prejudice, it affirmed its belief in the fatherhood of God and the brotherhood of man because God had made of one blood all nations. It then asked: "Why has this Gospel not wrought its normal work among the nations?"[6] To which there could be but one answer. This affirmation in Acts of the Apostles is not the Gospel at all, but an historical statement as to God's dealing with man by the act of creation. This one question revealed in unmistakable terms the theological bankruptcy of both the Church Peace Union and the Federal Council of Churches.

Both the Federal Council and the Church Peace Union renewed their activities for peace in 1916. Late in 1915 the Church Peace Union had passed a series of resolutions on increased armaments and soon reinforced this action in February 1916 with a letter to President Wilson deploring the actions looking toward military preparedness and calling on both Wilson and the Congress to bend every national effort toward working out a plan of international cooperation for peace that would make the recurrence of such a world war impossible.[7] It also mailed resolutions to ten thousand Prostestant ministers and Jewish rabbis throughout the country. Some thirty-six hundred replies were received. Among the signers of these resolutions and letters to President Wilson were men who either were or would be leaders of the Federal Council: Henry Sloan Coffin, Washington Gladden, John R. Mackay, William P. Merrill, and J. Edgar Park.

Although it is true that the work of the Church Peace Union must not be confused with that of the Federal Council of Churches, there was a very close relationship between them. This is attested by the fact that this volume on the work of the Federal Council on international relations contains the record of the Church Peace Union, to which the Council gave its blessing and with which it cooperated. There is no note of protest against this involvement in the official records of the Federal Council.

The report of the commission on peace for 1915 concluded with a kind of confession of failure to understand the world it faced when the commission was formed:

> When this commission was established, most of us thought that the conditions for securing permanent peace in the world were being rapidly fulfilled. Not only had the integration of the activities and

6. *Ibid.*, pp. 19-23.
7. *Ibid.*, pp. 43-44.

the interests of the great nations through commerce, science, travel, education, banking facilities, postal communication and numberless international societies been proceeding for several decades at a rapidly increasing rate, but two great international conferences at The Hague had been held by which important steps had been officially taken for the establishment of an international court of arbitral justice and of boards of arbitration and conciliation.[8]

As naive as this confession may seem to the more cynical readers of the latter half of the twentieth century, and as naive as it actually is, there is in these words a wistfulness that reveals a passionate, if misguided, devotion to a peace that could not be achieved. Nor can it be today, and for the same reason. The commissioners pinned their hopes of peace on human achievements in the technical, political, and cultural areas. A superficial understanding of the cause of international conflict could only lead to a superficial kind of remedy. The refusal of the ecumenical leaders of that day to accept the biblical doctrine of sin undermined their whole approach to the solution of every special economic and political problem.

The drastic difference between the idealism of the leaders of the Federal Council and the realities of the era produced in the leaders' outlook a tension that is vividly portrayed in the report of the peace commission:

> If they [the churches] hold themselves strictly aloof from international problems, if they say these are questions with which the churches are not concerned, they will of course do nothing [about the war]. It is indeed true that these problems have important political and economic aspects. But they are fundamentally moral and spiritual. If, because of the inactivity of the churches, the tragedy of war should overtake America, would not the impotency and bankruptcy of American Christianity be loudly and justly proclaimed?[9]

Underlying this plea for a greater involvement of the churches of America in the task of keeping war from our shores was the assumption that such action was and would continue to be the main duty or one of the main tasks of the church, and failure to become involved would be little less than an acknowledgment of the bankruptcy of American Christianity. Actually this assumption itself rested upon a superficial view of the causes of war in general and the nature of World War I in particular. Likewise it rested on the supposition

8. *Ibid.*, p. 155.

9. *Ibid.*, p. 158.

that the church in America could somehow guide the thinking and actions of the unconverted and unregenerate of this country into paths that, in the opinion of the leaders of the Federal Council, were specifically Christian. The only answer these leaders had for this tragedy was somehow to see to it that the American people were permeated with a Christian international idealism: "To infuse this into all world movements is the distinctive and supreme task and duty of the Christian Church. The time has come for mobilizing the Christian forces of America and of the world for establishing Christian internationalism."[10]

However, the report that insisted on propagating Christian international idealism also contained a confession that highlighted the tensions of the day in ecumenical circles.

> We confess with sorrow and with shame our failure in teaching and in guiding our people. We have not seen the world as it is. We have left to selfish interests the determination of our international policies. We have not cried out as we should against wrongs committed. . . . We have not insisted that the principles of righteousness, justice, and goodwill toward other peoples and races should control our legislation in matters involving their interests and welfare.[11]

The genuine spirit and sincerity of this confession cannot be doubted. Nor can one doubt its superficial conception of the depth of human sin. Willing to acknowledge that people are selfish, the framers of this confession were still unwilling to admit that human sin lies at the heart of the matter, and that instructing people in the principles of righteousness, justice, and goodwill is vain if not accompanied by an instruction in the meaning of human sin and the atoning work or Christ as its only remedy.

Amidst the darkness of the day this commission offered to men a series of affirmations as a platform of hope. The affirmations set forth a creed of the Federal Council, one that was essentially humanistic, although its humanism was partially concealed by references to Infinite Will: "We accept and affirm with all the strength of Christian convictions those Christian conceptions of man and society, of races, nations and governments, upon which the permanent welfare of mankind rests and through the universal adoption of which world justice can alone be established and durable peace alone be maintained."[12]

10. *Ibid.*, pp. 159-60.
11. *Ibid.*, p. 161.
12. *Ibid.*, p. 171.

This affirmation then went on to assert that above all nations is humanity and that all nations are members of one great human family. Therefore, no nation is or could be complete in itself. Thus all sovereignty (on the human level) is limited and relative, subject to the Infinite Will and to the ethical restrictions and limitations of all humanity.[13]

This definition of sovereignty, on the one hand, seems rightly to point to the biblical insistence that only God is truly sovereign. On the other, the statement is seriously undermined by the affirmation that sovereignty is also limited and relative to the ethical restrictions and limitations of all humanity. Are the limitations imposed by God on nations equaled by those imposed on them by the demands of humanity? Is this definition of sovereignty limited by limitations imposed on it by all of humanity? If this is true, on what ground may it be said to be true? It would seem that this can only be true in the light of the scriptural teaching on the role of government. But this affirmation will not accept this view of government. The only hope that this report could offer to the quadrennial meeting of the Federal Council of 1916 was the realization of the ideal of universal disarmament, a far cry from the real world of 1916, which was engaged in the greatest war yet known to man.

The Quadrennial of 1916

The second quadrennial conference of the Federal Council opened in St. Louis late in 1916, facing a discouraging situation. On the home front efforts to promote the formation of local and state federations had not been as fruitful as expected; prospects for keeping the United States out of the war raging in Europe were being dissolved by the renewal of unrestricted submarine warfare by Germany and Woodrow Wilson's stiffening attitude toward this practice. Launched in the midst of the buoyant optimism of the progressive era, it was coming of age in the midst of military preparedness and war. The hope that the twentieth century would be the golden fulfillment of the promises of the nineteenth was growing increasingly feeble in the face of such events. The optimism that had produced the belief that the Western world, if not the world as a whole, had evolved to a place where it would no longer engage in the folly of war had been rudely shattered by the events of 1914. For most Americans a policy of disarmament, such as that which had been advocated by the Federal Council, and even the arbitration of inter-

13. *Ibid.*

national disputes, no longer seemed too feasible as a means of preventing war. This change of feeling which gripped most of the denominations comprising the constituency of the council was a tempering and modifying influence in the thinking of many, if not most of those, who gathered for this quadrennial session at St. Louis.

Thirty-three denominations or groups were represented at the St. Louis Quadrennial representing over 17,000,000 Protestants. However, the composition of the council at this time raises some very important questions. To what extent were the members of the constituent denominations aware of the real purpose of this new organization and to what extent did the council represent the theological position of the member churches? It is quite apparent that there was a serious cleavage between some of these denominations and the theology of the social gospel and an even greater cleavage between the historic theologies of the denominations and the theology of the leadership of the Federal Council. The Lutheran General Synod, the Presbyterian Church in the United States of America, the Southern Presbyterian Church and the Dutch Reformed (or Reformed Church in America) were far more conservative than the leadership of the council.[14]

The 1916 meeting produced very little that was new in theology or practice. By December the relations of the United States with Germany had deteriorated to such a point that it seemed unlikely President Wilson would be able to avoid our entry into the conflict. This despite the fact that during the political campaign he had run on a statement that certainly implied that since he had been able to keep the nation out of war during his first term, he would be able to do so the next four years. In April 1917 the nation went to war and the Federal Council found itself facing a serious dilemma. Its commitment to international peace and pacifism now confronted the very real challenge presented by our involvement in the European conflict. Would the leaders of the Federal Council remain loyal to their commitment or somehow find an accommodation with the realities of the situation?

The dilemma was partially eased for them by the propaganda that the Wilson administration administered to the nation in rather heavy doses under the leadership of George Creel. The belief that it was a war against autocracy and a kind of crusade to make the

14. It is true, however, that even these denominations were, with some exceptions moving leftward in their theology, but they were still in the conservative or orthodox camp. Certainly few of their members were willing to subscribe to the radical views of the leadership of the council in 1916.

world safe for democracy did much to make the leaders of the Federal Council come to terms with the demands of the wartime situation. They realized that they had a commitment to the soldiers and the civilians at the same time and they were also convinced that if Germany should win the conflict, then the basic purposes of the Federal Council not only would be endangered but probably would not be realized at all. The argument that the war was morally justified was very appealing to thousands of ministers in those churches that made up the Council; the Council simply could not afford to maintain its prewar rhetoric against all wars. This would be the last justifiable war to end all wars.

The Federal Council and World War I

The American entry into the war in April 1917 brought much of the indecision to an end and the Federal Council took immediate steps to rally to the support of a war "not of our making." In May the Council held a specially called meeting in Washington and created the General War Times Commission to act as a liaison between the government and the churches, and to speak for the Christian conscience of a nation at war. The commission, in a report, declared that it was its duty to aid the religious life of a people at war, to awaken a new consciousness of the social ministry of the church, and, in the third place, to be loyal to the government and yet keep alive an international consciousness among the Christian people of this nation.[15]

This commission in turn operated partially through another committee agency known as the National Committee on the Churches and Moral Aims of the War. Its task was to educate the American people on the moral aims of the war, but actually it placed its emphasis upon the necessity of our involvement in the conflict to save democracy and to aid in the creation of the League of Nations after the war was over.[16] This group held meetings in some three hundred cities and towns with an attendance estimated at about one million people. During the war the Council expended a great deal of energy in its efforts to improve the chaplaincy service for the armed forces and in maintaining contact with French and Belgian Protestants.

15. *Federal Council Bulletin* 1, No. 1:2.

16. S. M. Cavert, ed., *The Churches Allied for a Common Task, Report of the Third Quadrennial of the Federal Council of Churches of Christ in America* (New York, 1921), pp. 159-61.

This rallying around the colors caused some adverse criticism of the Council among various groups. The Mennonite General Conference saw fit to withdraw its membership at this time. In response to this criticism from pacifist churches, the executive committee of the Federal Council meeting at Cincinnati in December 1917 declared that it is not the business of the church to run errands for the government.[17] The position of the Council at this time, more or less offically declared, seems to have been to aid the government in that moment of great crisis, yet, at the same time, zealously to uphold the principle of separation of church and state in a delicate and complex situation. This is an admittedly difficult task at any time, but it was greatly complicated by the avowed pacifist stance of the leadership of the Federal Council and the theological position of some of the constituents like the Mennonites and the Quakers. The situation was made more delicate because many active pastors, both conservative and liberal, accepted the official thesis that it was not only a war, but a righteous war, a crusade to make the world safe for democracy and the final effort to banish war from the face of the earth. Many of these ministers later confessed that they had been misled and repented of their fall from the grace of pacifism. In effect, the leadership of the Federal Council became isolated from liberal pastors, from liberals in the pews whose conversion to pacifism had been somewhat superficial, and even from those whose conversion was genuine, but who regarded this war as a legitimate use of military force.[18]

Some of its leaders also saw in this situation an opportunity to bring their goal of church union nearer to realization, arguing for such local unions among various congregations as a war measure on a temporary basis.[19] Frank Mason North, in a address before the second annual meeting of the General War Times Commission in September 1918, took an even more advanced position on unity when he gave a plea for unity and union, calling the situation the greatest opportunity presented to the church in America for achieving unity through organic union.[20]

These pleas for a greater unity and union among Protestants passed largely unheeded for the moment, but they received new

17. *Federal Council Bulletin* 1, no. 2:1.

18. The impact of the war on the ministry has been well told by Ray Abrams, *Preachers Present Arms* (New York, 1935).

19. *Federal Council Bulletin* 1, no 4 (April 1918): 12-13.

20. *Ibid.*, no. 10 (October 1918): 3-5.

momentum in the years right after the war when various plans for denominational union were put forward.

Although the Federal Council was caught up in the patriotism aroused by our involvement in the struggle designed to end all wars and to make the world safe for democracy, its leadership also saw that the war could be very useful in promoting a postwar league of nations of some kind. The idea of such a league had been in the thinking of most of the Council leaders since the inception of the Council in 1908. They had since that time looked hopefully to the Hague Court as the best means of preventing future wars. When as early as 1915 President Wilson began to speak along the lines of a postwar alliance to keep the peace, he caught the attention of the leadership of the Council. And even as a league of nations became Wilson's great hope for the postwar world, it became the same for the theological and social liberals in the Federal Council.

They reasoned that if the war would result in the establishment of a league of nations of some kind, then our involvement would have been worthwhile and even justified. But at the same time the specter of the church's becoming involved with the state hung over their deliberations. If the church should not become an errand boy for the state in the waging of war, could it fulfill this function in the pursuit of peace? For many leaders in the churches, both within and without the Federal Council, this was not a theoretical question to be discussed and then neglected, but a very practical issue that could easily wreck the ecumenical movement at this point in its history.

However, the Federal Council leadership was far from consistent in refusing to be an errand boy for the state and was not always careful in drawing that line between church and state as many of its member denominations desired. The Council consistently rallied to the defense of wartime prohibition, imposed on the country by the Wilson administrations as a war measure. The records of the executive and the special commissions created at that time reveal that prohibition was a constant theme of their discussions. The leaders quickly saw that this wartime emergency measure could be translated into a permanent prohibition measure and they rallied to the cause in supporting the government. Since the prohibition of intoxicating liquors was for them at that time a moral issue, it was not too difficult to apply the same logic to the cause of peace and to rally to the support of a postwar league of nations.

In 1919 the Commission on International Justice and Good Will issued a report that showed very clearly the drift of opinion in the leadership of the Council on this issue. It declared that the supreme hope for the future was in the League of Nations. This was the one worthwhile thing that had come out of the war.[21] This strong declaration was coupled with an equally strong affirmation that the United States must join the league in order to realize this hope: "There is one clear and incisive call to the Churches of Christ in America at the present time and that is the call for cooperation on the part of all men and women of good will to the end that our nation may speedily and heartily become a part of this grand international enterprise."[22]

The third quadrennial assembly of the Federal Council was held in Boston. Twenty member churches were represented and Frank Mason North was president. By the time it met, the issue of the League of Nations had been settled for all practical purposes. The institution the Council had declared to be the one sure hope for the future began to function without the presence of the United States as a member, a fact much lamented by most liberals, who regarded our absence as a crippling blow to the infant organization designed to maintain world peace and democracy. That much of the Council leadership concurred in this general feeling is quite evident from its public utterances of one kind or another. But the problem of the League of Nations as such ceased to command the attention that it had received for a time in the deliberations of the various commissions and committees of the organization.[23]

By 1920 the ecumenical movement was again becoming absorbed in domestic issues. Even before the Boston meeting the way had been prepared to focus its attention on the social gospel in its domestic implications. In 1919 a special committee on the war and the religious outlook gave a report, "The Church Facing the Future," that set the tone for the Boston meeting.[24] This committee, created in 1918 by the Federal Council and the General War

21. S. M. Cavert, ed., *The Churches Allied for a Common Task*, p. 157.

22. *Ibid.*, p. 158.

23. The history of the Federal Council of Churches is cluttered with committees and creations. They were created for every conceivable purpose with duties and membership that often overlapped and at times their chief effect is confusion for the serious student of the history of this organization. It is easy to get the impression that the leadership of the Council was convinced that the kingdom of God would be achieved by creating a sufficient number of committees on the deliberations of which the kingdom would be brought into being.

24. The Commission on International Peace and Good Will continued to pass resolutions upholding the principles of the league, however.

Times Commission, with Dr. Henry Churchill King as its chairman and William Adams Brown as vice chairman, declared that the new social order was the hope of humanity, a social order that Christ called the kingdom of God: "We conceive it to be the duty of the Church to point out wherein human life, as it is presently organized, falls far short of this ideal and fails to apply these principles and what changes need to be made.[25]

The report pointed out that the church had failed miserably in the areas of race relations and business practices and that these areas must be subjected to the rule of Christian ethics. The report insisted that apart from Christian individuals there can be no Christian society. However, the context of this affirmation does not support the idea that it was expressing the evangelical concept of being Christian; rather, it was using it in an ethical sense, insisting that there can be no society that reflects the Christian ethic apart from those individuals whose lives express this same ethical concept.[26] This restriction of the word *Christian* to an ethical content is quite evident in other parts of the report, which declared that the ideal of the Christian society is sealed in the biblical doctrine of the fatherhood of God and brotherhood of man; this in turn was immediately related to the ecumenical concept of the church: "There can be but one church in the nature of the case and the inward unity which the Christian conscience affirms craves outward expression."[27]

At this meeting the Commission on the Church and Social Service, which had been reorganized in 1919, issued a report in which it reaffirmed the basic content of the Social Creed of 1908, that Christian principles must be applied to industry because the human race constitutes a great family under the fatherhood of God. Thus, the primary responsibility of industry must be to secure the more abundant life for the masses of the people, and service must be the controlling motive in business rather than the expectation of profits.[28]

This report, however, did not stop with a simple affirmation of the principles of 1908. It went much further and outlined what the future work of the Federal Council should be in the area of social and industrial relations. It openly said that its future work should include study and research, and the preparation of study courses on social problems for churches, colleges, and other groups. Even more

25. Cavert, *op. cit.*, p. 39-40.

26. *Ibid.*, p. 40.

27. *Ibid.*, p. 51.

28. *Ibid.*, pp. 118-21.

important, perhaps, was the declaration that it must become involved in the field of social legislation to aid in reaching what it called "constructive measures."[29] In calling for the preparation for study courses on social problems and research in social legislation for the avowed purpose of influencing legislative activity, this report went much further than previous statements that called for direct action for the purpose of achieving liberal and radical social legislation. This committee was not at all squeamish about its program. If the church was not to be the errand boy of the government, the government was to be the agency through which the kingdom of God was to be realized. In using the state for this sublime purpose the committee was quite willing to surrender its former stand that the separation of church and state must be maintained. But this kingdom of God must be democratic in its nature: "If we talk democracy, let us act democracy." It might be ethically regarded as the kingdom of God, but politically it would be under the control of man, hopefully under the leadership of the Federal Council of Churches. In these reports we find the themes that would dominate the thinking of the Council in the decade of the twenties—race relations, the democratization (socialization) of industry, and democracy in all areas of our national life—all of which were to be coupled with an intensification of the movement for the organic union of the Protestant churches as the prerequisite for the success of this Christianizing of American society.

It is obvious that the issues that loomed large on the ecumenical horizon in 1920 were by their very nature controversial and were likely to bring severe criticism of the Federal Council from many sources, both from within the constituent churches and from denominations not affiliated with the Council in any way. A harbinger of the controversy to come can be seen in the criticism leveled against some of the activities by the Southern Presbyterian church, which entered a series of protests against some positions assumed by the Federal Council: "While there are many things in the reports of the Council [for 1914] which we heartily approve . . . there are actions which so do violence to the historic and scriptural positions of our church that we can do nothing else than to decline to accept the responsibility for them and enter our protest."[30]

The General Assembly of 1916 repeated this protest and also rec-

29. *Ibid.*, p. 123.

30. *Minutes of the General Assembly of the Presbyterian Church in the United States for 1915* (Richmond, Va., 1915), p. 39.

ommended that the Federal Council create a committee to channel communications with that body since the previous protest had gone unheeded. This was a valuable and practical suggestion, but it also went unheeded, at least in the sense that it didn't result in any positive action being taken. In the General Assembly of 1919, a committee reported a much stronger protest and spoke out vigorously against the resolutions on political issues passed by the Federal Council in its meeting at Cleveland in May 1919.[31]

Such protests hardly caused a ripple on the placid scenes of radical ecumenicity. The only other protest that received any official attention was the withdrawal of the Mennonite General Conference in 1917 because of the failure of the Council to take a bold stand against the war. The protests of the Southern Presbyterian church were aimed at the very heart of the Federal Council and its reason for being, whereas the Mennonite protest was aimed against what that group felt was a violation of its stated principles. On the other hand, the Cleveland meeting admitted the Christian Reformed Church and the Church of God in North America (General Eldership) into membership. Since both of these groups were quite conservative, their admission more than seemed to counterbalance, for the moment at least, the conservative protest from the Southern Presbyterian church and the Mennonite withdrawal.

This refusal of the Federal Council to pay any serious attention to its critics within its membership boded ill for those who later tried to defend the membership of conservative evangelical denominations in the Council on the ground that they had a moderating influence on its actions. Such a hope or assertion has no real foundation in the history of the Council up to 1920. When we look at the lists of those who represented conservative denominations during the first twelve years of its existence we are forced to conclude that they had relatively little influence on the final decisions of that body so far as its social and economic policies are concerned.

31. *Minutes of the General Assembly of the Presbyterian Church for 1919* (Richmond, Va., 1919), p. 55.

3

The Federal Council, 1918-1929

For the Federal Council the war years had been something of an interlude for its activities. In spite of its pacifist creed and actions, the Council had almost inevitably been drawn into the conflict to the extent that some of its leaders were easily convinced that the war against Germany was essentially a crusade against autocracy on the one hand and the war to end all war on the other. The Council also participated in a program to aid the chaplains in the armed forces. The very nature of the period was unfriendly to its programs of social and economic reform, and its work on the home front almost came to a complete halt. Its program for the reformation of American life received little attention and less action. Unlike its successor, the National Council of Churches, the Federal Council seems to have overlooked the possibilities of a war situation for bringing about radical reforms in American society. It is also true, of course, that the Wilson era did not offer the same encouragement for such reform as did the age of Franklin Roosevelt.

With the coming of peace in November 1918, the attention of the leadership of the Council was focused on what it felt were the bright hopes of the Versailles Conference and the League of Nations. Our entrance into the League of Nations would more than justify our involvement in the war. The league gave support to the belief that we had fought the war to end all wars and that it was now a mission accomplished. The leadership of the Federal Council was convinced that the church in America must use its influence to support Wilson's peace aims even as most churches had supported his war aims. Permanent peace must be the ultimate result of four years of bloody carnage such as the world had never experienced.

But the forging of a just and durable peace and the American involvement in the League of Nations were but one aspect of the challenge of the postwar era for the Federal Council. Its leadership looked upon the 1920s as the threshold of a new era in which the social gospel would thrive as never before and bring the millennium to this country. Once peace was established and a warless world a reality, the church would then be free to center its attention on the other ills affecting American society.

A new spirit of optimism over the Council's role in the affairs of the nation was quite evident at the quadrennial meeting held in Boston in 1920.[1] In its message to the churches, the quadrennial declared that the task of the Christian Church was "to help men realize that kind of life that befits free personalities who accept the standards of Jesus Christ."[2]

It was the duty of the church to show by deed what Christian discipleship means for the family, for the home, for industry, and for a proper relationship between the races. The very nature of the special program presupposed a new emphasis on an ecumenical cooperation, and Samuel M. Cavert, now the general secretary of the Council, issued a fervent but unrealistic plea for unity:

> Within the Federal Council there is full freedom for those who are now joined in common tasks to hold varying views as to the ultimate form in which the spirit of Christian unity may express itself. Some

1. At this meeting Dr. Robert E. Speer, secretary of the Board of Foreign Missions of the Presbyterian Church, USA, was elected president.

2. *Federal Council Bulletin* 4, no. 1 (January 1921): 1-5.

there are whose eyes are fixed upon the coming of a complete organic union in which the many groups while preserving their own
distinct methods of worship and work and their own special emphasis and point of view shall be organized in a single comprehensive
church. Others simply want friendly cooperation. Both groups can
meet in hearty accord in the Federal Council.[3]

The assumption that within the Federal Council there would be
full freedom for varying views on important issues was quite false.
In fact, the declaration that it was the task of the church to help
men realize that kind of life that befits free personalities who accept the standards of Jesus Christ clearly indicates that there was
no place for evangelicals in the Council. The most that the Council
could or would ask of cooperating groups was some kind of loyalty
to undefined standards supposedly set by Jesus Christ. Evangelicals
would have to set aside their belief in conversion and regeneration
if they wished to cooperate in these schemes for social reform.

The problem of industrial relations and labor unions was one of
the first to receive the enthusiastic attention of the Council. Bishop
Francis J. McConnell had sounded the call for action in an address
before the Boston quadrennial. In it he declared that it was perfectly fair to assume that anything that made for larger manhood
of the spirit of Jesus Christ has a religious significance.[4]

The Council responded to this call by urging collective bargaining
on the major industries of the country and entered into active contact with management for this purpose. These efforts to persuade
management to enter into collective bargaining on a nationwide
scale resulted in the first widespread criticism of the Council from
other than Southern Presbyterian circles. The Council attempted
to meet the criticism by holding in New York in March 1921 a
meeting that was claimed to be marked by a spirit of brotherhood.

The specified object of this attack was the Social Creed of 1908
and the Council was for the first time forced to declare its position
on the social issues.[5] It admitted that the Social Creed of 1908 had
come from the Methodist Social Creed of that year. It also attempted to defend itself by pointing out that several of the constituent churches had since that time adopted social creeds of their

3. *Ibid.*, no. 2, (April-May 1921): 2-3.

4. *Ibid.*, no. 1 (January 1921): 24.

5. This attack came from the Pittsburgh Employers Association and the basic issue
was the idea of a social creed itself.

own.[6] The use of a social creed to broaden the influence of the Federal Council into labor relations was regarded as unwarranted and directly contrary to the purpose of the church as it had been instituted by Christ.

The specific issue was the report of the Social Service Commission of the Council, a report that was quite critical of the conditions existing in the coal mines. Liberal church publications were not slow to respond to the challenge. The *Churchman* (Episcopalian) declared:

> Well, let the churches accept the challenge. Let Mr. Long and like-minded employers withdraw their money from the churches and from any church whose social ideals offended them. Any minister of Christ, any church in Christendom which would promise to confine its teachings to zones of agreement would be unworthy of stewardship in the Christian Church.[7]

The *Congregationalist* uttered a similar sentiment.

> Honestly now, could the church stand for anything less than this? Of course, there is room for differences of opinion with regard to just what a living wage is and as to the practical application of some of these outstanding principles, but in the main, the platform is one by which the Christian Church must stand or turn traitor to the Master.[8]

In his editorial opinion Samuel M. Cavert undoubtedly touched on the real issue when he wrote: "It is clear that the real issue is not any particular utterance or action of the Federal Council, but the whole question as to whether the churches are to include the problem of industrial relationships in their field of interest."[9]

The Council leadership was not at all deterred in its program by this outburst of criticism and sponsored a conference on church and industry in November 1921 in Boston at which Roman Catholics, Jews, Unitarians, and Universalists participated, The composition of this conference certainly belied the claim of the leadership of

6. The National Council of the Congregational Churches had adopted such a creed in 1910, as had the General Assembly of the Presbyterian Church, USA. The Northern Baptist Convention did likewise in 1911 and this action was followed by the Methodist Episcopal Church South in 1914. In 1919 the Board of Bishops of the Methodist Episcopal Church adopted a similar statement and in this same year the fortieth international convention of the YMCA adopted its sixteen articles.

7. *Churchman*, April 2, 1921, p. 54.

8. *Congregationalist*, March 31, 1921.

9. *Federal Council Bulletin* 4, no. 3 (April-May 1921): 54.

the Federal Council that it offered a meeting place where all Christians could find a unity of action in social matters.

The fact that Jews and Unitarians could participate in such a conference held under the auspices of the Council raised a serious question as to its basic Christian integrity.

Some leaders were becoming increasingly sensitive to the criticism that was coming their way, and in 1922 Dr. Samuel McCrea Cavert attempted to answer it. Brushing aside most of it as unworthy, he did admit that the charge that most ministers and rank-and-file members were not competent to discuss the difficult questions involved in labor relations, particularly the thorny question of what constitutes a just and living wage, had validity. But he quickly added that the church must become competent in this matter.[10] In assuming the offensive in this matter, Cavert set forth the justification for the entrance of the church into industrial affairs, which rationale became the standard for the next twenty years. Cavert insisted that the church must be free and not confined to a narrow zone of agreement, and that it has the right and the duty to speak since it is impossible to divorce Christianity from economics. The church must know the world in order to bring Christian principles to bear upon its activities. In its meeting in February 1922, the administration committee of the Council called for a national conference on Christianity and social questions to be held in either 1923 or 1924 for the purpose of dealing with the questions involving industrial shops and race relations. But it also declared that the purpose of such a conference would be to study these issues and not to entertain mere opinions or become an agency for propaganda. This avowal would have carried more weight if the committee had not appointed as members of this committee of 100 such radicals as Kirby Page, Sherwood Eddy, Worth Tippy, and Harry F. Ward. Even by 1922 these men were so impressed with the Russian experiment in communism that it is difficult to believe they could confine themselves to an objective study of these two areas of American life.

Dr. Cavert again took up the cudgels for the entrance of the church into the area of social concerns by attempting to pour oil on the troubled waters with an ameliorating plea:

Let us be done with setting the social gospel and the Gospel or the individual over against each other. Each is but a partial phase of one individual whole. The good news announced by Jesus is a message

10. *Ibid.*, 5, no. 2 pp. 14-15.

for the transformation of personal character, but character is a matter of social relationships. So there can be no real preaching of the gospel apart from its social meaning nor any effective proclamation of the social gospel that does not rest on an appeal to individual hearts and wills.[11]

Cavert was quite emphatic that in order to obtain its goals in society, the church through the Federal Council must definitely set itself to the task of molding public opinion:

So if we are to have a Christian society, Christians must come to a common mind on the meaning of Christianity for contemporary issues.

In the development of such a Christian public opinion an organization like the Federal Council ought to render an indispensable service to all churches.[12]

It is quite obvious that Cavert was calling on the Federal Council definitely to secure a common mind among the churches for the social task he and his colleagues envisioned for it. But it is equally true, that the creation of this common mind also entailed the creation of a common faith in the social gospel and its theological implications. Sharp theological divergences could not be allowed to continue lest the progress of the social gospel be impeded by such diversity. Yet in 1922 there seems to have been very little criticism of the direction in which the Federal Council was leading its constituent membership. Favorable reaction came from the General Conference of the Methodist Episcopal Church South, and the General Assembly of the Presbyterian Church, USA, which voted to give the sum of $30,000 to its work. The only discordant note came from the 1922 meeting of the General Assembly of the Presbyterian Church, U.S. (Southern). Here the question of the work of the Council brought on a sharp debate. A large minority was in favor of withdrawing because of the intrusion of the Council into the social and political realms. The assembly refused to make any appropriations for the program, but it also refused to withdraw from membership in the Council. By 1922 the southern Presbyterian Church had become the most persistent critic of the policies of the Federal Council.

By 1923 criticism inhabited other church bodies to such an extent

11. *Ibid.*, no. 4 (June-July 1922): 5.

12. *Ibid.*, p. 5.

that the Council felt it wise to send out speakers to the annual meetings of some of the constituent churches to defend the Council's intrusion into such issues as labor relations. These speakers were sent to the meetings of the General Assemblies of the Presbyterian Church, USA, the Presbyterian Church, U.S., the United Presbyterian Church, and the Reformed Church in America. The issue became most acute in the Southern Presbyterian church; there was another extended debate in the 1923 General Assembly over the activities of the Council in the areas of industrial relations and international policies. However, after a fervent plea by Robert E. Speer, the assembly voted to remain in the Federal Council.[13] The messages in behalf of the Council were then favorably received by the other churches. The Presbyterian Church, USA included the Council in its budget for the first time with an appropriation of $25,000. The Reformed church increased its from $1,300 to $4,000.[14]

By 1924, publications and public utterances of various Council leaders were beginning to reflect some of the tensions that its social policies were engendering. There was a growing awareness that these policies were endangering the traditional Protestant conception of church and state. In an editorial Samuel McCrae Cavert, executive secretary of the Council, sought to quiet this growing apprehension that the social and economic program upon which the Council was entering might endanger this tradition:

> We zealously cherish the conviction, on the one hand, that the church should be free from political control or support and, on the other, that no religious test should be required for public office.
> But that the church should not undertake to influence the state toward Christian ends surely was never in the minds of the founders of our nation nor could this be the desire of any Christian today.[15]

In response to the question, How is the church to help the state to become an instrument for the furthering of the right? Cavert offered several suggestions. In stating that the church should never become involved in partisan politics or align itself with one political party against the other, he insisted that the primary purpose of the church in public affairs was to quicken the conscience of men

13. *Ibid.* 6, no. 4: 27.
14. *Ibid.*, p. 27.
15. *Ibid.*, 7, no. 4 (July-August 1924): 7.

and to make them more sensitive to moral and spiritual issues. By doing this the church would develop a Christian public opinion on social and international issues and would be able to express this opinion in an effective manner. Having gone this far, he abruptly retreated and said that the church should not pass a corporate judgment on the issues of the day. But he coupled this insistence with an ambivalent statement that occasionally it must do so or deny its own nature. He cited such issues as American entrance into the World Court, support of the Eighteenth Amendment, and the prohibition of child labor as those exceptions on which the church should pass corporate judgment.[16]

The importance of his editorial lies in the fact that it served as a guide to the position assumed by the leadership of the Federal Council in reference to the questions confronting the nation from 1920 to 1932.

Cavert was quite correct in assuming that the Founding Fathers believed that the United States must serve Christian ends. He was equally correct in asserting that the church must never ally itself with one political party over against another. But in his efforts to explain how the church should influence public opinion toward these Christian ends and purposes, he ran into serious error. He assumed that somehow the church can create a Christian public opinion on social issues among those who are not Christian. How can the church make people more sensitive to spiritual and moral issues if they are spiritually dead in sin? Cavert never considered this basic question.

In 1924 the Federal Council was also emphasizing four additional principles inherent in the Social Creed: the gradual and reasonable reduction of the hours of labor; a living wage as a minimum wage along with the highest possible wage each industry can afford; the application of the Christian principle, carefully undefined, to the acquisition and use of property, a principle exceedingly stressed; and the most equitable division of the products of labor and industry that can be devised. These principles were given a new emphasis and urgency in the Labor Day message to the churches of 1924.

It becomes evident that the social thinking of the Federal Council by 1924 was openly assuming the direction that the logic of the Social Creed of 1908 demanded. The Council was not only asking the churches to direct the Christian conscience of America; it was also asking the church to think in terms of a socialistic collectivism.

16. *Ibid.*, p. 1.

The affinity with socialism lurked beneath the surface of most of its pronouncements during the period from 1920 to 1932 and was the object of most of the criticism directed against the Council. Some churches, notably the Southern Presbyterian, held to a view of the spirituality of the church, which view opposed any interference with economic affairs in the name of the Gospel. Others, while not opposing economic and social pronouncements per se, were very much opposed to any trend toward socialism by the Federal Council and reacted accordingly.

By 1926, leaders of the Council were becoming much more vocal in their public questioning of the legitimacy of the profit motive. Ernest Fremont Tittle held that a reasonable profit was legitimate but he raised the question whether it was legitimate to enter business to make a profit.[17] The implication of this article was that entering business for profit was not legitimate, but equally disturbing was his implication that the church had the right to judge what profits were fair and what profits fell short of the Christian ethic.

The leftward drift of the Council was even more evident in the plea made by Bishop Francis J. McConnell to its membership in 1925:

> It is the duty of the Church to see the actual contradiction in the world between the ideals proclaimed by Christ and the facts as we see them. . . . But let us remember that we do live under a capitalistic system and we breathe its air. Why should we not be inspiring in dealing with it?. . .I plead for the radicals in our churches. I mean the radical in the literal sense of honestly getting down to the root of things. . . . He holds the essential Christian ideal up high.[18]

This leftward movement did not escape public attention. Early in 1927 Congressman Arthur Free of California introduced a resolution into the House of Representatives calling for an investigation of the propaganda activities of the Federal Council, charging that it was radical and subversive.[19]

Fuel was added to the fire of indignation when Dr. Worth M. Tippy, of the Council's Commission on the Church and Social Service,

17. *Ibid.*, no. 5:14.

18. *Ibid.* 8, no. 2 (March-April 1925):13-14.

19. Rather abruptly and for reasons never made public, Congressman Free withdrew early in 1928 his plan for investigating the Council on the ground that he had used false information when he introduced it.

aided in the drafting of the *Appeal to Southern Industrial Leaders,* which was signed by forty Southern churchmen. Its purpose was to ask this leadership to raise the wages in the textile industry to the level of what was deemed a living wage.

The proposal that the Federal Council should be investigated for its propaganda activities caused the liberal and some rather conservative theological journals to rally to its defense. The *United Presbyterian* declared:

> There has been caution and care in the formulation of its pronouncements and in the definition of ways wherein the churches should act cooperatively. And we express our strong hope that Christianity, voiced and expressed by the Federal Council of Churches, will become more and more dangerous and threatening to every man who is unfriendly to the high morality of the Sermon on the Mount in our national life.[20]

The liberal *Christian Century* welcomed the proposed investigation by Congressman Free as an indication that the voice of the Council was being heard and its influence felt in political circles. It rejoiced that the churches were beginning to exercise a power in American life too long denied to them.[21]

For the first time since the Council was formed, the charges lodged against it forced the organization to take note of the growing criticism of its activities. The Council's Administrative Committee formally issued a reply to its critics. In reply to the charge that the Council was "continually adding to its program undertakings distinctly nonreligious in nature and outside the mission of the church," the committee said:

> If such tasks as the cultivation of public opinion in support of better social and industrial conditions, the prohibition of liquor traffic, and the development of other means than war for settling disputes between nations are non-religious in nature and outside the mission of the Church, then the Federal Council gladly admits the charge. To influence public opinion for such causes was one of the fundamental purposes for which the Council was created by its twenty-eight constituent members.[22]

20. *United Presbyterian,* March 24, 1927. The relatively conservative editor of this journal apparently failed to understand that the radical social outlook of the Federal Council bore no resemblance to the idealism of the Sermon on the Mount.

21. *Christian Century,* March 17, 1927.

22. *Federal Council Bulletin* 10, no. 4 (May 1927): 29.

In reply to the second major accusation, that the Council was in no way a representative body, the committee declared that it was absolutely false and insisted that the Council was organized throughout on a representative basis:

"The four hundred members of the Council as a whole, which meets once in four years, the one hundred members of the executive committee, which meets annually, and the twenty-eight members of the Administrative Committee, which meets every month, are appointed by the highest authorities in the several denominations that comprise the Council. No one, of course, would think of claiming that on any specific issue the 20,000,000 church members unanimously agree with the position taken by the members of the Council's governing bodies. . . . No one can deny, however, that the utterances of the Federal Council are made only after full consideration by those whom the denominations have themselves appointed to deal with such matters in the council.[23]

The tone of the defense became more indignant as the committee attempted to refute the third charge, which in essence stated that the Federal Council was working under the direction of radical groups affiliated with the Third Internationale.

There is no shred of truth in this allegation. The council takes its position without reference to or in connection with any organization except those of the churches, and the well known character and patriotic service of the men and women appointed by the various denominations to direct the program of the Council are in themselves sufficient answer to the baseless charge that they are associated with any groups inimical to the welfare of the country.[24]

These denials issued by the Administrative Committee were something less than convincing. Many evangelicals in the major denominations were absolutely convinced that the Federal Council was increasingly concerned with issues that were not the province of the church and certainly not part of its mission, and this report admitted that this charge was essentially true. What was omitted was a frank recognition that there was a basic theological division between the evangelicals and the adherents of the social

23. *Ibid., p.* 29.
24. *Ibid., p.* 29.

gospel and that social gospel was the basic creed of the Federal Council. Because of this fact it necessarily follows that the Council was not truly representative of the thinking of the vast majority of the membership of the constituent churches. However, it did represent the thinking of many of those in control of the ecclesiastical machinery of these denominations.

The refutation of the third charge against the Council was false. Leading members of the Council had been and still were very friendly to the Communist philosophy and were shaping the social creed of the Federal Council in that direction.[25] Even in 1927 the trend toward radicalism in the thinking of the Council leadership was evident; certainly some leaders were becoming well known for their radical utterances and activities.

The reply of the Council to its critics is worth noting at this point. It contained a note of defiance that was in sharp contrast to its assertion of dedication to speak for the churches and to voice their collective Christian conscience:

> It can not be too strongly emphasized that, in these and all other questions of public welfare, the Federal Council of Churches seeks to discover the high common mind of the constituent denominations and then to speak and act in their behalf. This is what the Council has done in the past. This is what the denominations expect it to continue to do in the future. Its course will in no way be modified by the unjustifiable attacks of the forces which would, if they could, stifle the voice of the churches and weaken their influence in the life of the nation.[26]

The determination of the leaders of the Federal Council to extend their missionary activities in behalf of the their social gospel could only call forth increased criticism from the Council's evangelical opponents. But close kinship between their social outlook and liberal theology became increasingly apparent and they inevitably spurned this evangelical criticism. Bishop Francis McConnell, long identified as one of the liberal leaders of the Council, wrote in *The Christlike God:* "Is not the tendency to deify Christ more heathen then Christian? Are we not more truly Christian when

---

25. The relationship between the Federal Council and radicalism of the Communist variety will be dealt with much more fully in chapter eight.

26. *Federal Council Bulletin* 10, no. 4 (May 1927): 29.

we cut loose from a heathen propensity and take Jesus simply for the character that He was and for the ideal that He is?"[27]

Samuel G. Craig, the editor of *The Presbyterian*, quickly alerted the Presbyterians to this open denial of the deity of Jesus Christ. Charles MacFarland of the Federal Council was not slow to reply, but his defense was far from satisfactory. It seemed to many readers little less than an admission that heresy coming from a Methodist bishop was to be accepted as orthodoxy.[28] Many felt that MacFarland's final statement that *The Christlike God* had strengthened his faith in God, in Christ, and in humanity was little more than a confession as to how far the Federal Council had drifted from historic Christianity.

The mounting criticism of its policies by 1929 forced the leadership of the Federal Council to answer the charges against it in much greater detail than was its custom. At the request of its editor, Dr. Frank Mason North prepared for the *Bulletin* "The Social Ideal of the Churches," which traced the history of the relationship between the social-gospel movement and the formation of the Federal Council.[29] Declaring that the main principles or convictions upon which the ever-widening principles are the social concern of the churches were then old enough (by 1929) to have become historic, North then traced the close relationship between this concern and the movement, which relationship resulted in the formation of the Federal Council in 1908. In his efforts to portray this social concern as historic, MacFarland clearly proved that the close affinity between the social gospel and politico-economic socialism had entered into the thinking of some of the major denominations by 1890. He quoted with favor the platform drafted by the Open and Institutional Church League and adopted in 1894, which said in part: "Thus the open and institutional church claims to save all men and all the men by all means, abolishing so far as possible the distinction between the religious and the secular and the sanctifying all days and all means to the great end of saving the whole world for Christ."[30]

In this attempt to defend the program of the Federal Council as it existed in 1929, North was actually admitting that it was the purpose of the leadership to obliterate the distinction between the

27. Francis J. McConnell, *The Christlike God* (Nashville, 1927), p. 137.

28. For this controversy, see *Federal Council Bulletin* 12, no. 1: 22-23.

29. *Ibid.*, no. 3: 13-14.

30. *Ibid.*, (April 1929): 14.

religious and the secular from the very beginning, thus substantiating the very charges this article was supposedly written to refute. To support this thesis he even went so far as to cite as evidence the Social Creed of 1908. The more evidence he cited to support the basic thesis that the social concern of the Federal Council was not a recent innovation, the more support he gave to those who contended that the Federal Council had been formed to advance a liberal and potentially radical social, political, and economic program in the name of Christianity.

The movement to involve the Council in radical social reform gained momentum as the effects of the Great Depression became more widespread in American life.

In its report for 1930 the executive committee of the Federal Council declared that unemployment conditions were so widespread that it called for the united efforts of all forces concerned with the problems of human welfare.[31] At the same time attention was called to the shocking inequalities of income in this country; the executive committee declared that "too large a share of the national income goes to those who must invest it, if it is to be profitable to them in activities which are already overdeveloped and over capitalized."[32] It also declared that "too small a share goes to those who would use it for food, clothing, housing, and other necessities and comforts of life." All of which was intended to serve as an introduction and justification of the main thesis of the report of the Commission on the Church and Social Service: "The Christian ideal calls for hearty support of a planned economic system in which maximum social values shall be brought. It demands that cooperation shall supplant competition as the fundamental method."[33]

The report further insisted this ideal called for a vigorous educational program using trained economists, social engineers, and leaders in business and labor: " The churches should be ready for a warm-hearted cooperation with every sincere attempt . . . to build a better social order, and they themselves should become a source of inspiration for such an effort."[34] This report called for an industrial as well as a political democracy with government ownership and control of industries for the better promotion of the common welfare.

31. *Annual Report of the Federal Council of Churches,* 1930, p. 133.

32. *Ibid.,* pp. 163-64.

33. *Ibid.,* p. 64.

34. *Ibid.*

The report called for the practical application of the "Christian" principle of social well-being to the acquisition and use of wealth, and for the subordination of the speculative and profit motives to the creative and cooperative spirit. This, of course, is a delightful socialistic millennium, which was being presented as the earthly goal of Christianity.

Basic to the achievement of this utopia was the demand for social planning along with the control of credit and the monetary systems and economic processes for the common welfare. More specifically, the report advocated practical goals, of which some were not contrary to orthodox Christianity while others were definitely hostile to the biblical world-and-life view. The safeguarding of all workers against harmful conditions of labor and occupational diseases and injury was in keeping with the ethical requirements of the Gospel. But the socialist influence was quite evident in the insistence that there must be a wider and more equitable distribution of wealth plus, for workers, a just share of the products of industry and agriculture. The key to this part of the report lies in the meaning attached to the word *just*. Rightly interpreted, this affirmation could be regarded as in harmony with the biblical view of economic activity. But other aspects of the report make it doubtful whether this biblical meaning is intended, because there was also an emphasis on the fair share of the products of industry apart from what the wage earner actually produced.

This report included what was to be the new social creed of the Federal Council of 1932. It would be the foundation for the Council's increasingly extensive involvement in social, economic, and political matters in the era of the New Deal.[35]

The Federal Council and the Problem of Peace and War, 1920-1932

Second only to its passion for social and economic reform was the concern of the Federal Council for world peace. Although it did not receive as much attention in the early years of the 1920s, it was never absent from the thinking of the leadership of the Council. By 1930 it was again rivaling social reform as a center of attention. Although the outbreak of World War I and American involvement in that conflict dulled the outward expression of the passion for peace, the international scene during the twenties offered tempt-

35. For the full text of this proposed creed, see *Annual Report of the Federal Council of Churches*, 1932, 72-73.

ing and fruitful possibilities for a new accent by the Council, which once again offered the hope of a warless world to a war-weary nation. Inspired by American leadership in calling the Washington Arms Conference, the Council issued in 1921 "A Declaration of Ideals and Policy Looking Toward a Warless World."[36]

This declaration modestly admitted that it was not the task of the church to detail the political methods and institutions by which the scourge of war was to be banished; this was the task of statesmen. It insisted, however, that it was the right and duty of the churches to declare in no uncertain terms the moral principles that are involved in international life and to insist that "our lawmakers and all those who represent the nation in its international relations shall observe these principles with the utmost care. We insist that the main issues shall neither be evaded nor obscured by the discussion of details."[37]

The report rejoiced that the Washington Arms Conference had made a good beginning with its agreement for a radical reduction of naval strength among the major powers and with its agreements regarding China and the maintenance of peace in the Pacific. But this was only a beginning. The Federal Council went on record as calling for a drastic reduction in the size of armies, air forces, submarines, and other forms of armament.

War itself must be abolished. To do this, institutions of peace must be established. The Council went on to affirm its belief that "peculiar duties and responsibilities rest upon the Christians in this and all other lands for the establishment of institutions of peace."[38]

And then, in spite of a professed willingness to allow the details of a warless world to be worked out by statesmen from the various nations, it went on to give details for the achievement of these goals, even spelling out how Germany, Austria, Russia, and Great Britain should be treated. It called for American participation in institutions for the formulation of international law and for the effective operation of an international court of justice. It specifically called upon President Harding to make good on his pledge that this country would become part of an international organization for the maintenance of peace.

To give support to this program the Federal Council called upon

36. *Annual Report*, 1921, pp. 11-16. This declaration was adopted by the executive committee on December 15, 1921, in behalf of the Federal Council.

37. *Ibid.*, p. 11.

38. *Ibid.*, p. 13.

each of the constituent churches to establish its own appropriate committee to cooperate with the Council's Commission on International Justice and Good Will. It also urged these denominations to provide adequate courses for their students for promoting the understanding and solution of international problems.

This declaration served as a guide for the activities of the Federal Council in its efforts to promote international peace, not only during the twenties, but also during the early thirties, until the rise of Hitler again brought war clouds to Europe. Future statements and decisions made after 1921 either were supplementary to this one or were efforts to apply these principles to specific situations in the realm of international relations. Late in 1922 the Commission on International Justice and Good Will began an active campaign for the realization of these goals by entering into a cooperative agreement with the Church Peace Union, the World Peace Union Foundation, the Young Women's Christian Association, the Women's Christian Temperance Union, the National League of Women Voters, and the General Federation of Women's Clubs for the realization of a world peace, by which the Council meant a warless world.

The Council's leaders during the 1920s were convinced that such a peace could be obtained. Thus the leadership gave to all efforts to obtain this goal a religious sanction by which it could enter into political campaigns to persuade the government of this country to enter into the League of Nations and the World Court, and to take many other actions looking toward the realization of the Kingdom of God on earth. After 1918 the Commission on International Justice and Good Will became the voice of the Federal Council both to the American people and to the government as to what should constitute the Christian approach to international affairs.[39]

During the 1920s the Council's influence was in the direction of internationalism and away from isolationism. As a result, the Federal Council supported American entrance into the World Court, and in 1923 it launched a campaign to arouse the U.S. Senate to take the appropriate action. At the public hearings held by the Senate on the World Court bill in May 1924, the Federal Council was well represented.

Early in 1926 the "Council sent to the churches its message on world peace which had been adopted by the National Study Con-

39. Its increasing importance is seen in the fact that by 1938 it had three secretaries and a budget of $121,400, in contrast to the $35,000 under which it operated in 1924.

ference of the Churches on World Peace held in Washington in December, 1925."[40] This message called for a reexamination of the Monroe Doctrine and its role in our foreign policy. It advocated our immediate entry into the World Court and our cooperation with the League of Nations in all of its humanitarian programs. Its demand that we enter the League of Nations was tempered with an insistence that we would use neither economic nor military sanctions when called for by that body in any future effort to avert war. This last demand is an interesting foreshadowing of a dichotomy within the ranks of the Federal Council and American pacificism, a dichotomy that would seriously weaken the Council's testimony for peace in the later 1930s. The Council greeted with enthusiasm the announcement of Secretary of State Frank Kellogg that he was ready to negotiate a multilateral treaty for the renunciation of war as an instrument of national policy, and committed itself to the task of bringing about the complete abolition of war from the world.

In its "Message to the Churches on World Peace," adopted by the Council's executive committee early in January 1928, the Council again advocated the reduction of armaments and the suspension of the naval building program. Again expressing its regret that the United States was not yet a member of the League of Nations, the Council nevertheless rejoiced at the increased cooperation between this country and various commissions of the league.[41] The ultimate acceptance of the Pact of Paris by most of the nations of the world, including Germany, Italy, Japan, and the Soviet Union, was attended with such reservations that made it of very little value as a means of outlawing war. This, however, did little to quench the zeal of the Federal Council in its search for peace.

The Rochester quadrennial passed a memorial calling upon this nation to renounce war and never use it again as a method of settling international dispute. It also besought the federal government to have war made a crime under international law and to obtain agreements assuring that all international disputes would be settled by pacific means.[42] It is quite evident that the leadership of the Federal Council allowed its enthusiasm for peace to blind it to the realities surrounding the signing of the Pact of Paris.

40. For the text of this report, see *Federal Council Bulletin* 9, no. 1 (1926): 12.

41. For the full text of this message, see *Federal Council Bulletin* 11, no. 2 (February 1928): 5-6.

42. *Ibid.* 17, no. 1 (January 1929): 9.

In 1929 it declared its hope that this pact would usher in a new era in human history, "an era free from the wrongs of war, an era glorious with the happiness, the property of brotherly humanity."[43]

Not surprisingly, the Federal Council supported the purposes of the London Disarmament Conference of 1931. But by 1931 the thinking of the Council's leadership was beginning to undergo rather profound changes as to the causes of modern warfare and was veering in the direction of an economic interpretation. This change of attitude became much more prominent after 1932. Increasingly the internationalists in this country ceased to rely on pacifism while those that remained steadfast in their devotion to pacifism turned from their earlier internationalism.[44] Yet in 1931 this potential cleavage was not strong enough to diminish the zeal of the Council so as to prevent it from passing a peace platform that in essence restated most of the positions the Council had held since 1920, including an emphasis upon reduction of armaments and the accompanying drastic limitations on armaments. Nevertheless, emphasis on the economic aspects of war did enter into the pronouncement; the Council affirmed its pleasure over the growing sentiment for an all-around reduction or cancellation of intergovernmental war debts as a step toward fostering international goodwill.[45] In 1931 the Council also supported Secretary of State Henry L. Stimson's policy of refusing to recognize the Japanese takeover of Manchuria. In taking this stand, the Council was much closer to representing the majority of the American people than it was in calling for a general disarmament policy for this country.

Changes in the thinking of the Council's leadership—as evidenced by the adoption of the new Social Creed of 1932—plus the growing unrest in much of the world and the emergence of Hitler in Germany resulted in a new role for the Council in the peace movement, a role which will be discussed in the next chapter.

The Federal Council and Labor

From its inception in 1908 the Federal Council was greatly concerned with labor problems and with improvements in the relationship between labor and management. Many of the leaders in

43. *Annual Report of the Federal Council*, (1929), p. 45.

44. For an interesting discussion of this growing cleavage, see John Hutchinson, *We Are Not Divided* (New York, 1941), pp. 208, 213-14.

45. For the full text of this peace platform, see *Federal Council Bulletin* 15, no. 1: 22.

the movement for its formation had this role in view for the Council even before 1908. The Social Creed of 1908[46] had pressed for "the right of workers to protection against hardships resulting from the swift crises of industrial change, for the use of arbitration in industrial disputes, for a living wage and the highest wages which each industry could afford." It also urged the end of child labor and the prohibition of dangerous occupations for both women and children.[47]

There were rather sharp differences of opinion in the conference of 1908 between those who felt strongly that the Federal Council should enter into the quest for social justice and the realization of the social gospel and those who felt that the Council should center its attention on advancing an ecumenical evangelism. Not a few delegates were suspicious of the insistence of Frank Mason North and Charles Stelzle that the church should befriend the workingman in order to bring him back to the pew; they feared that these liberals were concealing their real aim, which was to win American labor to the cause of socialism.

By 1920 the Council's activities tended to support these fears. By 1918 the Commission on the Church and Social Service was becoming actively engaged in the investigation of labor disputes. The first such study had been made by Charles Stelzle when he investigated the Bethlehem steel strike of 1910. This was followed by an investigation of the Colorado coal strike. In 1919 the textile strike at Lawrence, Massachusetts, was scrutinized. The tramway strike in Denver was the next labor disturbance commanding the attention of the commission, which also looked into the railroad strike of 1922. A department of research was created to aid this commission, which in 1920 started an information service known as a Bulletin of Information. Benson Landis joined the Department of Research in 1923 and a year later it was removed from the social services commission and made a separate commission.

In 1920 the Commission on the Church and Social Service issued a statement dealing with the application of Christian principles to the industrial life of the nation, which statement served as a philosophical or theological guide for the activities of the Federal Council in the economic and industrial life of the nation for the next decade.[48] Declaring that the human race constitutes a great

46. For the contents of this creed, see chapter one.

47. Frank Mason North had advanced the cause of labor in the conferences of 1905 as well as that of 1908.

48. For the complete text of this report, see the *Annual Report*, 1920, pp. 118-21.

family under the fatherhood of God, the statement insisted that the primary purpose of industry must be to secure the more abundant life for the masses of the people, that sound industrial organization must be based on the principle of righteousness, that the Christian spirit of brotherhood must dominate industrial activity, and that service must supersede the profit motive in all industrial and economic activity.

The Federal Council was not content to issue manifestos for the Christianization of American industry, but soon became more specific—and also more political—as it sought to apply these principles to particular issues. In 1922, in conjunction with the National Catholic Welfare Council, it condemned the twelve-hour shift for labor in the steel industry and also supported the proposed amendment to the Constitution banishing child labor. The Council aided in raising funds for the striking miners in Ohio and West Virginia and called conferences on the problems of management and labor, the first of which was held at Atlanta in 1920. Between 1920 and 1924 about one hundred and twenty similar meetings were held over the country. Very early the Council began the practice of issuing Labor Day messages to the churches. It would be tedious and certainly repetitious to discuss all of these messages; their content is remarkably similar and often the phraseology is almost identical.

The message issued in 1931, however, demands special attention. It was issued jointly by the Federal Council, the National Catholic Welfare Council, and the Jewish Rabbis of America, a fact notable in itself. But equally notable is the nature of its content. Appearing during the depression, the message was more openly radical than most (if not all) of the previous messages. Plumping for adequate relief measures to aid the unemployed and for a vast program of public works as a necessary part of this program, it also demanded an adequate program of social insurance against future unemployment, and old-age pensions. Of even greater importance was its insistence that the church must challenge the system that made such injustices possible.[49]

Although a keen sympathy for the laboring man had been evident from the very first of the Labor Day messages, the increasingly radical tone did not escape the observation of the many critics of the Federal Council. In reply the Council continually insisted that it was attempting to foster cooperation between management and labor and was not trying to foment class struggle in America. This repudiation of the Communist doctrine of class

49. *Annual Report*, (1931), p. 131.

73

struggle did not convince many of the Council's critics. The tempo and scope of the criticism increased during the depression.[50]

An examination of the thinking of those largely responsible for drafting these Labor Day messages substantiates the charge that a radical reconstruction of American economic life in the interest of collectivism was clearly envisioned in the messages. But this fact was concealed from the majority of the members of the churches that belonged to the Federal Council by the seemingly innocuous language that marked the messages.

The Problem of Race Relations

The problem of race relations in this country received the attention of the leaders of the Federal Council from 1905 on. Although neither the Social Creed of 1908 nor that of 1912 addressed itself to this problem specifically—and only by indirection at best—the leaders of the 1908 meeting at Philadelphia welcomed the participation of the Negro churches in the formation of the Council. The African Methodist Episcopal Church, the African Methodist Episcopal Church Zion, the Colored Methodist Church, and the National Baptist Convention all took an active part in its proceedings.

Involvement of the nation in World War I brought the issue to the forefront in the thinking of the Council. The General War Time Commission appointed a committee on the welfare of the Negro troops and in 1920 caused the Federal Council to issue at the Boston quadrennial a statement, "A Crisis in Democracy," as the answer of the church to the racial disturbances in this country resulting from the social dislocations brought on by the war.[51] This statement, the first to be issued by any ecclesiastical body, clearly identified the Federal Council with the integration movement. It was soon followed by other declarations and positive actions designed to implement its affirmations in this area of social concern.

In 1921 the Commission on the Church and Race Relations was created. It entered upon its task of improving race relations by sponsoring a series of conferences in various parts of the nation. The first of these was held in Washington, D.C. in July 1921. This conference issued a statement of its position that was widely quoted in the religious and secular press; it expressed the convictions of

50. For the criticism of the Federal Council during this decade, see pp. 123-127.

51. For the text of this statement, see *Annual Report*, 1920, pp. 143-44.

74

the Council on race from that time on. The statement justified the creation and role of this commission.

In organizing this Commission on the Church and Race Relations . . . we are animated by the conviction that the Christian religion affords the one adequate solution of the problem of the relations of the races to each other. Recognizing one God as the Father of all, and conceiving mankind as His family, we are convinced that all races are bound together in an organic unity; only on the basis of brotherhood can satisfactory relations be secured.[52]

On the basis of this conviction the commission called upon the churches not only to give serious attention to the race question, but also to provide a clearinghouse and meeting place for all Christian agencies to come together to deal with the problems of Negro and white. White churches were encouraged to support local conferences of white and Negro ministers convened to consider their common problem. The commission also requested that white churches aid in developing a public conscience that would secure for the Negro race equitable provisions for education and health services, housing, recreation, and other aspects of the common welfare. In 1923 the Federal Council began to sponsor its annual Race Relations Sunday, which also involved the exchange of pulpits by white and Negro ministers. In 1924 the Atlanta Quadrennial renewed these pleas for racial brotherhood and adopted its "Program of Applied Brotherhood," which denied the commonly held idea of the inferiority of the Negro race and advocated a program of education and economic justice for the Negro.[53]

The program for the improvement of relations between the Negro and the white races met with only limited success and much opposition during the 1920s, although there was some advance by 1926, at which time it was reported that about thirty cities had created interracial committees in cooperation with the Federal Council of Churches. But in this, as in other areas of domestic social reform, a more radical policy statement on race and the drive for improved race relations awaited the Social Creed of 1932 and the more favorable climate afforded by the advent of the New Deal.

52. *Ibid.*, 1921, pp. 79-80.
53. *Ibid.*, 1924, p. 82.

The Federal Council and Prohibition

Although the Federal Council was hardly a pioneer in the movement for temperance, the liquor problem early engaged its attention. The Council recommended total abstinence and condemned the liquor traffic. It justified its actions in this area on the grounds that the use of liquor is basically a moral problem and therefore the church must speak to it. But on this question, as on others, it is very doubtful that the Council was speaking for the majority of Americans. Nevertheless, it received support when the Anti-Saloon League began its all-out effort to secure an amendment to the U.S. Constitution providing for national prohibition. In the same year, 1916, the Council formed its Temperance Commission to cooperate with other organizations working for the same goal.

The drive for national prohibition received new impetus during the war as a result of the tremendous need for American grain in war-torn Europe. Our entrance into the war added a new justification for ending the liquor traffic. The Washington Conference of the Federal Council urged national prohibition of the making of liquor as a war measure. Between 1916 and 1919 the Temperance Commission was a beehive of activity. But with the passage of the Eighteenth Amendment, it virtually ceased operation. The Federal Council then turned to peace, the outlawing of war, and other areas of domestic social reform as projects of more immediate concern. In 1925 the Council issued a statement calling for the support of the prohibition amendment and its strict enforcement. Unlike other concerns that had engaged the attention of the Council between 1920 and 1932, the problem of temperance received little attention in the Social Creed of 1932, which contained a brief reference to the harmful effects of the use of liquor.

Why the Federal Council lost interest in this issue is difficult to answer. There is no doubt that in its early days it regarded the liquor issue as a serious moral question worthy of its interest and active support. There is evidence that the success of the dry forces in securing the passage of the Eighteenth Amendment lulled them to sleep during the 1920s; the victory of Herbert Hoover over Alfred Smith in the 1928 election further confirmed their optimistic assumption that prohibition was here to stay.

If this is the case, however, the silence on this issue in the Social Creed of 1932 is difficult to explain. Although it had been framed before Franklin Roosevelt's victory over Hoover in the November election of that year, it is nonetheless true that the issue of the repeal of the Eighteenth Amendment had already become important long before the election, both in the platforms of the Republican and Democratic parties and in popular discussion. It is almost unbelievable to assume that the framers of this document were unaware of the new efforts already under way to render the Eighteenth Amendment inoperative. Although there is no hint in any of the official documents that the problem of liquor had by 1932 lost its moral importance in the thinking of the Federal Council leadership, the absence of any strong statement in the new creed leads to the suspicion that economic issues such as poverty, unemployment, and social planning had replaced liquor as the burning moral evil of the day.

The Federal Council and The Problems of Marriage and Home Life in America

In its early days the Federal Council assumed a surprisingly conservative position in regard to most, if not all, of the issues centering around the maintenance of the sanctity of the home—marriage, sexual purity, divorce, and the closely related issue of the role and position of American womanhood in American society. In the New York conference of 1905 Bishop William C. Doane launched an attack on women's suffrage, birth control, the remarriage of divorced persons, and the whole trend toward gaining greater freedom for women.

This position gradually gave way to a more liberal outlook after World War I, partly because of the impact of the war effort on the economic status of women and partly because of a shift in thinking within the Council itself. The shift became evident in 1920 when at the quadrennial the Council issued its *The Church and Social Reconstruction* in which it placed a new emphasis on what it called the democratic rights of women.[54] This statement was a rather cautious declaration of the role of women in American society. There was no repudiation of the biblical view of the home or marriage. It simply recognized that there were other opportunities for women than remaining at home, and called for their wider participation in other activities.[55]

In 1926 the Council's executive committee formed the National

54. For the text of this statement, see *Annual Report*, 1920, p. 111.

55. *Ibid.*, 1929, p. 111.

Commission on Marriage and the Home with Everett J. Clinchy as its first executive secretary. In 1929 this commission issued *Ideals of Love and Marriage*, which condemned free love and the idea of companionate marriage, an idea that had been gaining popularity in recent years. But it was very cautious in its attitude toward remarriage of divorced persons. By 1929 a shift in the thinking of the Council's liberal leadership could be discerned. However, the shift was less than drastic; on the whole, it had not departed very far from the biblical view.

The trend away from the biblical teaching on these issues became very evident in 1931 when the commission released its "Moral Aspects of Birth Control."[56] This controversial statement was not an official statement of the position of the Federal Council but was released for purposes of discussion only. This nice distinction was not generally recognized by the membership of the constituent churches. Hence the statement aroused more controversy than any other proclamation, official or unofficial, released since the formation of the Council in 1908.[57]

This statement opened by insisting that birth control was nearing the status of recognized procedure in preventive and curative medicine, and since knowledge about contraceptives was being widely disseminated, the question of their use had become of great social importance. Therefore, the public had a right to expect guidance from the church on the moral aspects of birth control.

Admitting that "in conception we are in the presence of the wonder and mystery of the beginning of human life" and that sex relations have their origin "in the thought and purpose of God, first for the creation of human life, but also as a manifestation of the divine concern for the happiness of those who have so wholly merged their lives," the statement proceeded to discuss the moral problems that arise from these two functions of sex.[58] Having made this valid biblical admission, the report then voiced a humanistic consideration, namely, the relation of large families to poverty and, apparently for the first time, to overpopulation.

The committee was then moved to opine that the church should not seek to impose its view of contraceptives on the American public, either through legislation or through any other form of coercion.

56. *Ibid.*, pp. 80-84.

57. It seems to have been one of the factors leading to the withdrawal of the Presbyterian Church, U.S. (Southern).

58. *Annual Report*, 1931, p. 81.

And especially it should not seek to prevent physicians from imparting such information to those who in the opinion of the medical profession are entitled to receive it. But at this point the agreement within the committee came to an end, a majority holding that the careful and restricted use of contraceptives by married people was valid and moral.[59] This majority admitted that wider dissemination of knowledge regarding birth control could promote serious evils, such as increasing extramarital sexual relations, but the danger must be faced in the light of this fact. The remedy lay in the church and society giving more effective character-building training to the youth of the nation.[60] The storm of protest that greeted this report forced the Administrative Committee of the Federal Council to complain that the statement was not an official release by the Council and was being wrongly used.[61]

The change of direction, under way in the thinking of the majority of the Council's leaders and clearly seen in this trial balloon, became more obvious and more firmly entrenched as a result of the affirmations contained in the Social Creed of 1932.

The Federal Council and Evangelism

The importance of evangelism in the thinking of the founders and subsequent leaders of the Federal Council is not an easy matter to deal with. There were those at the Philadelphia Conference of 1908 who felt that evangelism must be a basic goal of this ecumenical project, but it is doubtful that they were by any means in the majority. The Social Creed of 1908 is silent on this matter. But in 1911 the Council created the Commission on Evangelism with Dr. William Roberts as its first secretary.[62] He had not been in sympathy with the social-gospel movement or with the movement to focus the interest of the newly organized Council largely toward social reform.

From the very beginning of its existence the Commission on Evangelism was beset with a fundamental weakness in the Federal

---

59. *Ibid.*, p. 83.

60. A small minority rejected this conclusion and insisted that abstinence should be the method used to meet the problem of too large families.

61. *Annual Report*, 1931, p. 93.

62. He was succeeded by Dr. Charles Goodell, who served until 1934. Jesse Bader, William Hiram Foulkes, W. S. Abernathy, and George Buttrick also held his position at various times.

Council of Churches, a weakness that made its program distinctly subsidiary to the Council's social welfare program. The Council's attitude was antitheological, in the historic sense of this term, and this attitude was reflected in the secretaries of the commission itself.[63]

The general attitude of the leadership of the Federal Council was that there should be a moratorium on theology and theological controversy in favor of a concerted action among the churches for the realization of the Social Creed of 1908. In 1932, at its Indianapolis quadrennial, the Council declared:

> Not differences of theological view or ecclesiastical polity but great common tasks, how to make Jesus Christ the Lord of every human life—this was the primary concern of all and in that concern they found themselves no longer separate groups, but members alike of one family of Christ. . . . The sure way of getting together is to work together on the basis of such unity as we already have.[64]

At this same quadrennial it was asserted that there could be no substitute for a personal religion. Such an assertion must be viewed in the light of the above declaration, and raises the very serious question as to what, in the eyes of the leaders of the Council, constituted personal religion and, therefore, what did they mean by evangelism.

A close study of the various affirmations on the necessity of evangelism and of a renewal of personal religion, in the commission reports, reveals minimal emphasis on the great biblical truths of sin, eternal punishment, regeneration, conversion, justification by faith, and related doctrines. The moratorium on theology imposed by the Council leadership made such an emphasis virtually impossible, even though some Council members personally held to the great fundamentals of the faith. This basic and pervading theological weakness was admitted by some who were sturdy defenders of the program and the Council. John Hutchinson admitted this openly: "Not a little of the Social Gospel preaching in the Federal Council has been an effort to clothe the new in traditional language and terms."[65] He even went so far as to admit that the history of the Federal Council was largely an effort to destroy the distinction

63. It would seem that Dr. William Roberts believed in evangelism in its historic meaning and this is quite likely the case with Dr. Charles Goodell, his successor.

64. *Annual Report*, 1929, p. 13.

65. *United We Stand*, p. 85.

between the sacred and the secular in American life.[66] Very seldom was this goal admitted in the reports and public affirmations of the Council's leaders, though occasionally there are brief statements or references that indicate its constant presence in their thinking. In 1924 Methodist Bishop Francis J. McConnell called for the conversion of our institutions.[67] Such an appeal clearly reveals how this concept of conversion was used. McConnell was actually calling for a revolutionary overhaul of these institutions. But he masked his goal by his use of biblical terms. That this was no isolated aspect of his basic thinking is clearly evident in his statements to the Council four years later: "We seek to bring about a social atmosphere and a condition of things in communities and throughout the world in which great saintliness becomes possible."[68]

Thus, much of the evangelistic activity of the Federal Council of Churches must be viewed as an effort to win the thinking of men to the Jesus of the social gospel rather than to the Christ of Calvary, even though in the literature of the Commission on Evangelism there are frequent references to the Christ of Calvary and his resurrection. It is difficult, if not impossible, to escape the conclusion that the Federal Council sponsored evangelism simply as a tool to win converts to the social program rather than to save men from sin. The frequent references to the necessity of conversion in the annual reports of the Council make this clear. Personal decisions to accept the social teachings of Jesus as the rule of life are necessary if individuals are going to accept the social gospel as the rule for American life.

In the first ten years or so of its existence the Commission on Evangelism seems to have contented itself largely with talk about the necessity of evangelism, but did little to implement this talk. Not until the advent of commercial radio broadcasts in 1921 did the Federal Council undertake any responsibility for the kind of evangelism it was urging on its constituent denominations. But in these early years of broadcasting by individual stations the opportunities for evangelism seemed quite limited and the Commission on Evangelism, on several occasions, expressed its doubt about attempting to use radio in its work. The creation of the National Broadcasting Company in 1926, with its chain broadcasting, changed the picture

66. *Ibid.*

67. *Annual Report*, 1924, p. 36.

68. *Annual Report*, 1928, p. 17. For a further treatment of this basic idea, see F. E. Johnson, *Church and Society* (New York, 1935), pp. 59-61.

considerably and by 1928 the commission was sponsoring three Sunday afternoon broadcasts for the whole nation. By 1932 there were twelve such network programs featuring S. Parkes Cadman, Harry Emerson Fosdick, Ralph Sockman, and Charles Goodell, none of whom was a noted evangelist, and two of whom, at least, were extremely liberal.[69] The records indicate that throughout NBC's history, the facilities of its network broadcasting were effectively closed to evangelical leaders who faithfully proclaimed the biblical message.

The Commission on Evangelism after 1920 became increasingly active in other phases of evangelism, among them the printing of many devotional tracts and pamphlets, too numerous to mention. These, like all other evangelistic efforts, reflected the basic desire to place a moratorium on theology in favor of a growth in secular saintliness. The coming of the depression and the appearance of the Social Creed of 1932 gave a new importance to the work of this commission, but in no sense did they engender a more evangelical type of evangelistic effort, although serious efforts were made to make evangelism more personal.

Criticism of the Federal Council, 1920-1932

Criticism of the Federal Council was much less severe and frequent in this period than it was after 1932. The Council did, however, receive criticism for three basic reasons. It was criticized by those groups who objected to its anti-theological character and doctrinal laxity, by those who objected to what they felt was its invasion of the secular sphere at every point, and by those who objected to its social, economic and political radicalism.[70] An examination of the minutes of the various general assemblies of the Presbyterian Church, U.S. reveals that it and the recently formed United Lutheran Synod objected to the Federal Council on all three grounds. The Council's consistent stand for the reduction of armaments also made the Council vulnerable to criticism from other groups who had little or no interest in its theological stance, but who were vitally concerned with maintaining the military strength of the nation.

69. On May 6, 1923, station WEAF in New York began its series of Sunday radio vesper services, and in October of that year it began its midweek prayer service on a donated-time basis. In January 1924 WJZ began its Sunday school on the air.

70. An analysis of the basic theological, political, social, and economic radicalism of the Federal Council is reserved for chapter eight.

Severe criticism was also forthcoming from those religious groups who opposed the posture assumed by the Council during World War I when it supported the war to save democracy and to end all wars.[71]

Mention has already been made of the rather persistent criticism of the Council by various general assemblies of the Southern Presbyterian church. The complaints against it were theological in part. Because of its theology this church also held to a strict "spiritual" view of the church, a view that insisted that the church as an organized body must not take part in secular affairs or play a role in the political life of the nation.[72] For many years the United Lutheran Synod refused to consider anything more than a consultative arrangement with the Federal Council on theological grounds. As early as 1922 it took sharp issue with the Council in regard to its doctrinal indifference:

> We believe in upholding our denominational integrity until Christian unity can come on the basis of a common faith. . . . We miss in the Constitution of the Federal Council and likewise in recent utterances of representatives of the principal churches cooperating with the Council any definite recognition of the necessity or importance of unity in the faith and its confession as a condition of relationships of cooperation in such a federal union as the Federal Council.[73]

It is ironic that until 1932 most of the criticism hurled against the Federal Council for its political, social, and economic philosophy arose not from the constituent churches, but from other secular sources that were apparently more alert to the implications of the Council's various pronouncements on international and domestic issues. After 1932 the close relationship between the radical nature of the Social Creed of 1932 and the radical position struck by the Council on many issues became more apparent. As a result, the evangelical opposition to theological liberalism in the Federal Council became much more vocal.

But the Council did not escape criticism from secular sources

71. Its stand on World War I caused a Mennonite group to withdraw from membership in 1917.

72. See the *Minutes of the General Assembly of the Presbyterian Church in the United States*, in passing, 1916-1931, particularly the 1931 minutes, pp. 60-62.

73. *Minutes of the United Lutheran Church*, 1922, pp. 74-75. Quoted in John Hutchinson, *United We Stand*, p. 80.

early in the 1920s. In 1923 the *Ohio Journal of Commerce* charged the Federal Council with spreading communism through the churches and early in 1927 Congressman Arthur Free introduced into the House of Representatives a resolution that openly called the Council a Communist organization.[74] The resolution was introduced just three days before Congress adjourned and no action was taken upon it.[75] Although the resolution caused little excitement at the time, some newspapers arose to defend the Council from the charges. Dean Shailer Mathews of the Divinity School of the University of Chicago and S. Parkes Cadman also denied the charges. Cadman's denial is of interest for its adroit avoidance of the issue: "The Federal Council is composed of some of the greatest individuals and organizations through the length and breadth of the land, including eminent bishops, college presidents, and editors. Their names are sufficient answer to the charge."[76]

However, the feeling that the Council was unduly allied with radicalism did not easily die. In June 1929 Dudley Knox, historian for the Navy Department, printed a similar charge in the *United States Naval Institute Proceedings*. Like Congressman Free, he later retracted his charge. It is difficult to discover just what pressures, if any, were brought to bear upon these two men. Yet each withdrew his charge. These early attempts to link the Federal Council with radical political groups did not meet with much popular response either within the constituent denominations or from the American public at large. After 1932 these criticisms would become more open and more vehement.[77]

To what extent were those early criticisms justified? There could be little doubt that communism had infiltrated into the Federal Council at an early date in its history. The instrument of this infiltration was the Commission on the Church and Social Service, the secretary of which for many years was Charles S. MacFarland. Associated with this commission were Dr. Harry F. Ward, secretary of the Methodist Federation for Social Action; Rev. Henry Atkins, secretary of the Congregational Brotherhood; and Rev. Alva Taylor, all

74. U.S., Congress, House, *Congressional Record*, Vol 76, p. 1614. For the attack of Maury Maverick see House, Vol 79, pp. 3042-3043.

75. In 1928 Free withdrew his resolution, claiming that he had used false information when he introduced it.

76. *Literary Digest*, March 26, 1927, p. 32.

77. They will be dealt with in chapter eight.

of whom were identified as being involved in Communist activity.[78]

The evidence suggests that the Commission on the Church and Social Services was the most important Council agency through which those devoted to communism could and did work. Accordingly, this commission became the most controversial agency of the Council; through the efforts of Ward et al. to have the Council speak for communism in the name of Christianity, the commission's reputation was ensured.[79]

The feeling in some circles that there was a connection between the Council and radicalism was based on sound evidence. Many of the leaders of the Council in the 1920s were friendly to Communist theory, if not Communist practice, and their liberal theology brought them into close affinity with various forms of radicalism. Certainly those occupying the important posts of leadership were thoroughly aware of the Communist influence at work within the Council, but it is very doubtful that the delegates who came to the quadrennial meetings had any real understanding of the behind-the-scenes debates of the various commissions and committees.

The 1920s in Retrospect

By the end of this decade the Federal Council had established itself as the leader of the ecumenical movement in this country, a position the Council never relinquished. Even though individual liberals might, and did, criticize particular actions or resolutions of the Council, they were solidly behind it as the great and only expression of the ecumenical movement in this country. If some criticized it for an occasional outburst by radicals, a liberal journal would criticize the Council for timidity.

There can be no doubt that the theology of the Council was liberal, with Unitarianism and higher criticism its chief characteristics. Its leadership was hostile to evangelical Christianity; it fully recognized that there was a basic incompatibility between conservative theology on the one hand and liberal and radical social and eco-

78. U.S., *Congress, House, Hearings Before the Committee on Un-American Activities*, 83d Cong., 1st sess., July 7, 8, 13, 14, 1953, pts. 6-8, pp.2057, 2075-77, 2177, 2084-85, 2169, 2171, 2201-2.

79. A complete discussion of the Council's relation to communism will be discussed in chapter eight.

nomic philosophy on the other. But it is also necessary to point out that there was a strong desire for the Council to reflect and to support the historic private morality of historic Christianity. This dichotomy appears repeatedly in its various resolutions on the sanctity of the home, its pronouncements against pornography and the evils of the motion-picture industry, and its strong emphasis on sexual purity and the holiness of the marriage bond.

4

The Federal Council, 1932-1941

The decade that opened in 1932 confronted the Federal Council with a new challenge, a world at home and abroad which was quite different from that which it had faced throughout most of the 1920s. The coming of the Great Depression gave it an unusual opportunity to accelerate and expand its various activities on the home front, steering them along a more radical course. But events in Europe and Asia would rudely shatter some of the Council's long-cherished assumptions concerning the possibility of peace in a world dominated by dictators. Although the leadership of the Council viewed the rise of Hitler with horror, it greeted the coming of Roosevelt's New Deal with enthusiasm, condemning the former while almost joyfully coming to terms with the latter. But in 1932 the leadership was happily unaware of the events that would soon bring another world war to Europe; it was much more concerned with preparing the

Council for tackling the many problems it faced on the home front as a result of the depression and the election of Franklin Delano Roosevelt to the presidency.

In preparation for the Council's expanded leadership in an age of depression, many Council leaders felt that their organization must be updated, even restructured, to enable it to meet the new challenges of the day. At the same time they were convinced that the Social Creed of 1908 was no longer a suitable expression of the Council's social and economic philosophy and that it too must be updated to meet the economic and social problems of the 1930s. This reorganization of both the structure and the thinking of the Council was the task of the 1932 quadrennial, which met at Indianapolis in December, just one month after Roosevelt's defeat of Herbert Hoover. It proved to be a most important, if not the most important, meeting of the Council after the Philadelphia conference of 1908, and would remain so until the meeting of 1950, which created the National Council of Churches. Reorganization of the Council was not the result of a sudden desire first expressed at this quadrennial. A special committee to study the function and structure of the Federal Council had been appointed by the Rochester quadrennial of 1928 to report in 1932.[1] This committee recommended that the Council should add five new areas of emphasis and activity to those already part of its work.[2] The new areas were: evangelizing the churches, cultivating the devotional life of church members, furthering Christian education (by which it clearly meant developing the social consciousness through the Sunday schools), serving as a common agency of the churches to remove the social evils of the day, social and racial injustice, and unemployment, and expunging war as an instrument of national policy by establishing a more Christian international order.[3] This committee also felt that it would be of great help to the Council in pursuing its goals if it could be made perfectly clear to the members of the constituent churches and to the American public at large that the Federal Council was a representative and not a hierarchical body and

1. For the content of this report, see *Annual Report*, 1932, pp. 29-56.

2. *Ibid.*, p. 28.

3. *Ibid.*, p. 30. This committee also discussed the question of the proper relationship that should exist between the Council and the issue of church union. Admitting that there was a great division of opinion on this matter, the committee simply declared that the function of the Council was to help the denominations express the unity that they already possessed.

that it had two distinct functions in the area of molding public opinion: (1) witnessing on moral issues on which there was sufficient common agreement to make a pronouncement possible, and (2) education through study and frank discussion of the issues on which there was insufficient common accord and publishing the results of such discussions on these issues.[4]

The special committee also recommended that the earlier report of the executive committee on restructuring the Council be adopted. This report was accepted. Under it the Council was to meet every two years rather than every four. Its membership was to be composed of three members from each of the constituent denominations, of which each would also be entitled to one additional member for every one hundred thousand members. The Adminstrative Committee was abolished. The executive committee was reconstituted to be composed of two delegates from each denomination and one additional delegate for each church possessing fifty thousand members over the first five hundred thousand.

In spite of the insistence of this committee that the Federal Council should give the appearance of being a representative body and not a hierarchical one, revision of its organization resulted in more centralization, and also placed greater authority into the hands of the larger denominations, which were decidedly the most liberal members of the Council. The conservative voice would be reduced to a whisper as a result of this reorganization.

The other important work of this Indianapolis quadrennial was the adoption of the Social Creed of 1932. This also was the product of previous agitation. Ground for such a development had already been broken by several pronouncements in the issues of the *Federal Council Bulletin* of 1932. The January issue featured an article by Toyohiko Kagawa, the Japanese churchman, who declared that the Christian message must include the reconstruction of society and nothing less. By this he meant Christian collectivism. "It is evident," he wrote, "that we must Christianize industry and get rid of the acquisitive motive in economic life. It seems to me that we cannot solve our problems on the basis of individualism."[5] His proposed Christian solution was the creation of Christian cooperatives after the pattern of the guild system.

The trend in the Council's thinking regarding social issues was clearly enunciated later that year in another article, "The Spiritual

4. *Ibid.*, p. 30.

5. *Federal Council Bulletin* 15, no. 1 (January 1932): 6.

Challenge of the Economic Crisis."[6] Written by the Reverend William Boddy of the First Presbyterian Church of Chicago, the article admitted that it was not the place of the church to outline an industrial program or structure for a new economic order. The Presbyterian minister declared: "It seems too that there is a new imperative facing the Cross, not as a dogma of theology, not as the source . . . of vesper hymns, but as a way of life. . . . In short, the church in this day must teach that Jesus had undertaken nothing less than changing man over, the whole range of his life, from an acquisitive to a contributive being."[7]

This drive for a Christian collectivism received a further boost from the 1932 Labor Day message prepared by the Commission on the Church and Social Service. The message was little less than a plea for a scientific redistribution of wealth not only in this country, but among the nations of the world as well. It declared that the kingdom of God could be advanced by the intelligent planning and direction of industry, credit, and finance for the common good, the extension of minimum-wage laws, and the payment of the highest wages possible in order to achieve the redistribution of wealth and to realize the kingdom of God.[8]

These declarations reveal not only that theological liberalism of the worst kind was rampant in the thinking of a large segment of the leadership of the Council, but also that political and economic radicalism was equally prominent. The groundwork had been laid for the new social creed; it was obvious that the Federal Council was now ready to lead the nation into the enjoyment of a materialistic kingdom of God through a Christianized collectivism, which would not be like the secular collectivist states of Europe because it would somehow be Christian.

The revised creed adopted at Indianapolis declared that the churches should stand for:

1. Practical application of the Christian principle of social well-being to the acquisition and use of wealth, subordination, speculation and the profit motive to the creative and cooperative spirit.
2. Social planning and control of the credit and monetary systems and the economic processes for the common good.
3. The right of all to the opportunity for self-maintenance; a wider

6. *Ibid.*, no. 9 (September 1932): 12.

7. *Ibid.*

8. *Ibid.*, pp. 23-24.

and fairer distribution of wealth; a living wage, as a minimum, and above this a just and fair share for the worker in the products of industry and agriculture.

4. Safeguarding of all workers, urban and rural, against harmful conditions of labor and occupational injury and disease.

5. Social insurance against sickness, accident, want in old age and unemployment.

6. Reduction of hours of labor as the general productivity of industry increases; release from employment at least one day in seven, with a shorter working week in prospect.

7. Such special regulations of the conditions of work of women as shall safeguard their welfare and that of the family and the community.

8. The right of employees and employers alike to organize for collective bargaining and social action; production of both in the exercise of this right; the obligation of both to work for the public good; encouragement of cooperatives and other organizations among farmers and other groups.

9. Abolition of child labor; adequate provision for the protection, education, spiritual nurture and wholesome recreation of every child.

10. Protection of the family by the single standard of purity; educational preparation for marriage, home-making and parenthood.

11. Economic justice for the farmer in legislation, financing, transportation and the price of farm products as compared with the cost of machinery and other commodities which he must buy.

12. Extension of the cultural opportunities and social services now enjoyed by urban populations of the farm family.

13. Protection of the individual and society from the social, economic and moral waste of any traffic in intoxicants and habit-forming drugs.

14. Application of the Christian principle of redemption in the treatment of offenders, reform of penal and correctional methods and institutions, and of criminal court procedure.

15. Justice and equal rights for all, mutual goodwill and cooperation among racial, and economic and religious groups.

16. Repudiation of war, drastic reduction of armaments, participation of international agencies for the peaceable settlement of all controversies; the building of a cooperative world order.

17. Recognition and maintenance of the rights and responsibilities of free speech, free assembly, and free press; the encouragement of free communication of mind with mind as essential to the discovery of truth.[9]

The creed closed with an appeal for a new age of faith:

We may legitimately expect that the collective mind of the nation

9. *Ibid.* 16, no. 1 (January 1933): 9.

will be equal to the intellectual and administrative tasks involved, especially under the stress of critical social conditions, if the moral qualities required are in sufficient power. What our people lack is neither material resources nor technical skills—these we have in abundance—but a dedication to the common good, a courage and an unselfishness greater than are now manifest in American life. The tasks are beyond us and their accomplishment will be indefinitely delayed or frustrated, unless there be a nationwide spiritual awakening which has social gains. Our supreme social need is spiritual awakening. In our extremity arising out of harrowing social conditions throughout the world, we therefore turn anew to Christ; for the faith of great endeavor, for an overwhelming disclosure of God in the life of humanity, for the dedication of innumerable individuals to the creation of a more Christian social order, and for the assurance that what needs to be done, with God's help can be done.[10]

There can be no doubt that the social affirmations of 1932 were, on the surface, much more radical than those contained in the original creed of 1908. But a closer study of the original statement reveals that it contained the seed of the declarations of 1932. The original made no demand for subordination of the profit motive to a new cooperative spirit and it did not openly call for the collective control of the economic processes and credit and finance for the common good, but neither can it be successfully denied that the idea of collectivism underlay the Social Creed of 1908. The economic conditions of 1932 were much more favorable for expressing the radicalism inherent in the earlier version.[11] The statement of 1932 enabled the Federal Council to greet the New Deal with its many radical proposals and supporters with open arms and warm enthusiasm. It also served as the platform on the basis of which the Council would erect its many projects to meet the social and economic crisis of the 1930s. The *Christian Century* greeted the new creed with enthusiasm and declared that in spite of the many difficulties involved in formulating it, the Federal Council made the bold choice and the right one.[12] The editor of the *Christian Herald* also gave an enthusiastic endorsement of the work of the Council. Similar endorsements came from the *Journal of Religious Education* and the

10. *Ibid.*, p. 9.

11. The Indianapolis quadrennial also gave a much fuller and more radical statement of its position in its 6,000-word exposition, "The Social Order and the Good Life," which served as the basis for the creed of 1932.

12. For a thorough commentary on this creed, see the *Christian Century*, January 4, 1933, pp. 6-8.

Christian Endeavor World. Commonweal (Roman Catholic) went so far as to declare that the Social Creed of 1932 made a great advance toward the practical application of Christian principles to the solution of many of the most pressing problems of the day and that it should receive the sympathetic approval of all Catholics; moreover, the first article of the creed seemed to agree with the spirit and practice of Catholic sociology.[13] Except for some scattered criticism from the more conservative Presbyterian and Lutheran journals, the new creed met with a surprising enthusiasm. Apparently some who did endorse it were only dimly aware of what it really meant for both Christianity and the American people.

With reorganization an accomplished fact and a new and more precise statement of its goals before it, the Council, sword in hand, was ready to battle for social justice at home and abroad and to slay the giants Greed and Injustice in the name of that Christian collectivism envisioned by Walter Rauschenbusch. The latter's growing number of disciples apparently were willing to import communism as the primary manifestation of the kingdom of God on earth—provided it be under American rather than Russian direction.

The Federal Council, Social Justice, and the New Deal

As the New Deal program began to unfold during the session of Congress that met from March to June 1933, the Federal Council looked with increasing favor on the Roosevelt administration and acted accordingly. At its September 1933 meeting the executive committee adopted a statement that interpreted the National Recovery Administration in the light of the Social Creed of 1932, and that constituted a qualified endorsement of the New Deal as it existed in 1933.

> We do not suggest that the national recovery program embodies the full social idea of Christianity, or that the success of the program would leave no desirable social goals unattained. The Christian conscience can be satisfied with nothing less than the complete substitution of motives of mutual helpfulness and goodwill for the motive of private gain, and the removal of the handicaps which our economic order now inflicts upon large numbers, particularly on certain occupational and racial groups. But we would call the attention of the members of our churches to the fact that the recovery program aims

13. *Commonweal.*, December 28, 1932.

a vigorous blow at some of the more grievous types of exploitation and injustice.[14]

The report then went on to praise the Roosevelt program for aiming crippling blows at child labor and for supporting the right of labor to organize as it was then guaranteed in the National Industrial Recovery Act of 1933. The statement also took a very high view of the codes provided for by this act because they called for a new kind of ethical functioning by the various groups in the economic order. Admitting that it called for a large degree of experimentation in the economic and political life of the nation and that "it is not to be supposed that a flawless program could be developed quickly in a time of great stress and anxiety," the executive committee felt that "whatever its inevitable weaknesses, the National Industrial Recovery program implies the practicability of a more cooperative economic order, socially controlled for the common good and a willingness to relinquish special privileges and power."[15] And even though the churches would not feel called upon to endorse every detail, particularly the technical aspects of the many measures that had been promulgated, the committee did urge the members of its constituent churches to give full recognition to the social and spiritual implications on the national recovery program and to cooperate in the attainment of the high ends toward which it was directed.[16] To implement these pronouncements, a special meeting of the Federal Council was called to meet in Washington early in December 1933 to face the emergency then confronting the churches and the nation and to take whatever action it could.[17] This special meeting produced a union of sorts between the New Deal and the Federal Council. Both President Roosevelt and Henry Wallace, secretary of agriculture, spoke and set forth the terms of the union from the point of view of the leadership of the New Deal.

14. *Federal Council Bulletin* 16, no. 10 (October 1933): 6.

15. *Ibid.*, p. 6

16. *Ibid.*, p. 6. In his *The Third American Revolution* (New York, 1933) Benson Y. Landis, assistant secretary of the Department of Research of the Federal Council wrote that the New Deal was trying to carry out a large part of the program of the churches that had been set forth in the Social Creed of 1932. He praised the Roosevelt "revolution" as a robust young collectivism waging a battle against the old rugged individualism.

17. The *Christian Century* (November 23, 1933, p. 1495) adroitly pointed out that the Council should come to the aid of President Roosevelt's formulation of a sharp ethical antithesis between property rights and human rights.

In speaking of the prosperity that he envisioned for our nation, Roosevelt said:

> It can be a prosperity built on spiritual and social values rather than on special privileges and special power. Toward this new definition of prosperity the churches and the governments, while wholly separate in their functioning, can work hand in hand. Government can ask the churches to stress in their teaching the ideas of social justice, while at the same time government guarantees to the churches . . . the right to worship God in their own way. The churches, while they remain wholly free from the suggestion of interference in government, can at the same time teach millions of followers that they have the right to demand of the government of their own choosing the maintenance and furtherance of "a more abundant life."[18]

Close analysis of this address reveals that the union Roosevelt proposed would mean the subservience of the church to the state. The Social Creed of 1932 had led the Council into a situation in which it would do the will and bidding of the state, a state that was on the way toward becoming a political collectivism for the sake of erecting an economic collectivism. The Council had come a long way from its early statements that it would never become the pawn of a political party and would never actively endorse or support a particular economic or political program.

The address of Henry Wallace was more forthright than Roosevelt's. Wallace openly called for changes in Protestantism that would bring it in closer harmony with the New Deal:

> I am wondering if the religion we shall need during the next hundred years will not have much more in common with the Christianity of the second and third centuries or possibly even with that of the Middle Ages than with the Protestants of the past one hundred years. The strong personal initiative conferred by the Protestants' religion must in some way be merged into a powerful religious attitude concerning the entire social structure. . . . I am not talking about welfare drives and other forms of charity which good men among the Protestants, Jews and Catholics alike support so loyally. The thing I am talking about goes far deeper. It is an attitude that will not flow from external compulsion but that will spring from the hearts of the people because of an overwhelming realization of a community of purpose. Perhaps the times will have to become even more difficult than they have been during the past two years before the hearts of our people

18. *Federal Council Bulletin* 17, no. 1 (January 1934): 7-8.

will be willing to join together in a modern adaptation of the theocracy of old.[19]

In this appeal to the Federal Council Wallace made it clear that Christianity itself would have to be changed in order to meet the needs of the day. The old theocracy must yield to the new. The old virtue of meeting the needs of those who had suffered hardships must give place to a new conception of a community of purpose. The basis for such a change is disclosed in the closing paragraph of his address:

> This spiritual cooperation to which I refer depends for its strength on a revival of deep religious feeling on the part of the individual in terms of the intellectual concept that the world is in very truth one world, that human nature is such that all men can look on each other as brothers, that the potentialities of nature and science are so far-reaching as to remove many of the ancient limitations. This concept which now seems cloudy and vague to practical people must be more than the religious experience of the literary mystic. It must grow side by side with a new social discipline. Never has there been such a glorious chance to develop this feeling, this discipline as in this country today.[20]

Wallace was pleading less for a new theocracy than for a new humanism that would be communal in nature. The new religious feeling must arise from the realization that the world is one and not from any knowledge of the Sovereign God of the Scriptures. It would be the product of sociology and of the new knowledge made available by science. Is it not both interesting and revealing that the leadership of the Federal Council would see a kinship between the philosophy of Franklin Roosevelt and Henry Wallace and its own concept of the realization of the kingdom of God? The insistence that the social aims of the New Deal did not fully meet the requirements of this secularized concept of the kingdom of God is nothing more than an acknowledgment that the humanistic theology of the Council was more radical in its implications than the philosophy of the New Deal architects, who faced the political realities of the hour and of what could and could not be pushed through Congress.

Nevertheless, the editor of the *Bulletin* was quite enthusiastic

19. *Ibid.*, no. 2 (February 1934): 6.

20. *Ibid.*, p. 7.

about this address. He stated that Wallace was a man of vision who envisaged a better social order and was devoting his energies to securing a cooperative instead of a competitive economic organization. As his address showed, Wallace had been influenced both by the Old Testament prophets and by the life and teaching of Jesus.[21]

The admiration of the Federal Council for the New Deal received repeated emphasis from its leadership from 1933 until the end of that decade, when the war in Europe took priority in its thinking. In this address to the Dayton biennial in December 1934, President Albert Beaven insisted that the church must take part in the drastic changes being wrought in the political, industrial, and economic life of the nation. He held that the church should never be content with things as they are, but very impatient. Said Beaven:

> It is not possible for the church to say in a voice commanding enough so that the world can hear, in the name of the Lord, that any proposal of society or government which asks for the backing of Christian people, but which would protect property at the expense of people, would protect the privileged at the expense of the underprivileged, would seek material profit rather than the enrichment of life, would rely upon force rather than justice, would manipulate and control the gifts of God in nature for the interests of the few as against the many, would breed the fears that destroy rather than the confidence that releases and strengthens, would exploit humanity rather than enlarge the life which humanity lives—cannot be consistent with the purposes of God and the teachings of Jesus and cannot have our support.[22]

This declaration of war against the old order, the Republican party, and all other opponents of the New Deal was an unblushing defense of radicalism. Basically it rested its case on the Communist divorce of property as a right from human rights. This separation is logically and theologically false, but it has been the stock-in-trade of American liberalism for over a century. Though false, it has tremendous appeal to all varieties of liberal thought. But it is essentially a Communist appeal.

After the Council's hearty endorsements of the general program of the New Deal of 1933 and '34, a curious silence about the Roosevelt domestic program was conspicuous both in the annual reports and in the issues of the *Bulletin*. There are occasional favorable

21. *Ibid.*, no. 1 (January 1934): p. 7.
22. *Annual Report*, 1934, pp. 26-27.

references to various aspects of the legislation, but the New Deal as such received scant attention after 1934, a fact which on the surface seems difficult to explain. Two factors account for the apparent lack of interest. First, the New Deal was a reality in American life. Roosevelt's personal popularity, reinforced by his political adroitness, had made it apparently secure from conservative attacks. It was so close to the demands of the Social Creed of 1932 that there was little more for the Council to do but applaud its success.

Second, the stirrings in Europe required the kind of action for which the Council was equipped and to which it was greatly inclined. The events of 1933 and '34 in Germany and Austria were creating fears that another European war was in the offing, and this prospect monopolized the attention of the Council's leadership.

The Federal Council and the War for Peace, 1932-1941

The rise of Hitler to power in Germany and the threat of another world conflict occasioned the greatest crisis yet to confront the Federal Council. It realized that it could do little to avoid the conflict in Europe or mitigate the severity of the Nazi persecution of the Jews. Probably for this reason the leadership of the Council was determined to use all the influence and power at its command to prevent the United States from again becoming involved in a European conflict. Once again the Federal Council would be launched on a great peace crusade, this one from 1934 until Pearl Harbor. The very enthusiasm of the Council's leaders for the New Deal made it possible for them safely to turn their attention to the problems of peace and war assured that their social program at home was in good hands.

This new crusade began with the acceptance of a rather popular notion of the day, that our entry into World War I had been greatly influenced and aided by the American arms industry. This belief was not only widespread in secular liberal circles, but also very attractive to the Council's liberals, who quickly saw that this approach could be used to aid their own radical approach to economic and industrial reform at home by casting suspicion on one segment of the industrial complex.

Thus in February 1934 the executive committee of the Federal Council endorsed a proposal for an official investigation of our arms industry to determine its influence on the shaping of a favorable

American popular opinion for our involvement in World War I.[23] A few days later it reinforced this earlier action by sending to Senator Gerald Nye a communication clearly stating its support of such an investigation.[24] Written by the president, Albert Beaven, on behalf of the committee, it contained a very strong statement of the feelings of the Council on this issue, probably one of the strongest statements the Council had ever issued.

> As president of the Federal Council and at the request of the Council's Executive Committee I am writing to urge you and your associates to let nothing prevent the continuance of our inquiry until all the pertinent facts relevant to the manufacture and sale of war materials by American firms are made a matter of official record. Moreover, we protest against the suggestion that these hearings if continued, be continued under the cloak of secrecy. The public is entitled to the facts irrespective of the effect which the publication of these facts may have upon individuals or groups of individuals in our own or other countries. The Christian thinking people of the nation are thoroughly aroused over this situation. A wave of moral indignation is sweeping through the churches against what appears to be a conscienceless and unscrupulous attitude taken by the armament and munition makers who are willing, apparently, to jeopardize the peace of the world for the sake of private gain. . . . The churches are determined to do all within their power to rid the world of war. They do not believe that this can be attained until the private traffic in arms and munitions is placed under strict national and international control.[25]

This statement is of great importance for several reasons. In the first place, it is obvious that the Federal Council had already come to the conclusion that the munition makers were guilty as charged and that it was the business of the Nye committee to confirm what the Council already believed. The Council was hardly assuming the neutral position, which was necessary for an impartial investigation of the issue.

Second, it is equally obvious that this investigation was to be used

23. *Ibid.*, p. 115.

24. *Ibid.*, pp. 142-43. Senator Nye as chairman of the Senate committee was charged with the responsibility of conducting the investigation of the munitions industry.

25. *Annual Report*, 1934, pp. 142-43.

for discrediting American industry by discrediting one segment of it. The campaign against the munition makers was part of the Council's program to extend strict governmental control and socialization of industry, even as the Roosevelt administration several years later would use the coming of war for the same purposes.

Third, this pressure from the Federal Council on a congressional investigating committee was a bold political action, a far cry from the earlier position assumed by the Council that it would not become involved in purely political or administrative matters.

The Council reinforced its support of the Nye committee by issuing the message "To Christians of All Lands" in behalf of international peace. In it the Council appealed to the churches worldwide to join in a crusade not only against war itself, but against all preparations that could lead to conflict.[26] Admitting that there was much in the international situation to cause concern, particularly the spirit of nationalism and a dangerous war psychology, the message asserted that the Christians of the United States could not lift the finger of condemnation against any single people anywhere, for all Christians were guilty. In that solemn hour it was the duty of the churches of Christ to stand firm and steadfast.

> Many Christian bodies in the United States have said that our churches should never again be used in preparation for war but should be used in the promotion of peace. They have said that the church should not sanction war or bless it. They have said that war is a denial of the gospel they profess. In any dilemma between loyalty to country or to Christ, they have said that they would follow Christ. . . .
>
> We invite the people of the churches of the world to join us in proclaiming anew our citizenship in a kingdom that is without geographical or racial division. By virtue of a common loyalty to the Lord, Christians everywhere have a kinship with one another. Their loyalties, accordingly, are first to God and after that to the nation of which they are a part. . . .
>
> We believe that the churches of Christ around the world should with all possible dispatch say to their respective governments that they cannot and will not give their moral support to war as a method of settling international difficulties, nor will they become a party to the mad race in armaments now in progress in so many parts of the world. . . .
>
> We believe that the hour has come when all Christians should

26. *Federal Council Bulletin* 17, no. 5 (May 1934): 6-7.

unite in urging the nations to make renewed effort to resolve existing international differences on a peaceful basis. We cannot and will not believe that the people of the world desire that a relatively small number of persons shall precipitate an international crisis that would seem to make inevitable a resort to military violence.[27]

In retrospect we can only wonder at the naive attitude toward the developing crisis displayed by the Federal Council of Churches. The Council obviously had little or no understanding of Nazism on the one hand or of the diplomatic and international realities on the other. But underlying this basic ignorance of the crisis confronting the church and the nation was a fatal illusion, that there was a large residue of good will and Christian virtue among the peoples of the West.

The Council was not content with drafting a letter urging peace on all Christians. It also adopted a concrete peace program in which it called on the Roosevelt administration to press for a multilateral nonaggression pact, as suggested by President Roosevelt, in which each nation would pledge not to send its armed forces across the boundaries of other nations. It also called on the administration to place an embargo on arms and credits to any or all nations that violated the nonaggression pact. It renewed its demand that the arms industry be placed under strict government control, that all offensive weapons be destroyed, and that the naval construction provided for under the Vinson bill be stopped at once. Its final demand was that the United States renounce the use of all military aviation except for peaceful purposes.[28]

That such a program would dangerously weaken the military power of the United States in a world that was threatened with totalitarian domination seemed not to concern the leaders of the Federal Council. They seemed to have little or no comprehension of the nature of totalitarianism, Russian or German. Still intact was their unbounded optimism in the power of the social gospel to maintain peace in such a world; it had not yet been shaken sufficiently to see that pacifism would simply play into the hands of the dictators of Europe and Asia.

But if the Council was blind to the implication of its activities in behalf of peace, there were many people in the country who were by no means unaware of what was involved in the brand of pacifism

27. *Ibid.*, p. 6.
28. *Ibid.*, no. 6 (June 1934): 7.

it was claiming as its own. As a result, a new wave of vigorous criticism arose against the Council because of the growing conviction of many that it was under radical control and opposed to the best interests of the American people.

The Federal Council helped to sponsor the National Conference on the Churches and World Peace, which met at Dayton, Ohio, in December 1934. The tone of this conference is evident from the resolutions passed and the affirmations adopted:

> Resort to military violence for the settlement of international, interracial, economics, or class disputes is sin.[29]
>
> We are convinced that in order to avoid a calamitous race of armaments with Japan the United States should be prepared to make substantial concessions by agreeing to abolish naval vessels and other weapons of aggression so as to make impossible a war across the Pacific.[30]

Taking the initiative provided by these resolutions and affirmations, the Council accepted the resolutions sponsored by its own Department of Good Will and International Justice that it endorse the neutrality proposals then before Congress. These would provide for this country a strong neutrality policy that would include an embargo on arms, credits, and loans to belligerent nations coupled with a declaration that Americans who traveled on the vessels of the belligerents did so at their own risk.[31] In its final form, the Neutrality Act of 1935 contained the essence of these demands, though it is doubtful that the similarity between the act and the position of the Council can be ascribed to the latter's influence, except insofar as the Council was itself voicing the general isolationist sentiment that was the inspiration for the passage of this innovation in the field of neutrality legislation.[32]

The rising pacifist feeling in the Federal Council by 1935 brought an old issue to a more acute form. Many members were having second thoughts about the cooperation between the Council and the General Commission of Army and Navy Chaplains. This relation-

29. *Federal Council Bulletin* 18, no. 1 (January 1935):4.

30. *Ibid.*, p. 11.

31. *Annual Report*, 1935, p. 39.

32. It should be noted that isolationism and Christian pacifism were not identical. There were many "secular" isolationists who were in no way related to the Federal Council and it is very likely that their influence played the greater role in the passage of this and subsequent neutrality acts.

ship had been established in 1917, just after our entrance into World War I, and had continued from then on. There was a growing feeling by some that such cooperation in itself actually sanctioned war and should be terminated. In 1936 a committee of the Council, in a report, opined that the Council's withdrawal from such cooperation could only mean chaos. Men in the armed services, insisted the report, needed the bread of life as much or more than civilians, and continuing the program would be not an endorsement or war, but simply a recognition that military men are also in spiritual need.[33]

At the biennial meeting held at Asbury Park, New Jersey, in December 1936 the Council sought to implement its position on world peace by adopting a nine-point program as a guide for the military and diplomatic policies of the Roosevelt administration. It called on the government to implement its Good Neighbor Policy for the Western world, to exercise moderation in its military policies, to enter the World Court, to extend the provisions of the Neutrality Act of 1935, to work for the national and international control of the arms traffic, to extend the reciprocal trade agreements provided for by an act of 1934, to make it clear that our armed forces could not and would not be used for protecting our overseas material interests, to improve relations with Japan, and to make the ROTC program in the colleges entirely voluntary.[34]

The Neutrality Act of 1937, the high-water mark of such legislation in the years before the outbreak of World War II, went even further in the direction desired by the Federal Council, although it fell short of the goal sought by the Council in the national and international control of arms traffic. But just how much influence the Federal Council had in its passage is difficult to answer for in 1937, as in 1935, the isolationist sentiment was a powerful factor in congressional thinking. Even though President Roosevelt on occasion professed great sympathy for the Council and its works, he most certainly did not approve of certain features of the acts of 1935 and 1937, both of which restricted his presidential authority in the application of neutrality to actual situations.[35]

These resolutions and programs, particularly the nine-point program of 1937, constituted the peace platform of the Council until the

33. For the content of this report, see *Annual Report*, 1936, pp. 155-59.

34. *Federal Council Bulletin* 20, no. 1 (January 1937): 7.

35. For Franklin Roosevelt's role in the struggle for the passage of neutrality legislation, see Charles A. Beard, *President Roosevelt and the Coming of War, 1941* (New Haven, 1948).

actual outbreak of hostilities in Europe in September 1939. But the return of war to Europe was a major blow to the hopes and basic conviction of the Council's liberals that an enlightened Christian conscience in Europe could prevail upon the various governments to settle their disputes by peaceful means. Early in October 1939 the executive committee through Dr. George A. Buttrick, president of the Federal Council, and Samuel McCrea Cavert, its general secretary, sent to President Roosevelt a letter expressing the committee's pleasure in the President's assurance that every effort of the government would be directed toward keeping the United States out of war: "We support you in your purpose that our government shall not join in this war. . . . We seek to keep the United States at peace in the hope that our nation may thereby render a greater service to mankind."[36]

After asserting that such a war should not be used for the sake of ending the depression at home, the committee then went on briefly to spell out its hopes for the future:

> We also support you in your purpose, expressed in your radio broadcast on September 3, that the influence of America should be consistent in seeking for humanity a final peace which will eliminate as far as it is possible to do so the continued use of force between nations. . . . We therefore urge our government to indicate at the earliest possible opportunity, the terms upon which it is prepared to cooperate with other nations in the establishment of peace in Europe and in the Far East, and in the development of some form of political world order in which certain aspects of the sovereignty of the individual state would be limited to the interests of the world community.[37]

This was a very peculiar position taken by the Council's executive committee in this letter to President Roosevelt; it revealed a serious ambivalence in its thinking. First, it urged Roosevelt to stay out of the war, then urged him to work for the acceptance of the kind of peace that could only involve him in the war. Woodrow Wilson had learned that to be a party to the peace negotiations after World War I, he must first take part in the conflict to earn that right. Thus, cooperation now with the belligerent nations of the young war, in hammering out the terms of a peace treaty, would almost inevitably force the United States into the conflict. It would

36. *Annual Report*, 1939, p. 126.
37. *Ibid.*

104

seem that the executive committee of the Federal Council had not correctly read Wilson's wartime diplomacy.

Second, there is in this document a tragic note that the fervent appeal for peace for the United States could not totally conceal. The leaders were aware that once again the world was engulfed in war and that the peace messages and proposals of the Council since 1934 had been powerless to prevent it. Beneath the wording of this message there seemed to lurk the realization that our entry into the conflict was only a matter of time.

Yet the Council leadership continued to hope that at war's end there would be a just and durable peace. At the 1940 biennial meeting it voted to create a commission on a just and lasting peace, with John Foster Dulles as its secretary. In the pronouncements of this biennial, held at Atlantic City, a more realistic attitude emerged toward a more somber realization of what was involved for Christians in the days ahead. The biennial drafted a statement on the war and the church, a statement that clearly reflects this change in attitude regarding an unyielding pacifism.[38] Beginning with a general insistence that all peoples have been guilty of pride, arrogance, and greed, which sins lay at the roots of the confusion and conflict, the pronouncement affirmed the superiority of democracy to other political systems because it offered a better opportunity for the social expression of Christian ethics than that offered by any other government. This conviction then led the signers of the document into a curious paradox. On the one hand, the very superiority of democracy placed upon Christian citizens the obligation to maintain true democracy. Christians are obligated to use only those means appropriate to that end: "To attempt to defend life by its mass destruction, liberty by the denial of civil liberties, the pursuit of happiness by the acquiescence in conditions which condemn millions of human beings to the misery of poverty, hunger, privation, is to attempt to cast out Satan by Satan. Both the judgments of God and the verdict of history refute its possibility."[39]

What therefore is the remedy for such a dilemma? Here the Council stumbled; it had no answer. If war was as bad as the Council declared it to be, then obviously the Christian could not attempt to cast out Satan by Satan. In spite of the impossibility of such a

38. *Ibid.*, 1940, pp. 15-19. It was signed by Georgia Harkness, Edwin L. Aubrey, Conrad Bergendoff, and J. Harry Cotton.

39. *Ibid.*, 1940, pp. 16-17.

task, the Council refused to reach the obvious conclusion. It did not absolutely close the door to war for Christians.

> We must hold before men the duty of absolute loyalty to God. The duty of the individual Christian to engage in war, or preparation for war, at the call of the State, is an issue upon which there is no agreement among Christians. We do not affirm either the pacifist or non-pacifist view to be the Christian position. We do affirm that within either position the Christian is obligated to radical obedience to the command of God, "Thou shalt have no other gods before me."[40]

Quite obviously, this pronouncement marks a retreat by the Federal Council from its previous statements. No longer is pacifism the Christian position. Now it is admitted that Christians do disagree on the problem of war. The reality of war had indeed a marked impact on the thinking of the Council by 1940.

The question immediately arises: Why did the Federal Council leadership retreat from its previous position of adamant opposition to all war as totally contrary to Christianity? It can be answered that political realities played a prominent part in this dramatic change in thinking. And there is considerable truth in this reply. But it is not the whole story by any means. The clue to the changing attitude of the Council toward war is found in an exchange of letters between President Roosevelt and Dr. George Buttrick, Council president, in December 1939 and January 1940. These letters shed considerable light on the question. In his letter to Buttrick, Roosevelt gave a very optimistic view of the possible results of the war: "I believe that while statesmen are considering a new order of things, the new order may well be at hand. I believe that it is even now being built . . . , in the hearts of masses whose voices are not heard, but whose common faith will write the final history of our time."[41] Roosevelt invited Buttrick and presumably his successor to visit Washington from time to time to share in the building of the new order that Roosevelt envisioned for the Western world. Buttrick replied to the President's letter in an equally cordial and hopeful tone:

> We join you in prayer that a lasting peace of justice and good will may soon bless mankind. Your invitation to a continued opportunity for conference is gratefully appreciated. The Federal Council of

40. *Ibid.*, p. 17.
41. *Federal Council Bulletin* 23, no. 1 (January 1940): 9.

Churches of Christ in America pledges itself through you to the people of America and of every church of the land to seek under God a world order in which unmerited poverty and cankering fear and the threat of war shall be banished.[42]

In tones less strident than in 1917, the Federal Council was preparing to give its blessing to World War II, even as it had blessed World War I for similar reasons. But it can hardly be denied that this change of direction was motivated by reasons of expediency and must surely have embarrassed many leaders of the Council. Had they not just recently told President Roosevelt that they must not seek to bring in the kingdom of God with Satan's instruments for that was nothing less than fighting Satan with Satan? But now the Council was doing just that. Also noteworthy, in his reply Buttrick threw away the last vestige of any pretense at upholding the policy of the separation of church and state. Council officials were to be in on postwar planning as they had not been under Wilson from 1917 to 1919.

The coming of Pearl Harbor brought a new crisis for the Federal Council, even as it did to the nation at large. Pacifism seemed to be a theoretical issue at best and no longer possible. The pacifist groups in the country, religious and secular, felt the strain of our involvement in the war. The isolationism that had characterized the pacifist movement during the 1930s had by 1940 given way to a noninterventionist internationalism, not necessarily a military interventionism, but certainly a diplomatic type of interventionism that could easily lead many pacifists into viewing the war raging in Europe as a crusade to save the world from the Nazi tyranny. Many of the leaders of the Federal Council felt this tension and yielded to the persuasiveness of this argument for military intervention. Their lingering doubts were dramatically removed by the attack on Pearl Harbor. Their hours of anxiety and anguish were over. The Japanese had decided the issue for them.

The Federal Council and the Problems of Labor, 1932-1941

The Social Creed of 1932 called for a more intensive interest by Christians in the problems of labor, which had been greatly intensified because of the depression and the increasing unemployment. It was a challenge to the Council as well as to the New Deal

42. *Ibid.*, pp. 9-10.

and neither the Council nor President Roosevelt could afford to neglect this problem, since both were committed to the cause of labor.

In its report to the Indianapolis biennial of 1932, the Council's Committee on Function and Structure had strongly recommended that the Federal Council should act as the common agency for all the denominations for the removal of the great social evils such as unemployment and other ills involving the relationship of labor and industry. The declared goal was the achievement of a basic standard of living for the masses of the country.[43]

In 1933 the Federal Council hailed the early efforts of the New Deal to aid the cause of labor:

> We have from the beginning asserted the right of employers and workers to organize. We therefore most heartily approve the effort of the national government to give a new charter to labor, guaranteeing the principle for which we have long contended—the right of workers to organize and bargain collectively through representatives of their own choosing.[44]

The Council continued to issue its annual Labor Day messages. That of 1933 may be regarded as the standard text for all that followed during that decade: "It is the church's business to teach, to inspire, to provide the moral and spiritual dynamic for basic change. The time is at hand, let us move forward more boldly in our economic life to the realization of our ideals of justice and human brotherhood."[45] This is the basic theme of these messages. All suggest that the Council was pleased with the New Deal program for labor as far as it went, but that ideally the program should have achieved an even greater degree of justice and brotherhood. In 1935 the Department of Research released a series of monographs dealing with various social and economic problems, including studies on economic insecurity and on the status of farm labor and industrial labor. The monographs were intended as study guides for ministerial groups and congregational use.

43. *Quadrennial Report*, 1932, pp. 28 ff.

44. *Annual Report*, 1932, p. 114. This specifically refers to the labor provisions of the National Industrial Recovery Act of 1933. When this act was declared unconstitutional by the Supreme Court, labor received a new safeguard in the National Labor Relations Act of 1935.

45. *Federal Council Bulletin* 16, no. 7 (September 1933.): 4.

By 1935, however, the Council seemed of the opinion that as fine as the New Deal was in many respects, it was not approaching quickly enough the kingdom of God as proclaimed by the liberal theologians. Although headed toward collectivism, the New Deal was not achieving the degree of social and political collectivism that would mark the realization of that kingdom so dear to liberal hearts. The Council offered a clear challenge to reluctant politicians who saw not the vision as clearly as they thought.

> To an increasing number it seems clear that both Christianity and social science point toward a more collective economy in which the strong shall bear the burdens of the weak and in which the weak shall be made strong.
> What is needed is a loyalty to Christian ideals and good will that is strong enough to break through a hampering social structure even though we are unable to see the distant scene.[46]

Such statements concerning the domestic program of the New Deal, however, became increasingly rare after 1935 as the Council turned toward the more pressing problem of world peace. The liberals were becoming greatly alarmed over the rise of totalitarianism in Germany and Italy (but not in Russia) and felt that unless Europe's drift toward war was reversed, the entire domestic program of the New Deal would be in dire jeopardy. It would be inaccurate and unfair to say that the Council was no longer interested in the problems of labor and industry; however, they no longer received the attention they once commanded. Weightier issues were the order of the day.

Evidence of the Council's lingering interest in the industrial area was the activity of James Myers, industrial secretary for the Social Service Commission (Department, after 1932). Myers, active in the labor movement, investigated the sharecroppers' strike in the South in 1936, the Little Steel Strike of Johnstown, Pennsylvania, in 1937, and the Detroit automobile strike of 1936 and 1937. Myers also established friendly relations with the American Federation of Labor and later with the Congress of Industrial Organization to such an extent that representatives of the Federal Council attended the annual conventions of these two labor groups.

In 1936 the Information Service, headed by Benson Y. Landis,

46. *Ibid.* 18, no. 4 (April 1935): 5.

published three important studies: *The Textile Strike, The NRA Challenge to Labor,* and *The Consumer Under the Recovery Program.* The first two dealt very directly with the problems of labor, and the third less so.

The Federal Council and Social Problems; 1932-1941

In spite of the progressive posture that the Federal Council assumed in the Social Creed of 1932, the Council failed at some points to fulfill the role it claimed for itself during the 1930s. Prohibition ceased to a great degree to be a major concern after 1932 though the Council by no means condoned the use of intoxicating liquors. Even the race question failed to command the attention that it had received during the 1920s and that seemingly had been promised in 1932. The Council, notwithstanding, continued to issue messages on race relations to the churches for use on Race Relations Sundays every February, but here and elsewhere the Council apparently came to see that declarations on racial equality could have little meaning and less weight in a world dominated by Nazism.

If the Council's interest tended to slacken somewhat regarding certain domestic social issues, it was intensified by the problems emerging from the growing influence of the motion-picture industry, which by 1930 was the object of mounting criticism from many sources. Responsible leaders in many areas of American life had come to regard the movies as a very dangerous influence on the moral fiber of the nation; in this conviction they were joined by the Federal Council.

As early as 1929 the executive committee had requested the research department to make a study of the motion-picture industry. The result was a report, *The Public Relations of the Motion Picture Industry.* Published in 1931, the report presented factual coverage of the films produced and the issues involved. Scrutinized were such questions as the publicity tactics used by the industry, the problem of censorship, and governmental control over the pictures produced for the public.

This early attempt to awaken public interest in this issue seems to have had little effect on the constituent churches and the industry. In 1934 the Council renewed its campaign for better motion pictures, apparently prodded into action by the Catholic Legion of Decency, which had called for a vigorous protest by Catholics

110

against the immorality in many of the films being produced. The Executive Committee adopted a resolution which was a strong indictment of the attitude of the industry toward its critics.

> The Federal Council can see as yet little evidence of intention by the producers of motion pictures to improve the moral quality of films. While there has been some evidence in other respects, the indecencies, the false ideals of life, the inducement to drinking, gambling and sensuality and the cynical attitude toward the sanctities of life remain unchanged.[47]

The Executive Committee also urged the churches to work for the end of the practice known as block-booking, a practice which denied to the operators of local theatres the right to choose what films they would or would not show. In 1936 the council professed its pleasure at the results of its efforts. However, many of the critics of the industry failed to find the improvement which the council professed to see. Whatever success the council was able to achieve was destined to be quite temporary indeed.

Evangelism

After 1932 evangelism received much greater emphasis than it previously received at any time in the history of the council. The reasons for this new emphasis on evangelism are not entirely clear. In the membership of the Council there had always been a small minority that believed in evangelism in its historic evangelical context. But this group never was able to persuade the Council to sponsor evangelism in this form. Other factors were undoubtedly at work after 1930 to bring this new emphasis. One cause was undoubtedly the impact of the depression on the morale of the people. The America of the early 1930s was a very different nation from the one that a few years earlier was convinced it had solved the problem of depressions and had entered an era of perpetual prosperity. The Council was no doubt reacting to the depression era. But this does not explain the call to evangelism that went out from the Council from 1934 on. Much evidence suggests that this call was directly related to the Social Creed of 1932. To realize the goals of this creed demanded commitment to the concept of

47. *Annual Report*, 1934, p. 133.

the kingdom of God, commitment that had been notably absent from the people at large and from the constituencies of the member churches. Thus the new emphasis on evangelism was again designed to attain a socialistic end rather than to reach lost souls with the Gospel of the Lord Jesus Christ.'

During the 1930s there was in the Federal Council Bulletin an accent on the necessity of evangelism and an insistence that there was no basic conflict between the preaching of the social gospel as such and the need of evangelism. There was considerable truth in this insistence. The advocates of the social gospel were cognizant of the fact that unless they could secure from men a deep dedication to the ethical principles of the Gospel and a deep commitment to the Jesus whom they presented as the living embodiment of these ethical ideals, there would be no motivating power for Christians to struggle for the realization of the kingdom of God in our national life. The phraseology of biblical evangelism generally marked these fervent appeals, often in a way that deluded the unwary, but the basic content was lacking. If sin was mentioned, and it frequently was, it was generally in the context of sins against society rather than sin against God, as the Bible deems it. Regeneration was skillfully enunciated as a new social awareness. The substitutionary atonement of Christ upon the cross was seldom if ever mentioned. Justification by faith was emitted. What evangelical elements could be found in this approach were Arminian at best, semi-Pelagian or Pelagian at worst.

One of the clearest statements on the role of evangelism in the life of the Federal Council was given by Samuel McCrae Cavert in 1935:

> The first and basic task of the Church is to help men gain and hold a sense of the spiritual meaning of life. . . . If the Church fails here it fails everywhere and becomes a broken cistern from which thirsty men can draw no water. The second great task of the Church is to hold before men the Christian ideal of life and to train them for Christian living. The idea that by some external magic we can secure a Christian society without training the individual Christian motives is a subtle illusion. We cannot permanently solve a single problem without changing the human heart.[48]

Obviously there is no clarion call to Biblical evangelism in this message. Rather, it is a clear statement that the hearts of men

48. *Federal Council Bulletin* 18, no. 10 (November-December 1935): 5.

must be basically changed if society is to be changed. The spiritual meaning of life mentioned above refers not to the work of the Holy Spirit in regeneration, conversion, and sanctification, but to a kind of life that possesses a transcendental quality rising above the mundane and purely material considerations and interests of daily existence. Notwithstanding, it must be admitted that the Federal Council entered upon its self-conferred task of evangelism with a new zeal under Dr. William Hiram Foulkes, who succeeded Dr. Charles Goodell as secretary for evangelism early in 1933, and then under William S. Abernathy, who took office in January 1935.

In 1934 the Council decided to use a new approach to evangelize every part of the nation. Accordingly, in 1935 a national preaching mission was announced for the autumn of that year. Chosen were some of the most famous liberal preachers in the country: E. Stanley Jones; George Buttrick; Lynn Harold Hough, dean of Drew Seminary; Albert Beaven, former President of the Federal Council and president of the Rochester-Colgate Divinity School; Bishop Ivan Lee Holt of St. Louis; and Paul Scherer. To give the mission an appeal to evangelicals, George W. Truitt of the First Baptist Church of Dallas and Methodist Bishop Arthur Moore of Atlanta were also named. The membership of the preaching mission was also almost exclusively drawn from Northern liberal circles, and of these, largely from the Northern Baptist Convention and Northern Methodist churches.

In calling for this preaching mission, the Council made its purpose undeniably clear. In a civilization on the verge of being destroyed by irreligion it had become imperative that Christianity gird itself for a real struggle to stress once more the reasonableness of the Christian faith in the personal God, its appropriate provisions for the deepest needs and aspirations of human life, and its redemptive, creative powers in organizing and shaping a bewildered society after the standards and ideals of the kingdom of God.[49]

The purpose of the preaching mission, was unabashedly humanistic and socialistic. "Conversion" of souls was for one end—the realization of the kingdom of God as that kingdom had been expounded by Walter Rauschenbusch, Harry F. Ward, and their numerous devotees in and out of the Council. It was evangelism for the purpose of manipulating the converts in order to gain their sup-

49. *Ibid.*, p. 7. The Council had tried to begin a Youth for Christ preaching mission in 1933 but it was unsuccessful (see *Federal Council Bulletin* [June 1937], p. 8).

port for a radicalism that by its very nature could only be hostile to evangelical Christianity.

Apparently aware that such a call to evangelism would arouse conservative hostility, the Council sought to absolve itself from such a charge by declaring:

> A social order is an abstraction. It [the Church] must forever judge time in the name of eternity. It must never consider itself committed to any one social order. It is the critic of that which is evil. It is ready to cooperate with that which is good.
>
> It [the Church] exists solely to let the light of Eternity shine in mighty judgment upon the way of Time, and every prophet and every order must come at last to that judgment. Its nature is imperial. Hitlerism and Fascism must not deny it. Democracy must not repudiate it. Capitalism, Socialism and Communism, however noble the forms they try to assume, unless they are endowed with such a conscience as only the Christian religion can give, will yet break upon it, and prove like the others a menace to the world.[50]

This amazing affirmation, apart from its basic errors, was simply an attempt to give to the preaching mission an appearance of ideological and economic neutrality. It was to preach not socialism, but the kingdom of God. But the kingdom of God that was preached was little less than a thinly concealed appeal for conversion to a socialistic kingdom somehow different from secular forms of collectivism but nevertheless collectivistic.

> If there be any remaining doubt as to the purpose of the mission E. Stanley Jones should set it at rest. We believe that we see the goal and we believe that men can get hold of that power to move on to that goal. That goal is the Kingdom of God on earth. The Kingdom of God is a new order standing at the door of the lower order. The higher order, founded on love, justice, goodwill, brotherhood and redemption, stands confronting this lower order founded on selfishness, exploitation, unbrotherliness, with its resultant clash and confusions. . . . it [the higher order] will finally replace this lower order, for it is God's order. We shall present Christ as the open door to that era. We shall unfold the possibilities of that era both within the individual and the collective will.[51]

50. *Ibid.*, pp. 9-10.
51. *Ibid.* 19, no. 8 (October 1936): 5.

The Council was very well pleased with the progress of the preaching mission during 1936 and it reported that missions had been held in twenty-eight cities and that the total attendance for the meetings was about twenty million with some twenty-three thousand ministers participating. It was continued in 1937 with an enlarged number of ministers participating. In 1940 the Council sponsored a new national evangelistic effort with the inauguration of the National Christian Missions program. The first one was held in Kansas City, Missouri, in September 1940 and the last in Los Angeles in March 1941; each mission lasted one week. The missions were held in twenty cities and over two hundred speakers took part. E. Stanley Jones took part in all twenty-two missions. Murial Lester of London and Adolf Keller of Geneva also played prominent roles.

In 1938 a university preaching mission was launched. Missions were established on sixteen college and university campuses. Sixty-six speakers were involved, most of whom were also connected with the national preaching mission. Some one hundred and thirteen thousand students attended these meetings, which were held at such schools as Ohio State University, and the universities of North Carolina, Wisconsin, Illinois, and Pennsylvania. The participating leaders were carefully picked for their ability to make liberal Christianity and the social gospel attractive to student audiences. E. Stanley Jones and T. Z. Koo were the featured speakers at many of the schools.

In 1939 preaching missions were held on the campuses of twenty colleges and universities. Many of the speakers of the previous year were again employed. However, the growing crisis in Europe and the outbreak of war in September 1939 brought a shift of interest and the university missions faded from the picture. That these concentrated efforts to present liberal theology had any great impact on the student mind is doubtful indeed. Liberal theology had no answer for the crisis confronting Europe and America.

As a part of its expanding emphasis on evangelism, the Council broadened its radio ministry. By 1939 the Council said that it had at least one Christian message on the radio every day of the year using the facilities of several networks. In 1939 Harry Emerson Fosdick, Ralph Sockman, Paul Scherer, Oscar Blackwelder, Daniel Poling, Harold Paul Sloan, Frederick K. Stamm, John Sutherland Bonnell, Jesse Bader (secretary for evangelism for the Federal Council), Joseph Sizoo, and Norman Vincent Peale were the featured ministers of the air for the Council. In general, these programs were on a high cultural level and were directed to the more educated classes of the country. Their theological tone was definitely liberal for the most part, though a few moderate evangelicals were included to give the programs a wider hearing among those who were conservative and preferred the evangelical message.

The following year (1940) the Council began sponsoring the annual Worldwide Communion Sunday, held in October. The first occurred on October 6, 1940. In this it continued a practice begun by the General Assembly of the Presbyterian Church, USA.

The Federal Council and Unity and Union 1932-1941

During the decade beginning with 1932 the ecumenical spirit received new impetus and the leadership of the Council became much more vocal in expressing its hopes for closer cooperation and unity among the churches than had previously existed. Although there was an emphasis upon unity of purpose within the Council, among the constituent denominations increasing emphasis was placed on the union of denominations and of the missionary and educational organizations that carried on a cooperative work as the agencies of many of these denominations.

This interest in union had been implicit in the formation of the Federal Council and was always a part of the vision of the more radical leaders of the movement. But before 1930 the accent fell on cooperative unity in the work the denominations could undertake jointly. The cooperative idea did not suddenly disappear after 1932, but receded before the new wave of interest in the organic unity of various denominations.

The new enthusiasm for organic unity was the result of several factors at work on the American ecclesiastical scene. The first of these was the declining interest in the distinctive doctrines of the various denominations. As doctrine retreated into the background, its potential for divisiveness was quashed and the way was cleared for organic unity, first among those churches of the same or similar doctrinal and ecclesiastical backgrounds and then of churches of very different backgrounds. Liberalism had produced a doctrinal indifference that paved the way for organic mergers on an increasing scale and several important unions took place in the 1930s. In 1931 a merger was effected between the Congregational churches and a group of Christian churches; the result was the Congregational Christian denomination. In 1934 the Evangelical Synod and the Reformed Church in the United States came together to form the Evangelical and Reformed Church. The largest merger, involving the most members thus far in American church history, occurred in 1939 when the Northern and Southern Methodist and the Methodist Protestant churches united to form the largest single denomination in the country then.

The Federal Council was influenced by these mergers and also influenced the movement for church union. After 1932 the Council's leaders were much bolder in openly urging such mergers than they had been before 1930.

Another equally important factor was the appearance of the Social Creed of 1932. This creed, much more advanced and open in its demand for a collectivist society in America than that of 1908, also demanded a unified and collectivist Protestantism as the agency through which the collectivists' kingdom of God would be realized in this country. Without a highly unified Protestantism the cause of collectivism would be seriously weakened in the America of the 1930s. Although this reason was not often openly stated in the official pronouncements of the Council's leadership, it was lurking just beneath the surface of these fervent pleas for the realization of the kingdom of God in this nation, as that kingdom was defined by Walter Rauschenbusch and his many votaries in the social-gospel movement.

At the Indianapolis quadrennial in 1932 Bishop Francis J. McConnell, the retiring president of the Council, sounded a note that would become increasingly prominent in succeeding meetings: "If we keep going steadily in this direction [toward a larger Christian unity], we shall eventually discover that we have union and do not have to create it. All that will be necessary will be to ratify something that has come into being without artificial promotion."[52]

This strategy of achieving union as a necessary result of the existence and activities of the Council was not new, but inherent in it and in the entire ecumenical movement from 1908 on and even before. Organic unity would be the eventual product of a growing unity of action. A hint of this realization appeared in the *Christian Herald* for February 1933. It declared that the Federal Council was

52. *Quadrennial Report*, 1932, p. 19.

117

the greatest collective achievement to the credit of North American Protestantism and that if it were to disappear, the work of organized Christianity could be seriously handicapped in many fields.[53]

The celebration of the twenty-fifth anniversary of the founding of the Federal Council in 1933 occasioned much testimony for the cause of organic unity. Samuel McCrae Cavert wrote: "Thoughtful observers increasingly agree that the Federal Council has abundantly demonstrated its indispensability to the effectiveness of Protestantism, providing a necessary center of collective activity and a united leadership in the most crucial, moral and spiritual problems confronting the nation and the world."[54] And then he added this pensive insight: "While itself not an agency for organic union, the Federal Council is constantly creating the conditions out of which union can naturally come."[55]

On the other hand, the *Christian Century* sounded a very critical note about the Indianapolis quadrennial and its "timid" stand on denominationalism:

> Our denominationalist system is spiritually bankrupt. The foundations on which the denominations have been accustomed to justify their existence have been steadily subsiding for many years. . . .
> Our sects are all operating on the momentum from the past, rather than on power generated in the living present. . . .[56]

The editor of the *Christian Century* cited what he delighted to call the fate of the denominational missionary enterprise—the "five times too many churches," the too many ministers and theological seminaries, and the too many missionary societies—as evidence that the churches were being forced into "all sorts of irrelevant and unspiritual stunts and vices in order to keep going." The editor insisted, "Surely the Federal Council will face this condition, surely it will not meet and sojourn again without making a constructive proposal for a united administration of Christian mission—not by a board, as proposed by the Laymen's Report, but by a united church."[57]

53. *Ibid.*, p. 12.

54. *Federal Council Bulletin* 16, no. 10 (November-December 1933): 4.

55. *Christian Century*, November 29, 1933, p. 1496.

56. *Ibid.*, p. 1496

57. *Ibid.*

The *Christian Century* was inclined to blame the constituent churches for the weakness of the Council as a unifying agency. It clearly realized that the Council was not self-constituted, but the creation of some twenty-eight denominations (as of 1933) and was condemned by these basic limitations to be something less than what the ecumenical enthusiasts of the religious journal had hoped it would be. The *Christian Century* became a self-appointed agency for prodding the Federal Council into taking a more active leadership in promoting Christianity. In 1935 it carried two articles, one by E. Stanley Jones and the other by Finis Idleman, calling for a profound reconstruction of Protestantism.[58] Idleman called on the Council to create a department of Christianity, insisting that in 1935 the mood of the church was favorable to such leadership.

Just before he returned to India, E. Stanley Jones gave an impassioned plea for the union of the various denominations as the Church of Christ in America, which would be composed of various branches such as the Baptist, Methodist, Presbyterian, and Episcopal.[59] It was actually a union of all Protestant churches using the Constitution of 1787 as a model. The various branches would come together on the simple doctrinal basis found in Matthew 16:16-19. He denied that he wanted to see the various denominations poured into one mold. But he did insist that his plan was not a federation, but a federal union. He defended his proposal on the basis of the dire need of unity, in view of the task confronting the church:

> But I do not see how the Christian Church can do the things I have suggested unless we get together. Our denominationalism simply cannot do the task. A divided church in a divided world has little authority. The next great step within Christendom is for the church to unite. I suggest that we drop our denominational label as separate churches and have one church, the Church of Christ in America—and under this central unity we have branches—the Baptist Church. . . . We would be brought together in the General Assembly of the Church of Christ in America.[60]

Fully aware that such a proposal would arouse tremendous opposition from denominational sources, Jones thought to allay the

58. For the complete text of this article, see *Christian Century*, October 9, 1935, pp. 1278-79.

59. For the complete text of this message, see *Federal Council Bulletin* 20, no. 4 (April 1937): 3-5.

60. *Ibid.*, p. 4.

fears that would and did arise because of this radical plan of union, a plan that went far beyond any previous position assumed by the Federal Council. Said Jones, "In the plan we would not be called on to give up any thing fundamentally good in any branch, but each would give its good to the best."[61]

E. Stanley Jones was something less than candid in his statements. The whole plan rested upon and breathed an indifference to the whole development of Christian theology from the Council of Nicaea on and it actually called upon the creedal churches—the Presbyterian and the Lutheran, for example—to surrender the heritage of the Reformation. Loyalty to biblical theology was to bow to loyalty to unity for the sake of unity.

In response to the call of the Asbury biennial of December 5, 1936, and to the pleas of the *Christian Century* and E. Stanley Jones, the executive committee in 1937 created a Commission on Christian Unity, declaring that such an action was the natural result of the national preaching mission.[62] The *Christian Century* commented on this development with cautious optimism: "The positive assumption underlying this action is that the Federal Council is not to be a static thing, . . . but a growing expression of the growing unity of the churches. . . . It also ought to become a positive influence in the cultivation of the spirit of unity among all the churches."[63]

In 1937 the Federal Council began to take a more active part in the international conferences looking forward to the creation of the World Council of Churches. Although the Federal Council had no official connection with the first World Conference on Faith and Order held at Lausanne in 1927, since the delegates were chosen by the various denominations, it was nevertheless quite interested in its proceedings because of its ecumenical significance and because Bishop Charles Brent, a long-time influence in the Council, was chosen president of this gathering.[64]

This conference was significant for the ecumenical movement in that it laid the basis for the Edinburgh conference of 1937. As a

61. *Ibid.*, p. 5.

62. *Ibid.*, no. 5 (May 1937): 6.

63. *Christian Century*, April 21, 1937, p. 513.

64. In 1926 the Federal Council had participated in the Stockholm conference. One hundred and fifty delegates from the United States attended and declared for the same social gospel, which had helped to bring about the formation of the Federal Council in 1908. This position met with great opposition from the German delegates.

result of this 1927 gathering, the Federal Council began to play an increasingly significant role in the international ecumenical movement. Developments were further strengthened by the connections of Dr. John C. Bennett and Dr. Henry Smith Leiper with the Universal Christian Council. At the Oxford Conference on Life and Work, the Federal Council was well represented by William Adams Brown, Walter Van Kirk, and Henry Sloan Coffin.[65] Delegates to the Edinburgh Conference on Faith and Order were elected by the denominations; the Federal Council had no official role in this gathering. Both of these conferences laid the foundations of the World Council of Churches.

The Commission on Christian Unity was actually organized and began to function in September 1937. By March 1938 it was able to report its accomplishments in promoting unity among the churches.[66] In its first report to the Council on its achievements the commission analyzed the various proposals for church union that had been brought forward and found them sadly lacking.[67] It was particularly critical of E. Stanley Jones's plan because it retained in the united church the denominational structure in the form of branches. The committee agreed that this approach, which allowed the several churches to retain their own doctrinal positions, forms of worship, and methods of government, was not compatible with the kind of unity discussed at the Edinburgh Conference on Faith and Order. The report denied that there was a basic disagreement between those who insisted on the definite authority of the Scriptures for ordering the creeds and worship of the church and those who insisted on the individual experience of divine grace as the definitive norm in the determination of creeds and modes of worship. The committee came to the conclusion that "we have not reached the time in the United States when any plan for union is satisfactory."[68]

The matter of unity and union came up again in 1939 when the Commission on Christian Unity presented a report to the executive committee as a response to a request from the 1938 General Assembly of the Presbyterian Church, USA asking for advice on the E. Stanley Jones plan for church union and a recommendation for "fuller unity in Christian service."

65. William Adams Brown was elected one of its cochairmen.

66. See *Federal Council Bulletin* 21, no. 3 (March 1938): 9-10 for the complete text.

67. For the text of this report, see *Biennial Report*, 1938, 21-24.

68. *Ibid.*, p. 23.

The executive committee gave two recommendations in answer to this request. First, it said that in view of the heartening progress being made in the reorganization of the World Council of Churches and in view of the recent unification of certain denominations and the prospective mergers of others, any comprehensive effort for American church unity should be postponed until such issues as the nature of the church were settled. The executive committee also decreed that the unity contemplated under the plan formulated by Stanley Jones could be realized through an increasing cooperation with the Federal Council of Churches.[69]

In 1941 the Federal Council went on record as agreeing with the request of the General Assembly of the Presbyterian Church, USA of May 1938 for greater unity of planning and activity in the area of home missions.[70]

Organizational Developments, 1932-1941

In 1932 the Commission on Goodwill Between Christians and Jews, which had been formed in 1922, left the Federal Council in order to become an independent organization. Admittedly, this type of organizational change was rare in the history of the Council. The trend was toward an increase in such commissions. In 1935 a committee was created to nominate and supervise the chaplains in the federal penitentiaries; in 1937 Seward Hiltner was named its chairman and charged with obtaining men for these positions, men who had training not only in theology but in psychology and sociology as well. That year, 1937, the Committee on Religion and Mental Health was created.

In 1940 the Council itself was reorganized, the first real change since the reorganization of 1932. At the Atlantic City biennial it was

69. *Federal Council Bulletin* 22, no. 9 (September 1939): 7-8. A conference had been held in Utrecht in May 1938 to draft a constitution for the World Council. The Federal Council sent Kenneth Scott Latourette, Lewis S. Mudge, F. H. Knubel, James DeWolf Perry, J. Ross Stevenson, William Adams Brown, Samuel McCrae Cavert, Henry Smith Leiper, and Dean Luther Weigle as delegates. By September 1938 the proposed constitution had received favorable action by the General Assemblies of the Presbyterian Church, USA and the Presbyterian Church, U.S., the General Council of the Congregational Christian Church, the General Synod of the Evangelical Church, the General Synod of the Reformed Church in America, and the Northern Baptist Convention. By the end of the year five other denominations had taken similar action.

70. A beginning of cooperation in this area had been made in 1935 with the signing of the National Comity Agreement by six of the larger denominations, but it applied only to towns with less than 1,500 population.

decided that each denomination should have three members in the Council with one additional member for every 100,000 members. To its delegation each church could also appoint laymen, but the total number of laymen could not exceed one third of the total number of delegates. There was also a provision that the churches could name an additional number of delegates up to twelve, but they were to be designated as representatives of state and local councils of churches. This last innovation was part of a concrete program designed to strengthen the Federal Council at the grassroots level and give it a wider popular appeal and support.

Of greater importance during this decade was the development of the Council's public image and denominational support. Although it began the era with the loss of the Presbyterian Church, U.S. from its membership—the most important defection in the Council's history from 1908 to 1950—its record was one of growth in membership. The increase in denominational membership would have been more impressive if the mergers between constituent Council members, previously referred to, had not occurred.

Although the Church of God withdrew from membership in 1933 because of the comity arrangements favored by the Federal Council in regard to the establishment of new congregations, this was the last defection during the decade. In 1933 the recently formed United Church of Canada became an affiliate member. Five years later, in 1938, the Syrian Orthodox Church joined, the first non-Protestant church to do so, thus changing the original nature and purpose of the Council. In 1940 the Protestant Episcopal Church entered into full membership, and the same year overtures were made by the Presbyterian Church, U.S. to rejoin the Council.[71] In 1940 there were twenty constituent members of the Council representing a total membership of about twenty million people.

A Decade of Growing Criticism of the Council and Its Work

Even in its early days the Federal Council was the object of severe criticism by those denominations that had been historically committed to pacifism, which in fact occasioned the first withdrawal from membership.

Other actions had also given rise to particular criticism by individuals and denominational assemblies. But from 1932, even within denominations that continued their membership, there

71. The Presbyterian Church, U.S. formally rejoined the council by the action of the General Assembly of 1941.

was a constant stream of criticism from the conservative evangelicals and frequent demands for withdrawal from membership. Such criticism frequently issued from the most conservative Northern Baptist and Lutheran churches. However, the most persistent criticism came from Presbyterian sources and from those more conservative churches affiliated in any way with the Council. One cause of this hostile feeling was the Council's custom of giving the impression that when it made pronouncements, it was not only speaking for the membership of the constituent denominations but also acting as the conscience of all the Protestant churches. But a study of the records of the various churches makes it quite clear that the Federal Council at no time spoke for such a vast number of Protestants.[72]

The second factor behind the hostility to the Council was the passage of the Social Creed of 1932 and the increasingly radical stance assumed by the Council on many issues in the New Deal era. Its increasingly liberal theology inspired a similar development in its economic, social, and political outlook. Thus the Council was subjected to an increasing amount of criticism from those who were not necessarily interested in its theological position, but who were much concerned with its espousal of pacifism and disarmament—especially in this period of growing international tensions and dangers—and its growing zeal for socialistic panaceas for economic and social ills.[73]

The first of these attacks came from Fred A. Britten, a member of the House of Representatives. On January 30, 1934, Britten delivered a highly critical address against the Council on the floor of the House.[74] Mr. Britten made some statements concerning the Council and its membership that were not true and others that lacked substantive evidence.[75] For this reason his charges did little

72. Officially the leaders of the Council again and again cautioned that they were not trying to assume such a role, but for the most part their denials were not too convincing to the American public.

73. Such fears were also voiced frequently in the churches by the theological conservatives, who regarded socialism as essentially an atheistic movement closely allied with communism and who also regarded the attitude of the Federal Council toward pacifism and socialism as little less than treason to both God and the state and the American heritage.

74. U.S., Congress, House, *Congressional Record*, vol. 73, part 7, pp. 1612-1613.

75. For the correspondence in this matter, see the *Christian Century*, April 18, 1934, pp. 520-22. This journal in turn denounced Mr. Britten for being the spokesman for military preparedness in general and a large navy in particular..

to weaken the image of the Council, and the reply by Sidney Gulick, executive secretary of the Council at that time, was a masterful job of evading the issue.

In a 1935 address Congressman Maury Maverick of Texas revealed the contents of a memorandum issued by naval intelligence that accused the Federal Council of giving aid and comfort to the Communist party. The same charges were repeated by Admiral Standley, chief of naval operations.

This attack could not be overlooked or ignored. The result was a conference between President Roosevelt and a delegation from the Council consisting of Bishop Ivan Lee Holt and Joseph Sizoo of Washington. The President gave them a very gracious reception and personally assured them of his high regard for the Council and that he had no misgivings about anything the Council did. He also informed the delegates that he had sent word to the Army and Navy Departments that without his specific consent they should make no comments favorable or unfavorable about any civilian organization.[76]

In 1938 a somewhat different attack originated with the testimony of Dr. Theodore Graebner, noted Lutheran theologian of Concordia Seminary in St. Louis. Graebner insisted that "religious leadership has become infected with political radicalism and outright bolshevistic communism to an appalling extent," and that the Federal Council meddled in political affairs for the purpose of supporting radicalism.[77]

The Christian Century rushed to the defense of religious leaders in general and the Federal Council in particular. It stoutly insisted that Dr. Graebner could not name any religious leaders infected with communism. The periodical defended the Council in a curious manner, by denying that it had meddled constantly in political affairs, "except those political affairs that are also moral affairs as many political affairs are or ought to be."[78] Since the leadership of the council insisted that religion must be secularized in order to bring all of life into the kingdom of God, this was actually an admission of the correctness of the charge hurled against the Council.

The Federal Council also received support from more conservative sources. In 1939 a special committee, appointed the previous year,

76. U.S., Congress, House, *Congressional Record,* vol. 78, p. 1614; for the attack of Maverick, see vol. 79, pp. 3042-43.

77. *Christian Century,* December 21, 1938, p. 1564.

78. *Ibid.*

reported to the General Assembly of the United Presbyterian Church that the changes against the Federal Council had been made by people who had no firsthand knowledge of the Council. It went on to insist that the Council was so thoroughly a representative body that any mistakes it might make could be corrected by the democratic functioning of the official representatives of the denominations in the Council.[79] This report, accepted by the General Assembly, also voiced a caution against indulging in the popular pastime of placing a Communist tag on constructive proposals for removing social injustices and evils. These various efforts to defend the Council against its growing number of detractors no doubt settled the issue for many liberals and the undiscerning among the conservatives, but they did not actually answer the specific charges against the activities and leanings of the Council.

It is obvious that during this decade there was a growing apprehension over the intrusion of the Council into the political life of the nation and an increasing suspicion that it was radically inclined, not only in its theology, but in its social and political outlook as well.[80] This concern resulted in an increase in the number of public accusations that the Federal Council was under Communist influence.

However, those who accused the Council of these radical leanings did not for the most part offer sufficient evidence to make a convincing case. In its public pronouncements, particularly in the Social Creed of 1932 and some statements of its presidents, there is no doubt that this leftward drift in theology and political and social thought was under way. But those who made the charges all too often did not offer the necessary documentation to convince the American public. The evidence was available. Many of the leaders of the Federal Council in this era were identified with various radical groups as individuals and in this capacity they frequently made statements that were proof of their radical allegiances of one kind or another. Thus the defenses offered by the Council itself and the *Christian Century* and some denominational statements were perhaps technically correct but, nevertheless, quite misleading. The Federal

79. *Federal Council Bulletin* 22, no. 6 (June 1939): 5.

80. In some of its pronouncements the Council undoubtedly did, receive public support. A case in point was its opposition, to Roosevelt's appointment of Myron C. Taylor as the President's personal envoy to the Vatican, if such an appointment represented a permanent development (*Federal Council Bulletin* 23, no. 1 [January 1940]: 8).

Council did have connections with radicalism, but they were carefully concealed from the rank-and-file membership of the Council and from the American public.[81]

81. Some of this would have become discernible if its critics had taken the time to study the official pronouncements and platforms of the Communist party in this country and compared these with similar pronouncements of the Federal Council.

5

The Federal Council in War and Cold War, 1941-1950

The bombing of Pearl Harbor and our immediate involvement in World War II brought new tensions to the Federal Council. Mindful of its reputation of pacifism and its support of Wilson's entry into World War I, the Council's leaders faced a tremendous dilemma. Should they once again come to the aid of Roosevelt and the nation and give their blessing to another world carnage? Or should they withhold it and maintain neutrality, which could only be interpreted as a lack of patriotism and, even worse, a refusal to take sides in what appeared to most people to be the most dramatic clash between right and wrong in modern history? Was not totalitarianism worse than war? If it were worse, then war was not the worst of wrongs, but merely the lesser of two evils.

This was the dilemma confronting the pacifists of the 1930s both within and without the Federal Council. But the dogmatic insistence of the Council that Christians could not engage in any war placed the Federal Council in a position much more embarrassing than the stance taken by the secular pacifists, who had not so closely united their opposition to war to the biblical position.

The Council made a valiant effort to extricate itself from this dilemma. In a message to the churches and the American people on December 30, 1941, the Council sought to justify the American entrance into the conflict by regarding the war as a second crusade in behalf of freedom. The language, strangely reminiscent of some of the Council's pronouncements in 1917, sought to justify Christians' participation in the conflict:

> The war which oppresses our world today makes a deepening crisis in civilization. The calculated treachery of recent aggressions has evoked instant condemnation. It is a manifestation of a great flood of evil that has overwhelmed nation after nation, destroying human rights and leaving men the victims of irresponsible force. . . . Yet we must realize that war is but the most shocking sign of the demoralization of modern life and international conduct. The laws of God have not been honored. Now the awful consequences are laid bare.[1]

In such a situation, the Council declared, American citizens had a threefold responsibility and American Christians had an even heavier responsibility:

> We have a threefold responsibility as citizens of a nation, under God, that is dedicated to human freedom; as members of the Church in America, which is called to minister to people under heavy strain; and as members of the worldwide Church which unites in a common fellowship men of every race and nation who acknowledge Jesus Christ as Lord and Saviour.
>
> As citizens we gratefully acknowledge a priceless heritage of freedom and democratic ideals for which earlier generations struggled and sacrificed. We cherish this heritage more deeply when we see it attacked by a totalitarian threat. We are resolved to defend it from the menace of rival systems from without and from degradation of abuse or neglect from within. It is our high obligation to bequeath our heritage unimpaired and strengthened unto those who follow us. We rededicate ourselves to the highest purposes of this nation and to its unfinished task of building a more truly free and democratic society.[2]

1. *Federal Council Bulletin* 25, no. 1 (January 1942): 3. For the full text, see pp. 3-5.
2. *Ibid.*, p. 30.

In the last phrase we see the real reason for the decision of the Council to bestow its blessing on entering into the conflict. Its leaders saw that war could be used for domestic, social, and economic purposes, the building of a more democratic society, by which they actually meant that the war could and must be used for achieving the social and economic goals set forth in the Social Creed of 1932. Indeed, the realization that the war could be used to bring about a democratic collectivism in this country was the motivating factor in the thinking of Franklin Roosevelt and the radical members of the New Deal. It lay behind Roosevelt's support of the *Report of the National Resources Planning Board (March 10, 1943)* and many of the legislative enactments of the war era.[3]

In order further to underscore the true purpose of the war, the Council declared:

> The Church must be in the vanguard of preparation for a just and durable peace. The great sacrifice of treasure and of life must not be in vain. We must build now the spiritual foundations for a better order of the world. This task is immediate and cannot be delayed.[4]

Recognizing the more immediate and practical necessities also, the Council called for the formation of a coordinating committee for wartime service, to be formed with representatives from the General Commission of Army and Navy Chaplains, the Christian Commission for Camp and Defense Communities, the Committee on the Conscientious Objectors, and the Commission to Study the Basis of a Just and Durable Peace. It also suggested that the president of the Federal Council should be the chairman of this coordinating commission. The Council also voted to collaborate with the Home Missions Council in constituting the Commission for Aliens and Prisoners of War.

Early in 1942 a report was given by a select committee which spelled out more precisely and in greater detail the choices or possibilities confronting the churches at that time.[5] The committee—composed of John C. Bennett as chairman, D. Elton Trueblood, A. R. Wentz, Holmes Ralston, among others—stated it was right for the church to declare that this worldwide human struggle would decide whether these three possibilities would exist for most of the

3. For a discussion of this aspect of the war, see C. Gregg Singer, *A Theological Interpretation of American History* (Nutley, N.J., 1964), pp. 266-75.

4. *Ibid.*, p. 4.

5. *Biennial Report*, 1942, pp. 11-21.

people of the world: (1) the possibility of an order of life in which men would have freedom from the terror of lawless rule; (2) the possibility of an order of life in which there would be progress toward social justice and racial equality; and (3) the possibility of an order of life in which the church would have freedom to preach the Gospel to the community at large and to train youth.[6]

The committee then issued a disclaimer of sorts, stating that the future of the church was at stake in the conflict. The war was not to be regarded as a crusade to save the church from destruction: "We do not claim that the existence of the church or of the Christian faith depends upon the outcome of the war. We do not believe that God would be defeated by the defeat of the United Nations."[7] If God would not be defeated and the church would not be destroyed, the Council was equally sure that if the Axis powers should win, then basic freedoms would be in great danger, even lost. Freedom of thought, conscience, worship, and economic opportunity were definitely imperiled.

The committee repeatedly insisted that while our involvement in the war produced a crisis, it simultaneously presented a tremendous challenge and opportunity for the church to be "the church"and to assume a position of moral and ethical leadership in every area of American life.

It called upon the church to solve the racial problems, paying particular attention to the problem of Negro segregation, not only in the South, but also in the North. At the same time, it reminded the church that it must also oppose anti-Semitism and took the opportunity to remind Christians that they must be particularly sensitive to the wave of anti-Japanese feeling then sweeping the nation.

The committee also called upon the church to give very careful consideration to the problem of economic reconstruction and called on church members to give special attention to the available materials on this subject such as a report of the section of the Oxford Conference of 1937 on *The Church and the Social Order*, the section of the Delaware Conference Report dealing with the economic bases of a just and durable peace and still another report issued by the British Churches on social justice and economic reconstruction.

All of these reports spoke of economic reconstruction and social justice in terms of collectivism, either implicitly or explicitly.

6. *Ibid.*, p. 11.
7. *Ibid.*

Whatever the differences in language, they all had one objective: collectivism was a necessary and desirable outcome of the war:

> The chief contribution of the Church, especially of the clergy and all who have a teaching function within the Church, is to keep alive the vision in men's minds of the true order of life as God intended it to be, an order in which the whole process of production has as its primary purpose the meeting of human needs instead of having the meeting of those needs as a by-product of the pursuit of profit; an order in which there is such complete equality for all children that the division of classes will become merely a difference of function and not a radical difference of privilege; an order in which the resources of the earth, land and water are controlled for the benefit of the total community with whatever forms of ownership in each case are conducive to such control; an order in which it is possible for all men to be employed and find in their daily work a vocation that can represent not merely a means of support but one in which what they do, because of its relation to the needs of the community, can be regarded as God's will for their lives.[8]

This paragraph reveals the real reason for the willingness of the Council to support the war. The war was to be a crusade for the establishment of a democratic collectivism; put more bluntly, its goal was the establishment of socialism in this country. The purpose of this conflict was not merely to check German and Japanese aggression—which was necessary—but, as a result the peace to come, to gain a socialistic victory at home as well.

The *Christian Century*, very early in the war, had rushed to the defense of this concept. Although this journal did not regard the war as a righteous conflict, it did declare that God was trying to speak to his people in it since "every event is a Word of God." The editor could give the conflict a conditional acceptance:

> War is the collapse of the divine order for which God is striving, with man's cooperation, to establish in this world. The collapse of this order is due to man's disobedience. God does not command us to fight. He condemns us to fight.[9]

In this attempted solution of the dilemma there is a most serious contradiction. The God who failed because man failed now con-

8. *Ibid.*, p. 18.

9. *Christian Century*, January 14, 1942, pp. 38-41.

demns man to fight as a kind of punishment in which both are involved. If war is wrong, as the Federal Council and the *Christian Century* had both insisted on many occasions during the 1930s, then this God who had previously declared that war is wrong is now condemning people to commit sin.

The 1942 report of the select committee devoted a great deal of attention to the kind of peace that was to emerge from this conflict. "The members of the Churches should be prepared now for a vision of the kind of world in which it will be possible to have peace as the result of a just ordering of the lives of nations."[10]

The select committee insisted that this could be accomplished through a development of a genuine cooperation of the peoples of all races East and West, and declared that "never in all history has there been so great a chance to bridge the chasms of race and to unite the people of the East and West in a world without imperialism." The church must also rally to the support of international institutions charged with the responsibility of maintaining the peace of the world.

The report of this committee, considered as a whole, was actually a new social creed, which in a sense replaced the more formally adopted Social Creed of 1932. The creed of 1932 had been drafted under the impact of a depression psychology to meet the needs of that day, whereas the report of this select committee was drafted to meet the needs of a nation at war. However, the 1942 report was by no means restricted to the war itself; rather, it used the war as a means of placing the social and economic philosophy of the Council into a new context. In this report was the not too subtle assumption that collectivism must be the result of our involvement in the war. Without the triumph of collectivism, identified as the kingdom of God, there would be no real victory. A military victory in Europe and Asia would be hollow indeed if it did not bring victory at home for radicalism. Thus the report dealt with those topics that had been included in the creed of 1932 and treated them at an even greater length.

The Federal Council was not alone in regarding the war as a stepping-stone to realizing social justice and democratic collectivism. Other liberal and radical church organizations had also seen the potentialities of the conflict and had begun to plan accordingly. But much of the inspiration for these other actions came from the pronouncements of the Federal Council, aided by the vigorous edi-

10. *Biennial Report*, 1942, p. 19.

torial policy of the *Christian Century*. To formulate the proper procedures for the realization of the kind of peace Council leaders had in mind, the Council called for a National Study Council to meet at Delaware, Ohio, early in March 1942. The theme of this conference was the creation of a just and durable peace. It flatly declared that economic security was as necessary as political security for all the nations if this goal was to be reached. The report called for more industrial democracy as the necessary basis for political democracy. This insistence on industrial democracy was nothing more than a thinly veiled plea for much greater government ownership of industry in the United States.[11] The Marxian assumptions lying behind these demands are clearly visible. A month later the Methodist Federation for Social Service issued a call for the social (government) ownership of all industry necessary to win the war and declared that it was imperative that the government should take over the automobile and steel industries as once, if this war was to bring about the kingdom of God.[12] At a meeting of this organization in May 1942, Harry F. Ward, professor at Union Theological Seminary in New York and long-time friend of radical causes, declared that collectivism would be the next step in society and that the task of the Protestant church was to ensure that this collectivism be democratically controlled and not fascist in nature. If there was any doubt about Communist influence in his thinking, it should have been dispelled by his suggestion that the dialectic of Karl Marx be used to determine the direction in which American society should move.[13]

The Presbyterian Church, USA, through its Committee on Social Education and Action, joined in the chorus calling for socialism at home, even though its position was more carefully screened from those members of the church who still regarded communism as a form of atheism and entirely incompatible with the Gospel and any version of the kingdom of God on earth. This committee declared that "ours is the duty to build a people's Christian loyalty into the social order and to open their imagination and loyalty to all the implications of world citizenship."[14] However, this committee was

11. *Christian Century*, March 18, 1942, pp. 349-50. See also March 2, pp. 389-97.

12. *Ibid.*, April 1, 1942, p. 430.

13. *Ibid.*, July 1942, p. 814. Harry F. Ward had drafted the Methodist Creed of 1908 and been influential in the drafting of the Social Creed of 1908 for the Federal Council.

14. *Ibid.*, June 10, 1942, p. 762.

very careful not to reveal these implications to Presbyterians, or anyone else.

Early in 1943 the Commission on a Just and Durable Peace, under the leadership of its chairman John Foster Dulles, formulated a statement of political propositions, popularly known as the "Six Pillars of Peace." This statement was intended to be a guide for the churches in their efforts to secure a postwar settlement that "would merit the support of thoughtful Christian people."[15]

The first of these pillars insisted that the peace treaty must provide the framework for a continuing collaboration of the members of the United Nations and in due course of neutral and enemy nations as well.[16] This pillar obviously had reference to the League of Nations of Woodrow Wilson and Point Eight in the Atlantic Charter of August 1941.

The second pillar declared that the peace treaty must make provision for bringing within the scope of international agreement those economic and financial acts of national governments that have widespread international repercussions. In this assertion the Federal Council set itself squarely in favor of the creation of an international collectivism just as it had called for a domestic collectivism. Its leaders seemed oblivious to the fact that they were using the war against collectivism for the purpose of creating one at home and over the world, the only difference being that the one they would help to create would be democratically controlled. The third pillar really reaffirmed the first one in its call for a postwar United Nations. The fourth reiterated the call for an international organization to protect the autonomy of subject peoples.

In the fifth pillar the Federal Council called for the same kind of strict control over military establishments which it had previously demanded for this country. The sixth demanded that the peace should establish in principle and seek to achieve in practice the right of every man to religious and intellectual liberty.

The "Six Pillars" aroused much interest both in this country and in Europe. It met with an interesting response in Great Britain where the *Times* (London) carried a lead article openly commending this statement of the necessary results of the war. Fourteen leaders of the British church, including the archbishop of Canterbury and the

15. *Annual Report*, 1943, pp. 62-65. The Federal Council published several analyses of these Six Pillars and a manual of instruction for use in local churches.

16. This United Nations had been formed in January 1942 and was essentially a league of·all those nations engaged in war against the Axis powers.

moderator of the Church of Scotland, accepted the pillars as the embodiment of the aims of the British churches for postwar reconstruction. Since the British churches had already rallied behind the socialist aims for Great Britain, their enthusiasm for the "Six Pillars" is hardly surprising.

In the summer of 1943 the Commission on a Just and Durable Peace worked with Catholic and Jewish leaders in formulating a declaration on world peace, which held that these propositions were essential to such a peace: moral law must govern world order; the rights of individuals must be assured; the rights of the oppressed and the weak must be protected; an international organization to maintain peace must be created; international economic cooperation must be developed; and a just social order within each state must be established.[17]

The war continued to disturb the conscience of the Council leadership, which was fully aware of the dichotomy involved in its support of the conflict as a means for achieving social justice, yet withholding blessing from it at the same time. However, the Council did take an even more active role in aiding the military chaplains than it had during World War I, a surprising development in view of the strong language it had used against Christian involvement in the conflict.

The Council greeted the Dumbarton Oaks proposals of 1944 with a qualified endorsement and reserved enthusiasm. Although the proposals fell far short of the optimistic hopes and demands expressed in the "Six Pillars of Peace," political realism demanded that they be recognized as a step in the right direction.

The Council was unhappy over the fact that the world organization proposals at this time seemed to advocate more a military alliance of the victorious powers than a league to keep the peace and that it seemed to be based primarily on the possession of force by those powers rather than on the principles of justice.

Yet the Council could and did see some merit in the proposals and took heart accordingly.

> With all of these defects, the proposals do, however, have the great merit of providing for a continuing and virtually constant consultation of representatives of the great powers, and of selected lesser powers under conditions which will subject what is done to the moral judgment of mankind. . . . If the proposals envision much

17. *Annual Report*, 1943, p. 66.

137

that partakes of a military alliance, at least that military alliance is to be put into a setting which will permit public opinion to influence its revolution toward a more adequate general organization. . . .

We believe that the proposed organization with such beneficial modifications as ought to result from further considerations by the prospective members can be developed into one that will commend itself to the Christian conscience.[18]

The Council followed the advice it gave to the nations participating in the Dumbarton Oaks Conference by suggesting its own revisions to the proposals accepted at that meeting. In January 1945 the Commission on a Just and Durable Peace sponsored the National Study Conference in Cleveland; 481 leaders from thirty-four different denominations were present. This group drew up nine recommendations for the improvement of the original draft of the United Nations charter.[19] At the invitation of the State Department, the Commission on International Justice and Good Will sent Walter Van Kirk, Frederick Nolde, and Bishop James Baker as representatives to the San Francisco Conference in April 1945 to air the commission's views on the defects of the Dumbarton Oaks draft. The changes the San Francisco Conference made in the former proposals can hardly be ascribed to the influence of the Federal Council. They were largely the result of the powerful influence of diplomatic and political factors on the statesmen assembled there in April 1945. But the leadership of the Council was much more pleased with the final product than it had been with the original draft.[20]

After his return from San Francisco, John Foster Dulles reported on the conference to the Council's executive committee. He asserted that no one could read the United Nations Charter as a whole without realizing that it could be a magnificent charter of human liberty. The committee then adopted "The Churches and the Charter of the United Nations," a statement prepared by Walter Van Kirk. Wrote Van Kirk:

The Charter . . . offers mankind an important means for the achievement of a just and durable peace. The new organization . . .

18. *Biennial Report*, 1944, pp. 185-86.

19. *Annual Report*, 1945, p. 53.

20. Curiously enough, the ecclesiastical liberals were, on the whole, much more pleased with the United Nations Charter than were the secular liberals. See *Nation* and *New Republic* for 1945 and early 1946 for the secular attitude toward the work of the San Francisco Conference.

138

can help governments to join their moral and material resources in support of a system of world order and justice. The churches of Christ in America have long held that the nations can better serve God's purpose for the world as they are brought into organic relationship with one another for the commonweal. The Charter signed at San Francisco marks a genuine advance toward this end. . . .

We believe it is the clear duty of our government promptly to ratify the Charter and thus to assure cooperation by the United States in the task of making the organization an effective agency for the maintenance of international peace and security.[21]

This statement represents an obvious intrusion by the churches into purely political questions. The excuse used was, of course, that our entry into and continued support of the United Nations was a moral issue and therefore a proper subject for concern and action by the Federal Council. But was it truly a moral issue, as the Council leadership used that term? Could a world organization representing many different political theories and containing a block of Communist-dominated states achieve the moral aims that the Council had in mind? The leadership of the Council consistently assumed that the aims of the Communists in and out of Russia were identical with those of our country in 1945 and urged our government to act on this assumption.[22]

Still another intrusion into the political realm occurred when the executive committee adopted a resolution prepared by the Department of International Justice and Good Will regarding the use of the atomic bomb.[23] Although the committee did not specifically mention President Truman or indict him or the military officials for using the bomb against Japan, it did voice great alarm that such a weapon had been devised and called for very strong international controls of this weapon: "Every possible safeguard to protect man from the consequences of his own pride and greed is the urgent business of the churches. The danger of atomic war is too great and imminent to neglect any means to lessen or delay it."[24] The conclusion to this line of reasoning led the executive committee back to its favorite theme, a collective social control of this weapon:

21. *Annual Report*, 1945, pp. 151-52.

22. The relationship of the Federal Council to the Communist ideology and other issues will be discussed later.

23. *Annual Report*, 1945, pp. 171-72.

24. *Ibid.*, p. 171.

Therefore we need to study and support all feasible social controls of all destructive atomic power. . . . Atomic bombs and rockets in the separate hands of competing states would tend to precipitate total war because of the mutual fears of annihilating aggression. Consequently the establishment of single world control of destructive atomic power is an urgent necessity. . . . We urge our government to state its intention to place the new discovery under a worldwide authority as soon as all the states will submit to effective controls. We also urge the government to press without delay for the creation of such controls.[25]

It is quite obvious that even as the Federal Council wanted to use the war as a means of bringing a socialistic collectivism to this country, it was now prepared to use the peace for advancing this same collectivism at home and globally. Collectivism would bring the kingdom of God, and thus salvation would come to the collectivized peoples. The historic Gospel was being used for purposes never intended. But this treacherous design was kept from the public by liberal usage of biblical terminology, which gave to these secular schemes a superficial coloring of true evangelical orthodoxy.

Collectivism, however, was not the only glaring weakness of these proposals. Equally dangerous, if not more so, was the willingness of the Federal Council to trust the safety of this country to a central control agency still unformed and designed to give Communist countries, including Russia, as well as other nations an equal voice in the control of atomic power. Even though we were the first to use this awesome weapon, there was absolutely no evidence for the Council to assume that international control would be more effective. Just how or why the Council could come to the assumption that an international organization, in which Russia and other Communist nations would have a voice equal to ours, would be a more effective instrument for controlling the use of the atomic bomb is a difficult question to answer on the face of it. But beneath the surface of this question lay another possibility, namely, the Council was interested not so much in the international control of the bomb per se, as in giving Russia a position equal to that of the United States in the determination of this and other related issues.

At its special meeting called to deal with postwar issues, the Federal Council in March 1946 stated:

25. *Ibid.*, p. 172.

140

In the initial use and continued production of atomic bombs the United States has given and is giving sanction to the weapons of mass annihilation. We believe that this policy must be changed. Our nation, having first used the atomic bomb, has a primary duty to seek to revise the trend which it began.[26]

Apparently the Federal Council was not willing to have the United States take unilateral action in the control and use of the atomic bomb on the theory that since we had introduced this weapon, we were guilty of a crime.

That the leadership of the Federal Council had Russia in mind in most, if not all, of its pronouncements on foreign policy became clear from 1946 on. In 1946 its Commission on a Just and Durable Peace adopted a draft on Soviet-American relations that makes this evident.[27] This statement began with the thesis that war with Russia must be avoided and that it could be without any compromise of convictions by the United States. The Council then suggested how this could be accomplished. The means of achieving this was by eliminating intolerance, which makes it impossible for conflicting beliefs to subsist and be propagated in peace. But this in turn made it necessary for the United States to eliminate certain prejudices and practices that, observed the Council, unnecessarily created tensions. Furthermore, the Russian and American people must cooperate at the scientific, economic, cultural, and religious levels, and the two governments must conjoin in the task of making the United Nations an effective agency for peace.[28] The fourth and concluding part of this "manifesto" insisted that the American people must demonstrate that the democratic institutions, which reflect the Christian doctrine of the sacredness of individual personality, can be made so vigorous that all peoples will want them. These four mandates issued by the Federal Council regarding America's domestic conduct furnish the key for understanding its position on our policy on the atomic bomb.

The leadership of the Federal Council was thoroughly convinced that both the Russians and the Americans could accommodate their existing political, economic, and social systems to each other without any great sacrifice of convictions by either party. But how

26. *Biennial Report*, 1946, p. 57.

27. The committee that drafted this statement was composed of Bishop Oxnam, Russell J. Clinchy, and Frederick Nolde.

28. For the full text of this statement, see *Biennial Report*, 1946, p. 62.

could the two nations cooperate on the scientific, economic, cultural, and religious levels without such a sacrifice? Such cooperation without sacrifice was and is manifestly impossible on the face of it. Communism and orthodox evangelical Christianity represent two diametrically opposed world-and-life views, resting on opposing presuppositions, employing entirely different methods, and striving toward contrasting ends for human society.

These questions would seem to be unanswerable and the four mandates hopelessly false and impossible. But there is an answer. We must remember that the Federal Council leaders identified Christianity with social reform and the coming of the kingdom of God; further, many of them regarded what they fondly called "the great social experiment in Russia" as a major step toward the realization of that kingdom on earth. Thus, in their thinking no great compromise was necessary, simply because both nations were moving toward the same goals.[29] The policy statements as published were undoubtedly devious and misleading but, properly understood, they clearly reveal what the Council leadership had in mind and where it sought to lead the unsuspecting Christians in the churches associated with the Council. Much more was implied in these declarations by the Federal Council than appeared on the surface.

In 1946 at a specially called meeting the Council, with great fervor, backed the establishment of the United Nations not only as a most important step toward world peace, but also as a major development toward the creation of a more just social and economic order. Particularly, it placed its imprimatur on UNESCO as an indispensable step toward world cooperation and urged our government to join it at the earliest possible moment.[30]

Quite evidently, the Council leadership held an optimistic view of the United Nations, UNESCO, and the possibility of a real peace emerging from the end of the war because it clung to an optimistic view of Communist intentions. It assumed, with the Roosevelt administration during the war and the leadership of the Truman era, that Russia was militaristic because its neighbors, Germany and Japan, were militaristic and that the defeat of these two powers would remove the necessity for such an emphasis upon militarism by the Soviet leaders. This belief was expressed again and again

29. It should also be noted that Franklin Roosevelt held similar views as to the future relationship that should exist between the United States and Russia. See Sumner Welles, *Where Are We Heading?*

30. *Biennial Report*, 1946, p. 185.

both in religious literature and in official pronouncements by Council officials—not to mention the flood of rose-colored literature from government sources. It became a prominent part of liberal dogma in those postwar years and exercised a powerful influence in determining American foreign policy toward Russia.

This happy belief rested on the assumption that communism was hungering for the same kind of a democratic society that America was seeking, and that the two systems could be brought much closer together than they had been, without necessarily becoming identical. The great similarity that could be achieved between them would sufficiently guarantee the avoidance of war between the United States and Russia.

The liberal assumption that both the United States and Russia were each in its own way becoming more democratic nations was delightfully alluring as a prospect for peace. But it was as false and dangerous as it was attractive. To assume that democracy itself makes a people a peace-loving nation is a serious error. Of course, the sunny thought that Russia was becoming democratic in the liberal sense of that term had no factual basis and was the product of the liberal optimism that colored many American attitudes and practices in the postwar era.

The increasing tensions between the United States and Russia as a result of Russian policy in both Europe and Asia prompted the executive committee of the Federal Council to rush to the aid of the statesmen on both sides of the Atlantic who were attempting to deal with the problem. In 1947 it issued a statement on what kind of a peace should be achieved in Europe. It should be a peace that would reorder Europe in such a way that a just accord could be reached between the Soviet Union and the West.[31] The statement also declared that cooperation between the major powers without compromising basic convictions about freedom and justice was indispensable if Europe was to be more than an arena of tragic world conflict.

The executive committee hailed the European Recovery Program, then being considered in Congress, as an unexcelled opportunity for strengthening the foundations of democracy in Europe, but also cautioned that aid to Asia was a necessary corollary to the Marshall Plan.

It is almost inconceivable that the membership of the executive committee could have been so blind as to believe that such a policy, however helpful or necessary it might be for the survival of

31. *Annual Report*, 1947, pp. 113-18.

Western Europe, could in itself solve or even soften the growing tensions between Soviet Russia and the nations of the West. It was apparently under the delusion that the destruction of the military might of both Germany and Japan would somehow transform the Soviet Union into a peace-loving nation.

In January 1948 the Federal Council's Department of International Justice and Good Will was reorganized, and the Commission on a Just and Durable Peace abolished. The department called on the churches to consider the moral issues involved in the European Recovery Program. In connection with this new aspect of its peace crusade, the Council held a meeting in Philadelphia that called on the churches to keep the creative and curative possibilities of this program in the forefront of their thinking; to guard against setting up conditions of aid to the nations of Europe, conditions that might threaten the independence of those nations; and to call on our government to encourage the cooperation of the United Nations in this venture.[32] The delegates to this meeting became so intoxicated with the vista of a newborn Europe that they even called for a voluntary allocation of the necessary goods during this critical period and for governmental control of their distribution in this country. To advance freedom in Europe, freedom must be surrendered at home.[33]

Some seven hundred ministers signed a petition in support of this statement, "Cross Roads of American Foreign Policy." It was presented to Senator Arthur Vandenberg and Speaker of the House Joseph Martin on March 11, 1948, as an expression of the opinion of the constituent churches of the Federal Council. This maneuver was obviously an attempt by the Council to influence Congress. Since it was a moral issue in the eyes of the Council leaders, it did not represent undue interference by the church in the affairs of state. Further to impress members of Congress with the importance of this issue, a mass meeting in support of the statement was held in the Washington Cathedral with a reported attendance of over two thousand people.

Tireless in its efforts in behalf of the United Nations, the Federal Council, through the action of its executive committee, called upon the Christian people of the United States to provide the necessary Christian judgments, formed through careful study and by

32. *Biennial Report*, 1948, pp. 105-06. It is interesting to note that Alger Hiss was chairman of a committee at this meeting, which drafted data on the role of the United Nations.

33. *Ibid.*, p. 106.

democratic processes.[34] Specifically the Council declared that in the battle against international disorder, men deeply needed Christianity's spiritual dynamic

> to establish fellowship, mutual understanding and cooperation with Christians and a peace-loving folk around the world, to go across all borders and behind all iron curtains with voluntary services, to stand firm against national vindictiveness, hysteria and the pride of power, and in hazardous days to keep faith strong that God's will can yet be done on earth—such indispensable services the Christian people of America must render now.[35]

As the war clouds once again hovered over both Europe and Asia in 1949, the Federal Council continued steadfast in its unending quest for peace. The Department of International Justice and Goodwill sponsored the Third National Study Conference on the Churches and World Order, which met at Cleveland in March 1949. Some 440 delegates attended. It issued a message to the churches titled *"Moral Responsibility and United States Power."*[36] It was approved by the executive committee of the Council.

Declaring that the United States held its power under God, the statement affirmed that this nation must resist the temptation to use its power irresponsibly and the temptation to flee the responsibilities of this power, for the corollary of power is responsibility.[37] The document admitted that Soviet Russia presented a great difficulty, but the conference cheerfully asserted its belief that war with that nation was not only not inevitable, but also improbable, if the United States would use its great power wisely. It called on the American government to keep open all available channels of negotiation and conciliation. It optimistically affirmed that two contradictory ideologies can coexist without armed conflict if they are propagated by methods of tolerance rather than intolerance. The statement asserted that the Soviet leaders were coming to realize that their methods of intolerance against a good society were in vain, for a just society is immune to the enticements of communism. Our long-range policy should therefore be directed toward justice and freedom throughout the

---

34. *Ibid.*, p. 169. For the complete text of this statement on the United Nations, see *Biennial Report*, 1948, pp. 165-171.

35. For the full text of this message, see *Biennial Report*, 1950, pp. 104-11.

36. *Biennial Report*, 1950, p. 104.

37. *Ibid.*, p. 170.

world. Thus this nation, to achieve this goal, should support the United Nations.

The message closed with an affirmation of faith that God still ruled his world and that this was the Christian hope in the midst of confusion and uncertainty. But this reference to the sovereignty of God in human history was removed from its biblical context; the statement refused to admit that communism with its atheism was and remains a revolt against Christianity and that by its very nature it must be both revolutionary and belligerent. The events transpiring in Europe and Asia certainly furnished no evidence for the naive assumption that the Soviet leaders had somehow been converted to the notion that tolerance was a more effective policy than intolerance. In fact, there was massive evidence to the contrary.

In early 1950 the Council's executive committee approved a revised version of a statement on the atomic bomb and the control of atomic weapons. The finished product revealed that within the committee there was much disagreement over this weapon.[38]

The last definitive statement issued by the Federal Council came in September 1950, when its executive committee issued a curious and ambiguous statement on the outbreak of war in Korea:

> In Korea the United Nations was confronted with the severest challenge to its authority and usefulness. A people groping toward the light of freedom was plunged into bloodshed by an act of aggression. We are heartened by the swift action of the United Nations in resisting this aggression. We are gratified that the forces combating invasion in South Korea serve under the flag and command of the United Nations. We are resolutely opposed to the idea of a preventive war. . . . We can and do support the United Nations in mobilizing collective security resources from its member states for the purpose of establishing the conditions of peace in Korea. At this moment in history the United Nations offers promise that mankind, if it has the will to do so, can repel aggression and advance the cause of peace and justice through the cooperative endeavor of the world community. This will be the more true if, when the fighting in Korea is over, the United Nations can take steps which will vouchsafe to the entire Korean people the freedom to which they are entitled.[39]

38. *Ibid.*, pp. 89-91.
39. *Ibid.*, p. 131.

This statement on the outbreak of hostilities in Korea clearly revealed the dilemma facing the liberals in the Federal Council. Admitting that aggression had been committed, the leaders refused to name the aggressors. It also avoided the use of the term *war*, clung to the idea of collective action under the banners of the United Nations, and refused to admit that the real force for resisting this aggression was not the United Nations but the United States. To admit that the United Nations had been powerless to prevent this latest resort to arms was too much for the Council's liberals, who had rested their hopes for peace on the United Nations. Rather did they prefer to regard the military action in Korea as a collective action to secure peace. It is ironic that in the last year of its existence the Federal Council was once again the unwilling witness of war and that its last major pronouncement on the international scene had to be a guarded blessing to the idea of collective military action as another step in the search for a collectively enforced peace.[40]

The Federal Council and Labor and Industry, 1941-1950

The report that the special committee gave to the Federal Council early in 1942, which report justified our participation in World War II as a means of achieving the kind of society for which God was striving, served as a kind of blueprint for the other activities of the Council on the home front during this decade. While the attention of the Council mainly focused on the war, the Council's leaders did not forget that the war was a means to an end, and issued social and economic statements to guide domestic policy in achieving the new social order struggling to be born amidst conflict. Mention has already been made of that section of the special report calling for an economic order in which the desire to meet human needs took precedence over the profit motive.[41]

The report did not stop here, however; it declared it to be the duty of every Christian minister to guide the members of his congregation in their economic understanding, to help his members understand in detail how the actual conditions in the economic life of the nation and the world ran counter to the vision outlined

40. In 1950 the executive committee did renew its support of the Genocide Convention, then before the United Nations General Assembly; it also gave a guarded endorsement to American cooperation with UNESCO, naming Reinhold Niebuhr as its delegate to the National Commission on UNESCO.

41. *Biennial Report*, 1950, p. 18.

in the report. To achieve this goal, the Federal Council stood ready to help:

> We believe that the American Church needs to have the leadership of the Federal Council of Churches in this field as it does in that of the Commission to Study the Basis of a Just and Durable Peace. We recommend that a program of intensive study be begun in cooperation with the denominational agencies for social action which will relate the best that has already been thought concerning the meaning of Christian faith for economic relationships to American economic life now and in the years of postwar reconstruction. With the study there should go forward the effort to make Christian cooperation in thought and action in the concrete application of Christian principles to economic life a task for every church.[42]

The statement of purpose here is too clear to be misread or misunderstood. It was the avowed intention of the Council to call upon every individual minister and congregation to accept the Council's leadership in advancing the cause of economic collectivism under the guise of Christian economic cooperation. And both the war itself and the postwar period of reconstruction were to be used for this single purpose.

Although the declaration called for vast economic changes on the home front as part of the victory that must come in the war, similar pleas were seldom heard from the pulpit. The Council had hoped and intended otherwise. Liberal ministers, following the lead of the secular *Nation* and *New Republic* and the religious *Christian Century*, did make some such calls upon their congregations. However, overall this program received relatively little support from the pulpit. For most ministers, maintaining the spiritual life of the members, meeting the demands of wartime upon the churches, and comforting the bereaved were their chief concerns.

The Federal Council renewed its demands for economic planning in its 1944 Labor Day message to the churches. Using the approaching end of the conflict as a springboard, the Council insisted that American Industry and labor in cooperation must find a way to maintain full production for consumer needs after the war as they had cooperated to maintain full production to meet the demands of the wartime economy. The object of full production was full employment for the returning veterans. Full employment was the key to a continuing postwar prosperity:

42. *Ibid.*, p. 19.

Therefore, the Christian Church, proclaiming the essential worth of personality, would be remiss in its solemn duty did it not re-affirm this Labor Day its belief that a Christian society is under a sacred obligation to so organize itself that every one willing and able to work may be guaranteed some meaningful occupation. The Christian Church must point out that a society which can do this under the pressure of total war must also do so under a peacetime economy.

Thoughtful Americans are looking beyond the present crisis and formulating plans that will guarantee a greater security in the post-war world. Failure of society to so organize itself as to achieve such security would constitute the admission that the ends now being fought for at such staggering costs in lives and materials are not worth maintaining once the sacrifices have been made and the victory of arms assured.[43]

Although it modestly disclaimed that the church—and presumably the Federal Council—was not called upon to devise schemes of social organization or technical plans for industry, the Council nevertheless displayed the permeating influence of a very distinct economic philosophy in its thinking, a philosophy that called for collectivism. Now while it may be true that the Federal Council did not offer a blueprint for the exact form that collectivism should take, it is impossible to believe that its leaders were unaware that the economic philosophy involved in this message called for economic collectivism. They could hardly have been blind to the fact that the secular liberals, whom they regarded as their allies, were advocating a definite socialistic collectivism for both Europe and America as a necessary result of the military victory.

This same philosophy was reiterated in the Labor Day message of 1945. However, by 1945 the Council had become much more specific in its challenge to labor and industry. The Council challenged both groups to make possible a high standard of living based on a high level of production, a standard that would ensure good housing and adequate social security.[44] To achieve these goals, the Council advocated the acceptance of a plan for a guaranteed annual wage and for making permanent those goals that had been achieved under the New Deal, particularly the right of collective bargaining, a right which many liberals felt had been seriously

43. *Ibid.*, pp. 166-168.
44. *Annual Report*, 1945, p. 160.

threatened by the wartime labor legislation and by the rising tide of opposition to many of the provisions of the National Labor Relations Act of 1935. Further to fortify its position on these issues, the Council called for a new emphasis on work as a vocation under God. But such a biblical view of work found its sanction in the Puritan theology, which the Federal Council emphatically rejected.

To implement its labor platform of 1945, the executive committee became quite specific the next year. It counseled an increase in the minimum wage, provided for in the Fair Labor Standards act of 1938, from forty to sixty-five cents an hour immediately, and after two years of employment, to seventy-five cents an hour.[45]

In March 1947 the executive committee created the new Department of the Church and Economic Life, which took over the functions of the older Division of Industrial Relations.[46] The new department was to be composed of representatives from agriculture and consumer groups as well as from business and labor. This move was designed to give the Council a greater voice and influence over the total economic life of the nation, in the interests of its version of the social gospel.

Early in 1948 this department sponsored a national conference on the church and economic life at Pittsburgh. It was attended by some three hundred and fifty delegates representing the church, industry, and labor. The conference reached conclusions generally in accord with the position of the Federal Council. The executive committee specifically gave its approval to the following declaration of this conference:

> The Church cannot provide blueprints; it can give perspective. Every system is to be judged by Christian standards, which transcend it, and the judgment is likely to issue in commendation of some aspect of that system, condemnation of others, and indifference to still others . . . .
> Profits are characteristic of a money economy and are defensible, subject to proper methods of accumulating and distributing them. . . .
> The Church must reaffirm the supremacy of the law of love, under which all human devices must be judged . . . .
> The Church should seek to make its membership inclusive of all elements of our economic life, and thus avoid the stultification of a class church . . . .[47]

45. *Biennial Report*, 1946, p. 191.

46. James Myers, who had been industrial secretary for twenty-two years, retired and Arthur Fleming became the first executive secretary of the new department.

47. *Annual Report*, 1947, p. 9.

In its report on its present policies, the Federal Council insisted that it drew Christian representatives of management, labor, and capital together for the purpose of solving their mutual problems in the light of their common Christian commitment. It maintained that it upheld the legitimate rights of both labor and management, stressing that in both cases rights do not exist apart from obligations and responsibilities.

In regard to communism, the report of the Council insisted that it worked within the general framework of free enterprise, seeking to correct its abuses and make it more effective in serving the ends of a democratic society. The Council reiterated in 1947 an official statement of the executive committee of 1946 rejecting the Communist philosophy:

> Marxist communism in its orthodox philosophy stands clearly opposed to Christianity. It is atheistic in its conception of ultimate reality and materialistic in its views of man and his destiny. Its utopian philosophy of history lacks the essential Christian notes of divine judgment, divine governance and eternal victory. Its revolutionary strategy involves the disregard of the sacredness of personality which is fundamental in Christianity. Such differences can never be resolved by the compromise or surrender of faith by Christians.[48]

This rejection of communism would have been much more impressive if the policies of the Council and the statements and actions of many of its leaders had been consistent with this stand. However sincere the Council may have been in assuming this posture, it is also true that in many official pronouncements in regard to war, subversion, race, industry, labor, and related issues, its positions all too frequently paralleled the official platforms of the Communist party in this country.

Apparently aware of the frequency of the charges that it was Communist in its outlook, the Council issued a defense of its position, deploring the tendency in some quarters to label as communistic constructive programs of social advance. It was convinced that such misrepresentation actually played into the hands of the Communists. To create the impression that efforts to overcome unemployment or abolish poverty or correct social injustices were communistic was to render a grave disservice to America.[49]

48. *Ibid.*
49. *Ibid.*

This, of course, was a clever and unconvincing evasion of the issue. The critics of the Federal Council were not saying that efforts to achieve these goals were communistic. Rather were they charging that many of the particular aims of the Council and the methods it chose to achieve those aims were communistic.

As the decade drew to a close discerning members within the various constituent churches became increasingly convinced that the Federal Council was not nearly as friendly to the free-enterprise system or as hostile to communism as it said it was. Accordingly the tempo and intensity of the attacks on the Council mounted. The growing conviction that the Council was basically unfriendly to free enterprise naturally arose from the increasingly frequent demands by the Council for some formal economic collectivism, demands that could not be reconciled with the free-enterprise system in this country.

The Federal Council and Its Race Question, 1941-1950

The growing racial friction of the war years and the postwar era was accompanied by a growing demand by Negroes for an end to segregation and for greater participation in American life. Plainly, this situation challenged the Federal Council to play a role in this area of American social life.

The Social Creed of 1932 had provided some direction on this matter. And the declaration on the war issued by the Council in 1949 definitely challenged American churches to support the dissolution of segregation, not only in the South, but in the North as well. The war psychology gave the Council the opportunity and the incentive to become more aggressive in its attacks on segregation and racial discrimination at all levels.

In its document, "The Issues at Stake in the War," the biennial meeting held at Cleveland in 1942 declared that a victory for the Axis powers would be a setback for racial brotherhood and a political order more fully expressive of the unity of mankind as one family under God.[50] In his report to the Council on the state of the church, the executive secretary paid considerable attention to our race problem and the role the churches must play in achieving a solution for it. For this role he laid down a theological basis, which is interesting but hardly biblical:

50. *Biennial Report*, 1942, p. 37.

152

Christian teaching about the essential unity of the human race as created by God and as redeemed by Christ is so clear that there really can be no controversy about its meaning. Whether we approach the subject by the road of Christian ethical teaching about the idea; or by the road of Christian theological teaching about the actual nature of man, we come out at the same point.[51]

And the conclusion to which this line of reasoning came was that segregation was wrong and must be abolished in this country. Not only was it un-Christian, it was also undemocratic. If segregation were not abolished, grave consequences would follow:

Now that the colored races are in a position to assert their power, we can either change our ways and overcome our racial prejudice, knowing that it is a dread disease, or we can expect to enter a new period of inter-racial conflict that will be more disastrous than previous world conflicts. We are at a moment of decision. We know what is the right direction and already we see how the judgment of God may descend upon us if we do not take it.[52]

In 1943 the Council gave shape to its pronouncements on segregation in the South and on the Negro problem in general by creating the Commission on the Church and Minority Peoples. Dr. Will Alexander was its first chairman.

It should be noted that in its denunciations of segregation and of prejudice against Jews and other minority peoples, the Council declared that such prejudices were contrary to the democratic philosophy. Not infrequently, in its various messages and declarations on race and labor, the Council seemed to assume that democracy and Christianity were equivalent frames of reference and sources of value, and that the Council had the custodial responsibility of maintaining inviolate the democratic philosophy as one of the main fruits of Christianity. The Council also utilized the wartime psychology to emphasize anew the observance of Race Relations Sunday. In 1943, reports from 140 cities in thirty-five states indicated an unusually large number of interracial pulpit and choir exchanges; 156 pulpit exchanges took place in the Chicago area alone.[53]

51. *Ibid.*, p. 14.

52. *Ibid.*, p. 15. This report also condemned anti-Semitism and the treatment of the Japanese on the West Coast.

53. *Federal Council Bulletin* 26, no. 4 (April 1943): 13.

In spite of the efforts of the Council and many secular groups to achieve racial peace, mob violence broke out in 1943. In December or that year Henry St. George Tucker, president of the Council, issued a special appeal for an even greater emphasis to be placed on the race issue in the observance of Race Relations Sunday in February 1944:

> In these critical days of war abroad and group conflicts at home, we have come to realize how close to the surface is the spirit of mob violence. Our democracy is in the balance. Doubt is cast on the sincerity of Christians. We confess individually and corporately our failure to appreciate and understand all peoples as members of a common brotherhood. Where Jesus succeeded with ease and naturalness in such things, too often we have been awkward and insincere . . . . By friendly, personal understanding of people in differing groups we can solve the great American race problems. With mutual understanding and good will there is promice of steadfast united loyalties and cooperation toward ultimate solutions.[54]

Running throughout the pronouncements on the race problem are basic assumptions that not only find no support in the Scriptures, but are quite contrary to their plain teaching. Perhaps the most insidious of these assumptions is that which assumes that there is one common brotherhood on earth and that all men are children of the same God. However appealing such a belief may be, it can find no support in the Bible. The biblical doctrine of sin shatters such an illusion. Both the Old and New Testaments contain crystal clear statements that make such a belief impossible.[55]

In its annual Race Relations message issued for use on February 13, 1944, the Council stressed this belief and appealed to I Corinthians in support of its position:

> The belief that all men and women are children of one Heavenly Father has been a part of our Christian heritage through the centuries. The inherent right to life, liberty and the freedom to pursue the satisfactions of life is rooted in that Christian conviction. This is one of the many reasons for our world-wide struggle for the four freedoms.[56]

To this doctrine of universalism was added the usual plea for

54. *Ibid.*, no. 10 (December 1943): 5.
55. See particularly Ephesians 2 and Romans 1-3.
56. *Federal Council Bulletin* 27, no. 1 (January 1944): 8.

154

democracy. The minority groups, said Council leaders, had a growing resentment against white domination—which was undoubtedly true—and felt they were being deprived of the position that was properly theirs in a democratic society. Thus it was mandatory for Christians to speak with prophetic voice and act with apostolic conviction for men must and can achieve redeeming attitudes, methods of common understanding, ways of friendly living, and convictions of spiritual unity.[57]

In 1944 the Federal Council began to be much more specific in its attacks on the racial issue. Through its executive committee, it adopted in March of that year a statement concerning discrimination in employment.

> Discrimination in employment because of race, creed or national origin, is one of the great moral issues before our nation today. The right of a worker to be employed and paid solely on the basis of his character and ability is so clear, just and Christian that it should be protected in law. . . .
>
> We therefore urge our government to establish permanent procedures for securing the objectives which have been sought by the Committee on Fair Employment Practices.[58]

In 1946 the Department of Race Relations became one of the most active of all the agencies of the Federal Council. It could report that by that year sixteen denominations had placed Race Relations Sunday (the second Sunday in February) on their calendars for the year. The annual message from the Council in 1945 revealed a new aggressive spirit in the Council against segregation. The message declared segregation to be tyrannical as well as unjust; simultaneously it challenged the constituent churches to welcome people from all races into their memberships.

And yet, at this time, the Council was attuned to the reaction that was arising against this opposition to segregation: "We must oppose all charlatans and demagogues, giving no quarter to those who fan into flame racial animosities."[59]

The war against racial segregation was given priority at the special meeting of the Federal Council in March 1946 to consider the problems of the postwar era. The Council issued a statement renouncing segregation as a violation of the Gospel and instructed

57. *Ibid.*

58. *Ibid.*, no. 4 (April 1944): 15.

59. *Annual Report*, 1945, p. 44.

155

its constituent members to do likewise.[60] During the year the General Convention of the Congregational-Christian Churches, the Disciples of Christ, the Northern and General Baptist Conventions, and the General Assembly of the Presbyterian Church, USA adopted similar resolutions.[61]

The Council, however, did not content itself with declarations on segregation as a sin. It became active in the civil rights movement in the Truman era. In June 1947 the executive secretary of the Department of Race Relations testified before the Senate Committee on Labor and Public Welfare in behalf of the full-employment bill, then before Congress. In November the executive committee commended the report of President Truman's Committee on Civil Rights and urged the Council's constituent churches to give careful consideration to this report as being an expression of the Christian attitude on the race problem.[62]

During 1948 the Council stoked its interest in the battle for human rights by intensifying its political action on the national and international levels. This was in response to the role assumed by the Truman administration in the growing controversy over segregation at home and to the interest of the United Nations leadership in the problem as an international issue.

By a vote of 26 to 8 the executive committee authorized the Department of Race Relations to appear before any congressional hearings in regard to an antilynching bill then under consideration.[63] This action occurred in consequence of a previous action by the executive committee that permitted representatives of the Federal Council to appear before congressional hearings, but the representatives could testify only in regard to the principles underlying a bill and not on specific provisions of a bill itself.[64] The Presbyterian Church, U.S. (Southern) dissented from the position of the Council in its support of antilynching legislation. (A denomination dissenting from the official position of the Council could have its dissent recorded.) At the same time, the executive committee passed a resolution exhorting the Truman administration to adopt the Declaration and Covenant of the United Nations providing an

60. For the full text of this statement, see *Annual Report*, 1946, pp. 116-126.

61. *Ibid.*, p. 51.

62. *Ibid.*, 1947, p. 37.

63. *Biennial Report*, 1948, p. 182.

64. *Ibid.*, p. 74. The representative had to have authorization to do so from either the executive committee or the president of the Federal Council.

international bill of rights; and in September 1948 the committee appointed a special committee to draft a statement on human rights for consideration by the 1948 biennial meeting of the Council.

The report, as adopted, added little that was new to the thinking of the Council or the constituent churches on the race issue. It did outline the basic rights of all men and declared that these rights could not be obtained in a system of racial segregation. Whereupon the Council reaffirmed its renunciation of segregation in our society, terming it unnecessary, undesirable, and a violation of the Gospel of love and brotherhood.[65] As proof of their sincerity on this matter, the churches of America must work for a nonsegregated church and a nonsegregated society.

The report further defined the duty of the state in this area:

> It is presumptuous of the state to assume that it can grant or deny fundamental rights. It is for the state to embody these rights in its own legal system and to insure their observance in practice. . . . The churches are likewise bound to offer a continual challenge to the conscience of the community and to seek to influence the government in its appropriate sphere to safeguard the rights of all.[66]

In 1949 the Federal Council, through the action of its executive committee, took still further action in the area of race relations. It filed a brief with the United States Supreme Court as *amicus curiae* in *Sweatt* v. *Painter*.[67] This case involved the right of a Negro to secure equal protection of the law under the Fourteenth Amendment in the realm of professional education. Sweatt had been denied the right to enter the law school of the University of Texas by that state's supreme court, and the case had come to the Supreme Court on a writ of certiorari.[68]

The friend-of-the-court brief marked the beginning of a new era for the Federal Council in its social policy. For the first time it entered into the legal struggle for the achievement of its social goals. No longer was the Council content merely to monitor the social conscience of the members of the churches or of the American people at large. It was now ready to surrender the last vestiges of its

65. For the full text of this declaration, see *Biennial Report*, 1948, pp. 52-55.

66. *Ibid.*, p. 55.

67. The Presbyterian Church, U.S. dissociated itself from this brief by its vote in the executive committee.

68. *Biennial Report*, 1950, pp. 152-157.

meaningless claim that it was concerned to keep church and state separate, and to plunge its member churches into the mainstream of American political life.[69] In 1950 the Supreme Court rendered a decision ordering the University of Texas to admit Sweatt to its law school.[70] To what extent the filing of the friend-of-the-court brief influenced the thinking of the Court is impossible to determine. The decision seems to have been the result of the liberalism of the justices of the Court. The brief does represent the same liberal philosophy even though its liberalism was couched in religious jargon. Needless to say, the Council was jubilant at the outcome of its first venture into the realm of practical politics. There is little doubt that this initial foray encouraged the National Council to become even more active in the political arena after 1950.

In 1950 the executive committee issued its last message on race relations, but it had nothing new to say. It had all been said in many previous messages. This last statement, however, did give clear insight into the theology of the liberal leadership of the Council. The message is rooted in the traditional view of the social-gospel movement, to wit, that God is the Father of all men—Christians and unbelievers—and therefore all men are brothers. This liberal view ignored the divisive influence of original sin and the historic Christian insistence that there is a deep cleavage in humanity between the believer and the unbeliever, between the regenerate and the unregenerate. Their refusal to accept this biblical truth and include it within the framework of their social philosophy has doomed the liberals, secular and religious, to ultimate failure in their utopian quests. Their judicial and legal victories blinded them to the fact that they were destroying the fabric of the very Constitution they were using, that eventually their achievements would destroy constitutional government in our country, and that the ultimate result would be the death of the democracy they thought they were creating.

The Federal Council and the Social and Cultural Scene, 1941-1950

The 1942 statement on what the war must mean for American society served as a guideline for the work of the Federal Council in

69. It is interesting to note that in this same year, the Council was showing a great concern over the repeated rumors that President Truman was considering giving to Myron Taylor, his personal representative at the Vatican, the rank of ambassador. See the correspondence between Truman and Bishop Oxnam, *ibid.*, pp. 157-158.

70. *Sweatt v. Painter* et al., 339 U.S. 629.

other areas also. The demands of the war on the Council's leaders diverted their attention from the social and cultural issues, except as they either directly or indirectly impinged on the war effort. But they never lost sight of their goal of using the peace as a stepping-stone to vast social changes, not only in the area of race relations but in every other facet of American life as well.

The annual reports of the war period reveal a deep awareness that the war would bring major changes in American life, changes that would offer a serious challenge to the Council. But preoccupation with the problems of the war itself, along with an uncertainty as to what would emerge from the war precluded anything but the most general type of planning to meet these changes.

When peace did come and the Council felt free once again to contemplate the domestic scene, it not only attacked old issues with a renewed vigor, but delved into new ones as well. Curiously reversing its thinking, the Council, through its executive committee, issued statements regarding birth control. These statements stand in sharp contrast to the posture the Council assumed later. A declaration in 1946 counseled large families for those who could afford to support more than one or two children:

> For the individual family, there is nothing more satisfying even though it may involve real sacrifice, than to have at least three or four children. . . .
> The people we send out into the next generation are more important than all our material achievements, however brilliant and world shaking these may be.[71]

In keeping with its wartime aim, stated in 1942, regarding the necessity of a renewed emphasis upon the freedom of the church to train its young people, the Council further affirmed that a good family is the highest of achievements. Wise national policy would require that our resources and our activities be so organized as to favor good home life and the rearing of children fitted by inheritance and training to make a durable contribution to the life of their times.[72]

This insistence on the integral relationship between a strong Christian home and an equally strong national life continued to be the keystone of the thinking of the Federal Council during the last five years of its history. The Council was acutely aware that if Christian homes were to fulfill their mission of producing Christian

71. *Biennial Report*, 1972, p. 178.

72. *Ibid.*, p. 179.

young people, then the home itself must be strengthened and the rising divorce rate must be halted:

> Our concern is much more than to keep homes intact. We want them to be sound, happy, and intrinsically worth preserving. We want homes in which difficulties and hardships lead not to self-pity but to more sympathy and concern for each other and to a firmer will to succeed. Only on a foundation of such homes can we produce individuals, communities and a nation able to meet the needs and pressure of our times.[73]

To achieve homes of this kind the Federal Council called on the churches and the communities of the nation to provide skilled educational and counseling help. Undergirding this appeal was the insistence that God is the author of the love that draws families together and that his resources are available for all homes. Apart from the universalism in this statement, this document reveals an interesting, if transient, conservatism in the Council's thinking on the problems of the home. In 1948 the Commission on Marriage and the Home prepared a bibliography of some five hundred titles on family life, and sponsored the National Conference of Church Leaders on Family Life in November.

The Council also took another look at the postwar problem of alcohol in American life. During the war years little attention was paid to this issue and less said about it. But by 1946 the Council was ready to alter its approach. In 1947 the Seattle biennial convention of 1946 issued a major statement on alcohol.[74] The Council called for the creation of clinics to treat alcoholics, and urged the churches to be persistent in reaching youth as well as adults with the facts concerning the dangers of using alcohol as a beverage. But the old zeal for national prohibition was lacking. The Council stated that national prohibition was not its immediate goal. Rather, it looked to other reliable remedies such as the enforcement of the laws regulating liquor licenses. It was particularly concerned that sales to minors be prohibited. More dangerous was its demand that the taxing power of the state be used to discourage the use of alcoholic beverages. The statement concluded with this admission: "Beverage alcohol is a serious problem and cannot be ignored. It is also a complex problem and cannot be solved at once. As Chris-

73. *Federal Council Bulletin* 29 (November 1946): 16.

74. *Federal Council Bulletin* 30 (1947): 15-16. It was based on the report of a special committee created in October 1946.

tians we intend to act, taking those specific steps which we believe will lead us most surely to Christian goals in relation to alcoholic beverages."[75]

The Problem of Federal Aid to Education

The Federal Council became interested in many areas of American life with the return of peace in 1945. None of the new concerns became so thorny as the problem of financing our public schools. It not only raised the specter of federal control in the minds of many people but, for the Council, also raised the issue of the separation of state and church—at the very time the Council had assumed the lead in opposing any formal diplomatic ties with the Vatican. Again, however, the Council leadership felt that it was a moral issue. Thus it must speak out on it and help to develop a type of federal aid to the schools that would not result in financial aid to parochial and other kinds of religious schools; the latter would indeed be in violation of both the letter and the spirit of the first and fourteenth amendments to the Constitution.

Admittedly, here was an issue that the Council had not faced before the war in a decisive manner. During the war the concentration of workers in industrial areas had brought to many schools crowded conditions with which not a few communities were unable successfully to cope. Likewise, the inflationary pressures following the cessation of World War II enhanced the financial problem confronting local school boards. The issue became a lively, and at times an acrimonious, topic of conversation. During the Truman administration the matter was debated both in and out of Congress. Whether such federal aid should be given to parochial schools, and if so, in what form, soon became a vexing problem. The decision of the Supreme Court in the *Everson* case, a ruling that seemed to open the way for such aid by upholding a New Jersey statute allowing the state to pay the bus fares of parochial school students, aroused much public controversy.[76]

In 1945 the Council had shown a certain sensitivity to the church-state issue when the executive committee adopted a statement questioning the value of compulsory Bible reading in the public schools. However, its doubts arose from the feeling that such a

75. *Ibid.*, p. 16.

76. 330 U.S. 1. Although popular fears about state aid of education were reduced by the decision of the Court in the case of 1948, they were not set to rest by any means.

reading seemed not to create a superior religious life.[77] At this time the Council was apparently in favor of some kind of weekday program of religious education.

In 1947 the Council became much more concerned with the whole problem of public education and the executive committee voiced its alarm over the serious shortage of teachers that was developing nationwide. The executive committee urged that sufficient federal funds should be appropriated to raise teachers' salaries and to prevent the lowering of education standards. But it took a strong stand against federal funding of church-related schools and schools practicing segregation. Somewhat paradoxically, it also resisted any federal control over those schools to receive funds.[78] The committee was apparently unaware that the withholding of federal funds was a form of federal interference and control. Apparently such control was not dangerous when it coincided with the social policies advocated by the Council.

This demand for federal aid to education was by no means restricted to the Federal Council. It had already become an important political issue and the Council was merely joining in the secular hue and cry. There was considerable political pressure from Roman Catholic sources to include their schools in any program of federal aid. In the South the demand for federal aid was considerably tempered by the fear that such aid might well be tied to a policy designed to end school segregation there. Many Roman Catholic leaders and some Southerners optimistically believed that it was possible to have federal aid without federal control. Many educators also shared these fantasies. Both federal aid and federal control of the public schools came after the Federal Council had been replaced by the National Council of Churches in 1950.

Evangelism in War, Cold War, and Peace

The war broadened the social interests and concerns of the Federal Council from the national to the foreign scene. Early in the war it created a commission to deal with overseas relief and displaced persons as part of its social ministry. It was in active contact with the Protestant churches of Great Britain and Europe, acting as a relief agency for the distribution of aid to the Christians who were victims of the war. Although the Council in its various pronounce-

77. *Annual Report*, 1945, p. 163-64.
78. *Ibid.*, 1947, p. 90.

162

ments reflected an awareness that underlying the wartime crisis there was an even more basic spiritual crisis threatening the nation, its leadership failed to respond to this spiritual challenge with the appropriate emphasis on evangelism that might have been expected. In fact, not until the special meeting in Columbus in March 1946 did evangelism command the serious attention of the Council's leadership.

At this special meeting, called to consider the problems of peace, it was insisted that there must be a moral and spiritual preparation if the American churches and people were to meet the challenges of the postwar world. The Council declared that to meet the needs of this hour, the church of Christ must be strengthened in body, mind, and spirit. The first stirring of a new emphasis came in 1947 when the executive committee accepted the suggestion of Jesse Bader, the secretary of the Department of Evangelism, that a year for evangelism should begin with World Communion Sunday in October 1949. Preparation began in early 1948 with a conference for teachers of evangelism held in Louisville. This was the first of its kind and over four hundred attended.

In 1948 the executive committee enthusiastically accepted the proposed united evangelistic advance of 1950 with a statement on the nature of the Gospel. This statement might well have been the high-water mark of the Council's evangelical pronouncements about the task of the church in the field of evangelism.[79] Although the document clearly reflected a neo-orthodox concept of the mighty acts of God in history, it did so in a context that was rather different from most of the pronouncements on evangelism in the past. The united evangelistic advance was clearly spelled out in detail both as to its aims and as to the methods to be used. The statement enjoined the quickening of the ministry and the winning of the vast unchurched multitudes of the nation for Christ. Each new convert was to be carefully instructed in the meaning of the Christian faith and assimilated into the local church. The evangelistic advance was to consist of a Christian teaching mission, a visitation evangelism effort by local churches, and a preaching mission. The whole effort was to last for fifteen months. National teaching ministries were also planned for one hundred communities. In 1949, university Christian missions were held in thirty schools, most of them being small and all in the North. In addition, E. Stanley Jones held ten preaching missions, also as part of this new evangelistic advance.

79. *Biennial Report*, 1948, pp. 49-55.

The reports to the Council about the evangelistic advance suggest that it was well received in terms of the attendance at the various missions. The Council regarded it as successful. But no final assessment was possible because the evangelistic effort continued until the work of the Council ended in December 1950. The available evidence regarding the contents of the messages presented at these missions suggests that the basic purpose of the crusade was to bring about a moral rather than a spiritual rebirth in the church, and that it was designed to aid the spread of the social gospel.

The use of the radio continued to be an essential part of the evangelistic ministry of the Council, even though after the war certain organizational changes occurred, plus some experimenting with TV as the decade closed. During the war years the Council maintained twenty-three different radio programs of the network variety; for the most part, they were conducted by big-name liberal pulpiteers.[80] In 1945 the Federal Council had 578 programs over the three major radio networks; forty-five ministers took part.[81]

In order to take advantage of the greater facilities available in radio after the war and in order the use these new facilities for the advancement of the ecumenical movement, the Federal Council created the Protestant Radio Commission in 1947. It began operation on January 1, 1949. Paul Calvin Payne of the Presbyterian Church, USA, was its first chairman. The commission sponsored the Protestant Radio Hour among other programs, and continued to function under the National Council of Churches.

The Federal Council and the Ecumenical Movement, 1941-1950

The coming of war in no way diminished the zeal of the Federal Council for the development of an ecumenical Protestantism. Although the wartime emergency made it more difficult to plan for denominational unions, the same emergency served to convince the leadership of the Council that a much greater degree of unity was necessary if the church was to express the kind of witness to Christianity that the ecumenical leaders had in mind. The disunity

80. A few like Norman Vincent Peale could be classified as vaguely evangelical rather than liberal.

81. *Annual Report*, 1945. Among those participating were H. Ray Anderson of Chicago, Oscar Blackwelder, John Sutherland Bonnell, S. M. Cavert, Harry Emerson Fosdick, Bishop Bromley Oxnam, Daniel Poling, Samuel Schoemaker, and Joseph Sizoo. In theological outlook they range from a broad evangelicalism to extreme radicalism.

in the secular world put a new premium on the unity in the Christian church. During the war years plans were formulated for bringing all the interdenominational agencies together under a new roof, to be known as the National Council of Churches. At the same time, the ultimate goal—organic union of all denominations—was never forgotten.[82] In its wartime meetings the Council pleaded for a spirit of Christ and fellowship that would transcend the divisions caused by war, and for American Christians not to let a spirit of hatred poison their attitude toward Christians in those nations with whom we were at war.

By 1944 the Council was using the war situation as a definite reason for achieving a closer relationship among all Christians—Protestants, and Roman and Eastern Orthodox Catholics. Declaring that differences between Protestant and Catholic churches were small in contrast to existing differences between Christian and non-Christians, the Council in 1944 affirmed that we take our stand on the common faith of Christendom: faith in God the Creator, Redeemer, and Sanctifier. By so standing together we would invite men to share that faith and challenge all to conform their lives to the principles derived from it.[83] The Council was very insistent in that it was the part of Christian statesmanship to foster mutual understanding, fellowship, and cooperation between the Protestant churches and the churches of the Eastern Orthodox heritage. The reasoning behind this appeal clearly reveals that the ecumenical movement no longer would be confined to Protestant groups but would also include the Eastern Orthodox churches, perhaps even the Roman churches.[84] Organic union of the churches was the ultimate goal of the ecumenical leadership, but its realization was impossible during a war emergency.

The advent of peace in 1945 brought the Federal Council opportunities to make fresh appeals to American Christians for an ecumenical approach to the problems of postwar America, and to take a bolder leadership in the movement for achieving union among denominations. But between these two opportunities a certain tension existed. Many liberal leaders much preferred the avenue of cooperation to the more frontal approach of merger because of the many practical difficulties involved in the latter strategy. They

82. The formation of the National Council of Churches will be discussed in chapter six.

83. *Biennial Report*, 1944, p. 7.

84. *Ibid.*, pp. 9-10. The Eastern Orthodox church was admitted to the Federal Council in 1944.

realized that cooperation could result in a *de facto* union of sorts, a union that would be a reality before the many opponents of such mergers were aware of what was happening.

The leadership of the Federal Council was keenly aware of the necessity of maintaining an instrument for achieving organic union. Yet it emphasized in its public messages that it was a council of churches and not a superchurch. Not infrequently it called itself an instrument of cooperation and not of union, and stated that it rested on the conviction that within the framework of the denominational system there was sufficient spiritual unity to justify and to require that the churches work together. Furthermore, the Council was not an association of diverse and heterogeneous faiths, but a fellowship of churches, which all confess Jesus Christ as divine Lord and Savior. Beyond this the Council would not go; it studiously avoided matters of doctrine.

Basically the Council was an instrument for expressing the witness of its member churches to those social principles that are derived from our Christian faith.[85] This emphasis on the role of the Council in providing a common witness for the various churches in the area of Christian service could not conceal the underlying hope of many that this common action would ultimately provide the basis for a unity of organization.

The push for church union gained momentum as a result of the first meeting of the World Council of Churches in Amsterdam in 1948, and of the planning for the formation of the National Council on the home front in 1950.

Organizational Developments Within the Council, 1941-1950

The war years occasioned some changes in the structure of the Federal Council, but the many challenges to the Council arising from the complex issues of the ensuing peace and cold war inevitably occasioned many more changes, some of them important.

During the war years special committees and commissions were created to aid displaced persons in this country and Europe, to promote foreign relief, and to secure chaplains for our armed services.

85. For a comprehensive statement on the ecumenical purpose of the Council, see *Federal Council Bulletin* 29 (November 1946): 3-4.

In 1942 the Council's executive committee created a special committee on relief and reconstruction in Europe. In 1943 the Commission on the Church and Minority Peoples was created to assume a pastoral care over all minority groups in this country.

In 1944 the executive committee created the Commission on the Ministry with Dr. John Oliver Nelson its first executive secretary. This commission was regarded as necessary for meeting the needs of ministers as those needs were rapidly developing in the postwar world. But it was designed also to meet the needs of those ministers who were dedicated to the preaching of the social gospel more than was approved by their denominations. In addition, it was intended to provide those ministerial services not provided by the regular denominational agencies charged with this responsibility. In 1945 the Council opened a Washington office to maintain better contact with the activities of the federal government and to have a more effective voice in internal affairs.

As a result of the Pittsburgh conference on the church and economic life, in February 1947, the Department of the Church and Economic Life was the same year organized for the express purpose of making the Council's philosophy more effective on economic planning and practice. Also in 1947 the Department of Religion and Drama was created, to utilize drama in the life and worship of the church. All of these newly created agencies reflected the Council's determination to bring every aspect of American culture within the orbit of its influence, ostensibly to shed on these areas a spiritual influence, but actually to secularize the church.

The temper of the times was also evident in the changes occurring in the membership of the council and in the rising tide of criticism that beset it. The latter traced to the new areas of activity into which the Council had entered and the increasingly radical tone of its pronouncements on foreign affairs, the economic life of the nation, and the problems of race and segregation. Some churches left the Council, largely the smaller and most evangelical denominations. The denominations that chose to remain within the ecumenical fold experienced growing and intense dissent, much of it expressed with great vehemence in their periodicals and at their annual conventions and assemblies.

The Presbyterian Church, U.S. resumed its active participation in the Federal Council in 1942. The United Lutheran Church, however, refused an invitation to become a full member and retained its consultative relationship until the Federal Council ceased to exist in late 1950. This same year, 1950, the Church of the Brethren was readmitted after an absence of many years.[86]

As early as 1928 and again 1937, the executive committee had decided that all of the Orthodox churches were eligible for membership in the Council. Accordingly, the Ukrainian Orthodox church was admitted in 1942 and a membership invitation extended to the Armenian Apostolic and Polish National Catholic churches. This decision to admit to membership Orthodox churches of the East was significant in the life of the Council and marks a departure from its traditional Protestant stance. The Council was now willing to renounce its Protestant background and heritage in favor of becoming more ecumenical and less distinctly rooted in the Reformation.

At the same time, a shift took place in the Council's attitude toward the Roman Catholic church. The change surfaces in the Council's annual messages calling for the celebration of Reformation Sunday. During the first thirty years of its history the Council had been quite opposed to Roman Catholic theology and practice. But then a subtle change set in. The Council remained quite anti-papal, but also more tolerant toward the Roman Catholic church in America. The annual Reformation Day messages and appeals, in turn, were no longer so vehement in their tone; after 1940 they bade the churches of America to remember their Protestant heritage of individual liberty and liberty of conscience, but any mention of the Roman Catholic church was carefully muted to avoid offending American Catholics.[87]

In November 1944 the Universalist church applied for membership in the Federal Council. The executive committee departed from its usual practice and simply voted to refer the application to the biennial meeting for consideration. When the Evangelical Czech Moravian Brethren applied for membership the same year, the committee approved it and sent it to the biennial meeting for final action. The application of the Universalist church presented a problem because that organization did not subscribe to the deity of Jesus Christ in the manner required by the Council.

In 1945 the Russian Orthodox church was admitted to Council membership because it held to the early ecumenical creeds of the

86. This church had withdrawn in 1917 because of its opposition to American entry into World War I; it felt that the Federal Council had abandoned its stand against war and bestowed its blessing on the war effort.

87. For a detailed statement on this emphasis, see *Biennial Report*, 1944, pp. 7-10.

Christian church and thus met the requirement of belief in the Trinity.

In 1946 the problem of this doctrinal requirement assumed a new importance; the request of the Universalist church was turned down with eight voting against membership, four for granting, and one voted in favor of further study in a special committee. In a plenary session of the executive committee the request was turned down by a vote of 63 to 70.[88]

The Seattle biennial of 1946 also turned down the application for membership from the General Convention of the Swedenborgian church, the Liberal Catholic church, and the North American Old Catholic churches, but reason was not given for these refusals. Further complication arose in 1947 when the Religious Society of Friends of Philadelphia applied for admission to the Council. This group was the result of the union of two groups of Quakers—one orthodox, which had been a member of the Council, and the other a Hicksite or Unitarian group, which had not been a member. The application was accepted. In 1950 the Augustana and Danish Lutheran synods were received into membership.

In this period of ten years only one denomination withdrew from the Federal Council. The Reformed Episcopal church, with a membership of about 10,000, departed in May 1945.

Because of the great increase in church membership after 1945 and the addition of these new member churches, the membership of the Council reached new heights. The leaders could in one sense assert that they spoke for a very large percentage of the Protestant churches of this country as they interpreted their representative character as spokesmen for the combined membership of the churches in the Council.[89]

Dissent and Protest Against the Federal Council

The very fact that the Federal Council claimed the right to speak for the member churches sparked serious dissent from many members in the constituent denominations.

No sooner had the Southern Presbyterian church resumed its place as a member of the Council than it immediately called on the Council to place itself on the doctrinal basis as proposed at Utrecht

88. *Federal Council Bulletin* XXX (January 1947): 16.

89. Of the larger denominations only the Missouri Lutheran Synod and the Southern Baptist Convention steadfastly refused to join the Council.

for the World Council of Churches.[90] The resolution of the 1941 General Assembly of that church also affirmed its own basic theology and the relationship of that theology to pronouncements of the Federal Council of Churches:

> In accord with her doctrine of the sufficiency of Scripture, the Presbyterian Church in the United States declared that she does not accept any pronouncement of the Federal Council, its agencies or secretaries, which goes beyond the teaching of the Holy Scripture as part of the official position or testimony of the church, as law or recommendations binding the conscience of her members, but only as the opinion of representative Christian gentlemen.[91]

This is probably the clearest statement of a position of a member denomination to be found in the official reports of the Council and represented a deep unrest in that denomination concerning the statements and activities of the Council. To a lesser degree the same distrust was present in other constituent denominations, and as the decade drew to a close it became even more pronounced, so much so that the Council was finally forced to reaffirm its fidelity to the historic ecumenical creeds and their trinitarian position.[92]

In 1943 the General Assembly of the Presbyterian Church, U.S. again rebuked the Federal Council for the actions and pronouncements of its representatives. The Council was forced to reply to this complaint and clarify its position. It reiterated the stand taken by the executive committee on September 18, 1942, to wit, that the Council expected that the utterances of its secretaries and ministers speaking under its auspices would not be at variance with its constitution: "However, no secretary of the Council and minister speaking under its auspices can make any pronouncement in its behalf. The Executive Committee, made up of representatives officially appointed by the denominations, has the sole authority to make pronouncements for the Council."[93]

90. *Biennial Report*, 1942, p. 195.

91. *Ibid.*, p. 195.

92. This same distrust caused the Reformed Episcopal Church to withdraw from the Council. Earlier it had also been an important factor in the disruption in the Presbyterian Church, USA that led to the formation of Westminster Theological Seminary in 1929 and the founding of the Orthodox Presbyterian Church (formerly Presbyterian Church in America) and the Bible Presbyterian Synod in the later 1930s.

93. *Annual Report*, 1943, p. 143.

The Presbyterian Church, U.S. was not satisfied with the effectiveness of this hopeful directive issued in 1942. The Council therefore felt compelled to give a more specific reply to satisfy the Presbyterian General Assembly. In its reply the executive committee stated its belief that its secretaries and ministers clearly understood and followed the directive of September 1, 1942.[94] This reply was something less than candid and did not satisfy the suspicions of the conservative elements in the Presbyterian Church, U.S. and other constituent denominations. But that was as far as the Council was willing to go in its efforts to meet the complaints of the more conservative churches in its membership.

Actually the policy statement of September 1942 was little more than window dressing. The various secretaries of the Council were well aware of the extreme liberalism dominant in the executive committee and only acted accordingly. The source of the trouble was in the hierarchy that controlled the thinking and activities of the Council. The real problem was the Council itself; more specifically, the executive committee, which frequently espoused radical causes and made radical pronouncements and then claimed that these were the expression of Protestant thinking.

The executive committee was not entirely unaware of or indifferent to the growing criticism of its pronouncements and activities. In 1944, the first time in its history, it issued a defense of its role. It asserted that of its ninety-odd members, generally fifty or more attended its meetings. The committee insisted that it took its work very seriously. In fact, its debates were representative of various points of view, frequently prolonged, and even agonizing: "The average church member may be confident that these convictions are represented, at least approximately, by at least some of the members of the committee. Furthermore, he may be assured that they are represented completely and without any restraints except those imposed by Christian fellowship."[95]

This was a curious kind of defense—and something less than the truth. Truly orthodox Reformation theology, Lutheran or Reformed, seldom had any adequate representation and seldom, if ever, influenced the thinking of either the Council or the biennial conventions in their final deliberations on social, theological, and economic issues. Conservative denominations—particularly the Southern Presbyterian and United Presbyterian churches—frequently de-

94. *Ibid.*, pp. 143-44.
95. *Federal Council Bulletin* 27, no. 1 (January 1944): 5.

171

fended their membership in the Council on the ground that they had been able at various times to exert their conservative influence and prevent the Council from adopting more radical positions and programs, but little or no evidence for this contention exists in the available literature on the Council.

In March 1947 the executive committee again felt called upon to prepare a statement on the present policies of the Federal Council of Churches. It reiterated the evangelical nature of its doctrine.[96] The committee emphasized that it had refused to admit into membership any denomination if its doctrinal position was not clear on the person of Jesus Christ as the divine Lord and Savior. But the committee also reiterated its refusal to go beyond this simple requirement on the ground that it had no authority to draw up a common creed or a form of government or worship.[97] It is true that it had no power to draw up a common creed. But it is equally true that the phrase regarding Jesus Christ as divine Lord and Savior was not a satisfactory statement of the evangelical position, that it was in fact the lowest common denominator and as such furnished absolutely no guarantee for the evangelical stance of the Council. The phrase itself was open to too many variant interpretations to guarantee a basic evangelical theology and outlook for the Council. The Council's history is itself a powerful testimony to the fundamental weakness of this creedal requirement. Many within the Council could and did sign it, men whose theologies were a far cry from the Apostles' Creed or the Nicene Creed, let alone the detailed, explicit evangelical creeds of the Reformation era.

Obviously, this meager statement of the evangelical position in no way prevented the Federal Council from indulging in radical statements on social and political affairs. Its political, social, and economic outlook and activity bore little or no resemblance to the theological orthodoxy it claimed for itself. All too frequently its pronouncements on social and economic issues and on peace and war were derived from humanistic and Communist sources and coated with an evangelical veneer to make them more acceptable to the membership of the churches.

Toward the end of the decade the tempo of attacks on the theological and ideological outlook of the Council picked up considerably and its leadership became increasingly sensitive to these on-

96. *Annual Report*, 1947, pp. 229-35.
97. *Ibid.*, pp. 4-5.

slaughts. Criticism of the Council was closely allied with the popular awareness of the Communist menace posed by the various activities of Russia on the one hand and the increasing influence of domestic communism on the other. The great similarity between statements of the Federal Council and those of Communist sympathizers and party members in high places in this country convinced large segments of the American public that the Council was under Communist influence to an alarming degree.[98]

At its 1948 biennial meeting the Council sought to allay such criticism by, once again, reaffirming its doctrinal position:

> The Executive Committee of the Federal Council records its understanding of the Council's position as being in full accord with that of the World Council. In the preamble to its constitution the Federal Council asserts its faith in Jesus Christ as Divine Lord and Saviour, which is an affirmation of the deity of Christ in keeping with the historic faith of Christianity.[99]

But such an affirmation was no longer sufficient to quell the doubts of an aroused and even angry public. The Council itself was responsible for the hostile attitude within the churches because of its own statements and actions that clearly revealed that whatever its affirmation of faith may be, its heart was elsewhere.

In 1948 the executive committee adopted a report on the House Committee on Un-American Activities. The report was hardly calculated to quiet the fears of those who were now convinced of the ties between communism and the Council. The document clearly revealed a basic sympathy with radicalism:

> As Christians and as citizens were are concerned for the safeguarding and extension of our democracy and the individual liberties inherent in it. From that standpoint we have examined the procedures, the record and the long history of the House Committee on Un-American Activities, including the latest excursion of the Committee into the field of religion. Individuals who should be assumed innocent until proven guilty have been labeled guilty without having a trial. Time and time again the Committee has been used to falsify, intimidate and smear. In the light of the Committee's now long and clearly undemocratic record and in the interests of our democracy

98. The problem of the relationship between the Council and communism and other forms of radicalism will be discussed in chapter eight.

99. *Biennial Report*, 1948, p. 257.

we call for the Committee's abolition. We call for a new democratic committee on civil liberties.[100]

The report, which was approved by the biennial session, is a crystal-clear statement of the liberal opposition to the work of this House committee, chaired by the anti-Communist Martin Dies. It infuriated conservatives in the member churches and prompted a storm of criticism in the conservative religious press as well as in segments of the conservative secular press.[101] It reinforced the growing conservative conviction that the Council had become an instrument of communism for the destruction of both the American constitutional system and free enterprise.

Many critics regarded the call for a new democratic committee on civil liberties as a subterfuge and that what the Council really had in mind was a new committee whose zeal for democratic procedure and devotion to liberalism would make it tolerant of the Communist philosophy and its sympathizers in America.

In 1950 the Council began to react to the criticism, which was now coming in like a flood, against its activities. In its January meeting it took note of charges hurled against it in John T. Flynn's *The Road Ahead*; in a pamphlet published by the American Council of Christian Laymen, the Council called these outbursts serious misrepresentations of the facts of the case.[102]

Somewhat later the executive committee approved Council membership in the All-American Conference formed to combat communism.[103] This was an obviously strategic move to remove some of the sting from the repeated charges that the Council was soft on communism. Finally, in April 1950 Samuel McCrae Cavert undertook to answer Flynn's charges against the Council. He did so by pointing out some errors in *The Road Ahead*, thus implying that Flynn's basic charges were also in error.[104] Specifically, he tried to refute the charges that Bishop Oxnam, E. Stanley Jones, and John

100. *Ibid.,* p. 268.

101. For the attacks on the Federal Council by religious journals, see the *Christian Century, Southern Presbyterian Journal, Christian Beacon.* For secular treatment, see *Newsweek, Time* and *United States News.* After 1946 the secular journals paid an increasing amount of attention to the meetings and activities of the Council.

102. *Biennial Report,* 1950, p. 81.

103. *Ibid.,* p. 114.

104. *Federal Council Bulletin* 35 (April 1952): 16-17.

C. Bennett were in varying degrees admirers of Russia and friendly to communism.[105] Cavert's refutation at this point is quite unconvincing.

The few defenses that the Federal Council put forth in its own behalf were quite unconvincing to the man in the pew and his secular ally, the man in the street. The National Council of Churches became heir to this growing suspicion, that the ecumenical movement was the handmaiden of a liberalism that was friendly to communism and unfriendly to the American heritage.

105. This issue will be dealt with in chapter eight.

6

The Origins, Formation, and Early Years of the National Council of Churches

The movement for the formation of the National Council of Churches had long been in the making. For many years liberals had been dissatisfied with the basic structure of the Federal Council of Churches. The conviction that the Federal Council was inadequate for the tasks that these liberals sought to impose upon it took shape with the advent of the New Deal. The emergence of this politically radical movement opened up new areas of activity for the Council, areas it had never faced before. It had been born in the relatively tranquil period of the first decade of the nineteenth century and its constitution reflected the theological and political conditions of the day. Even though its Social Creed of 1908 contained the germs of a radical social and economic policy, this policy was only latent at best, not actual. And, as previously noted, conservative theological and political elements existed in the Council at its beginning that were opposed to any radicalism by the Council. But the Great Depression destroyed this relative tranquility in our national life, and replaced it with a depression psychology that welcomed the radical political and social experimentation by Franklin Roosevelt's administration.

The depression also presented a tremendous opportunity and challenge to ecclesiastical radicalism. But the very challenge and opportunity demanded a much stronger form of ecumenical organization than that offered by the Federal Council. The editors of *Christian Century* had in the early days of the New Deal declared that the Council was inadequate for the tasks and opportunities presented by the New Deal:

> The Federal Council has exhausted its present commission. New conditions require that it be recommissioned with a new charter in which the dictinction between the ecclesiastical and nonecclesiastical functions shall no longer obtain. . . . Protestantism needs to be set free from the inertia and the impotence of sectarian divisions.[1]

The basic issue is visible just beneath the surface of this editorial. The editors were really dissatisfied with the structure of the Federal Council. A council of denominations working together for common purposes was no longer acceptable. To meet the challenge of the new day, church union rather than denominations working in cooperation was a prime necessity. The Federal Council, on the other hand, still looked upon itself as the common agent of cooperating denominations in the achievement of their common goals in the economic and political life of the nation and insisted that it had not been created to bring about actual denominational mergers.

Although liberal publications and ecclesiastical groups sounded the call for a reorganization of the Federal Council many times during the 1930s, the Council took no steps toward its own restructuring. In 1937 and 1938 it became very much interested in the Oxford and Edinburgh conferences looking forward to the formation of the World Council of Churches. The evidence suggests that the leadership of the Federal Council hoped that the appearance of such a strong ecumenical organization in Europe would pave the way for the creation of a stronger council in this country.

But not until 1942 did the Federal Council take any positive action regarding its own reorganization. And then it did so under the

1. *Christian Century*, December 20, 1933, p. 1600.

mounting pressure resulting from our involvement in World War II and the accompanying demands upon the council in meeting the various problems resulting from the war. These first faltering steps were reinforced in 1946.

Charles Clayton Morrison supplied a new incentive for a stronger organization, in the columns of the *Christian Century:*

> Protestantism has not learned to live in the modern world. It has carried over from the era of individualism its structure of organization and its simple procedures that seemed appropriate to them. Everything around it has changed, the whole structure and psychology of society, but Protestantism proceeds as if it were still living in the middle eighties.[2]

For ecumenical leaders like this editor, Protestantism must conform to the modern world. Thus it must surrender its individualism for the blessings of democratic collectivism, a theme very dear to the hearts of the leaders of the ecumenical movement. A later issue carried the argument further:

> Protestantism cannot win America until it rids itself of the illusion that the American mentally is still individualistic and that the churches are gaining because they are recruiting individuals into their membership. The American mind is not predominantly collectivist in its structure. It is molded by a relatively few massive blocks of secular interest. . . . Protestantism, on the other hand, is sectarianized, localized and individualized. It has neither the organization nor the techniques for gaining entrance or commanding the respect of collectivities.[3]

The remedy for this alleged weakness of the Protestant church was to submit to the demands of a collectivist society and mentality. In short, the remedy was to be found, not in the Federal Council, but in something above and beyond this form of sectarian cooperation—an ecumenical church. This new organization must be a union of the major denominations and, it was hoped, of even the smaller churches as well. A secular collectivism must be paralleled by an ecumenical collectivism. A stepping-stone on the road to this ultimate goal would be the formation of the National Council of Churches. It would be a transitional organization, finding its strength

2. *Ibid.*, May 15, 1946, p. 618.
3. *Ibid.*, p. 619.

179

in the merger of the various constituent denominations along with the various interdenominational agencies that had cooperated with the older Federal Council but had never become a part of it.

Like that of the Federal Council, the avowed objective of the National Council was to be the realization of the kingdom of God on earth through the proclamation of the social gospel. America must be made truly Christian, by which the ecumenical leadership meant that it must become truly collectivistic and socialistic. This theme was prominent in the deliberations at the Columbus meeting of the Federal Council in 1946 and at Cincinnati in 1948.[4] America must be Christianized, but to become Christianized it must become socialized. In socialism the kingdom of God would come to America.

Not only was this thinking dominant in the policy of the Federal Council after 1945; it was also voiced by many leaders of those denominations that were in the Federal Council. Methodist, Northern Baptist, Congregationalist, and Presbyterian Church, USA leaders carefully prepared the stage for the drama that was to be unfolded in Cleveland in November 1950, in the formation of the National Council.

Although the leaders in forming this new ecumenical venture insisted that it was not merely a reorganization of the Federal Council, the spirit that pervaded the Cleveland meeting and its membership made it exceedingly difficult to differentiate between it and the biennial assemblies of its forerunner. The same theological and social liberalism that had increasingly marked the meetings of the Federal Council also permeated this assembly.

The *Christian Century* triumphantly asserted that the churches were meeting in Cleveland to achieve an object more significant for Protestant Christianity than any one action since the passage of the Virginia Statute of Religious Freedom in 1785.[5] It added:

> The National Council will give the churches a voice to which attention must be paid. It will provide a platform on which cooperative Protestantism can speak to this "nation under God." It will afford a field of action from which a leadership respected by all the churches may be counted on to emerge.[6]

Certainly the leadership at Cleveland was determined to make

4. For the major decisions of these two meetings, see *Biennial Report*, 1946 and 1948.

5. *Christian Century*, November 22, 1950, p. 1383.

6. *Ibid.*, p. 1384.

these dreams of a new and more powerful ecumenical organization come true. The various addresses breathed this ecumenical optimism. The old leadership was very evident in all this. Frederick Nolde, Edwin T. Dahlberg, Episcopalian bishop Henry Knox Sherrill, Franklin Clark Fry, Samuel M. Cavert, and Bishop Frederick Stamm (the last president of the Federal Council) not only provided impressive evidence that the National Council would be the old Federal Council in a new form, in spite of vehement denials, but also provided the evidence of the continuing theological and social radicalism that would motivate the new organization.

The meeting was composed of nearly five hundred voting delegates, though the opening service was attended by only about four hundred people at which Ralph Sockman, a long-time radio minister for the Federal Council, gave the opening sermon. The enthusiasm of the gathering was dimmed by neither the worst snowstorm to hit Cleveland since 1913 nor the war clouds that hung heavily over the American horizon because of the Korean crisis.

On Wednesday morning, November 29, 1950, Franklin Clark Fry proclaimed that the National Council of Churches was officially constituted, and the first session got under way for business. The National Council was composed of twenty-nine denominations. The roster of members was that of the old Federal Council with one addition: the United Lutheran Church was a full member of the new body. The twenty-nine denominations[7] claimed a membership of over thirty-one million members. For this reason the National Council advanced the claim that it spoke for the great bulk of Protestant Christians in America. The only large denominations refusing to join were the Lutheran Church, Missouri Synod and the Southern Baptist Convention.

Agencies that had never been a formal part of the Federal Council were not included within its successor. The Foreign Missions Conference of North America, the Home Missions Council of North America, the International Council of Religious Education, the Missionary Movement of the United States and Canada, the National Protestant Council on Higher Education, the United Council of Church Women, and the United Stewardship Council all became part of the new organization.

7. This represents only a small percentage of the total number of denominations in the nation. Small conservative evangelical Presbyterian, Lutheran, Baptist, and Methodist churches as well as large groups like the Church of Christ, Church of God, and Church of the Nazarene refused to join the Council.

The first major task of this assembly was to draw up a constitution suitable for the enlarged membership and tasks of this Council. The constitution, as finally accepted, contained a preamble that on the one hand managed, with effort, to maintain enough of an evangelical tone to allay discontent in those member churches having large evangelical minorities, and that on the other hand advanced the idea of an ecumenical purpose to gain the loyalty of those who looked to the new Council to produce a much more aggressive ecumenical, social, and economic program than had been possible under the constitution of the Federal Council. The preamble read in part:

> In the providence of God the time has come when it seems fitting more fully to manifest the essential oneness of the Christian Churches of the United States of America in Jesus Christ as their divine Lord and Saviour, by the creation of an inclusive cooperative agency to continue and extend the following general agencies of the churches and to combine all their interests and functions.[8]

Membership in the Council was declared to be open to any communion that would accept the purpose as enunciated in the preamble of the constitution. However, membership in a division of the Council would be open to any church board whether its denomination was a member of the Council or not. Denominations and boards choosing not to become charter members of the Council could join later if they received a two-thirds vote of the Council members.

Each member denomination was allotted five members on the General Assembly of the Council and an additional member for each 100,000 members or fraction thereof. At least one half of the total number of delegates was to be nominated by denominational boards and agencies. State councils of churches were given membership in the Council if they were constitutionally responsible to the denominations in their area. City and county councils could nominate ten representatives for election by the National Council to membership in the General Assembly on the same basis. According to these membership provisions, the General Assembly was created to have about six hundred voting members.

Under the General Assembly there was an executive body known as the General Board, which was to meet every two months and which was charged with the responsibilities of seeing that the general policies laid down by the General Assembly were carried out. This board had most of the powers of the General Assembly; it

8. *Christian Century*, December 13, 1950, p. 1482.

could not, however, elect new denominations to membership or change the constitution or the bylaws of the National Council. The membership of the General Board was elected by the denominations and by state and local councils of churches. Each denomination and council of churches was to elect one seventh of its delegation to the National Council as members of the General Board. Each division of the Council was also to name three members (one man, one woman, and one youth). The main functioning bodies under the General Assembly and the General Board were to be the divisions.[9]

The constitution provided for four divisions: Christian education, foreign missions, home missions, and Christian life and work. The Division of Christian Education was given the functions of the International Council of Religious Education and the National Protestant Council on Higher Education. The Division of Foreign Missions replaced the former Foreign Missions Conference. Similarly, the Division of Home Missions replaced the former Home Missions Council. The Division of Christian Life and Work assumed the role of the Federal Council itself. Membership for these four divisions was achieved by dividing the membership of the General Assembly into four equal parts; each of these would form an assembly of each division.

Under the divisions there were three kinds of departments. The first kind was general departments, like the Department of United Church Women and a newly created Department of United Church Men, to which no parallel existed in the Federal Council.[10] The second, joint departments, was created to administer the work that could be regarded as the concern of two or more divisions. Joint departments were intended to deal with family life, the Christian life, service, stewardship, evangelism, and religious liberty. The third type of department was intended to serve the Council as a whole, its divisions, and the local and state councils of churches, besides other agencies constituent to the Council.

This in essence was the organization of the National Council. It was complicated, much more so than that of the Federal Council. It was also far more centralized and intended to be so. For it was designed to carry out the increasingly complex task of making the social gospel a reality in American life.

This view of the functions of the National Council was enunciated

9. The General Board of the National Council largely corresponded to the executive committee of the Federal Council while the divisions replaced the former departments.

10. The Department of United Church Women replaced the former United Council of Church Women.

in its inaugural message adopted on December 1 by the first General Assembly.[11]

Disclaiming any intention of becoming a denomination and insisting upon the autonomy of each member denomination, the assembly put forward its role in the life of American Christendom. It did so, however, in a way that left many doubts. Its self-styled role certainly bore many of the earmarks of the role of a denomination. The assembly clearly stated that it would offer the churches a means of approaching the government and its civil agencies in secular matters of concern to the church. It is quite obvious that the architects of the National Council harbored none of the misgivings of the ecumenical leaders of 1908 who launched the Federal Council on the stormy seas of ecumenical activity. All secular concerns were declared to be spiritual and therefore under the guardianship of the National Council.

The inaugural address, on the other hand, was lavish in its insistence that the National Council was devoted to liberty and that all true Americans could rest assured that it was the ally of our national freedom:

> The council stands as a guardian of democratic freedom. The revolutionary truth that men are created free follows from the revelation of God in Jesus Christ, and no person who knows that God as Father has given him all the rights of sonship is likely to remain content under a government which deprives him of basic human rights and fundamental freedoms. The nation may expect in the National Council a sturdy ally of the forces of liberty. The council stands for liberty with the richest content. It stands for the freedom of men to be as the Lord God meant them to be. It stands for Christian freedom—including the freedom to pursue happiness with justice and to create conditions of happiness for others.[12]

Having thus assured the nation that the Council was on the side of freedom, the assembly hastened also to assure those who might suspect it of being soft on communism that nothing could be further from the truth: "The Council is opposed to materialism as an end in itself. It is the foe of every political system that is nourished on materialism and of every way of living that follows from it.[13]

Having sought to allay the fears of those who might see in this

11. *Christian Century*, December 13, 1950, pp. 1484-85.

12. *Ibid.*, p. 1485.

13. *Ibid.*

184

highly centralized Council a threat to the American heritage, the assembly then attempted to assure those who looked to the Council for stronger and more aggressive leadership in bringing the social gospel to bear in every sphere of our national life:

> Knowing that men too often dream in marble and then build with straw, we whose very human lives are separate from sin and ignorance can make no boast of past or future excellence.
> But this we have done: By God's grace we have forged an implement for cooperation such as America has never seen before. . . . The council is our churches in their highest common effort for mankind. . . . The council itself is a demonstration of his [Christ's] power to unite his followers in joyous cooperation. Let nation and nation, race and race, class and class, unite for their aims in his broad purposes for man, and out of that unitedness there will arise new strength like that of which we ourselves already feel the first sure intimations.[14]

This entire inaugural address was a concealed notice of the radicalism to follow. Beneath the meager layer of evangelical language and illusion can be seen the hard-core dedication to a liberalism that was really a radicalism. The assertion that the Council stood as "a guardian of democratic freedom" actually did not mean what it seemed to convey at first glance. For this phrase was quickly nullified by the statement that this kind of democracy is rooted in the "revolutionary truth that men are created free" and that this freedom "follows from the revelation of God in Jesus Christ." This is a grave distortion of the biblical doctrine of freedom and an attempt to interpret the Scriptures in the light and in support of the humanistic doctrine of freedom. The democratic view of freedom, to which this document renders homage, is a far cry from the biblical view of freedom and any reconciliation of these views is impossible.

On the other hand, this document intimately links democratic freedom with a revolutionary concept that is much nearer to Communist theory than to that liberty promised believers in the Gospel.

It is difficult to believe that the General Assembly's choice of words in these paragraphs and the confusion of biblical and democratic concepts of liberty were accidental. Rather, it is more natural and logical to conclude that the inaugural message was part and parcel of a well-developed plan to bring the ecumenical movement

14. *Ibid.*, p. 1482.

185

to a new height of power and achievement through a neatly centralized Council with an unequivocally radical statement of its goals and purposes. This is the unmistakable thrust of the addresses given at the Cleveland meeting.

These initial statements of the National Council, however biblical they may seem at first glance, were actually revolutionary in character; without question, the Council was prepared to enter into the economic, social, and political conflicts of the day with an organized power and influence not possible under the old Federal Council. And it would do so under the impetus of a theology more liberal than that to which its predecessor had occasionally pledged allegiance. The National Council thus assumed a position generally in harmony with that held by the political parties in this country that represented the socialist and the communist positions.

Basic to the promotion of radicalism in American life was the tacit assumption that underlay nearly all the pronouncements of this Cleveland meeting, namely, that the distinction between the secular and the sacred must be removed from the thinking of the American church. In his address to the first General Assembly of the National Council on December 1, 1950, Bishop Henry Knox Sherrill called for a church extended and applied to every aspect of American life. He declared that "there can be no artificial division between the sacred and the secular, for the Gospel has to do with international relations, with peace and war, with the atom bomb, with economic conditions, with family life, for nothing human can be alien to the love of God in Christ."[15] This statement was foundational to all the pronouncements and the acts of the National Council from that day on.

The general direction that the National Council would take in pursuing its secular goals under the guise of applying spiritual principles surfaced in an early pronouncement of the General Board, on May 16, 1951:

> The churches have special responsibility and a special contribution to make to the world and to the nation in relation to other nations. As the instrument of God's purposes they are concerned with peace, freedom and justice for all peoples. . . . Through the worldwide outreach of the missionary agencies they give the most effective and sustained demonstration of the ecumenical reality of the church. They contribute to the strengthening and building up of a living world

15. *Ohio State Journal*, December 2, 1950.

community and they gain an insight and perspective that should be brought to bear on American policy.[16]

Not only was the church to speak directly to American foreign policy but its missionary program must reflect the basic purposes of the social gospel as well. Indeed, this pronouncement called for a veritable revolution in the missionary message and program:

> Missionary work is at once a powerful expression of faith in God's purpose in history and of practical concern of the needs of man everywhere. Our representatives overseas are witnesses to the fact that God cares for all men. They demonstrate concern for human values as they apply to the peoples of all race. They prompt human welfare.[17]

Missionary effort thus should be nothing more than another kind of social welfare work. Its message must be the social gospel in word and deed. But there should be no mention of sin and its punishment or of the redeeming work of Christ upon the Cross. The total thrust of this important document was this: it was a call to Christians to a new loyalty to the philosophy of liberal democracy on the one hand, and to the cause of the United Nations on the other. But this call for loyalty to liberal democracy was also a summons to support a pagan concept of the origin and powers of government. In practice this document was a social program for the churches to aid in the abolition of poverty, and to advocate measures for maintaining mass employment and controlling inflation. It declared that it was the task of the church to develop a sound balance between freedom and justice in economic life (a thinly veiled call for the introduction of socialism in American life) and called for the promotion of international trade. In spite of our participation at that time in the Korean War, the Council asserted that the United States must not close the door to further negotiations with Soviet Russia and that it should encourage all efforts to bring all armaments, including nuclear weapons, under international control. In its total effect, this remarkable document resembled much more closely the platform of a confused political party than the pronouncements of a group of churches engaged in proclaiming the Gospel of redemption.

16. "The National Council of Churches Views Its Task in Christian Life and Work" (May 16, 1951), *Pronouncements Issued by the National Council of Churches of Christ in the United States of America, Through February 1961* (hereinafter *Pronouncements of the NCC*), pp. 9.1-1 to 9.1-6.

17. *Ibid.*, pp. 9.1-6.

The emergence of the National Council was greeted with varying degrees of enthusiasm not only by the *Christian Century* but also by the liberal religious journals in general. It also met with approval from religious journals of some conservative denominations on the grounds that it meant a new era of cooperation in those areas where such was necessary for preaching the Gospel at home and abroad. It is difficult to believe that the editors of these latter periodicals were not aware of the real meaning of the work of the Cleveland meeting. In general, Methodist, Northern Baptist, and Presbyterian papers were quite enthusiastic while a sharp division of opinion existed among Lutheran journals, those of the United Lutheran being rather favorable and those representing the Lutheran Church Missouri Synod and some smaller Lutheran communions were quite critical. The *Southern Presbyterian Journal* and Southern Baptist publications were sharply opposed to the whole development that took place at Cleveland. The fundamentalist press was virtually unanimous in its opposition to the formation of the Council, looking upon it as the triumph of a godless ecumenicalism in the member denominations.

The Augustana Lutheran declared that "the hour has struck when Evangelical Christianity needs to meet the perplexing problems of our day with a united front and to speak with a united voice. Unquestionably the Cleveland meeting may be regarded as perhaps the most significant in the religious history of America."[18] This sentiment characterized much of the Protestant press of the larger denominations, except for the *Southern Presbyterian Journal* and the *American Lutheran*, each of which asserted that it was the business of the church to bring the Gospel of Jesus Christ to those who do not yet know Him and then withheld its opinion of the new organization. "How the National Council will do this work—or undo it—will be the real test of its worth."[19] This was to be the final test by which conservatives would judge its performance.

Church assemblies also voiced their enthusiasm for the newly formed Council. The Presbyterian Church, USA, meeting in its 163d General Assembly in May 1951 at Cincinnati, gave full support to it. The (Southern) Presbyterian church, U.S., at its General Assembly in Orlando, Florida, overwhelmingly defeated a proposal to withdraw from the Council. The commissioners voted that "our Assembly continue to remember the work of the National Council in

18. Quoted in *National Council Outlook*, March 1951, p. 17.
19. *Ibid.*

prayer, that we seek to interpret its purpose to more people and that appropriate support be given the organization by our Assembly."[20] But the commissioners also took the precaution to instruct the representatives to the Council "to take all possible steps to insure the Presbyterian Church, U.S. from being misrepresented in any deliverances or pronouncements on economic or political questions by any lobbying groups of the National Council of Churches in Washington and in the public print."[21]

The secular press gave more space to the formation of the National Council of Churches than it usually allotted to news of the churches. The *New York Herald Tribune* remarked:

> The spiritual merger comes at a time of world crisis greater than any mankind has known since Protestantism was born more than four centuries ago. . . . The new council through an enlarged cooperation and unity which is both spiritual and practical in its markings, can keep the Christian religion what it always has been—a foundation force of freedom, democracy and peace, a power both in the hearts and hands of men.[22]

The *Pasadena Star-News* went to great lengths to establish the fact that the new organization was a council of churches and not a national church and that these two should not be confused. It declared that there was a real value in the varied approaches, from the ornate liturgy of the Orthodox church on the one hand to the nonritualistic service of the Church of the Brethren on the other. It stated that "one national church would tend to fuel a monopoly of religious power, therefore the uniqueness of the several churches is basic. At the same time the spirit of unity is essential"[23] For this reason it concluded that the Council was vital to the religious life of the nation. The *Cleveland News* voiced the same opinion and added that the spiritual brotherhood evident in this cooperation of the churches should stand as a symbol for other divided groups in our war-torn world.

20. *Ibid.*, p. 28.

21. *Ibid.* As far as I can tell, this is the first admission by any member church that the Council was engaged in lobbying. In its meeting at Des Moines, Iowa, the General Assembly of the United Presbyterian Church (later merged with the Presbyterian Church, USA) requested that "the cardinal Protestant doctrines be presented to the public in a positive manner, to offset the subtle propaganda against Protestantism in the secular press today."

22. *Ibid.*, January 1951, p. 15.

23. *Ibid.*, p. 20.

Little evidence exists to warrant the conclusion that the great bulk of church members looked on the emergence of the National Council with either understanding or approval. Most of them took little interest in such ecclesiastical gatherings or their solemn pronouncements, and the Cleveland meeting was no exception. But this lack of general interest soon turned to a vigorous concern as the Council came under attack by various patriotic groups and became involved in congressional investigations concerning communism in this country.

The National Council and the Cause of Peace

The Council was no less interested in peace than its ecumenical predecessor. The outbreak of the Korean War in June 1950 brought this issue into sharp focus. But the very sharpness of the focus caused the Council to be strangely silent on the Korean War as such throughout most of the conflict and to content itself rather with appeals for the support of the United Nations. On May 16, 1951, the Council's General Board adopted a statement urging the United States to cooperate with the people of the world's undeveloped areas by providing technical assistance. Further, the Truman administration should not close the door to further negotiations with Russia. The document also insisted that the United States should encourage efforts to bring all armaments, including atomic weapons, under international control, and called upon our government to be steadfast in its loyalty to the United Nations.[24] In November 1951 the General Board endorsed the disarmament proposals laid before the General Assembly of the United Nations by Great Britain, France and the United States.[25]

But the war confronted the Council with dilemma that it was apparently unwilling to face and that it could not solve. Not only was this country involved in a conflict because of an act of aggression by North Korea against South Korea, but this act of aggression was well known to have been inspired and aided by Soviet Russia. The fact that President Truman had declared it to be a part of the exercise of the police power inherent in the charter of the United Nations also complicated the position of the National Council. To denounce the war would be tantamount to severely criticizing a

24. *Pronouncements Issued by the National Council of Churches, Through February, 1961*, p. 22.1-1.

25. *Ibid.*, p. 5.1-1.

position adopted by the United Nations, and would also seemingly place the Council in the position of defending Russian Communism at a time when Americans were beginning to be very critical of the Russian regime and fearful of the infiltration of communism into this country.

With the end of hostilities in 1953 and the beginning of the peace negotiations that same year, the National Council became more courageous. Its president, William C. Martin, acting at the request of the General Board, called the Fourth National Study Conference on the Churches and World Order, which met in Cleveland in October 1953 with over four hundred and fifty delegates present. The conference spoke out against the proposed Bricker amendment to the Constitution and called for negotiations between the East and the West for ending the Cold War.[26] The Bricker amendment was hotly opposed by the liberals of that day because they regarded it as a threat against international cooperation.[27] The conference also called for universal disarmament and support for the technical assistance program sponsored by the United Nations.[28]

The repeated insistence by the National Council, and its sponsored offspring (like the Cleveland conference), on universal disarmament in the face of the well-known facts concerning the Korean War, is almost inexplicable. Throughout the decade of 1940 to 1950 these liberals had asserted unto monotony that once Hitler was defeated, Russia would become a friendly, democratic power, and with a dogged persistence they clung to this belief. But they could no longer sell this myth to the American people. Russian Communism had shown its true colors. It had launched a war in Korea in spite of its pretensions to peace and its membership in the United Nations. Nevertheless, the leadership of the National Council, cooperating with the liberal and radical journals like the *Nation* and *New Republic*, continued to call for disarmament, apparently in the expectation that if the West would disarm, Russia would do likewise. It is possible that some of these liberals actually believed this, but doubtful whether all of them did. More likely, they were interested in re-

26. The official report of this conference, *Christian Faith and International Responsibility*, was published in December, 1953.

27. The amendment, introduced into the Senate by Senator Bricker of Ohio early in 1953, provided that treaties and executive agreements with foreign powers should not become effective until they had been enacted by both houses of Congress. It also provided that when treaties involved matters normally regulated by the states, they must also be passed by all the states.

28. *National Council Outlook*, December 1953, p. 13.

moving any possible hindrance to the spread of communism in Asia, Eastern Europe, and even Africa.[29]

It is also important to note that the National Council acknowledged its involvement in the Cleveland meeting when it declared that it was committed to translating the resolutions of this conference into action. Not infrequently the National Council, following the example of its predecessor, would disown statements by such groups on the grounds that they were not made by the Council or its authorized representatives and did not therefore represent the position of the Council. Such a disclaimer in this case could not be made.

The National Council continued to oppose universal military training, which was finding popular support in the Korean War period. At the same time, it called for increased U.S. foreign aid to the underdeveloped nations of the world.

In 1955 a group of Protestant, Catholic, and Jewish leaders launched a crusade to have the United States enter into an expanded program for world development, human progress, and international peace. This group advocated also that this aid program be separated from the programs of military aid and be administered by private, non-governmental agencies so as to allay any suspicions of imperialistic aims by the United States. Although this interfaith gathering was not sponsored by the National Council, some of its leaders were present.[30]

In 1955 the Council took active steps looking toward more friendly relations between the United States and Russia by inviting representatives of the Russian Orthodox Church to visit this country in 1956 as part of a two-way visitation plan. The direction of the National Council's thinking was by 1955 quite evident in the pronouncements of its Division of Foreign Missions. At a meeting in Dayton, Ohio, in December 1955, this division called for a new vision of a single world mission of the entire Church of Jesus Christ.[31] There was no mention of this meeting in the National Council's records, but it was covered by the Communist *Daily Worker* of May 5, 1955. The reticence of the Council concerning activities of

29. It is worth remembering at this point that the liberals in Roosevelt's cabinet had insisted that if the Allied powers in World War II would only destroy the military might of Germany and Japan, then Russia would be free to disarm in safety. Germany and Japan, they stoutly maintained, had forced Russia to become militaristic.

30. *National Council Outlook*, November 1955, p. 17.

31. *Ibid.*, January 1956, p. 11.

its leaders can be easily understood in the light of the thrust of this gathering. To accomplish this goal the report insisted that there must be global reorganization of the entire missionary program. This meant that it was to become interracial and interdenominational in character so that the Gospel could be proclaimed in deed as well as in word. This not too subtle repudiation of the mission programs of the various churches was as fallacious as it was misleading. The evangelical missionaries of the preceding two centuries or more had never restricted their work to preaching the Gospel but had adorned their proclamation of the Word of God with appropriate deeds. This proposal for reorganizing the missions program was actually a call to substitute for the preaching of the Gospel a program of social up-lift stripped of any evangelical foundation. More, it was a thinly disguised move to replace Christianity with socialistic and communistic goals. The missionary work of the Christian church in this country was to become an arm of American radicalism for the realization of its international goals.[32]

In 1956 the National Council sent a delegation consisting of eight leaders to visit the Russian Orthodox church. The visit, which took place in March 1956, aroused a storm of controversy from evangelicals in the member churches and from political conservatives. Upon their return from Russia the leaders signed a statement in which they appraised their visit:

> The experience was predictable. We were received with generous hospitality. . . . There seems to be no interference with worship in the church. Congregations were large and devout in the relatively few available churches.[33]

But they admitted that there was a predominance of older people in these services and that no religious education of any kind was permitted outside the home.

This report declared that the Soviet government had discouraged any active persecution of the Christian church, but that it had increased the aggressiveness of scientific education as the means of ultimately eradicating religion in Russia. In other words the church

32. Among those at the Dayton meeting were Henry Knox Sherrill, bishop of the Episcopal church and first president of the National Council; Walter Van Kirk, Charles Parlin, Eugene Carson Blake, Franklin Clark Fry, Roswell P. Barnes, and Paul Anderson.

33. *National Council Outlook*, April 1956, p. 3.

in Russia in 1956 had more outer freedom than had formerly been the case, but was being confronted with a more subtle challenge.[34]

In June 1956 a delegation of Russian churchmen visited this country, representing four different churches in the Soviet Union under the leadership of Metropolitan Nicolai of Moscow, who was head of the Department of Foreign Affairs of the Russian Orthodox church. He was charged with being an agent of the Soviet Secret Police by segments of the American religious press.[35]

This exchange of visits by the Russian and American churchmen was by the liberal press widely heralded as a potentially great contribution to world peace. At the conclusion of the visit of the Russian delegation Eugene Carson Blake, president of the National Council, issued a statement, with the approval of the Russian delegation, to the effect that there was a general agreement on the nature of the peace that Christians seek and that freedom and justice are the most essential elements of such a peace.[36]

The optimism voiced by Eugene Carson Blake and other Council leaders that Christians "could hold the world together" was considerably chilled by the Russian invasion of Hunary later in 1956 and by the ensuing crisis in the Middle East. As Council president Dr. Blake sent a message congratulating President Eisenhower and strongly supporting his policy of acting through the United Nations in an effort to halt the Middle East crisis: "We welcome the prompt action by the United Nations to stop armed conflict in the Middle East and effect withdrawal of hostile forces." Blake urged the government to work through the United Nations to secure just and durable political settlements in the Middle East and to work for long-time solutions for the various economic and social issues of that region.

In regard to the Hungarian crisis, Blake spoke strongly in behalf of the action of the United Nations:

> We welcome the United Nations action condemning the use of Soviet military force to suppress the efforts of the Hungarian people to re-assert their rights. . . . The churches have steadfastly supported and sought to strengthen the United Nations. . . . We now welcome the increasing appreciation of the United Nations in our country and

34. For further comment on this, see *ibid.*, pp. 4-5, 6-7, 25-26.

35. See *Lutheran News*, September 7, 1964.

36. *National Council Outlook*, December 1956, p. 7.

194

abroad for its effective use of moral power as an operating force in a world where war has become an anachronism.[37]

Applaud as he might the good intentions of the Eisenhower administration and the "moral power" of the United Nations, Eugene Carson Blake failed to understand that Russia was not moved by similar moral considerations and that the Russian Church had little or no influence on the political and military decisions of the Kremlin.[38] Although the invasions of Hungary did not result in a general European conflagration as many had feared, it is questionable whether the Eisenhower administration or the United Nations had even a little influence on Soviet policy. During 1957 the National Council contented itself with the reaffirmation of its previous statements against militarism and in favor of disarmament and the extension of aid to underdeveloped areas. This year saw no momentous decisions being made or startling statements on world peace coming from the meetings of the council or its agencies. The fourth General Assembly meeting in St Louis in December, 1957 admitted that within its own ranks there was a difference of opinion on national defense and its relationship to the maintenance of peace.

> We hold that military might provides no sufficient security. While most of us think that our nation should maintain an adequate national defense, some of us feel that all armament is futile, but we all agree that even if there is a shield of arms, larger constructive work must be undertaken on many lines for peace with justice and freedom. Even when arming our nation, we believe, we must persistently seek workable agreements for universal inspection, controlled reduction and regulation of all armaments including nuclear weapons.[39]

The resolutions also admitted that questions were now arising as to the adequacy of American foreign policy to meet the demands imposed on it by recent technological advances. They urged the United States to assume a new initiative in diplomacy, making a maximum use of the United Nations and its agencies. In short, these resolutions called for a new diplomacy guided by moral and spiritual insights:

37. *Ibid.*, p. 22.

38. There is no evidence available that the Russian Church even tried to exert an influence on the Kremlin in the direction of peace.

39. *Ibid.*, January 1958, p. 21.

Our nation in partnership with others . . . should seize the present crisis as an opportunity to give an increased moral and spiritual leadership to the world. In this we must avoid self-righteousness and moralism, but develop domestic and foreign policies and practices which will give more compelling witness to our fundamental concerns as a nation for human rights and human values, for independence and interdependence, for freedom and responsibility, for justice and peace.[40]

On the surface these resolutions seemed to breathe a high-mindedness and Christian outlook for the problems confronting the Western world. But beneath these glittering and deceptive generalities there lay a thinly concealed demand for the application of a social, economic, and political radicalism intertwined with a suitable internationalism that in turn would reflect the radicalism that dominated this triennial session of the National Council.

In its *Message to the Churches of Christ in the U.S.A.*, the Fifth World Order Study Conference of the National Council of Churches, meeting in Cleveland, Ohio, in November 1958, gave additional emphasis to the challenge imposed upon the churches, the challenge to maintain peace in an era threatened by the spreading knowledge and application of atomic energy to nuclear weapons.[41] This message renewed the plea for universal disarmament, but insisted that it is a process involving spirit and will as well as conferences and treaties. Thus Christians must urge the government of the United States to show the way to international control of atomic energy and the suspension of nuclear tests under appropriate safeguards and inspection.

After praising the United Nations for its vitality and its contributions to peaceful settlements of international disputes and to change, the conference cautioned American Christians against resorting to drastic criticism of that international agency. Instead, Christians were to seek new ways to "defend, sustain, and enhance" that institution "as a diligent servant of the world's welfare."

This message to the churches of America at one point outdistanced recent declarations of the National Council. Christians were asked not only to support the United Nations with a new determination, but also to rethink the nature of the Cold War itself. Churchmen in this country were to reassess their attitudes to relations with coun-

40. *Ibid.*, p. 24.
41. *Ibid.*, December 1958, p. 20.

tries controlled by Communists. In such a review the Christian proceeds from his boundless faith in the overwhelming power of God's love and the ultimate triumph of God's righteousness. . . .[42] The Christian must formulate a philosophy of American foreign policy that reflects this boundless faith as well as the difficulties that confronted America in 1958. And here the message presented the ultimate suggestion, which clearly revealed the thinking of the Cleveland conference of the National Council:

> Stronger efforts should be made to break through the present stalemates and find ways of living with communist nations. Sometimes this is called "co-existence." But we are concerned with something more than the minimum meaning of the word. Our relationship with the communist countries should combine competition between ways of life and cooperation for limited objectives. . . . We should avoid the posture of general hostility to them (the communists) and cease the practice of continual lectures by our leaders.[43]

This message clearly exposes the yearnings of the Fifth World Order Conference. In spite of its admission of differences between the Western view of life and communism, there were grounds of accommodation that the West in general and the United States in particular must find to avoid nuclear war. Other sections of the message were directed toward the goal of making a case for communism; particularly, that it was not the mortal enemy of the West, as it had been pictured, and thus there was a basis for limited cooperation.[44]

The Cleveland conference took a decidedly optimistic view of the future:

> There is a real hope that new generations within the communist countries will be less fanatical in the ideological convictions and that they will be more preoccupied with peace, with economic self-being and with tentative experiments in cultural freedom than with attempts to dominate other nations. It is not to be expected that they

42. *Ibid.*, p. 21.

43. The insistence that our leaders must not lecture the Soviet government was a thinly disguised rebuke to John Foster Dulles and his foreign policy, which liberals in and out of the National Council delighted to call "brinkmanship." This rebuke is interesting in the light of the fact that Dulles had been the leader of the 1943 Cleveland conference and had drafted for that body the famous "Six Pillars of Peace."

44. *National Council Outlook,* December 1958, p. 21.

will formally renounce what we consider to be their errors. It is enough for the kind of living together described above if their emphasis and priorities change.[45]

At this point the basic error in the philosophy of the Cleveland conference and the National Council comes clearly into view. Communism with its atheistic assumptions is not truly in error. We of this country only think it is in error. We must change our viewpoint about the nature of communism, for world peace is more important than truth, and we must compromise our convictions in regard to Christian doctrine and practice to achieve world peace.

But this passage also reveals another popular liberal assumption, which will withstand neither logical analysis nor historical investigation. If the Communist countries would become more interested in promoting the economic well-being of their citizens, they would become less imperialistic in their interests. This is, to say the least, a curious assumption, especially so when we remember that these same liberals in the Council frequently charged capitalism with causing war because of its preoccupation with economic well-being. Apparently a capitalistic quest for well-being issues in war whereas communistic zeal for this goal reduces the chance of war. Such logic was vegetant at this conference on world order.

At its December 1958 meeting, held in Chicago, the General Board of the National Council affirmed the value of the work of the Fifth World Order Study Conference, but insisted that the conference did not speak for the Council. Nonetheless, the board called upon member denominations to study the text of the conference's message, thereby giving it a somewhat official, if not outright, approval.[46]

To disclaim that the conference spoke for the National Council was unconvincing, to say the least. The conference was convened by the Council's Division of Christian Life and Work and its Department of International Affairs. How much more official could it be? Six hundred delegates from the Council's thirty-three constituent members and selected by them attended the meeting.

There is no doubt that the National Council felt it was on the defensive regarding the Cleveland conference; it was actively seeking to retreat from the conference's findings:

45. *Ibid.*

46. *Ibid.*, January 1959, p. 17.

198

The Church should make it very clear that in publishing the findings of such a conference it is not speaking on the same level as when it gives voice to the Christian revelation that God entered human history in Jesus Christ in order that he might redeem the world and restore human life to its true center in himself. This is the unique Word that the Church must give the world, but this Word calls men to faithful obedience within all the callings of the world. The church must nurture that obedience and can best do so as it enables its members to take council together under the power and guidance of the Holy Spirit.[47]

The council sought to justify its equivocal support of the message of the Cleveland Conference by arguing that the report had been drawn up by political scientists, men experienced in governmental affairs, missionaries, and business leaders who placed their wisdom and experience at the service of the church and of the nation. Thus "it is folly to say that such men, many of whom have served in the very highest levels of government business and church circles ought not to speak about practical decisions."[48]

The inference that such a group was an organ through which the Holy Spirit would speak to the church and the world was theologically questionable and even absurd when we take a closer look at the composition of that Cleveland Conference. According to the Church League of America one half of the ministers attending this Cleveland Conference had been affiliated with one or more of the units of the apparatus charged with prompting the Communist line in this country. Twenty of the delegates had a record of having been affiliated with ten or more Communist front groups.[49] Thirty-five of the delegates had sponsored a report issued by the seven ministers who had visited Yugoslavia and been quite impressed with the Tito regime, even to the point of clearing him of the charges of being a dictator. Nineteen members of the conference were affiliated in some way either with the Fellowship of Reconciliation or with the members of the Church Peace Mission, both of which were regarded as quite radical. According to the Church League of America's study, thirty-one of the delegates had supported the fake peace campaign

47. *Ibid.*, January 1959, p. 17.

48. *Ibid.*

49. *The Record of the National Council of Churches*, rev. ed. (Wheaton, Ill., 1972), p. 76.

put on by the Communists.[50] The league also pointed out that, according to the records of the House Committee on un-American Activities, Edwin T. Dahlberg, active in the affairs of the National Council and one of the Cleveland delegates, was also a member of a committee of five that had initiated the formation of one of the front organizations in the Communist peace campaign, namely, the Committee for Peaceful Alternatives to the Atlantic Pact.[51]

Another member of this conference having an imposing record of radical interests and activities was A. J. Muste, who had a proclivity for conducting "peace talks and attending Communist conventions and rallies as an 'impartial observer.' "[52]

There can be no legitimate doubt that the membership of this Cleveland conference was so penetrated by Communist sympathizers that it was virtually a mouthpiece for the Communist philosophy.

The radical nature of the conference is clearly visible in its resolves and recommendations.[53] These resolutions insisted that the United States should show a greater willingness to solve international disputes through the organs of the United Nations, including the World Court, and should press for the creation of a permanent United Nations police force for the maintenance of international peace. The resolutions asked the United States to abolish its Selective Service System, which was to expire in June 1959. The conference called on the United States to extend trade and travel with Red China, Eastern Europe, and the Soviet Union. In the same manner and for the same reasons our government should encourage association and fellowship among the various professions and groups across the Iron Curtain, involving the exchange of firearms, students, and religious groups. The United States should evolve more seminars and conferences for social and other scientists from

50. *Ibid.*, p. 77.

51. *Ibid.*, p. 77. According to the Church League of America, this is not the only instance in which a president of the National Council played the role of founder in such a front organization.

Dahlberg had been chairman of the Department of Evangelism of the Federal Council and later held a similar post under the National Council. He had signed the open letter to President Franklin Roosevelt protesting the deportation of Harry Bridges and had also been a member of the Citizens Committee to free Earl Browder. Both of these men were known Communists.

52. For a complete account of the activities of Edwin Dahlberg and A. J. Muste, see Edgar C. Bundy, *Apostles of Deceit* (Wheaton, Ill., 1966.)

53. For the complete series of recommendations, see *The Record of the National Council of Churches* (1972), pp. 70-75.

the Soviet bloc and the West. Restrictions on the travel of Soviet visitors in this country should be lifted, and the report commended the efforts of the State Department to have the Soviet government lift its restrictions on American visitors to Russia. The United States was urged to encourage religious and philosophic dialogue above the level of political struggles: "In particular, all opportunities should be utilized through the World Council of Churches and other channels, for meetings of churchmen from the Soviet churches and the West."[54]

These suggestions were actually a call for the use of the church as a forum or sounding board so that the Communist philosophy and atheism could be given a hearing in the Christian West. These proposals were actually treason to the whole Western heritage and could hardly be viewed in any other light.

The resolutions and message issued by this Fifth World Order Study Conference at Cleveland in 1958, although not part of the National Council as such, certainly represented the thinking of its leadership and greatly influenced the future thinking and actions of the Council in regard to foreign and domestic affairs. They were the most radical statements yet to be made by either the Council or any meeting that it sponsored. All future policies accepted by the Council have their origins in this conference. From here on the National Council would assume an increasingly radical posture as to both domestic and foreign issues. The radicalism inherent in the Council from its inception would now blossom as it had not before.[55]

The humanism now triumphant within the National Council took steps in 1960 to ensure its triumph in national policy. On June 2, 1960, the General Board, by a vote of 69-3, issued a pronouncement stating that the United States must persevere in the quest for disarmament and insisting that the American government should support the United Nations as a forum for airing grievances, ratify the Genocide Convention, and restore its leadership among the nations of the world by supporting the Covenant of Human Rights.[56] To make it clear that these declarations meant that the General

---

54. *Ibid.*, p. 72.

55. The new tone became quite evident early in 1959 when the General Board by a vote of 64-0 (with one abstention) upheld the right and the duty of the churches and their councils to study and comment upon issues of human concern, no matter how controversial they may be (*Pronouncements of the NCC*, p. 14. 2-1).

56. *Ibid.*, pp. 25. 2-1 to 25. 2-3.

Board was no longer interested in maintaining the sovereignty of the government of this country and was much more concerned with the creation of some kind of a world government, the fifth General Assembly declared that American citizens should be prepared to subordinate their will to that of the United Nations.[57]

The National Council and the Economic Issues, 1950-1960

We have seen that Bishop Henry Knox Sherrill, the first president of the National Council of Churches, stated at the Cleveland General Assembly that the church must be involved with every aspect of national life. He repeated this at the Denver convention of the Council in 1952, and his successor Bishop William C. Martin approved this position. However, the Council and its various agencies became so engrossed in the area of foreign relations, the war in Korea, and the limitation of nuclear and other armaments that they did not exercise the kind of leadership in economic affairs during the Council's first five years that its many friends and equally numerous critics expected. But neither were the problems of labor and industry totally neglected. The Council on several occasions reaffirmed its belief in the right of collective bargaining and the right of the workers to a decent wage. Not until after the Korean War did the Council begin to give to domestic issues that same degree of attention that foreign policy had received.

In accordance with its developing philosophy, the General Board took part in the 1955 labor convention, which saw the amalgamation of the American Federation of Labor and the Congress of Industrial Organizations into a single labor organization.

In 1953 the National Council sponsored the publication of *Goals of Economic Life*, the first of a six-volume series titled *The Ethics of Society*, *Goals*, the result of a three-year study under a Rockefeller Foundation grant, was sired by a group selected by the Department of the Church and Economic Life. Its chairman was Charles P. Taft. Serving with him were Arthur Fleming, president of Ohio Wesleyan University, and Waldo Beach of the Duke Divinity School faculty. The volume had fifteen authors, among whom were Kenneth Boulding of the University of Michigan, Ralph Linton of Yale, and John C. Bennett and Reinhold Niebuhr of the Union Theological Seminary faculty in New York.

The general thesis for this first volume was that welfare eco-

57. *Triennial Report of the National Council of Churches*, 1960, p. 234.

nomics (the welfare state under another name) was the best, if not the only, solution to the problem of finding a balance between the individual and the economic group. Underlying this thesis was another one: free enterprise could not achieve this balance. Collectivism, at least in the shape of the welfare state, was the coming form of economic organization and activity. Though implicit rather than explicit, these assumptions formed the context of this work. Kenneth Boulding insisted that the economically progressive society knows that poverty can be abolished only through increased productivity. This led to the conclusion (which he did not draw in obvious terms) that society must organize itself in such a way that production is for the elimination of poverty rather than for profit.

The Communist overtones of this kind of thinking were too obvious to ignore. The leadership of the Council promptly took appropriate action. In October 1954, by an overwhelming favorable vote of 77-4, the General Board endorsed a four-thousand-word statement, "Basic Christian Principles and Assumptions of Economic Life." In this the board apparently tried to offset some of the severe criticism aimed against its earlier statements. It now announced that free democratic institutions are superior to other forms of political and economic organization and that it was a misconception to regard socialization as an easy road to economic justice, since looking to the state to correct every economic evil simply creates its own evils.[58]

But it is equally false to believe that a maximum of individual freedom will of itself create a good society. Thus it is a major responsibility of the church to conserve and promote justice and freedom. It must accept a prophetic role and call on men to recognize the meaning of God's lordship over their economic activities since all natural resources are a gift from God and every form of ownership must be scrutinized so that it may not distort the purpose of God's creation. Rejecting the union of political and economic power as a dangerous road to follow, the statement asserted that Christians should strive for a minimum standard of living for all.

The most important intrusion of the National Council into the economic and industrial life of the nation during the 1950s occurred in April 1956 when its Department of the Church and Economic Life sponsored a conference at Pittsburgh in conjunction with the major Protestant denominations of the nation. By using this approach the

58. *National Council Outlook*, October 1954, p. 3. For the complete text of this statement, see p. 14.

Council was resorting to a device used occasionally by the Federal Council, generally for the purpose of increasing the cooperation of other ecumenical groups with its program. There is no doubt that the National Council had this purpose in mind. It is equally obvious that it had another end in view—using these jointly sponsored conferences to share the burden of making radical pronouncements by insisting that these conferences did not speak for the Council.

This Pittsburgh conference followed the usual approach. It drew up a *Message to the Churches* setting forth its economic philosophy. This message offered hope to the world and a challenge to the Christian conscience.[59] It stated:

> We are entering a new age in the history of mankind. For the first time in human experience it appears possible that enough can be produced to meet the basic needs of man. We may refer to this new period as an age of abundance in contrast with past ages of economic scarcity. The promises of this economy are great but its perils are so real that we cannot evade the challenge which this age brings to the Christian conscience. . . .[60]

The underlying assumption and only partially concealed implication of this opening paragraph is rather clear. The challenge of making this abundance available to all is so great that our economic system must be restored to meet it. It was a call to collectivism. Free enterprise could not meet it. That free enterprise had failed was seen in the fact that even in this country there were still pockets of poverty. But the Christian conscience must look beyond America's borders to other areas of the world. Christians must act accordingly: "Under God, this age of abundance, bringing a rich experience of interdependence to men and nations, can be an age in which the church of Christ undertakes its tasks with new urgency."[61]

Specifically the Pittsburgh conference urged the United States government to assume the lead in launching a drive for an economic development fund to aid backward countries. Two to five billion dollars was the goal. These funds were to be made available without any military or political strings attached. The whole program would be administered by some international agency under the guidance of the United Nations. This conference was actually

59. *Ibid.*, p. 3.
60. *Ibid., May 1956, p. 3.*
61. *Ibid.*, p. 3.

204

asking this country to take the lead in creating such a fund (and probably providing most of it) without exercising control of any kind as to how it would be used. Control would belong to the United Nations alone. The gift of such a blank check could and probably would mean that it would be used for the creation of Communist states in Africa and elsewhere. Free enterprise was to be used for financing regimes friendly to communism.

It is little wonder that the National Council preferred to have an allegedly unaffiliated conference make such a plea. When popular opposition against the program would reach white heat, the Council could solemnly announce that the Pittsburgh conference did not speak for the Council.

The 1956 Pittsburgh conference resulted in a new crusade by the National Council to achieve social justice in this country. Involved in this program was a coordinated effort to provide material for use by local churches to help their members understand the meaning of the Christian faith and its principles in their economic activity. This material covered problems in international economic relationships, foreign trade and aid and Soviet economic competition, and the problems of surpluses and their distribution. Through its Department of the Church and Economic Life the Council concerned itself with such issues as the extension of the minimum wage to agriculture and other groups of workers, and federal aid to agriculturally depressed areas. This department also was able to have its executive director selected as a member of the newly created Clergy Advisory Committee of the American Motors Corporation and of the United Automobile Workers.[62] It also listed other religious groups with which it cooperated such as the Ecumenical Institute, which had a reputation for being a decidedly radical agency.

The Department of the Church and Economic Life counted as its most important activity direct involvement in the prolonged and bitter steel strike of 1959-60. Calling upon representatives from the churches, labor, industry, government, and education, the department authored *The Ethical Implications of the Dispute in the Steel Industry*, an in-depth study of this nationwide strike, which was proving exceedingly detrimental both to the steelworkers and to the general public. By 1960 the department had brought out three new studies in addition to the earlier multivolume series on various economic issues and ethics. By its own admission it had issued a

62. *Triennial Report*, 1960, pp. 140-43.

series of policy statements and pronouncements covering most of these same topics.[63]

To give witness to its vital interests in settling the steel strike, the General Board authorized the president of the National Council to inform the principal parties to the labor dispute that it, the General Board, would be willing to help the two parties reach a settlement.[64]

There can be no doubt that the Council through its agencies was using every means at its command to bring its liberal-radical economic philosophy to the attention of as many congregations of the constituent denominations as it could. The study ended on the optimistic note that this program was meeting with a new success and that the climax would come in 1962 with a meeting of the Fourth National Conference on the Church and Economic Life, which, hoped the Council, would bring about a new era of cooperation between the National Council and the denominations, an era marked by the realization of these economic goals.

The National Council and Social Welfare[65]

Although the problems of social welfare had always engaged the serious attention of the Federal Council of Churches, they loomed larger in the thinking of the National Council. Countless discussions on social welfare were held and as many plans hatched for dealing with it. This greater attention was partly due to the fact that the National Council possessed a more extensive machinery for conducting such studies and formulating plans for solving these social issues. But it also was due to the feeling among its leadership that the very prosperity that swept many segments of the American people after World War II placed a stigma upon the nation for allowing any social or economic inequalities to exist. Such prosperity must not allow poverty to coexist with it. But even these two factors do not fully explain the continued emphasis the National Council placed on social welfare. Lurking behind them was another and very important force at work. Social welfare planning and activity offered an excellent vehicle for the National Council to give a practical and ef-

63. *Ibid.*

64. *A Summary of Resolutions of the National Council of Churches: 1951-1961.*

65. In treating the National Council I will use a format different from that used for the Federal Council; the National Council gave different weight to some of the major concerns they held in common.

206

fective expression to its radical social theory under the guise of simply applying the Christian ethic to specific social problems, some of which were and still are a true concern of evangelical Christianity and others of which are not and must not be.

The note that the National Council must be a socially sensitive institution not only was sounded by Bishop Henry Knox Sherrill, its first president, but was reiterated in one form or another by every successor to that office and in the affirmations of the General Board and the triennial assemblies. There was a general agreement among its leadership that "a fourth great emphasis in the National Council, therefore, is on the church as socially sensitive to all the human conditions bound up with the missionary spirit. . . ."[66]

Social sensitivity received expression in many ways, not a few of which became very controversial. On November 10, 1952, a letter, signed by Walter P. Reuther, president of the United Auto Workers; John Ramsey, public relations director of the Organizing Committee of the CIO; and by Ted Silvey, secretary of the National CIO Community Services Committee, stated that these men had worked closely with the Department of the Church and Economic Life of the National Council and that "labor and the Churches should stand shoulder to shoulder in the fight for justice and brotherhood in industrial economic life." The letter frankly asked for contributions for this purpose and stated that checks should be made payable to the National Council of Churches.[67] This frank admission of a close relationship between the National Council and the United Auto Workers greatly compromised the Council. Many felt its leadership was much more friendly to the cause of labor than it was sympathetic to the problems confronting the businessman.

The National Council and Race Relations

During this decade the problem of race relations became the overriding issue for the Council. It took precedence even over the problems of labor.

The 1954 decision that ended legalized segregation in our schools gave great impetus to the crusade to end racial discrimination generally. The National Council, following the lead of the Federal

66. *National Council Outlook*, April 1951, p. 16.

67. *The Record of the National Council of Churches*, p. 72. The fact that this letter was also sent out on stationery of the Council caused much comment; it was speculated that the National Council, in its zeal for social welfare, might welcome the voice of the even more radical labor groups.

Council, had already taken a strong stand against this practice in every area of American life. In 1952 the General Board issued a very strong indictment of segregation and urged member churches "to cooperate with the organizations in the formulation and execution of a communitywide plan to eliminate patterns of segregation."[68] The suggestion that the churches should work with other groups to eliminate the pattern of segregation in American life is important. Such cooperation necessarily meant an involvement of the various denominations in programs devised by liberal and radical elements that either were strongly in sympathy with the Communist philosophy or were actually voicing the Communist party line in this country. Many of these radicals were quick to see that they could use agitation against segregation as an aid in fomenting revolution here. It is difficult to escape the conclusion that some of the National Council leaders were fully aware of the revolutionary nature of the movement with which they were willing to cooperate.

Even in 1952 the thinking of the Supreme Court was evident. In control of left-wing liberalism, the Court was headed in the direction of eliminating segregation at every level of American public education—from kindergarten to graduate school. Although the Council leadership was anxious to give the drive against segregation a religious sanction, it was also willing to work with the enemies of the Gospel to achieve a goal that was at once religious and humanistic.

And even though the National Council raised its voice in vigorous opposition to the union of church and state, the issue it felt was involved in President Truman's plan to send an ambassador to the Vatican, the Council showed an amazing lack of concern over its own denial of the very important principle it was so strenuously urging on the President of the United States. In the area of desegregation, as well as in peace and disarmament, the Council repeatedly obliterated the wall of separation between the two institutions.

Meeting in Evanston, Illinois, a few days after the Supreme Court announced its decision in the segregation cases,[69] the General Board hailed them with delight and called them a milestone

68. *National Council Outlook*, September 1952, pp. 9-10.

69. *Brown* v. *Board of Education of Topeka* (347 U.S. 483) and *Bolling* v. *Sharpe* (347 U.S. 497). These two decisions brought legally enforced segregation in the public school to an end, but they did not actually sanction much of what took place in the area of integration in the public schools during the next twenty years.

in the achievement of human rights. The board recognized that carrying out the Court's historic ruling would involve many problems and said that "implementing this decision will test the goodwill and discipline of the people in many communities." The board added:

We know that the churches and individual Christians will continue to exert their influence and leadership to help the authorized agencies in the several communities to bring about a complete compliance with the decision of the Supreme Court. The law of neighborliness is the great guide available to Christians as they deal with this situation in their local communities.[70]

Christians as such, as well as the church as a corporate body, were to join in the liberal crusade to achieve a wholehearted popular compliance with this decision. It would seem that the National Council was on the verge of taking a very dangerous step, namely, becoming an agency of the state for the enforcement of this particular decision, which happened to occupy a high place on the list of liberal priorities. We shall see that after 1960 the Council took a quite different attitude toward its role in law enforcement in areas where many liberals were violently opposed to such participation.

The mind of the Council became even more clear when in September 1954 the General Board by a vote of 77 to 4 (one abstention) issued a policy statement that condemned not only racial but other kinds of group discrimination and then criticized the great contrast between the rich and the poor in American society.[71]

In this conjunction of racial discrimination and poverty a pattern was emerging that increasingly characterized the position not only of the National Council, but also of liberalism in general. In fact, the National Council was merely pursuing a policy dear to liberal secular movements for a number of years, one originating in the platforms of the Communist party in this country and now being owned by the Council. This curious adoption of Communist and left-wing programs for its own use makes it rather clear that much of the Council's social and economic thinking was more than a little conditioned by sources other than the Bible.

Early in 1955 the National Council, through its General Board, began to show a renewed interest in the plight of the American

70. *National Council Outlook*, June 1954, p. 8.

71. *Pronouncements of the NCC*, pp. 12.1-1 to 12.1-5.

Indian. By a vote of 71 to 0 the board resolved that each Indian tribe should be assured of its right to preserve, to the extent consistent with the general welfare, its own cultural identity.[72] The resolution called on the federal government to enter upon very careful social planning in those cases in which it would terminate its special relationship with a tribe so that such termination would not in practice result in the abandonment of that tribe.[73]

In a burst of enthusiasm over the civil rights movement in 1956, the General Board authorized the president of the Council to send a communication through Martin Luther King to the people of Montgomery, Alabama. In it the Council expressed its appreciation of "their influence on Christian discipline which has significantly mitigated the community tension in the situation arising from the problem of segregation in public transportation."[74]

In 1957 the campaign of the National Council in behalf of the Negro took a new and even more controversial turn. Its Department of Racial and Cultural Relations published a pamphlet or reading list, "The Negro American," that caused a furor. The list included several books dealing with sex that used vile language, plus a number of recommended titles that were either by Communist authors or by those affiliated with various Communist-front organizations. Apparently the Council had come to the conclusion that communism offered a stronger argument for the abolition of segregation than did the Scriptures.

In October 1957 the General Board commended churches and individuals who were working for desegregation in the schools. It also endorsed a telegram that Eugene Carson Blake, Council president, had sent to President Eisenhower commending him for his action in sending troops to Little Rock, Arkansas, to aid in enforcing desegregation of the public schools there.[75] That constitutional scholars viewed Eisenhower's action as seriously infringing on constitutional limitations on the federal government

72. *The Record of the National Council of Churches*, pp. 63-64.

73. *Ibid.*, p. 19.1-1. This resurgence of interest in the plight of the Indians was to have a nearly tragic conclusion at Wounded Knee, South Dakota, in 1972.

74. *A summary of the resolutions of the National Council of Churches: 1951-1961*, p. 24. This had reference to the efforts by Martin Luther King and others to end segregation on the buses of Montgomery, one of the earliest of these efforts. The irony of this message lay in the fact that the statements of the National Council, many keen observers felt, had helped to bring on the crisis.

75. *Ibid.*, pp. 17, 311.

had little or no effect upon either the National Council's General Board, or the Council's president, Blake.

At its St. Louis General Assembly, held late in 1957, the Council continued its agitation against segregation. It declared that this practice was "contradictory to the teachings of Jesus" and that the majority of the communions in the Council had spoken out against a racial exclusion policy.

> The General Assembly of the National Council is grateful for the effective Christian witness which many churches and individual Christians are bearing in communities disturbed by tension and confusion in connection with the problems of desegregation. We join them in urging responsible local community action and obedience to the mandates of the Supreme Court. . . . We assure the churches and our fellow Christians in these agonizing situations of our sympathy and prayers of our resolution to assist them in ways that may be helpful, including continuing practical support when they suffer hardship as a result of their loyalty to Christian principles.[76]

During 1958 the National Council itself made no more declarations on the issue of race; it preferred, rather, to work through the Fifth World Order Study Conference, which met in Cleveland in November of that year. The Council continued agitating in behalf of desegregation, but paused to note the swelling chorus of criticism of its declarations and pronouncements on race. As in the areas of economic issues and foreign policy, the Council preferred to work through conferences that were not an integral part of the Council so that it could disown any pronouncements that would cause undue criticism.

The Council maintained its appeal for desegregation in 1959 but did so on a noticeably lower key, probably in the hope that it would be less offensive to the American public within and without the institutional church. By the end of this decade the Council was facing a torrent of criticism, to which it was becoming increasingly sensitive.[77]

In its message for Race Relations Sunday in 1959, written by Dr. Edwin T. Dahlberg, The Council observed:

The Supreme Court decree outlawing segregation in the public

76. *National Council Outlook*, January 1958, p. 24.

77. See chapter 8 for the National Council and its critics.

schools came like a burst of sunlight and hope to millions of people who had been denied justice and equality in education. Now the clouds of fear and violence have rolled over the entire American scene; they darken our efforts toward integrated housing, education, recreation, industry, and religion.[78]

Alarmed over this growing violence and fear, Dahlberg asked, "What is the matter?" He had, however, answered his own question, perhaps without realizing it. For he had admitted that ending segregation in the schools was only the prelude to terminating it in every segment of American life, particularly in those very areas where segregation meant more to the white people of this country than it did in the area of education.

The Council ended the first decade of its existence with a series of confirmations regarding race relations. These simply reiterated its openly stated position and solidified its previous stand.

The Council and Welfare Programs

In the area of aid to the needy and minority groups the National Council showed an interest that probably went beyond that displayed by the Federal Council. In so doing it virtually accepted the concept of the welfare state, which had long been urged on the government by various social planners.

Historically in this country, as in England, France, and Communist Russia, the concept of the welfare state had been viewed as a kind of secret weapon that could be used to destroy not only the American morale, but also such institutions as the home and the church. Lester Frank Ward, generally regarded as the father of American sociology, undoubtedly had these aims in mind. He became the inspiration for his followers, who developed these aims in their writings and social planning, particularly in the New Deal of Franklin D. Roosevelt and the Fair Deal of Harry S. Truman.[79]

The National Council's growing interest in social welfare was directly the result of its increasingly identifying the philosophy of democracy with the Christian view of life. This meant that the

78. *National Council Outlook*, January 1959, p. 22.

79. In the Roosevelt era Harry Hopkins was the leading architect of the welfare state. But with the creation of the Department of Health, Education, and Welfare, Lester Frank Ward found a much more formidable champion, which had both the money and the legal power to carry out his policies.

Council must inevitably become a champion of those policies in our national life that reflected this democratic outlook and must oppose those that contradicted this humanistic approach to the issues of the day.

In 1955 the National Council, through its Department of Social Welfare, sponsored the First National Conference on Social Welfare in Cleveland, Ohio. Some fifteen hundred attended, including some of the leaders in the sociology field. Its purpose was to examine the broad problems in this area of our national life and to suggest broad avenues of approach to achieve solutions. Additionally, it was to break the ground for future activity rather than to plan specific programs of action.

A second such conference was held at Atlantic City, New Jersey, in May 1957. It took a positive stand in regard to the relationship which it felt should exist between the churches and the welfare problem. Social welfare is an integral part of the ministry of the church, not an option.[80] Consistent with this philosophy of social welfare, the conference urged that the National Council and its constituent members enter into constructive relations with secular welfare agencies in achieving common tasks and realizing commonly held goals.

By 1960 the Department of Social Welfare was able to spell out just what these two conferences on welfare had really meant in their pronouncements, and called for a greatly expanded ministry in this area:

> More national and regional consultations are needed to explore the role of the church in meeting urgent demands for foster homes, retirement homes, treatment centers for the mentally retarded and emotionally disturbed children, halfway houses for alcoholic and narcotic addicts, and services for unmarried parents.[81]

This report insisted that the problems involved were so great that they could be solved only on an interdenominational level. Only the National Council through its Department of Social Welfare could undertake a full-scale analysis of the social, economic, and cultural trends and suggest the problems that would emerge as a result. It would seem that the National Council was interested in creating roles of sufficient magnitude to ensure its own future

80. *Triennial Report.* 1957, p. 123.
81. *Ibid.,* 1970, p. 139.

usefulness and to increase further the dependence of the denominations on its centralized planning.[82]

In his 1960 report to the National Council reviewing a decade of its history, Roy G. Ross paid a great deal of attention to the social witness of the Council in race relations, economic justice, and the broad problem of human welfare:

> The church is inevitably concerned about undue concentration of economic power which stifles individual and small group initiative . . . about distribution of the benefits of our economic system so that all who participate are compensated; about irrational discrimination in matters of age, race and creed. . . .[83]

Secretary Ross was not unaware of the meaning of what he was writing. The Council was to undertake reformation of every aspect of American society in terms of the liberal gospel, which the Council claimed as its own and which it was urging on the various churches, members, and nonmembers. It was, he candidly admitted, a tremendous task. Basically it called for a change from a concept of missions (the traditional view of missionary endeavor) to that of mission—the total mission of the church.[84] It involved a general reorganization both of the National Council in its missionary program and of its constituent members in their respective programs. Ross added a veneer of theological urgency to this call for a crusade to achieve a totally secular liberal society:

> The churches today are called to a renewed task of redemptive endeavor. The form of the endeavor will be revealed only as we seek to obey the leadership of the Spirit. The task is as great as that which confronted our forefathers at the time of the Reformation. . . .
> Only a new surge of intelligent and obedient devotion can answer our present apostasy and the rising tide of paganism. Let us therefore determine to renew and deepen our insight concerning His will for our lives and our social order through study and prayer. Let us bear a more sure and complete witness to our Oneness in Jesus Christ. Let us utilize the National Council of Churches in the fullest

82. It might not be amiss to point out at this juncture that the Denver Triennial of 1960 created a General Policy and Strategy Committee entrusted with the task of initiating necessary policies and programs and to act as a clearinghouse for the operation of the Council in all of its various arenas of interest (see *Triennial Report*, 1960, pp. 88-89).

83. *Ibid.*, p. 17

84. *Ibid.*, p. 21.

possible measure for proclaiming that Jesus Christ is the Living Lord of all of life.[85]

The theology of this appeal is elusive, hardly biblical, and would serve as a very, very poor substitute for that theology the Reformers rediscovered in their struggles to reform the church. The Council's theology for 1960 was actually nothing more than an appeal to spiritualism with "spirit" being undefined even though capitalized.

Just how this program was successfully to stay the rising tide of apostasy and paganism, which the Council leaders professed to see, still remained to be explained. The proposal was little more than an attempt to offset the paganism of the decade with a highly refined spiritual paganism having almost nothing in common with historic Christianity but much in common with the materialism the Council sought to combat. The decade beginning in 1961 would put this social philosophy to its most severe test to date, and it would be found wanting. The Council's pretense to spirituality would be brutally swept aside as it yielded to the demands of a revolutionary era with scarcely a whimper, yet the while piously protesting that it was making the Gospel relevant to an age addicted both to revolution to destroy the establishment and to drugs, sex, and rock as the acme of its cultural aspirations.

Some inkling of the nature of the Council's envisioned social policies can be seen in the action of the 1960 Triennial Assembly, which resolved that

> the churches be urged to work for the availability of adequate public assistance for all needy people, the elimination of state and local residence requirements for public assistance and the replacement of federal aid for certain categories of people by a simple program based solely on need.[86]

Although the Council had not ceased to be interested in the problems of alcoholic beverages, it had paid to them less attention than did the Federal Council. However, by 1958 the problem of alcoholism could no longer be avoided or treated with indifference. The threat drunkenness posed for the nation was serious, so much so that even the liberals could no longer evade its implications for their own utopian aspirations.

85. *Ibid.*, p. 30.

86. *A Summary of Resolutions of the National Council of Churches, 1951-1961*, p. 31.

Hence, in February 1958 the General Board turned its attention from other goals to alcoholism and issued a statement declaring its belief that "the use of alcoholic beverages is a serious threat to the health, happiness and welfare of many people and to the stability of families and communities.[87] While noting that alcoholics are "persons in need of diagnosis, understanding, guidance and treatment," the board also pointed out their "need of pastoral care and the divine love which the church can bring them."

The basic assumption of this statement was clearly expressed in the statement that alcoholism was an affliction, a kind of sickness, that required treatment. But in no place was there any recognition that alcoholism is sin, a particular form of sin. Thus the treatment that the Council prescribed for this illness was both medical and educational:

> Alcohol education in the churches should cover all aspects of the use of alcohol, drinking, drunkenness, and alcoholism—and should be conceived in long-range terms. . . . Each individual should be helped to an understanding of the problems arising from alcoholism and an appreciation of the church's role as a redemptive fellowship in the lives of alcoholics and their families.[88]

The Council then offered its latest solution for this continuing problem. It affirmed its belief in a vigorous program of continuing education based on the findings of theological and scientific research "as the necessary means for developing attitudes toward and making decisions on the use of alcohol." It explained that such education, to be an effective social control, ought to be motivated by a moral concern to which all religious groups in our country should make their contribution.

But the National Council was trapped by its own sociological theories, which were deeply influenced by psychological determinism. The alcohol problem, observed the Council, could not be studied in isolation for it was related to other social problems such as poverty, disease, bad housing, and inferior education. Thus any cure must include improvement in these conditions as well as provide mental health clinics. In general, the Council shunned any commitment to the legal prohibition of the use of alcohol, but it

87. *National Council Outlook*, April 1958, p. 8.

88. *Ibid.*, p. 8.

did endorse the concept that the general public must be protected from those whose drinking endangers others. The legal controls relative to beverage alcohol should be aimed to reduce its use.

In 1959 the Council evinced a radical upturn in its social thought in at least two areas. The first concerned the issue of capital punishment. Although neither the Council nor its General Board issued any specific pronouncement against capital punishment, the tone of its publications became increasingly hostile toward this practice. The editorial staff of the *National Council Outlook* traced the growing opposition of the denominations and local councils of churches to this particular form of administering justice in the United States. Further, the *Outlook* created the unmistakable impression that it was contrary to the biblical ethic and did not actually deter the commission of serious crimes.[89]

The thinking of the Council on another social issue surfaced also in 1959 when one of its more vocal leaders, Mrs. Cynthia Wedel (later the first woman president of the Council), took up the cudgels for women's equality in the church.[90] Although the Council took no formal action in this area during the rest of this decade, a pattern of thought was emerging that would produce fruit in the life of the nation and of the council during the 1960s.

The National Council and Labor, 1951-1960

Although the National Council increasingly yielded to the demands of the radical nature of its theology and social philosophy in most areas of American life, it showed an unexpected and peculiar reluctance to become unreservedly the voice of labor as had the Federal Council after 1930. The National Council was not uninterested in the problems confronting labor and continued to lend a sympathetic ear and voice to its more legitimate demands. But at the same time it began to take a more critical attitude toward the activities of the leaders of the unions and their dubious policies. The Council was not always consistent in its attitudes or policies toward labor, but this curious trend is nevertheless visible.

The National Council continued the policy of the Federal Council in issuing annual Labor Day messages. But as there was little more

89. *National Council Outlook*, March 1959, pp. 21-22.

90. *Ibid.*, May 1959, pp. 18.

to be said on this subject, most of the messages were seldom more than reaffirmations of the stand of its predecessor.[91]

On November 10, 1952, the Council allowed its name to be used in a letter sent out by Walter Reuther and other labor leaders. The missive declared that the Council's Department of the Church and Economic Life should stand shoulder to shoulder with the unions in the fight for economic justice; it did not spell out the details of what this cooperation with labor might mean. The implication of this budding alliance was clearly evident for the business and industrial leadership of the nation to see.

But the National Council was interested more in sponsoring conferences that would call for the more radical changes in labor's role than in taking the lead itself. In its 1954 Labor Day message it contented itself with the observation that collective bargaining is a significant part of the American worker's Christian experience, and with commending workers who exercised the right to organize into labor unions to obtain a decent living and a measure of economic security for themselves and their families. This was hardly a radical departure from previous messages, but it did conceal the basic economic and social philosophy of the Council from public view.

By 1957 the Council had, on the surface at least, lost some of its earlier enthusiasm for the unionization of American labor. It issued a pronouncement on the appalling corruption that had been recently revealed in the labor movement as well as in management, and urged both groups to correct the specific abuses brought to light.

In 1958 the General Board reaffirmed the right of employees to organize for collective bargaining, but coupled this with the recognition of the right of employers likewise to organize for the purpose of bargaining collectively with labor. Then the board reminded both groups that the interest of the consuming and general public should be protected against possible collusion in such mutual organization for collective bargaining.[92]

At first blush one is surprised at the General Board granting that employers and management had such a right; indeed, one finds it inexplicable in the light of the Council's general and economic

91. In its first message for Labor Day 1951 it paid tribute to the labor movement for its historic flight against injustice which had been carried on against enormous odds and often with little means except devotion and courage (*The Record of the National Council of Churches*, rev. 1972).

92. *Pronouncements of the NCC.* p. 10. 1-1.

218

philosophy. But we must remember that by 1958 the Council was coming under an increasingly severe public attack for its alleged communistic affiliations and sympathies. Although the records of the Council seldom indicate why such actions were taken, it seems certain that this constant criticism was having some effect. There at least existed the necessity of admitting that management did have some rights under the law and that if the right of labor to organize is part of its Christian experience, it would be indelicate, if not actually contradictory, to deny such an experience to employers.

In 1958 the Council turned its attention to the problem of unemployment, which was termed a basic injustice against each person and family suffering from it. The Council reiterated its 1954 affirmation that "large scale unemployment or continued unemployment for any considerable number of persons able and willing to work is intolerable. It ordinarily indicates defects in or relaxation of social economic safeguards."[93]

Starting from the dubious hypothesis that unemployment is a concern of the church, the Council then pleaded for governmental intervention as the solution to the problem. It even took the next step of broadly outlining the best method of solving it:

> Social responsibility has been accepted and should be maintained for adequate unemployment compensation. At most it will require an increase in the amount, duration and coverage of unemployment compensation now available under the present laws. Here both the federal government and the state governments bear a responsibility. We urge the desirability of agreement on a standard of compensation which bears a fixed relationship to both a desired minimum and the wages paid at the time the worker was laid off.[94]

Next the Council boldly suggested that the state governments extend the duration of such coverage by fifty percent, then gave some additional unasked-for advice to the federal government:

> The government should give continued consideration to both short run and long term measures to restore and maintain employment levels. The government has a responsibility to use, when needed as stabilizers and other aids, the vast resources available in its fiscal,

93. *Ibid.*, p. 28. 1-1.
94. *Ibid.*, p. 28. 1-1.

monetary, public works and other economic powers. It also reminded the government that these powers should be used with
due regard to their effect upon the economies of other powers.[95]

This counsel was nothing less than a thinly concealed hint that it
should invoke the economic theories of John Maynard Keynes, theories designed to lead to socialism—and to war.[96]

The economic picture in this country in 1959 prompted the National Council to issue through its General Board a pronouncement
on the ethical issues in industrial relations, particularly with the
problem of the responsible use of power. Admitting that big business, big labor, and big government were necessary features of
contemporary technological society, the message averred that
such bigness "tends to enlarge the powers of men to act for good or
evil." From the Christian viewpoint the issue could be resolved
by answering this query: Is the power associated with bigness used
in a responsible manner?

> Collective bargaining is one of the major areas in which this respon-
> sibility on the part of labor and management is exercised. It is one
> of the main means by which a free society preserves the free mar-
> ket place. Failure in social responsibility by labor or management
> means that the public may express its will through government in-
> tervention. This creates a dilemma of real ethical importance. On
> the one hand, it is well recognized that government intervention
> can lead to the impairment of freedom and responsibility in the
> economy. On the other, only government has the authority to rep-
> resent the total public concern. In its role as the whole people
> acting together, government can make a positive and fruitful con-
> tribution in the just reconciliation of interests of all the elements in
> the economy.[97]

This seemingly neutral stand by the Council regarding government intervention in collective bargaining can mislead the unwary. The Council, aware of the rising chorus of criticism against
its policies and alleged Communist sympathies, felt obliged to
make these pronouncements to conceal its basic sympathy with
labor. That this was the case is evidenced by the fact that the Council almost never in its history has found a major labor dispute that

95. *Ibid.*

96. Keynes himself was aware of the logical conclusion to his theory.

97. *"Ethical Issues in Industrial Relations of Concern to Christians,"* Pronouncements of the
NCC, p. 21. 2a.

did not warrant governmental intervention plus its own sympathetic support.

That its sympathy lay with labor in 1959 can be easily detected in this same pronouncement. After admitting that wage increases resulting from collective bargaining may bring a price increase, the Council went on to explain its view of the relationship between wages and prices:

> The process of fixing prices includes many complex factors in addition to labor costs. This can lead to widespread misunderstanding particularly by the general public. For example, in collective bargaining labor is generally expected to explain and defend its wage demands before both management and public opinion. In collective bargaining there is no similar expectation that management account to labor or to the public for factors other than wages that lead it to price increases. . . .
>
> However, we have here an ethical problem which should be taken fully into account; namely, that labor which does not share directly in price setting is often held responsible by the general public for price increases whenever wages are increased.[98]

Although some truth dwelt in this contention, this statement was sufficiently misleading to prevent the Christian public from gaining the necessary insight into the issue to lead it to higher ethical practices, as the Council suggested.

The Council expressed its indignation at the recent revelations by committees of Congress charged with the task of investigating corruption in both labor and management. The unethical practices that had been brought to light reflected, said the Council, the unhealthy moral condition of American society. It summoned the people of the various churches to hold fast to a sense of responsibility for high integrity in their own lives and in the affairs of economic organizations, especially their own.[99]

The Council finally made several suggestions for safeguarding the rights of labor union members: periodic reviews of the provisions requiring union membership as a condition of employment, protection of union members from abuses through provisions in the union constitutions, and free and regular elections of union officials.

The final major Council pronouncement of the 1950s on social wel-

98. *Ibid.*, 21. 2b. In the board the vote for this pronouncement was 73 for, 16 against, and 12 abstentions.

99. *Ibid.*

fare concerned the role of the churches in supporting a policy of national health care. The Council stopped short of advocating a national health service like Medicare, but was obviously anticipating this kind of service. Advocating the expanson of prepayment programs for medical care, the Council said:

> With the rising cost of medical care, serious or extended illness has imposed economic burdens which are beyond the capacity of many individuals and families to meet from current income. There is need for churches and church members to study the economic aspects of health services. . . . Flexibility on the part of all health professions and the public, willingness to try new methods, cooperative planning, analysis and evaluation are required to meet the needs of the people.[100]

In the areas of social welfare, labor, and health services the National Council of Churches, from 1951 to 1960, was obviously heading toward increased governmental activity and intervention. Occasional criticism of specific federal actions and programs could not obscure this. As a result, its pronouncements, as in the economic arena, increasingly occasioned severe criticism of its radical social philosophy and the actions recommended.

The National Council and Education

The National Council hailed the 1954 decision outlawing segregation in our public schools. But this victory was not the extent of its interest in education. It became vitally interested in federal aid to public education and in improving the quality of religious education being offered by the constituent denominations to their respective memberships.

The issue of federal aid to public education had been raised in connection with the overcrowding that resulted from massive concentrations of war workers in certain areas. Many small communities, suddenly faced with an influx of children, were just not prepared. Federal aid in these emergency situations had opened the door for such assistance on a much wider scale, and the liberals in government and the National Council were not slow to seize the opportunity. They began stumping for a public school system that would be virtually federalized in control, leaving local school boards with more honor than responsibility. The outbreak of the Korean War in 1950

100. *Ibid.*, p. 30. 1-2.

222

and the resulting upswing in industrial activity for national defense provided an additional argument for federal aid.

The liberals were and are very much in favor of such a program because it would give the federal government additional control over our school systems. This, of course, was necessary to reach the goal of complete school integration. Of even greater importance in the long run, the liberals realized that a federally funded public school system was an ideal situation for "the proper indoctrination of the youth of the nation in the liberal philosophy." To them the public schools offered the most suitable arena for behaviorist manipulation of American youth.

During the 1950s this second purpose was seldom mentioned in public discussions of federal aid. But it was never far from the minds of those who composed the educational hierarchy of what became the Department of Health, Education, and Welfare and of the lesser educational bureaucracies of the nation. The leaders of the National Council, fully aware of what was really involved, were quite content to cooperate with these "secular" forces.

The first real sign of what the Council was thinking appeared in the activities of the United Church Women during the 1951-52 biennium. At that time the ladies took a stand favoring federal money for school lunch programs, school construction grants, and school construction in critical housing areas. In 1954, the day after the Supreme Court announced its decision in the segregation cases, the General Board issued a pronouncement calling on the federal government to come to the aid of education.[101]

Recognizing the critical situation confronting education in this country, the General Board urged the federal government to make contributions to education. The contributions would be "applied exclusively to the aid of tax-supported public schools on condition that the funds be paid over to agencies of the several states and administered by them in accordance with their several statutory regulations and allocated according to a formula that would move toward full educational opportunity in the public elementary and secondary schools, in the various sections of the nation . . . in both urban and rural districts, and for groups of different racial or national origins."[102]

Such a program was to have adequate safeguards against the imposition of federal control in matters of educational policy. This last safeguard was added to reduce the fears of many that federal money

101. *Ibid.*, p. 13. 2-1. The vote was 33 for, 8 against.
102. *Ibid.*, p. 13.2.

meant federal control. Actually this safeguard was from the very beginning almost meaningless. The Supreme Court decisions outlawing segregation had already inaugurated the era of federal control over the local public schools, and it would ultimately mean that schools refusing to comply with this decision would either not get federal funds or lose money already allocated for them. It was an empty gesture, but it served its purpose. No leader of the Council really expected that federal control would not follow federal funds and it is doubtful that they had any real fear of federal control. More likely, they favored it.

At times the Council's public statements on the schools of the nation are somewhat confusing. In 1953 the General Board affirmed its belief in the schools as an institution essential for democracy and refused to believe that they were "godless."[103] In spite of the continuing insistence by the National Council that there must be rigid separation of church and state, its General Board went on record as stating that the public schools have a responsibility concerning the religious foundation of our national culture and that the schools can and must say that human ethical values have their ground and sanction in God. At the same time it also said that "no impairment of separation of church and state is involved in the assumption of such responsibilities."[104]

To implement this goal the General Board voted in 1954 to create the Department of Religion and Public Education. It was given the responsibility of making its consultation service available to state departments of education, local school boards, administrators, classroom teachers, faculty members of liberal arts colleges and schools of education. This project was based on the assumption that public education in America was open to the watered-down theism offered by the National Council, an assumption that was and is open to great question.

In 1956 the Council sponsored a conference at St. Louis on the question of religion and the public schools in an effort to reach general agreement on this matter. Its report was commended to the constituent denominations in the hope that the National Council would be able to make a general policy pronouncement on this issue.

In its report to the triennial meeting of 1960 the Department of Religion and Public Education provided a good summary of its activi-

103. *National Council Outlook*, March 1954, p. 17.

104. *Pronouncements of the NCC*, p. 13.1.

ties since its formation.[105] Its study document "Relation of Religion to Public Education" was well received by the churches and was reprinted in the *International Journal of Religious Education* in April 1960. The United Presbyterian Church in the USA[106] went so far as to publish an elective unit for adults dealing with the issue of religion in the public schools.

To say the least, the thinking of the National Council on the issue of religion in the public schools was confused and confusing. On the one hand, it stood for its version of a theistic foundation for public education, and on the other, it zealously insisted on the proper separation of church and state, by which it meant that any religious teaching in the schools should be denominational or creedal in character and not evangelistic in purpose. The theism it advocated as the proper basis for its program was actually humanistic with enough biblical and religious phraseology larding its statements to mislead the unwary into thinking that the Council was advocating a continuation of the historic national policy of religion in the schools. Which certainly was not the case.

The National Council and Religious Education

From 1951 to 1960 the National Council devoted much attention to making suggestions for what it felt would be valuable improvements in the educational program of the local churches of the constituent denominations. Endless time and effort were spent in developing various programs to achieve this goal. Actually the entire program of the Council was educational in its design and was dedicated to awakening the social conscience of the various churches and to developing a theology that had social improvements as its goal. There were very few concerns or activities of the Council that were not—and are not—closely related to this all-consuming passion. Religious education was calculated to fashion an ecumenical movement that would in turn bring the strength of a united Protestant (even Catholic) church to bear in support of the social gospel, the old concept now being reinterpreted in the 1950s.

This insistence that the whole church must teach was early emphasized, in fact soon after the National Council was organized.

105. *Triennial Report*, 1960, pp. 120-21.

106. This denomination resulted from the 1958 merger of the Presbyterian Church in the U.S.A. and the United Presbyterian Church of North America.

The Council, contended many, represented a determined effort to train children, youth, and adults in an understanding of the Christian faith and the Christian life.[107] The road ahead would not, however, be easy:

> Our task is intensified by the secular outlook that has come to a dominant position in education. . . . The default of American education on the side of religion throws a tremendous responsibility on the church. We cannot be satisfied merely to have Sunday School—not even if it is a good Sunday School. The whole church must become a teaching church.[108]

The general feeling of the Council in its early years was that its greatest achievement was the completion of the Revised Standard Version of the Bible, presented to the public of both the United States and Canada in September 1952. This version soon became the target of conservative Christians in many denominations because of its tendency to change the King James and other versions at crucial points involving basic doctrines of the faith. Perhaps the target of most criticism was Isaiah 7:14, wherein the committee refused to translate the Hebrew word *alma* as *virgin* and simply translated it as *young woman*. Biblical scholarship was clearly on the side of those who insisted that it should be interpreted as *virgin*, from the meaning of the Hebrew term, from the context of the passage, and from the New Testament's own interpretation in Matthew 1:23. In spite of vigorous efforts by the leaders of the Council and the liberals in the major denominations in behalf of this new version, it never really replaced the King James in either the hearts or the minds of the Christian people of this country. It now faces serious competition from newer versions—some even more liberal, others generally evangelical.[109]

The National Council developed an intense interest in what it fondly called Christian higher education. Here it became much more involved than had the Federal Council.[110] In July 1957 the Council,

107. *National Council Outlook*, April 1951, p. 16.

108. *Ibid.*

109. There was also criticism of the Council because it retained the copyright to the new version; obviously it was using it as a means of obtaining additional income for various programs of the Council.

110. The Federal Council had been very active in its evangelism on our college campuses, but had placed less emphasis on bringing its own philosophy of education to the attention of both faculty and students.

through its Division of Christian Higher Education, sponsored a meeting of Protestant church-related colleges at Lake Junaluska in North Carolina. The general trend of the discussion emphasized the difficulties confronting these schools, largely financial. But also insisted on was the unique role to be played by these schools, and their fundamental importance in American society. Dr. John O. Gross, chairman of the Commission on Higher Christian Education, contrasted these schools with atheistic totalitarianism and said:

> Our Christian colleges may find in this period their greatest hour. Just as the monasteries of the Dark Ages preserved for the succeeding generations the great spiritual truths which later burst forth in the Renaissance and Reformation so the Christian college may serve this day and the oncoming generation.[111]

Although Dr. Gross was badly misinformed on the role of the Renaissance in initiating those sparks of spiritual truth, he was correct in insisting that those colleges, which he regarded as Christian, have signally failed in the task to which they were called and have supported the very degenerate forces in American society, which forces he deplored.

The National Council overlooked no aspect of the activities of the constituent churches in its overall quest to bring them under its direct control or influence. By 1957 the Council was expressing alarm as to whether the church at large was prepared to meet the challenge of the rising tide of students seeking admission to America's colleges and universities. As part of its answer to this question the Council decided that it should strengthen and coordinate its work with these college students by merging in 1959 the United Student Christian Council, the Interseminary Movement, and the Student Volunteer Movement into the National Student Ministry Federation. This was an obviously successful effort to eliminate the last vestige of denominational effort on our campuses and thus relegate any surviving evangelical witness on them to the sidelines. The federation was created to reflect faithfully the ecumenical concerns of the National Council in its theology and its religious activities. During the 1960s on many of these campuses the federation's ministry would become revolutionary in character.

Closely related to this work among the students was the Faculty Christian Fellowship, which sought to enlighten faculty members in

111. *National Council Outlook*, September 1957, p. 23.

227

the ecumenical crusade. Retreats were held in various parts of the country and professors invited to take part to explore the role of the church in American society, as, of course, that society was viewed through the ecumenical lenses of the Division of Christian Higher Education. In addition, the Council sponsored the *Faculty Forum* to enhance its mission among faculty members. The Commission on Higher Education also sponsored the Second Quadrennial convocation of the Christian Colleges, which pondered the theme, "The Vocation of the Christian College." Some five hundred delegates attended. The six study sections dealt with such questions as the theological foundation of the Christian college, the relation of the church to the campus, the Christian college and the world mission of the church and the outgoing role of the Christian college in American higher education.[112]

This convocation, held at Des Moines, Iowa, paved the way for the formation of the Council of Protestant Colleges and Unversities, which was formally constituted in January 1959. Dr. Fred G. Holloway, president of Drew University, was its first president.[113]

In the late 1950s the National Council undertook still another project in the area of Christian education. Again the same general purpose was in view. The Sunday school program, long in the eye of the Council, was now regarded as a fertile area for developing the ecumenical outlook in the minds of young and older church members.

Although the plan was not formally announced until the meeting of the Division of Christian Education at St. Louis in February 1961, the planning had been in progress for several years.[114] Known as the Cooperative Curriculum Project, the plan was designed to bring a new dimension to interdenominational curriculum planning. It was based on the concept that all the program-building agencies of the church must be regarded as part of the curriculum process. The resulting curriculum, it was insisted, would allow each denomination to preserve its own identity in the materials that reached the local churches. However, there would be an underlying unity in the program so that the Sunday schools of the cooperating denominations would be presenting a general point of view, namely, the ecumenical theology and outlook of the National Council.[115]

112. *Triennial Report*, 1960, pp. 123-24.

113. In 1960 James M. Godard, vice president of the University of Miami, became the executive director of this council and opened an office in Washington, D.C.

114. The project involved twelve different denominations, not all of which were members of the National Council.

115. *Presbyterian Journal*, March 15, 1961, p. 7.

In summary it can be said that during this decade the work of the Division of Christian Education was formative in most of its activities. The foundations were being laid and the agencies created that would bear the desired fruit in the tumultuous days of the 1960s. The fruit would be the involvement of the churches in the civil rights movement with its attendant disorders, the campus unrest, the acceptance of the New Morality in many of the denominations, the intensification of the ecumenical movement for denominational unification, and the condoning of civil violence for many other causes, most notably for achieving "peace" in Vietnam.

The National Council and Evangelism

From infancy the National Council insisted that its emphasis must be evangelistic.[116] It stressed its obligation of propagating the truth of God, as revealed in Christ, to the seventy million Americans who professed no religion. But herein the note of universalism was evident and the uniqueness of the Gospel tacitly denied. The crisis facing the nation in 1951 was the time for churches not to stress their differences, but "to stand together for what they hold in common, the great central truths of the Gospel." In these terms, then, the Council sought to define the task of evangelism:

> Today the great dividing line is not between one denomination and another, but between those who believe and those who do not believe that God is the Sovereign Reality and that in Jesus Christ he has entered into human life for man's redemption. On this crucial issue we must confront men with the necessity for a decision of faith. We must never forget that it is the business of the church to win souls—to secure real commitment of the self to Christ and what he stands for. The whole church must become an evangelistic church.[117]

This call for an evangelistic effort clearly reveals the philosophy that motivated it. It was philosophically rather than theologically motivated. The commitment was to what Christ stood for rather than to what he had done. There is no note here for redemption from the guilt and power of sin, no note on the substitutionary atonement of Christ. The spotlight is on what Christ stands for, which is nothing more than calling for a commitment to the social gospel rather than to Jesus Christ as Lord and Savior. It was the kind of evangelism

116. *National Council Outlook*, April 1951, p. 16.
117. *Ibid.*

that had characterized the Federal Council. In both cases the real concern was evangelism for social action, but the Federal Council seemingly was more conscious of the need for some kind of change in the heart of those being asked to commit themselves to the social gospel.

The National Council of Churches apparently was never inclined to the kind of preaching mission in which the Federal Council had engaged. To be sure, the National Council was eager to use college and university students for its own purposes, but it never utilized the kind of an evangelistic approach to them which its predecessor had employed.

It must not be inferred that the National Council had no interest in evangelism at all. Suitable reports were made at the triennial meetings from the appropriate agencies as to what had been accomplished and what further plans were being made for the proclamation of the social gospel, but it is difficult not to conclude that the National Council preferred other means for accomplishing its goal. This was no doubt partly due to the fact that the evangelistic crusades of Billy Graham had seized the public attention to such an extent that the kind of preaching mission sponsored by the Federal Council would have been quite difficult, if not virtually impossible, after 1950. Because of this, university preaching missions would face the growing importance among college students of distinctly evangelical movements such as the Intervarsity Fellowship.[118] Young Life, Youth for Christ, and High School Born Againers were also making their influence felt among high school groups at the same time and in such a way that the agencies of the Council were not equipped to meet such competition.

Throughout the first decade of its history the National Council continued to pay its respects to evangelism, but never with the fervor that marked its involvement in many of the decade's social and political issues.

The Department of Evangelism appointed the Reverend Charles B. Templeton as its first full-time evangelist.[119] His early preaching missions were well attended. Preaching missions for migrant workers also were commenced, in 1951-52, as they were for servicemen in army camps and on naval bases. Visitation-evangelism campaigns were also held in fifty communities in America and Japan. The thrust

118. In the late 1960s and 70s Campus Crusade for Christ was a formidable rival to the efforts of the National Council to attract the college mind.

119. He subsequently left the ministry for other work.

in evangelism, however, took the form of Christian teaching missions, which reached four million people in 1952 in a house-to-house religious census.[120] University Christian missions on thirty-six campuses were conducted to help make their religious-emphasis weeks more relevant during these same two years. During much of this decade the Council paid relatively little attention to work evangelism; rather, the accent was on the civil rights movement, the economic issues of the era, and above all, the peace movement. From 1955 to 1957 Christian teaching missions were held but had little visible impact on the churches.

In 1955 the Council's Division of Foreign Mission said that a new vision of a single world mission of the entire church of Jesus Christ was necessary and called for a global reorganization of the missionary enterprise.[121] This new form was to be interdenominational and interracial in character and must proclaim the Gospel in deed and words. Seemingly innocuous, this pronouncement was really a call to end denominational missions as such and put the entire project into the hands of the National Council. Foreign missions were to become foreign mission and the content was to be the social gospel.

The National Council and Religious Broadcasting

From its beginning the National Council not only continued the use of radio broadcasting inherited from the Federal Council, but also was quick to see the vast potentialities of television. A series of programs, adapted for such use, were soon developed.

In 1951, its first year of operation, the Broadcasting and Film Commission reported that it had placed ninety-nine ministers and fifty-seven laymen on regular commercial radio and television programs. Admitting that it was impossible to compute the size of the audiences, the commission was quite sure that it had reached tens of millions of people with the witness of the National Council to Christ. But the commission was also aware that it would soon wear out its welcome with the public with this kind of an approach if it did not present interesting people with a dramatic story to tell.[122]

This commission later reported that during its first year of operation it had produced 1,058 radio and television programs with an

120. *National Council Outlook*, December 1952, p. 15.

121. *Ibid.*, January 1956, p. 11.

122. *Ibid.*, February 1952, p. 29.

average production of over twenty programs a week with 442 network radio programs and 161 network television programs.[123] Further to implement its work it conducted workshops in thirty-three cities in which 809 ministers and laymen were trained in the use of radio and television for religious purposes.

In 1954 Dr. S. Franklin Mack of the Presbyterian Church, U.S.A. was named director of the Broadcasting and Film Commission, and it began to assume a much more aggressive tone in its activities.[124] In early 1955, it began, through the National Broadcasting Company facilities, a new series, "Thy Kingdom Come," which was to explain to the nation the Council's intention to bring the American people under the sway of the social gospel. To attain this goal the budget was increased from $1,160,000 in 1954 to $1,405,000 in 1955. Ralph Sockman remained as the minister for the National Radio Pulpit while Bishop James Pike of the Episcopal Church presented "Frontiers of Faith" for the television audiences. Throughout the year 109 new television programs were produced by the commission.

This new aggressive spirit of the National Council in the broadcasting field came into full bloom with the adoption in June 1956 of the General Board's pronouncement "Advisory Policy Statement on Religious Broadcasting."[125] This statement was little less than a declaration of war against the evangelical programs then on air. A belligerent spirit was masked behind a stated concern for the religious health of the American people. The Council recorded its concern that the religious programs be of the highest quality, be designed to serve the spiritual needs of the American people and to strengthen their religious foundations, and be presented on television and radio. The churches and synagogues of America, stated the Council, have an obligation to provide such a responsible broadcast ministry to all people.[126]

Arguing that the licensed stations have an obligation to provide adequate time and facilities for broadcasting religious programs as a public service, the Council then contended that the networks

123. *Ibid.*, May 1952, p. 23.

124. During 1954 nearly five hundred individual radio and television programs were sponsored by this commission involving 38,400 actual broadcasts compared with 37,000 in 1953.

125. *Pronouncements of the NCC*, p. 8.1-1.

126. *Ibid.*

and individual stations have a responsibility to provide the time and facilities free as a public service.

But the pronouncement did not stop here. The General Board took an additional step, which clearly revealed its basic purpose in adopting such a statement. The board advised against the sale or purchase of time for religious broadcasts and held that this practice is inconsistent with its own basis of operation and, by implication, with the position of the broadcasting industry as expressed in the television code. In keeping with this declaration, the Council held that the scheduling of sponsored or paid-for religious broadcasts in all or a major part of the time allotted for religious broadcasts could not be deemed an adequate discharge of the public service obligations to religion by a network or a station.[127]

The Council was trying not only to gain more time for its own type of religious broadcasting, but also to drive the other programs, which were paid for, off the air. It appealed to one clause in the Television Code of the National Association of Radio and Television Broadcasters as a basis for this demand.[128] An inconsistency in this pronouncement emerges in the paragraphs asking the networks and individual stations to give due consideration in their allotment of time to the Protestant and Orthodox Churches, as well as to the representative strength of the councils of churches, both local and national. Yet the Council was quite unwilling to tolerate similar consideration to the evangelical programs. The loyalty of the National Council to the doctrine of religious freedom was a one-way street.

In March 1957 Dr. S. Franklin Mack, chairman of the revitalized Broadcasting and Film Commission, released a plan that would win virtually all broadcast listeners and viewers to programs with a spiritual content. The plan was designed to appeal not to just the faithful few, but to that larger group accustomed to calling itself Christian and to the unchurched who avoided virtually all religious broadcasts![129]

Dr. Mack estimated that to help religious broadcasters discover the real potential of television and radio for the spiritual undergirding of American life would require a capital fund of ten million dollars yielding an income of three hundred thousand dollars per year.[130]

---

127. *Ibid.*, p. 8. 1-2. The vote for this resolution of the General Board was 67 for, 10 against, 1 abstention.

128. *Ibid.*, 8, 1-1.

129. *National Council Outlook*, April 1957, p. 8.

130. *Ibid.*, p. 9.

In response, the Broadcasting and Film Commission agreed to a proposal of close cooperation with Roman Catholics and Jews for developing national television programs of broad religious appeal; it also endorsed a plan under which it would work more closely with the independent religious broadcasters, to consider objectively the role of the independent producers and sponsors.[131]

Beneath this seemingly innocuous agreement lay the announced purpose of coming to an agreement with the group that was largely responsible for the vast number of evangelical programs on the radio. There were virtually no such programs on the networks, and this plan was designed to strike a blow against evangelical broadcasting at its roots—the independent radio station. That this was the real aim is clearly seen in a report given to the commission concerning its work in 1956, during which the commission produced nearly two hundred television programs that were viewed over 465 of the nation's 475 television stations. Over five hundred radio stations carried 271 different religious programs.[132] In the light of these statistics it simply cannot be argued that the National Council was being slighted in any way in the allotment of time for religious broadcasts.

The real intent of this new aggressive policy was to drive evangelical programs off the air in favor of the ecumenical type of broadcast with its broad religious appeal, but with little or no Gospel.

The commission spent the rest of the decade endeavoring to relate the goals adopted in 1957. It met with some success. Its showcase NBC-TV program, "Frontiers of Faith," was cited as a factor in NBC's receiving the outstanding program award for 1958 in the field of religious broadcasting. But it was not, and has not been, successful in driving evangelical broadcasts off the air.[133]

The National Council of Churches and Church Union

From the day of its inception the National Council of Churches

---

131. *Ibid.*

132. *Ibid.* The commission was quite proud of the fact that in addition to ministers these broadcasts featured poets, ballet dancers, film stars, newspaper reporters, and jazz musicians.

133. It has been successful at times in its aggressive policy of having the licenses of certain radio and TV stations revoked or their renewal withheld until they changed their policies. The National Council waged unrelenting warfare against the radio broadcasts of Rev. Carl McIntire, probably its most outspoken critic in this country.

had denied that it was created to bring about the union of the various denominations or that it was a kind of superchurch. However, its influence from 1951 on has been undeniably used to effect such unions. So great has been the suspicion of this in many quarters that the Council has felt obliged frequently to gainsay that this was its purpose. The suspicion was deeply rooted, too deeply rooted in the minds of many to be removed by empty-sounding avowals to the contrary. After all, the very plan to replace the old Federal Council with a stronger ecumenical organization gave the lie to the Council's pious disclaimers. This stronger organization was essential to accomplishing the many important tasks that its liberal leadership had assigned to the ecumenical movement. It was to bring the whole country under sway of the social gospel for the purpose of socializing America, and to achieve this challenging goal the church as a whole had to be under the liberal scepter. The underlying philosophy of the Council was clearly presented by Dr. Samuel McCrae Cavert at the Denver triennial in 1952:

> The fact is that American Christianity in its organizational life has entered into a new era. To a large extent our grandfather's time was one of sharp controversy among the denominations. In our father's time the age of controversy had given way to one of toleration, but each denomination held aloof from the others. Ours is the first generation of American Christians that could be described as living in an era of cooperation.[134]

This same Denver assembly sent a letter to the Christian people of America denying that it was a superchurch or that it had any desire to become one. It insisted that all of the churches have a prophetic role to play in American life and that it was "their duty to sensitize the conscience of the nation and of all classes and institutions within it."[135] The National Council was founded to bring united strength of the churches to bear on national issues. Nevertheless, in spite of such denials, many observers, particularly those in the evangelical camp of American Protestantism, remained unconvinced. They were much more impressed by the appeals for Christian unity as a backdoor approach to the union of the churches under the banners of the Council.

The plea for unity was reaffirmed at the Boston triennial of 1954:

> Underlying our common task of work is a deep and abiding unity of

134. *National Council Outlook*, January 1953, p. 13.
135. *Ibid.*, p. 14.

faith in Christ as Divine Lord and Saviour. We have discovered new strength and effectiveness in our common enterprises through the National Council of Churches. When we speak unitedly as Christians we affirm a oneness in Christian experiences which we believe is an increasing reality among us.

While we have begun to sense our unity, we are not always clear what practical obligations it places upon us. We have the vision of unity as a principle, and now we must translate it into actual practice. We must provide the best pastoral and lay leadership for the unified community programs of the local councils of churches.[136]

By 1956 the leadership of the Council was quite willing to speak openly of "breaking down the walls" of separation and to call for organized union among the various churches. The editor of the *National Council Outlook*, after reviewing the organic unions either already completed or under way in 1957, played down the historical factors that had once occasioned disunion and looked with hope on the current crop of possible mergers. He found support from two leaders of diametrically opposed views on most issues: from Billy Graham, who said that the "spiritual awakening now sweeping the country is one of the greatest forces working toward uniting Protestantism"; and from Reinhold Niebuhr, professor at New York's Union Seminary, who opined that "the organized pressures of history will bring the churches closer together."[137]

Bishop Henry Knox Sherrill, the first president of the National Council, was much more forthright, however: "Church cooperation is a very important step toward church unity. Before we can have organic unity, we must know and trust one another."[138] To Sherrill, cooperation, although good, was not an end in itself. It was the means toward a greater end—organic union. Nothing short of organic union was the goal that both Bishop Sherrill and his successor in the office of president envisioned. The suspicions of the critics of the Council were well based, and the frequent assertions by various Council leaders that such a union was not their goal were something less than honest.

In November 1957 the ecumenical movement in America took another step forward with the meeting of the Oberlin Conference on Faith and Order under the sponsorship of the United States Confer-

136. *Ibid.*, January 1955, p. 20.
137. *Ibid.*, October 1956, p. 25.
138. *Ibid.*

ence for the World Council of Churches. In attendance were 279 official delegates from thirty-four denominations of the United States and from five Canadian churches. Five American churches were represented that were not members of the National Council including the Roman Catholic church and the Southern Baptist Convention. It was the first such conference to be held on American soil and drew over five hundred in attendance.[139] Its theme was "The Nature of the Unity We Seek." Its leadership was quite representative of the ecumenical liberals. Dr. R. H. Edwin Espy exulted as he surveyed the work of this conference:

> There can be little question that Oberlin marked a new ecumenical thrust in the life of the American churches. Its representativeness was in itself significant. Its substantive quality was outstanding. Its process was germinal leading to new ground gained, but more important, staking out the next territory for further advance. . . .
>
> Theologically and analytically, perhaps the greatest achievement of the conference was the beginning of a recognition that the concern of each of the divisions was inextricably woven with the concerns of the other two divisions. If this truth can become normative for future Faith and Order research, if we can seek an integrated analysis of all the forces which divide us, we will be helped a long stride forward toward the unity we seek.[140]

In his presidential address at the 1957 triennial meeting, Eugene Carson Blake made it very clear that among the constituent denominations there was a developing unity that he regarded as a harbinger of hope, and he expressed the feeling that the Southern Baptist Convention and Missouri Lutheran Synod would soon join. In his report to this triennial, Roy G. Ross, associate general secretary, insisted that "we [of the National Council] must not be content until all who acknowledge the preamble of our Constitution are banded together in their search for the full knowledge of the mind of Christ and a more complete manifestation of their unity."[141] He also summoned this meeting to be ready to follow up the interest developed by the recent Oberlin Conference on Faith and Order: "Though the council has been given no clear mandate to work specifically in the field of faith and order, it seems unthinkable that we should not have

139. *Ibid.,* November 1957, p. 18.

140. *Ibid.,* p. 21.

141. *Triennial Report,* 1957, p. 21.

a vital interest and role in studying together fundamental questions concerning Christian unity."[142]

This ascending accent on Christian unity was featured in the "Message to the Member Churches"[143] adopted by the Fifth General Assembly of the National Council at San Francisco in December 1960:

> We are grateful for the steady advance of understanding and mutual trust among us. We look forward to the time when each member denomination, recognizing the authenticity of Christian discipleship in all others, will entrust to any of them the care of human souls and responsibility for advancing Christ's mission in the world. And we call upon all churches to continue to pray and labor for the full unity, visible and invisible, of the People of God.[144]

This message went further than previous pronouncements on the matter of Christian unity; specifically, it contained terminology whose meaning could not be doubted. The hesitancy and ambiguity that had characterized previous statements on the subject were absent, and the real force and goal of the ecumenical movement became crystal clear: "We are called upon to face the truth that the autonomy, or even continuing identity, of our denominations is not the paramount issue, but rather our openness to the intent of Christ for His church in these times, recognizing that such openness may lead in directions which are new and unfamiliar to us."[145]

The attitude of the National Council toward the Roman Catholic church underwent a vast change in the period from 1950 to 1960. In 1951, along with most liberal as well as most conservative religious opinion, the National Council registered a strong protest when President Truman first proposed sending an ambassador to the Vatican. The Council chose Reformation Day 1951 to issue a very strong statement condemning the action on the ground that it violated the basic American principle of separation of church and state.[146] It also

142. *Ibid.*, p. 22.

143. For the full text of this message, see *Triennial Report*, 1960, pp. 232-34.

144. *Ibid.*, p. 232.

145. *Ibid.*, p. 233. There was considerable truth in this accusation, and the Council was not unaware of its own weakness in this respect. In this history of the National Council I have not dealt with the efforts to reorganize it, largely because it was a continuing effort and, for the most part, ineffectual; also because in chapter seven I will deal with the critically important impasse that overtook the Council in the late 1960s, forcing the Council to deal with its own structure in ways in which it never had since its formation.

146. *Pronouncements of the NCC*, pp. 29.1-2; 29.2-2.

asserted that this action was totally unnecessary for the purpose the President had in mind; at the same time, though, it took pains to point out that the protest was against Truman's action and not its Roman Catholic friends.[147]

Although the Council never formally repudiated this statement its attitude toward the Roman Catholic church was greatly modified by the end of the decade; it changed radically after 1960 and Vatican II.

By the end of the first decade of its history the National Council was ready to announce its real purpose and shed its cloak of deception. Cooperation and unity no longer were enough to achieve its goals; only organic union could. The oft-repeated assertion that the Council was simply the agent of the churches was still true in part, but it was giving way to an emphasis that was new and yet not new. It was new in the sense that it had not been openly stated very frequently, but that was all. Never had it been long absent from the thinking of the Council's liberal leadership. But by 1960 the liberals felt that the Council had achieved a position of such influence in America's ecclesiatical community that it could expose its real goal with a measure of impunity, which had not been the case at the Cleveland convention of 1950 or in its formative years.

Growing Criticism of the National Council

Almost as soon as it was born the National Council of Churches was subjected to bitter and prolonged criticism, much more incisive and widespread than ever the Federal Council experienced.

At times it was difficult to distinguish clearly between types of charges brought against the Council, but most fell into one of three categories. Some critics were convinced that it was a sprawling bureaucracy, top heavy with committees and boards, and laden with confusion.

Other individuals and churches criticized the National Council for its frank intrusion into the political, economic, and social areas of American life, areas traditionally regarded by American conservatives as lying outside the domain of the church. Thus pronouncements on issues touching these areas were deemed violative of the separation of church and state.[148]

147. *National Council Outlook*, December 1961, pp. 15-16.

148. For a detailed study of this, see Edgar Bundy, *Collectivism in the Churches* (Wheaton, Ill., 1961) and *Apostles of Deceit* (Wheaton, Ill., 1966). These are thoroughly documented and clearly reveal the radical involvement of this liberal leadership.

A third kind of criticism, often implied in the second, concerned the National Council's official pronouncements and activities. Specifically, they mirrored the Communist philosophy. The Council's liberal leadership was all too often actively involved in or sympathetic to the Communist movement in general and Russian communism in particular. As the decade advanced this kind of charge advanced in the minds of the Council's critics. By 1960 this had achieved the status of religious conviction, especially to the evangelicals in most, if not all, of the major denominations. The Council leadership became increasingly sensitive to this charge, it might be added.

Although this kind of criticism approached tidal wave dimensions after 1960, it came alive in 1951 when it became evident that the radicals of the Federal Council leadership had gained control in its successor.[149] There can be no reasonable doubt about the Communist orientation of both the older Federal Council of Churches and the National Council. The dominant liberal leadership of these two groups unhesitatingly sponsored and joined, at one time or another, nearly every Communist front group that appeared on the American scene between 1920 and 1972.

Many have sought to excuse this on the ground that they, the front members, were not in the Communist party. Even if they were, many good Americans were also supporting these causes and even joining the party in the 1930s and 40s, it being modish in the Roosevelt era. Doubtless it was the in-thing for good liberals then, but by no stretch of the imagination does this argument excuse the leadership of the National Council, which was formed at a time when most Americans were becoming painfully aware of what Russian communism meant to the world and was doing to this country.

To say that many good Americans were becoming interested in communism as a possible solution to our economic woes after 1929 in no way absolves these ecclesiastical leaders for the simple reason that they held responsible leadership in a council of churches that confessed its belief in the God of the Bible and in Jesus Christ as Lord and Savior. The atheistic nature of communism, both Russian and American, was too well known for these leaders successfully to disclaim any knowledge of its true character. It is most dif-

149. These pronouncements lay at the heart of the constant complaints by the Presbyterian Church, U.S. (Southern), which was still heavily influenced by the Thornwellian doctrine of the spirituality of the church.

ficult to escape the conclusion that they flirted with communism of all varieties because they believed it more relevant to the needs of twentieth-century America than was the Gospel of Jesus Christ. They were not unwilling, however, to use the Gospel and their zeal for evangelism to cloak their interest in—even devotion to—a philosophy of life that in its atheistic assumptions denied every basic biblical statement concerning God, man, sin, good, evil, the existence of the soul in man, and heaven and hell. If these men really believed that some kind of synthesis between the Scriptures and the Communist philosophy was probable, their ignorance is inexcusable; if they did not, then their deceptiveness is equally inexcusable and gives the lie to their lofty ethical declarations against war, economic plight, and racial injustice.

No sooner had the National Council taken its place in the ecclesiastical life of the nation than its affinity with the Communist cause came under public attack—with far more vehemence than that attending previous similar attacks on the Federal Council. These early attacks on the National Council came to a head on March 17, 1953, when Congressman Donald Jackson, a Republican from California, said on the floor of the House of Representatives that Bishop Bromley Oxnam, a leader in the Federal and National Councils, had "served God on Sunday and the Communist front for the balance of the week over . . . a long period of time."[150]

Similarly, against Bishop Henry Knox Sherrill, the first president of the Council, was lodged a charge that he had sponsored the Congress of American-Soviet Friendship. Herbert Philbrick, an operative with the Federal Bureau of Investigation from 1940 to 1949, added excitement to the situation. Before the Senate Internal Security Subcommittee he testified that in the Boston area during this period he knew of seven or eight ministers who were underground agents of the Communist party and that they had been selected by the party for the specific purpose of doing its work under the guise of serving the church.

The National Council took the position that investigations of conspiracies to overthrow the government of the United States were a proper function of the government. No reason existed why men pretending to be clergy, but using their role to shield Communist activity, should not be investigated and exposed. Indeed, conspirators in any area of life who seek the violent overthrow of the government of the United States should be discovered, tried in

150. U.S., Congress, House, *Congressional Record*, vol. 99, pp. 2024, 9597.

American tribunals, and, where found guilty, punished.[151] But the Council also said that following up such leads was a very different matter from "investigating the churches as a group or their clergy as a class."[152]

The liberal leadership on the Council further declared that while "it is important to detect a conspiratorial communist who wears the robe of a clergyman it is equally important not to confuse a liberal Christian who is an honest advocate of social reform with communism. This is something which is now happening to a damning and inexcusable degree."[153]

The Council would have had a much stronger case against the House Committee on Un-American Activities had it paused to consider the situation and acted accordingly. It raised its voice in protest against what it felt were the unwarranted charges against the activities of Bishop Henry Knox Sherrill, Bishop Bromley Oxnam, and other leaders of the Council, but it never stopped to ponder the fact that what they regarded as the liberal Christian program for reform all too often coincided with the Communist Party platform at the time. Thus it was very difficult, if not impossible, for the House and Senate investigating committees to distinguish between liberal Christian reform and communist demands, for frequently they were one and the same thing. Liberal Christianity was much closer to the Communist Party ideology than to evangelical orthodoxy.

Later in 1953 the General Board created a Committee for the Maintenance of American Freedom.[154] In creating this committee Bishop William Martin, president of the Methodist Council of Bishops and of the National Council, charged it with the duty of watching developments that threaten the spirit of liberty, and to help the churches recognize any Communist infiltration into American life.[155] The sincerity of the National Council in creating such a committee would have been less suspect had Bishop Martin not appointed Bishop Sherrill as its chairman and Bishop G. Bromley Oxnam as a member.

At the same May 1953 meeting the board issued a pronounce-

151. *National Council Outlook*, May 1953, p. 11.

152. For complete text, see *Pronouncements of the NCC*, p. 141.1.

153. *National Council Outlook*, May 1953, p. 11.

154. This committee had been organized at the March 1953 meeting of the General Board.

155. *National Council Outlook*, June 1953, p. 12.

242

ment expressing its confidence in the loyalty of the lay and clerical leaders of the constituent churches and its conviction that these churches were among the greatest bulwarks of freedom in the United States. Then, by way of reinforcement, it added, "The National Council of Churches is and always has been unalterably opposed to communism."[156]

Liberal religious publications, notably the *Christian Century* and those representing the liberal denominations, rushed to the defense of the National Council and its beleaguered bishops. The conservative religious journals were reluctant to raise their voices in protest. Even though to varying degrees the latter probably accepted the Council's contention that any widespread congressional investigation of the churches or the ministry might raise a question about the relation of church and state and the constitutional guarantees of freedom and religion, they seemed to be more impressed with the probability that communism had infiltrated into the National Council and some of its constituent denominational members and that this threatened the church and the state far more than the investigations being carried on by Congress.

The efforts of liberal churches and politicians to minimize the Communist threat in this country were largely offset by the Russian tactics in the Korean War and the revelations of the McCarthy and other congressional committees concerning Communist infiltration into the federal government, the colleges and universities, as well as the churches. As a result, charges that the National Council was also infiltrated became an important part of the ecclesiastical scenery after 1950 and have continued to be an important cause of criticism by various evangelical bodies and secular organizations concerned with the maintenance of American political and economic freedon. Their fears were during the decade reinforced by the Council's various statements and publications on economic and social issues; these showed a distinct friendliness toward collectivism and an equally distinct hostility toward the American tradition of free enterprise and constitutional government.

In fact, the National Council had, and has, an uncanny ability to issue pronouncements and policy statements that justify these fears. In March 1954 the General Board, on the recommendation of the Committee for the Maintenance of American Freedom, issued a statement on threats to American freedom. The state-

156. *Pronouncements of the NCC*, p. 11.1-1.

ment flatly said that "one such threat has come from procedural abuses by Congressional Committees" and recommended certain reforms it deemed necessary.[157]

Although the policy statement did not name the committees, it was obvious that it clearly referred to the House Committee on Un-American Activities, of which Congressman Harold Velde was chairman, and the famous McCarthy committee of the Senate. This committee, because of its prolonged hearings and successful uncovering of Communist infiltration into the various agencies of the federal government, gave birth to the "McCarthy era," a term liberals effectively used to reproach Senator McCarthy personally and anyone else who shared what they referred to as the McCarthy mentality, meaning anyone who counted communism a distinct threat to American Freedom and security.

Such indirect attacks on congressional committees and those who opposed communism intensified the suspicion that the National Council was indeed friendly to communism and occasioned a flood of literature attacking the Council for its attitude. But the Council was not without friends in other quarters. The *New York Times* said that the Council's statement of March 1954 gave strong reinforcement to the growing demand that Congress take effective action to control its own investigating committees. The *Chicago Sun Times* said that "the American people would be wiser to trust their spiritual leaders than politicians with the McCarthy lust for power."[158]

The fears of many Americans were aroused anew by two events of 1956. The first was the appearance of a "Message to the Churches and Economic Life" in April. This was the work of the Third National Study Conference on the Church and Economic Life, which was sponsored by the National Council. Although it contained a phraseology intended to be deceptively neutral at some points, this report was certainly not unfriendly to some form of collectivism for the future guidance of American economic activity.

The second event was the promotion of exchange visits with Russian clergymen. This closely linked the ecumenical and international interests of the National Council with an undue and even dangerous interest in the Communist experiment on Russia. This exchange, coming at a time when Russia was actively fomenting

157. *National Council Outlook*, April 1954, p. 18.

158. *Ibid.*

crises in Hungary and the Middle East, stood in sharp contrast to the reports given by the American churchmen on their return from their visit to Russia and strengthened the growing conviction in many circles that the Council was interested more in promoting communism than in advancing the Gospel of Jesus Christ or promoting the American way of life.

The "Message to the Churches of Christ in the U.S.A.," issued by the Fifth World Order Study Conference at Cleveland in November 1958, was hardly calculated to set at rest the swelling doubt concerning the dedication of the National Council to American and Christian ideals. Rather did it cause what was probably the most violent criticism of the Council since its founding eight years before.[159]

The reaction of many people in and out of the church to the findings of the Cleveland conference prompted the National Council at the end of its first decade to strike out more openly against the growing army of its critics. At its meeting in Hartford, Connecticut, in February 1959 the General Board issued its "Hartford Appeal," which delineated its case with clarity if not with logic.[160] Declaring that every organization must, on occasion, confront the issues that test its purposes, and try its values and that the issues arising out of the message of the Fifth World Order Conference was of such a kind, the General Board took its stand on the right of Christian churches and their councils

> to study and comment upon issues, no matter how controversial in the realms of politics, economics and social affairs, in view of their common faith in Jesus Christ as both Lord and Saviour. In exercising this right and fulfilling this duty, the National Council has repeatedly been charged by enemies and criticized by worried friends as being soft toward communism.
>
> Reiterating our loyalty to the God and Father of our Lord Jesus Christ and our opposition to atheistic communism, we declare that the basic challenge to the council and to the churches does not arise solely from specific viewpoints or conclusions expressed by them.
>
> The issue is the right of citizens of whatever race or creed and of any peaceable organization he chooses to join or form, to discuss freely and to express judgments without exposure to attacks upon motive or integrity for daring to exercise the right to do so. Such a

159. See pages 239–242.
160. *Pronouncements of the NCC*, p. 14.2-1.

right is especially vital to the Church, which owes a duty to lead and inform, so that its members may be aided in reaching morally valid judgments in the light of their common faith.[161]

The Board then called upon its member churches to uphold these rights and required a response from them to this appeal.

This artfully worded document had merit if it had been the work of a secular organization. But it was open to severe criticism because of its assumptions. There can be no doubt that the church of Jesus Christ must have the right to speak out in proclaiming the Gospel of redemption. But the church is not a secular organization; it is a divinely instituted and empowered institution. When it speaks, it must speak as directed by the Scriptures through the enlightening power of the Holy Spirit. When the church abdicates this high role and chooses some lower and secular role, like that found in the report and "Message" of the Cleveland conference, then it speaks no longer as the church of Christ, but as a secular, perhaps even a revolutionary, organization and must be judged by the role it has chosen for itself. When the church sponsors conferences that seem to favor collectivism and other forms of economic activity that are certainly not the product of Christian theism, then it cannot demand that it be judged as the church of Christ in the eyes of men. By 1958 the National Council was an overtly secular, even a radically secular, organization parading under the guise of a Christian frame of reference. In issuing the "Hartford Appeal" it was asking to be judged in the light of the high ground of a biblical theology that it had virtually abandoned.

As the first decade of its life drew to a close, the National Council found itself in another serious controversy, again involving its relationship to communism. The issue was raised in a manual written for noncommissioned air force officers for their training program. The manual stated that Communist influences had been successful in penetrating certain religious groups, and the National Council was specifically named as one of them.[162] When this became generally known there was a new public outcry against the Council. The House Committee on Un-American Activities held a hearing on the matter, and Richard Arens, chief counsel for the committee, stated:

161. *Ibid.*

162. This statement occurred in the section of the manual dealing with the subject of internal security.

246

Thus far in the leadership of the National Council of Churches of Christ in America we have found over 100 persons in leadership capacity with either Communist front records or records of service to Communist causes. The aggregate affiliations of the leadership, instead of being in the hundreds as the Chairman first indicated, is now, according to our latest count, in the thousands, and we have yet to complete our check, which would certainly suggest on the basis of the authoritative sources of this Committee that the statement that there is infiltration of fellow-travelers in churches and educational institutions is a complete understatement.[163]

Although the offending material was later withdrawn, it further strengthened the conviction that the National Council was more Communist that Christian in its orientation, and that its assertions of loyalty to Christ and the Gospel were actually meaningless and served as traps for those unversed in the art of Communist duplicity. As a result of its own pronouncements and affiliations, the National Council found itself increasingly on the defensive during the first half of the 1960s. After 1965, seemingly tired of its double role, it openly participated in the ongoing revolutionary struggle in America.

163. House of Representatives, Hearings Before the Committee on Un-American Activities on Issues Presented by Air Force Reserve Center Training Manual, February 26, 1966, pp. 5-6.

7

The National Council, 1961-1972

Its Basic Mission in This Decade

The 1960s brought no vital change of direction in either the thinking or the activity of the National Council. Rather did these years witness the further development of the state of mind it had acquired during its first ten years. Undoubtedly the contents of the Council's political, social, and economic pronouncements indicated greater aggressiveness and ever-deepening conviction of the rightness of its accompanying activities and programs. But none of these developments indicated a change of direction, only the extension of a program whose broad outlines were easily discernible by 1955.

In his report to the 1960 triennial, Roy Ross had insisted that the church look upon its task as mission rather than missions. This seemingly insignificant change of emphasis conveyed monentous meaning for the future of the Council. Mission embraced a call to the Council to accent anew its role in maintaining international understanding and creating world government among nations that were willing to surrender any portion of their own sovereignty to such an organization. Involved in the solution of such issues was the further challenge of redeeming our national culture in such a way that we would be truly a nation under God.[1]

Beneath what seemed to be a call for national righteousness lay a thinly concealed invitation to follow the Council down new and more treacherous paths of radical thought and practice. Aware of the barrage of criticism against it by segments of its member denominations, the Council took steps to bolster its defenses. In April 1961 it issued a statement asserting that the pronouncements, resolutions, and other actions of the General Assembly had precisely the status and weight of being actions of such a representative assembly, and that although the National Council had no authority over its constituent churches or their memberships, it had a right to expect from them either loyal support or loyal opposition.[2] The member churches must either loyally support the radicalism of the Council or be loyal in their opposition to it. As the Council's second decade drew to a close, the impossibility of fulfilling this injunction became increasingly clear, so clear that it was threatening the very life of the Council.

The National Council and the Problems of War and Peace

During the first four years of its second decade of life the Council paid remarkably little attention to the issues of war and peace. It was content with the statement of one of its executive secretaries, that the sharing of American wealth with those in need was radically necessary for survival in the international struggle.[3] In 1965 the National Council worked, apparently in secrecy, for the

1. *Triennial Report*, 1960, p. 12. This redemption of American culture was for the purpose of developing our nation into an instrument of world order. The creation of a world order was the dominant thrust of all references to "the mission of the church."

2. *The Record of the National Council of Churches*, rev. ed. (Wheaton, Ill., 1972), p. 94.

3. During these ten years the attention of the Council increasingly centered on the civil rights struggle. The cause of civil rights virtually became the Gospel for much of the Council leadership, superseding even the crusade for pacifism, then the chief concern of the ecumenical movement.

passage of the Nuclear Test Ban Treaty, not by open resolutions supporting it, but by communicating with state and local councils of churches in the home states of those members of Congress whose support for the proposal was in doubt.[4]

In 1965 the Council, spurred by the intensifying war in Vietnam, suddenly became conscious again of its role in the peace program and acted accordingly. Meeting in St. Louis, the Sixth World Order Study Conference, called by the president of the National Council, recommended that the National Council of Churches urge the United States to end its opposition to the admission of Red China as a member of the United Nations. The study conference also counseled that careful study be given by this country to "regularizing diplomatic communication with Red China and to the conditions under which diplomatic recognition may be appropriately granted."[5]

The philosophy underlying this approach to our diplomacy was also quite evident in the conference's proposal that the United States halt its bombing of North Vietnam for an indefinite period "in order to create more favorable circumstances for negotiations."[6] In addition, our government was to work for a cease-fire in Southeast Asia and to request the United Nations to convene a peace conference.

The sympathy of the Sixth World Order Study Conference was not confined to communism in China and Southeast Asia but extended to that in Cuba. With unblushing audacity the conference recommended that the United States should not take unilateral action in opposing communism there but work with the Organization of American States and the United Nations. We were also to lift our embargo on travel to Cuba and on the sending of food and material for the purpose of welfare work there.[7]

Although the National Council strenuously insisted that the pronouncements of study conferences did not represent its position, the General Board nevertheless issued a "Message to the Churches" on Vietnam in December 1965. The document explained that war in a nuclear age settles hardly anything and may destroy everything.[8] It also warned that unilateral action by the United States

4. *The Record of the National Council of Churches*, p. 135.

5. *Ibid.*, p. 144.

6. *Ibid.*

7. *Ibid.*, p. 145.

8. *Policy Statements of the National Council of Churches*, p. 25.4-3.

in Southeast Asia would not lead to peace; the United States must, instead, unite its peace efforts with those of other nations through the United Nations. It then called upon American Christians to make "peace-making the priority of their Christian witness and to support the efforts of the National Council in its approach to the World Council of Churches and Pope Paul VI in a common effort to mobilize the worldwide Christian community in support of a just alternative to war."[9]

Accompanying the "Message to the Churches" was a policy statement adopted by the General Board on the same day. Modestly it counseled the Johnson administration concerning a course of action for ending the Vietnam War. The United States was to reaffirm and manifest its readiness for unconditional negotiation in such a way as to remove any uncertainty about official policy relating to the ending of military action. Further, this could be appropriately accomplished by halting our bombing of North Vietnam. The statement also suggested that the United Nations convene a peace conference as soon as it could.

The policy statement laid bare the totally unrealistic attitude of the National Council toward the Communist problem in Southeast Asia. In proposing a peace settlement, the document called on our government to make it crystal clear that a primary objective of settling the Vietnam War was the independence of South Vietnam. That war-torn land was to be free from outside interference, with complete liberty to determine the character of its future government by the peaceful, free, and verified choice of its people. It mattered not that the choice might result in a coalition government made up of nationalists and National Liberation Front members, or in being united with North Vietnam, or in operating as an independent and nonaligned state, or in becoming with Cambodia and Laos a buffer zone between Communist and non-Communist spheres of influence.[10]

Finally, our government was immediately to make available to Southeast Asia, in fulfillment of President Johnson's proposal, reconstruction assistance and funds for long-range economic development. In defense of this proposal the Council said that "in a world of revolution, rapid change and sharp conflict of ideologies, Christians have an opportunity and duty to be a reconciling and

9. *Ibid.*, p. 25.4-4.

10. *Ibid.*, p. 25.4-2.

healing force between nations and peoples and races where possible.[11]

The policy statement plus the accompanying "Message to the Churches" perhaps more clearly than any previous utterance by the Council, revealed the pro-Communist outlook of that body and its close affiliation with the radical left in this country. Although tinged with Christian piety, the basic orientation toward radicalism cannot be denied.

These two documents stopped just short of indicting the United States for responsibility for the Vietnam War. Stopping it, though, lay within the power of the Johnson administration; by exercising that power it would show its trust in the good intentions of North Vietnam and the National Liberation Front. The documents show no awareness of the Communist designs on Southeast Asia. The belief that Southeast Asia could and would solve its problems in a peaceful manner if we would only withdraw was either naive beyond belief or a studied attempt to allow communism to take over Southeast Asia. That the latter was probably the real design of National Council policy becomes more obvious in the policy statement adopted by the General Board in February 1966 in regard to Communist China.[12] That it could hardly be ignorance of what was occurring in Asia is readily seen in the opening statement of the document:

> We realize that the People's Republic of China is in a stage of communist development and nationalistic reassertion which makes her outspokenly aggressive toward some of her neighbors and at the present time an opponent of peaceful coexistence with the noncommunist world. We oppose these trends, however, even while recognizing the increasing belligerence of the mainland China government. We as Christians, and therefore as witnesses to a Lord who reconciles us all, recommend the following actions.[13]

The statement then called on the Johnson administration to create a commission on United States policy regarding Com-

11. *Ibid.* This statement passed the General Board with 93 in favor, 10 opposed, and 6 abstentions.

12. The vote on this was 90 for, 3 against, 1 abstention ("*Minutes of the General Board*", February 22, 1966, *Matthews Collection* [Presbyterian Historical Foundation, Montreat, N.C.).

13. *Ibid.*

munist China. It was to be composed of public officials and private citizens. The United States, without prejudicing its own policy concerning diplomatic recognition of Taiwan and under conditions that would take into account the latter's welfare, security, and political status, would develop a new policy of support for the admission of Red China into the United Nations. The statement also counseled our government to permit free travel between the two nations and to allow the sale of food and other strategic items to China, following the example of Canada and the United Kingdom.[14]

This avowed recognition of the aggressive policies of Communist China is excused by the Council on the ground that Red China was simply passing through a necessary stage in its development and would, it was hoped, soon pass into a new era of peaceful coexistence, which transition the United States should aid—even reward —by pioneering the way into an international organization that by its own charter was to be composed of the "peace-loving nations" of the world. Incongruities abounded in this proposal, a fact happily overlooked by those so zealous for the expansion of communism in Asia that they were willing to allow a Communist nation into an organization whose police force would be used to maintain the peace in Southeast Asia after the United States had withdrawn its troops.

Further sustaining and strengthening its radical image, the General Board at this same meeting issued a policy statement on American policy toward Southern Africa. Suffice it to say, the Johnson administration was counseled to aid the radical and leftist governments at the expense of the conservative ones.[15]

In 1967 the National Council issued no important statement on the war in Southeast Asia but did make a pronouncement on conscientious objectors. Specifically, it advocated extension of the coverage of existing legislation to those opposed to a particular war, declared or undeclared. It also requested that the statutory requirement of showing "religious training and belief" be no longer required to qualify for classification as a conscientious objector on the ground that it was unnecessary to "validate the operation of the human conscience" and that it gave preference to the religious conscience over the nonreligious conscience.[16]

This statement, humanistic in its assumption, was a curious contradiction of the position earlier assumed by both the Federal

14. *Ibid.*

15. *Ibid.*, February 23, 1966.

16. *Ibid.*, February 23, 1967.

254

Council and the National Council. From its earliest days the Federal Council had insisted that pacifism with its attendant right of being a conscientious objector was a Christian position by which a Council member bore witness to his Christian profession. But if the religious or Christian conscience is not be be preferred over the non-Christian conscience, then pacifism ceases to be a Christian position *per se* and is no longer the means of any meaningful Christian witness.

In 1968 the National Council once again was moved to advise the Johnson administration and charged, in a policy statement, that the government was operating on the basis of an oversimplified world view. That is, it saw the world as being divided into two camps, the Communist and non-Communist, with a third world occupying a neutral position. The statement charged that to an increasing degree the United States had been making unilateral decisions on the use of military power, which all too often had been utilized to maintain the status quo.[17] The document concluded that this country had grasped, wrongly, but one horn of the apparent dilemma in its efforts to establish the imperatives of peace, failing to seize the more creative solutions.[18]

And what were these creative solutions? The National Council was quite willing to make them available and did so. It was vital that the United States put new policies into effect in Vietnam. America must avoid provocative military actions toward China and should work to reduce and minimize its military presence in that area. As a contribution to equilibrium there (presumably between non-Communist and Communist groups), this country should give appropriate military and economic assistance to Asian nations seeking it, but under conditions that would not thwart necessary social change. In other words, the United States should aid those nations seeking to build a Communist state and not prevent the triumph of communism anywhere in Asia. Instead of trying to isolate Red China the United States must take positive steps to bring that nation into the international community. At the same time the Council suggested that our government take far more imaginative steps to create conditions for cooperation between the United States and the Communist countries of Eastern Europe, the Soviet Union, and Cuba.[19]

The thrust of these pronouncements on foreign policy was that

17. *Ibid.*, February 21, 1968.

18. *Ibid.*

19. *Ibid.*, February 20, 1968.

this country should overlook the basic cleavage between the ideology of the West and the communism of Eastern Europe and Asia and cooperate with these nations in the economic, political, and cultural areas. At bottom was the conviction, shared by the Council with other liberal and radical groups in this country, that communism posed no threat to America and that we must learn to coexist with atheistic communism in the world of the latter half of the twentieth century rather than run the risk of nuclear warfare.

In accordance with these assumptions, the National Council soon took the next logical step. In September 1968 the General Board issued a policy statement calling for a mutual halt in the production and deployment of strategic offensive and defensive missile systems, including the antiballistic missile system, and in the production of fissionable material for military purposes. It advocated the passage of a comprehensive test ban treaty. To implement these policies, the United Nations must be strengthened as a peacemaking and peacekeeping agency. Accordingly, its members could make available trained special forces to the United Nations for peacekeeping operations.[20]

The overall effect of these proposals would have been to place the United States at the mercy of Russia and other Communist powers and to render this nation a second-class military power. It is not unimportant to observe that the Nixon administration implemented many of these liberal demands, despite conservative protests. Also of importance, these proposals closely followed the platforms of the Communist parties in this country. This continuous parallel policy can scarcely be regarded as accidental. There can be no doubt that Communist groups in America and the National Council of Churches were urging on America almost identical foreign policies. But then, why shouldn't they? They held almost identical philosophies.

At its Detroit triennial assembly in December 1969, the National Council adopted still another resolution on the war in Vietnam. It declared, in part:

> We do not agree with the historical explanation which the present United States Administration (Nixon) and previous administrations (Kennedy and Johnson) have given as to the origins of the Vietnam conflict and the justification of United States intervention. In particular the notion that the Vietnam War is essentially a case

20. *Ibid.*

of communist aggression and of American and Allied defense of freedom and self-determination against aggression is misleading and has failed profoundly to do justice to the complexity and diversity of the historical, political and social conditions of Vietnam.[21]

Here was a deliberate distortion of the known facts. The complexity to which it alluded was the product of the liberal mind and press in this country and was part of the general effort to misrepresent the invasion of South Vietnam by North Vietnam as something other than an unprovoked military attack. It was part of the liberal thesis that this country was under control of a military and industrial complex that exploited the American fear of Communist aggression for mercenary purposes. This policy statement not only reflected the widespread liberal thesis but attempted to sanctify in church circles this interpretation of the conflict.

At the same December meeting the General Assembly passed a resolution on peaceful dissent quite in keeping with the liberal thesis:

> We believe that the organization of legitimate, peaceful and legal demonstrations of political dissent and moral protest against U.S. policy in Vietnam is to be commended, not condemned. In particular, as one method of dissent we recognize the legitimate, peaceful and legal nature of the Washington Moratorium of October 15, and of the November 12-16 march on Washington sponsored by the New Mobilization Committee to end the war in Vietnam. We commend those whose conscience leads them to peaceful participation in such events and, in particular, church members, for their willingness to make a public witness in support of the resolution passed by the churches.[22]

This resolution must have been passed by that triennial assembly with tongue in cheek. It is very difficult to understand just how the participants were voicing their Christian convictions regarding the war in Vietnam. The marches cited were hardly calculated either to inspire or to express such convictions. The Council surely was not unaware of the great gulf between the idealism expressed in the resolution and the barnyard conduct marking these marches.

After 1969 the National Council was drawn to other issues. The

21. "Resolutions Adopted by the General Board," June 1969, *Matthews Collection.*
22. *Ibid.*

war in Vietnam was no longer as important as it had been in ecumenical thought.

Its final blast against the policies of the Nixon administration in Southeast Asia came in early 1972. The medium was "Ecumenical Witness," a conference composed of Protestant, Roman Catholic, Orthodox, and Jewish leaders. It met in St. Louis in January of that year. The conference, initiated by the General Board of the National Council, unanimously charged the government of the United States with immoral practices in Southeast Asia and recommended that Congress cut off all funds for the war.[23]

This decreasing emphasis on the conflict was due in part to the rising hope for an early end to the hostilities because of the new approach of the Nixon administration. It also was due to the fact that the issue of race relations became the dominant concern of the Council in 1969. It must be added, little remained for the Council to say about Vietnam.

The National Council and Economic Issues, 1961-1972

Very early in the decade the National Council intruded into economic issues that were none of its concern and had no relationship to the Gospel. In February 1961 it adopted a resolution in support of a program for the improvement of economically depressed areas of the country. The program included vocational training, the extension of unemployment compensation, and urban renewal.[24]

In November 1962 the Council's Division of Christian Life and Work sponsored the Fourth National Study Conference at Pittsburgh; 450 delegates attended. Using the theme "Ethical Implications of Rapid Change in the United States" as the basis of its discussions, the conference published its findings in 1963: *The Church in a World That Won't Stand Still*. This work reflected the blossoming radical stance assumed by the Council, but it did not add much to reports issued by previous study conferences. But the implication that the church must keep pace with the rapid social and economic changes of the second half of the twentieth century was clearly in line with the basic ethical relativism of the Council. The Division of Christian Life and Work was thoroughly imbued with the spirit

23. *Tempo Newsletter*, January 1972.

24. *A Summary of the Resolutions of the National Council of Churches, 1951-1961*, p. 6.

of change and chose as its emphasis for 1963-64 "Being a Christian in a Rapidly Changing World."

In 1965 the General Board adopted a policy statement, "Christian Concern and Responsibility for Economic Life in a Rapidly Changing Technological Society."[25] Probably the most important statement issued by the National Council on economic issues since 1960, "Christian Concern . . ." spotlighted problems arising from the vast technological changes occurring in America. "Man has unleashed in the world vast forces accelerating economic and social change" in his pursuit of scientific and technological knowledge. The statement continued:

> We have pushed our machines with their mechanical minds and vast power outward into space among the stars, inward into the secrets of matter and men, and into the fields, the factories, the mines and the market places. A world without hunger, nakedness or human beasts of burden is now a real possibility, no longer a visionary dream.[26]

Asserting likewise that these forces and powers are of God, the document then declared that man is responsible under God to utilize his new powers in managing change "in ways that will enrich human personality and nourish the growth of human community."

The statement pointed out that a result of these developments was widespread loss of the sense of individuality and personal worth. There is of course much in this analysis that demands our agreement. But the report then went on cleverly to use it for justifying economic collectivism in America, while seemingly paying tribute to the doctrine of individual moral responsibility:

> The rapidly expanding dimensions of man's power over the earth and its physical resources call for new and deeper commitment to the Christian doctrine of stewardship in the light of the reexamination of traditional interpretation. Stewardship must be seen as a transcending and disciplining concept over prevailing concepts of private property. It must also be extended to include commitment to a realistic policy of population and family planning.[27]

25. "Minutes of the General Board," June 1969, *Matthews Collection.*

26. *Ibid.*

27. *Ibid.*

Individual responsibility was actually negated by the allegedly necessary reinterpretation of "private property."[28] There was throughout this report a basic hostility to the concept of private property; for example: "The exercise of the traditional right of private property must be conditioned by the right of all mankind including future generations to enjoy the resources and fruits of the earth. Legal ownership of resources does not confer unlimited rights of use or misuse."[29] Clearly the Council was waging warfare against the traditional American concepts of private ownership and free enterprise. In so doing it chose to overlook the contradictions in its own position, not the least of these being the fact that the very technological advances it claimed would now banish poverty, hunger, and nakedness were mostly the achievements of private enterprise.

The National Council made no major pronouncements on economic and technological issues after this one. However, the trend of its thinking was quite evident. Never did it retract the basic assumptions contained in the 1965 document. The failure of the Council to make pronouncements between 1966 and 1972 can be attributed to its all-consuming passion for the civil rights issue on the one hand and its growing realization that it needed a drastic overhaul if it was to survive into the 1970s.

The National Council and the Cause of Labor

Because of the National Council's obsession with the civil rights movement during the decade, the problems of labor received less direct attention than they had from 1950 to 1960. The Council even ceased the practice of making Labor Day pronouncements on the plea that the time had come for practice rather than proclamations on the Christian virtue and dignity of honest toil. All of which does not mean that the Council muzzled itself regarding labor. Indeed not.

In 1965, in fact, the Council entered the struggle then going on in this country to repeal section 14 (b) of the Taft-Hartley Labor Act of 1947. The repeal of this section would have had the effect of legalizing compulsory unionism in all states. J. Edward Carothers, secretary of the Council's Department of the Church and Economic

28. In the original draft the phrase "in the United States" appeared immediately after "private property" but was deleted in the final draft.

29. *Ibid.*

Life, appeared as a spokesman for the Council before the Special Subcommittee on Labor of the House Committee on Education and Labor. In his testimony Carothers stated the Council's position, or most of it. He fudged about the Council's support of compulsory unionism.[30]

In 1966 the Council made bold over what it felt was the plight of farm workers, pointing out that in the all-out war that the Johnson administration was waging against poverty the farm labor front was a major concern and that poverty in America would not be overcome until this group, among the lowest paid in the nation, rose above the poverty line. To accomplish this, quoth the Council, all discrimination and exploitation, the sins behind the farm workers' second-class citizenship, must be eliminated.[31]

In 1967 the Committee on the Church and Economic Life of the Department of Social Justice issued a statement declaring that public employees should not be denied the right to strike simply because they were employees of the state. Herein the leftward thrust of the Council clearly surfaces. Compared with this, the Federal Council's sentiments and early expressions on labor problems pale.

Direct statements on labor were much less frequent after 1960, the Council being inclined to combine the cause of labor with that of the Negro and other minority groups, after the pattern of secular liberalism in this decade. This is patent in the 1969 report "Crisis in the Nation," which will be discussed later in this chapter.

The National Council And Social Issues

After 1960 the National Council and its various agencies were increasingly inclined to make pronouncements on nearly every social issue that confronted the American people. It would be virtually impossible here to examine all of these in any detail—and probably of little value—so we will scrutinize the important ones.

In February 1961 the General Board blazed a new trail in the area of social thought by condoning birth control. Previous pronounce-

---

30. *The Record of the National Council of Churches,* pp. 139-44. While Carothers was testifying, the chairman of the committee received a telegram protesting his appearance and his claim to represent the position of the thirty-nine million members of the churches in the Council. In making this claim, Carothers was challenged by the chairman of the committee.

31. *Ibid.,* p. 151.

ments on this issue were far less liberal than this new one, as were those of the Federal Council before 1950. The 1961 pronouncement was unusual in that it contained a preamble that was somewhat apologetic in tone.[32] Acknowledging that some member denominations had already issued statements expressing the same basic conviction now espoused by the Council, the preamble also admitted that differences of opinion existed to such a degree that representatives of the Orthodox churches felt it necessary to abstain from voting.[33]

The ethical basis of the pronouncement derived from what the Council called the contemporary need and not from any biblical source. It appealed to recent advances in medical science for its justification. The dramatic reduction in the death rate, particularly among children, and the new medical knowledge of human reproduction were specifically cited as factors making it necessary now to consider how the Christian doctrine of parenthood was to be made relevant to the needs of husbands and wives. After elaborating the biblical view of marriage, its purposes and nature, the document then announced that responsible parenthood carried the obligation to weigh the claims of procreation by the total purpose of marriage and the situation of the family in society. Then followed four basic reasons for family planning: the right of children to be wanted, loved, and trained in the fear and admonition of the Lord; the prospects for the health of the future child; the health and welfare of the mother-wife; and the general social situation, meaning the prospect of rapid population growth, which would put dangerous pressures on the social order.

The pronouncement went on to state that Christians agreed that the limitation of procreation might be right and proper for the parents under certain conditions, but disagreed over the circumstances of such limitations. Specifically cited was the position of the Orthodox churches on this matter. In contrast to the Orthodox reliance on the traditional teaching sanctioning marital abstinence as the means of family planning, most Protestant churches, said the document, now upheld the use of contraceptives as well as periodic continence to be morally right when the motives were right. The general Protestant conviction was that motives, not methods, formed the primary moral issue, provided the methods were limited to the prevention of conception.[34]

32. *Pronouncements of the NCC*, pp. 31. 1-1 to 1-3.

33. The pronouncement passed 83-0, with 4 abstentions.

34. *Ibid.*, 31.2.

But the Council hastened also to insist that Protestant Christians were agreed in condemning abortion or any other method that destroyed human life, except when the health or life of the mother was at stake. The destruction of life already begun cannot be condoned as a method of family limitation. The ethical complexities involved in the practice of abortion related to abnormal circumstances need additional study by Christian scholars.[35]

This refusal to accept abortion as a solution ran counter to the secularism of the 1960s, with which the Council was so closely associated. The General Board was also thoroughly cognizant that the acceptance of abortion, except where the mother's life was at stake, would cause a violent reaction in the member denominations. However, the door was now opened just a bit; wider use of abortion would await later findings of Christian scholarship. Obviously the last word had not been spoken. The position of the Scriptures needed further interpretation so that the biblical ethic could be made more relevant to the needs of contemporary society.

The liberal bent of this document is transparent in its final appeal for family planning and its denunciation of many legal impediments to gaining the knowledge necessary for such planning:

> For most couples, family planning requires access to appropriate medical information and counseling. Legal prohibition against impartation of such information and counsel violates the civil and religious liberties of all citizens including Protestants. . . . Legislation or institutional practices that impair the exercise of moral and professional responsibilities of family-serving professions should be opposed.[36]

Not only was the National Council opposing legal provisions for the dissemination of knowledge about contraceptives—provisions which had long stood the test of time and court decisions—but it was opening the door to the widespread use of such knowledge and devices by the unmarried. In taking this stand the authors of the pronouncement were making a mockery of their opening expressions of loyalty to the biblical doctrine of marriage. It can hardly be argued that they were unaware of the implications of their position. Contemporary literature dealing with this burning issue painted a starkly real picture of the consequences of the unrestrained dissemination of such knowledge; history since the laws on this subject were stricken has more than vindicated their fears.

35. *Ibid.*
36. *Ibid.*, p. 13.

Closely associated with this enthusiastic endorsement of a planned and responsible parenthood was a 1963 policy statement on the status of women.[37] The statement counseled the United States Senate to ratify the convention proposed by the United Nations dealing with the consent to marriage, the minimum age for marriage, and the registration of marriages. The convention had been referred to the member nations by the United Nations and was simply another expression of the liberal attitude toward the role of women in modern society. The General Board called on the Council's member churches to consider in addition to this convention such questions as the rights and responsibilities of women in community life and in the life and work of the church, and to press for the passage of laws that would recognize the equality of men and women in the family and society.

Beyond an introductory statement that the Christian faith, at its best, had led to the elevation of women, no attempt was made to provide biblical justification for the contents of this pronouncement. It was candidly sociological and humanistic at bottom, and it attempted to bring the United States into line with the social policies of the United Nations.

In an effort to strengthen its whole social program the General Assembly of the National Council, at its 1963 triennial meeting, adopted a pronouncement on human rights that hailed the fifteenth anniversary of the Universal Declaration of Human Rights. The declaration had been hatched in December 1948 by the General Assembly of the United Nations. Its fifteenth anniversary now gave the Council an appropriate opportunity to counsel the United States to ratify this document.[38]

Although the Council's pronouncement opened with the usual attempt to give its contents religious sanction, the very fact that it sought to bring the United States under the influence of the United Nations mocked even this slight concession to Christian principles. The effort to give this pronouncement biblical sanction is found in the opening paragraphs:

37. *Triennial Report*, 1963. It passed 68-3 with no abstentions.

38. *Matthews Collection*, December 8, 1963. The Council's document is also important because the vote on it was 347 for, with no votes against or abstaining. This is one of the very few pronouncements or policy statements that received such a huge vote. Most of those issued by the General Board received fewer than 100 votes and were attacked because they represented not even a majority opinion of the members of the board, yet gave the impression that they were representative of the National Council membership at large.

Christians believe that man is made in the image of God, that every person is of intrinsic worth before God, and that every individual has a right to the fullest possible development of life abundant and eternal. Denials of rights and freedoms that inhere in man's worth before God are not simply a crime against humanity; they are a sin against God. . . .

Christians also share with people of other faiths and of goodwill in deep concern for the dignity of man and in profound respect for the unalienable rights with which he has been endowed by his Creator, including life, liberty and the pursuit of happiness.[39]

Significantly the attempt at religious sanction is directed not to the Scriptures as such, but to what Christians believe, and, by implication, to what they believe at this point in history. The frame of reference is humanistic, not biblical. By abandoning the scriptural norm the framers of this pronouncement could take great liberty with the historic Christian concept of the nature and extent of human rights. For a starter, no mention is made that the rights enumerated—general, political, civic and economic—have their origins in those duties that man owes to God the Creator. Rather it insists that general rights are inherent in all persons because of our personal worth and dignity.

Thus rights in this statement are ends in themselves and not the necessary means by which men are to fulfill their divinely imposed duties. As a result the list of rights that modern man may claim is greatly expanded over the four basic rights found in the Bible: life, liberty, property, and marriage. The National Council was pleased to regard other items as rights—receiving, when absence of opportunity or other unavoidable causes bar employment, a proper standard of relief payments from public sources; earning a standard of living able to promote the welfare and security of the individual and family; working in decent and healthful conditions; and having free choice of employment for just compensation with protection against unemployment. The report also insisted that one had the right to acquire vocational, professional, or job training solely on the basis of ability and character, and to engage in social action on economic issues. Even more farfetched was the assertion that to enjoy freedom of association with other persons regardless of racial or other distinctions, one must have the right to social welfare, health, and other community services.

The National Council challenged the churches to promote human

39. *Pronouncements of the National Council*, p. 17-6.

rights and to encourage the state fully to recognize these rights in laws with teeth. Here was a boldfaced call to the churches to collaborate with the Council in creating an absolutist state to enforce this code of rights. In the name of democracy the Council was hoping that Christians would support a plan to create a despotic democratic state that would destroy man's God-given rights in a vain quest for a system in which every one could claim for himself many rights without recognizing or accepting any of the responsibilities man owes to God. The Council was engaged in a stupendous task of creating a magnificent humanistic structure—overlaid with Christianity, and founded on sand. The Council became a pastmaster in maintaining a religious image while at the same time cooperating with liberalism and radicalism. The Council constantly affirmed that it took an active role in social and economic affairs because it believed in a God of compassion and justice.

This pronouncement on poverty proved to be but the first of many that would issue from such deliberations in connection with a new program to end poverty in this country. The 1964 General Board urged constituent communions of the Council to take appropriate action on the "Report of the Consultation of the National Council on Persistent Pockets of Poverty," a project sponsored by the National Council, and to develop sound public and private measures toward the elimination of poverty. Some member churches obeyed this request. In May 1964 the Methodist General Conference took such an action, followed by the General Convention of the Protestant Episcopal Church the same year. In 1965 the American Baptist Convention and the General Synod of the United Church of Christ took similar actions.

In December 1966 the General Board issued a more radical call for action against poverty.[40] This policy statement declared that the church has a clear and compelling mandate to war against the evils, the suffering, and the human misery associated with involuntary suffering. Before the twentieth century, however, the church could not cope with this problem because of the primitive nature of human technology. But now in industrially developed countries it is possible to end poverty, and the church must use these technological improvements for this purpose.

Such a solution is now possible because of socioeconomic defects, dislocations, and maladjustments. Thus poverty is the result of various environmental factors such as inadequate national eco-

40. "Policy Statement of the General Board," December 3, 1966, *Matthews Collection.*

266

nomic growth, recessions and depressions, the lack of educational opportunities, the lack of training in consumer education and money management, and low wages and low incomes. These factors along with unsatisfactory social conditions condemmed segments of the American people to perpetual poverty.

Since the diagnosis of the disease of poverty was largely environmental in character, although the statement did make a passing reference to the importance of personal attitudes, the cure must be found in changing these environmental factors which cause poverty. The Council volunteered its remedy:

> Essential to the effective involvement of the poor in community-wide and church programs is the creation of a supportive atmosphere for the self-organization of the poor. The history of the human struggle for justice and equity reveals the instances in which the establishments of this world have voluntarily transferred power to the powerless or of their own free will granted redress of grievances to the exploited and the dispossessed. For the contemporary poor, as for other disadvantaged groups in history, self-organization for counter-rivaling power is an essential ingredient of any successful war against poverty.[41]

The thoroughly Marxian interpretation of history was also an invitation for revolution, or at least mass protests, which would lead to social upheaval. Let those who refuse to see the Marxian assumptions in the thinking of the National Council consider this statement very carefully and if any doubt remains, then the following should remove any remaining doubt:

> These indigenous organizations may often adopt unconventional modes of expression and action. In evaluating such activities account must be taken of (1) the lack of access to conventional channels of communication on the part of these groups, and (2) the tremendous hidden power of the beneficiaries of the status quo to defend their positions of privilege merely by inaction or by mobilizing the political, legal communications channels which they control.[42]

This is nothing less than justification for illegal activity on the

---

41. *The Record of the National Council of Churches,* rey. (1972), pp. 150-51. This statement originated in the Division of Christian Life and Mission of the Commission on the Church and Economic Life. The division passed it 34-0 and the commission 27-0. The vote of the board was not recorded.

42. *Ibid.*

part of these groups, nothing less than justification for revolutionary protest such as we experienced from 1965 to 1970. The word *unconventional* must be interpreted as revolutionary and nothing else.

But this policy statement did not stop with an endorsement of such unconventional or revolutionary activity. It counseled the churches to become a part of this unconventional approach to social problems.

Meaningful, effective, and lawful counteractivities of the unorganized poor deserve the understanding support of the churches. If occasionally such activities violate the law, the churches have an obligation to understand and interpret the basis of such protests, and to participate in a reappraisal of the laws, customs, institutions and traditions that provoke the reaction of the poor. In other words, where violence results, then the church has the task of reappraising and, by implication, changing the laws, customs, traditions, and institutions that stand between the poor and their goals. Underlying this is the assumption that the poor are, by the bare fact of their poverty, advocating such a total reconstruction of society. This, of course, is a basically Marxian interpretation of the situation. It is a far cry from the biblical ethic to which the National Council habitually claimed allegiance in theory and just as habitually ignored in practice.

This statement praised the Economic Opportunity Act passed by Congress and said that two of its basic principles were quite in harmony with the Christian conscience, and with the inherent dignity and worth of every man. Further, in a democratic society every person is entitled to a voice in shaping decisions and policies affecting his life.[43]

Early in 1967 the Division of Christian Life and Mission began one of those almost innumerable reorganizations that have characterized the National Council, and created four new departments: Social Justice, International Affairs, Church Renewal, Church and Culture. The Department of Social Justice was responsible for dealing with the church's relationship to economic life and social welfare, religion and race, civil and religious liberty, migrant ministries, Indian-American affairs, and the Anti-Poverty Task Force. The reorganization was the opening gun in the new frontal assault by the Council against poverty and racial injustice. As part of this renewed campaign it summoned other departments in the Council to its aid. One result was the Department of Education

43. "Minutes of the General Board," December 1966, *Matthews Collection.*

268

for Mission's congregational study program for 1966-67: "Affluence and Poverty, Dilemma for Christians."

The newly reorganized Division of Christian Life and Mission sent in 1967 to the General Board a report on crime control and public morality. At best a hodgepodge of interesting counsel and disturbing contradictions, the report opened by insisting that the National Council welcomed all government efforts to strengthen law-enforcement agencies and that it was endeavoring to create a climate of public opinion favorable to sane law enforcement for the poor and the wealthy, the Negroes and the whites. It then promptly expressed its fear that current trends in law enforcement tended frequently toward repressing social discontent rather than toward its alleviation. The best plan was to prevent crime because it was more humane and also cheaper. The report also supported the Supreme Court decisions sharply limiting the police in obtaining confessions, using wiretapping devices, employing polygraph tests, and applying "stop and frisk laws."[44]

In endorsing this report the General Board enunciated its own view of law endorcement, a view that mocked the declaration that it welcomed efforts to strengthen law-enforcement agencies:

> The General Board of the National Council calls on the churches to encourage the development of a more humane and responsible value system which will serve as a guideline for a new public morality. . . . We further urge that the churches work for the establishment of morally and socially oriented priorities which will relieve the frustration of those caught in personal and community disorganization by inadequate and unjust social structures.[45]

Here was a flagrant suggestion that the Council's constituent denominations repudiate the biblical value system undergirding American jurisprudence and seek to develop a new system more humane. The Decalogue was to be supplanted by Freud and his companions in arms in the field of sociology and social service. By "more humane" the General Board was pandering to a theory of crime and its control that would relieve the criminal of his guilt and place it on society, which tolerates an "inadequate and unjust social structure." Social disorganization, said the Council, was the cause of crime. Society must accept the blame for this and not punish the criminal since it is not his fault.

44. *Ibid.*, June 1967.

45. *Ibid.*

By 1967, in the area of social thought and practice (as in nearly every other aspect of its work), the National Council had virtually abandoned the pretense of seeking theological justification for its activities. Instead it was relying upon Marx, Engels, Freud, and modern behaviorism in both psychology and sociology for guidelines for the new public morality it was seeking. Neither the National Council as an organization nor its leaders as individuals had openly formally endorsed communism or cited it as an important segment of the New Left or the overall radical movement in America. The Council had without ceremony replaced Freud and Marx for Moses and Christ. By 1967 its new philosophy was an accomplished fact.

Those critics of the National Council who seek to base their case on its leaders' formal involvement in Communist or Communist front organizations, as important as this involvement undoubtedly is, have deprived themselves of a very formidable weapon. Lack of Council involvement, however, has been a very effective weapon; it was intended to ward off congressional inquiries, which had in the 1950s become embarrassingly difficult to handle in the face of the documentary evidence presented.

The surreptitious introduction of Marx and Freud into the thinking of the Council was accomplished virtually unnoticed by the members of the denominations involved. Not so with the radicals, who were keenly aware of the change and of the actual and potential value of this organization to their social revolution.[46]

Notwithstanding its success at stealth, the Council was careful to disarm the suspicious minds and create the impression that communism was not really the menace it had been pictured in those years just after World War II. Accordingly, the Department of Research was pressed into service and obliged with a new interpretation of communism designed to pacify those who might still harbor antiquated notions of Soviet Russia: "The primary political fact we must register today is that it has become manifest that there is no longer any such thing as world communism."[47]

The rise of national independent movements in the various countries under Soviet control had precluded the possibility of an enduring monolithic world communism, according to the department's report. This development made it mandatory for Russia to

46. Indeed, when the time and place were appropriate, leaders of the National Council frequently expressed their position to radicals in the civil rights movement.

47. "National Council Information Service," October 28, 1967, p. 3.

respect the aspirations for national independence and the consumer desires in these states. The report did admit that it was not clear whether Russia would "soon respect civil liberties and civil rights." Events in Czechoslovakia certainly sustained the validity of such doubts, as they did the admission that religion had a much easier time when Russian clergymen were not a part of revolutionary agitation against the Communist regime in Russia.[48]

But the report closed on the optimistic note that there was long-term hope for Christianity in Russia. It urged American churches to press for a peaceful solution of the issues dividing the United States and Russia.

As the Department of Research sought to allay the fears of many Americans about Russia, the General Board began preparing the member churches for the changes it felt necessary in their thinking. In regard to the antipoverty program, it stated in 1967 that "a society in which abundance replaces scarcity and social structures are increasingly complex, a reappraisal of tradition, of dealing with poverty, is necessary." Thus the church must rethink its role as a servant prophet, which is to say that the church must turn from the Scriptures to the more contemporary and relevant social guidelines found in behaviorism.

As a result of the World Conference on Church and Society, held in Geneva in 1966, the National Council issued a call for a United States Conference on Church and Society for Detroit in October 1967, to receive and study the report of the Geneva conference and to consider the issues involved therein.

The six hundred participants assembled in Detroit were to represent agriculture, business, the media, labor, the home, professional protest groups, the ministry, low-income and poverty groups, and the various geographical regions of this country.[49] Although not organically related to the Council, the assembly was given its unofficial blessing. However, by the time the assembly convened, the Council was so embroiled in controversy with the various groups of black churchmen that the conference's pronouncements were mostly neglected except as they became a part of the whole racial involvement of the Council.

In fact, by 1967 the Council was so engrossed in the racial crisis

48. *Ibid.*

49. Sixty percent was to come from the member churches of the National Council while twenty-five percent was to be elected by state and local councils; guests and consultants were to make up the remaining fifteen percent.

sweeping the nation that it devoted comparatively little attention to other areas of social concern and issued only one other major policy statement of a social nature during this period. In February 1967 it entered into the arena of controversy involving church-state relations in the field of social and health services. At this time the General Board issued a policy statement seeking to justify the entrance of the church into the medical-care issue.[50]

After polite and misleading reference to the Acts of the Apostles and to the Reformers, the statement again enunciated the favorite theme of the Council's liberals. Seeking to convey the impression that they were walking in the footsteps of Calvin, Luther, and Zwingli, these liberals insisted that only in the twentieth century had productivity reached a point offering a theoretical probability of eliminating poverty. This goal could alone be achieved by a coordinated program involving both private and public agencies. Ever helpful, the National Council suggested fourteen guiding policies to its member churches for their social service activities. The basic goal was to encourage the member denominations to create a specialized ministry in the area of health services and to develop a program that would parallel the federal and local programs as well as serve as a pattern for these secular agencies. To implement this at the grass-roots level, the Council urged every local church to develop a committee to encourage study, discussion, and action for such local problems as divorce, delinquency, alcoholism, mental illness, and problems of the aging.

Church-related agencies were also to have the responsibility of shaping a sound public social policy. But in a curious reversal of form, the Council then declared that church-related service agencies offering social, psychiatric health rehabilitation, and housing and neighborhood development services could accept public funds for such services provided certain safeguards were observed. The thrust of the remaining proposals was to place such church social service agencies under the control of the governmental bodies engaged in these kinds of programs.[51]

The philosophy underlying this pronouncement clearly emerges in the General Board's attempt at justifying these proposals:

Accompanying this growing diversity in the structures of national

50. "Minutes of the General Board," February 1967, *Matthews Collection*.

51. *Policy statements, Church-State Issues for Social and Health Services in the USA*, February 22, 1967, p. 30. 2–14.

life has been a growing recognition of the importance of competent planning within and among all resource sectors of the society: education, economic development, land use, social health services, the family system and congregational life. It is not generally recognized that an effective approach to problem solving requires a comprehensive planning process and coordination in the development of all these resource areas. Access to and use of these resources are equally important; the civil rights movement and the nation's poverty program have had indispensable contributions to make in this regard.[52]

This actually invited the National Council's constituent denominations and their loyal churches to become part of an all-embracing planned society in which the churches would have a voice in the planning program. Their own social programs would now be merged with those of the bureaucratic state. The Gospel would thus be muted by the new gospel of erasing poverty and establishing full-orbed equality.

Would the National Council have made such a pronouncement after the 1968 election? Quite likely, the General Board in February 1967 was assuming that Lyndon Johnson or one wearing his mantle, committed of course to his Great Society, would be the victor in 1968 and that liberalism would still be in the saddle in national affairs. It is unthinkable that the board would have suggested such close collaboration between church and state social service agencies had the state fallen under conservative control, which is how the Council viewed the Nixon victory.

The National Council and the Crisis in Race Relations, 1961-1972

During this period the issues of peace and war, the cause of labor, and even poverty and other social problems bowed to the racial conflict. So much so that to many observers the National Council equated its concept of racial justice with the very Gospel of Jesus Christ. The 1960 election of John Kennedy to the presidency set the stage for a new wave of liberal thought and action in the nation and the Council. Liberals and radicals were aware that a subtle alteration in the nation's intellectual and moral fabric was under way, even though they were unable precisely to describe it. Aided and abetted by Supreme Court decisions, radical action was increasingly employed to obtain drastic social changes, particularly

52. *Ibid.*, p. 30. 2-2, 2-3.

in the field of civil rights. The National Council soon became a leading spokesman for such activity.

As has been noted, Council interest in the Negro cause was not of recent origin. Concern for racial equality had been an inherent part of the social gospel from the infant days of the Federal Council. But the radicalism that gripped the national mood after 1960 gave it new impetus in both word and deed. Official pronouncements of the National Council soon reflected the change.[53]

Within a few months of its organization the General Board pioneered the path the National Council would take in the civil rights controversy. It commended, via a pronouncement, nonviolent protests.[54] This placed the Council in the camp of those who favored widespread protests against segregation, so long as the protests were peaceful and lawful.

The pronouncement gave the needed impetus to the various Council departments to initiate their particular forms of protest and action against segregation. In his report to the Denver triennial of 1963 Edwin Espy observed that 1962 "may well turn out to be the year of Christian decision in regard to race. Time will tell whether the spirit of Oxford, Mississippi, or the spirit of the National Conference on Religion and Race will leave the deeper mark on history."[55]

In 1962 the National Council also prepared the way for the first Religion and Race Conference, which met in Chicago in January 1963. This conference represents a milestone, being the first time delegates from the National Council, the National Catholic Welfare Council, and the Synagogue Council of America met together in an ecumenical spirit for ecumenical purposes. The National Council was now ready to bring non-Christian groups into the ecumenical fold, at least where common goals existed. It was also willing to

53. The activities of the Council were bewildering in number in the decade under consideration; it would be of little advantage to discuss them in detail. This section of the chapter will investigate the basic philosophy behind the Council's support of the civil rights movement and its more important pronouncements and actions. The bibliography will provide a mountain of source material for those interested in pursuing this subject.

54. *Pronouncements of the NCC*, pp. 24-25.

55. *Triennial Report*, 1963, p. 4. The reference to the spirit of Oxford relates to the attempt of James Meredith to enter that stronghold of educational segregation, an attempt that, although ultimately successful, caused an outburst of unmeasurable civil commotion in Oxford and that heralded the great violent protests to come.

join with the Roman church to promote common social programs. The ecumenical movement was no longer to be regarded as Protestant or even Christian; rather, it had now become a political agency flying the colors of the Gospel for achieving goals distinctly secular in nature. The Council was no longer even pretending that its program had theological sanction. Further evidence of the changing theological climate of the National Council is the June 1962 action of the General Board approving a resolution expressing gratification for the warmer relations with the Roman Catholic church in many parts of the world as a result of Vatican II.[56]

The year 1963 brought a flurry of new activity on several fronts. The National Council prepared the way by announcing the cancellation of its annual Race Relations Message. Rather than passively listening to "messages primarily designed to salve the conscience," the emphasis should be placed on doing. No longer was the Council willing to sit on the sidelines and cheer the contestants in this new crusade; it was throwing down the gauntlet. It would enter the arena.

Accordingly, the General Board, in late February 1963, approved a resolution committing the National Council to continue its inter-religious activities in the area of race relations and authorized the Department of Racial and Cultural Relations to coordinate the development of resources and the development of personnel for the implementation of the program.[57]

In June of this year President J. Irwin Miller challenged the member churches of the Council to end racial discrimination in their own ranks. At the same time the General Board approved a report of the President's Committee of Six on Race and called for the appointment of a commission on religion and race for the purpose of taking vigorous action in the field of race relations.[58] The General Board thereupon created the commission with a membership of twenty-five persons drawn from the member churches and from those involved in the civil rights struggle. Bishop Arthur Lichtenburger of the Episcopal church was chairman and Eugene Carson Blake of the United Presbyterian Church, USA was vice chairman.

The commission was authorized to encourage negotiations, demonstrations, and direct action in places of particular crisis, and to

56. Ibid., p. 185.

57. Ibid.

58. Facts About the Commission on Religion and Race of the National Council of Churches, February 1965.

mobilize the necessary resources in the hope of sparking legislative and executive action that would bring dignity, equality, and justice to all Americans.[59] This authorization embraced a challenge to the churches to put their own houses in order by desegregating all the institutions of the church, and to develop and implement long-term plans and strategies "so that a continuing design of action will move us steadily toward the moral goal of full human rights for all."[60]

In connection with these actions, the General Board, at this meeting (June 1963), passed a resolution recognizing the use of economic pressure in racial crises as a legitimate means of attaining a moral end: "The proper warrant for the exercise of any power is the necessary accomplishment of an ethically valid purpose, such as, in this case, the Christian concept of justice."[61]

Specifically the board declared that the Council upheld the validity of orderly nonviolent demonstrations as expressions of just and righteous indignation against laws, customs, and traditions that violate human personality.[62]

To be sure, the board added the safeguard that these laws, customs, and traditions must be brought into conformity with the law of God. The specific type of action approved was the sit-in demonstration. It seemed not to occur to the board that the kind of sit-in then being used was in itself a violation of the right of private property.

The National Council of Churches was now officially launched into its role as a leader in the civil rights movement. The real import of this decision was not lost on its liberal partners, secular and religious. The Council, through the aforementioned commission of twenty-five members, was now committed to the task of organizing boycotts and demonstrations against segregation and of lobbying in Congress in behalf of civil rights legislation.[63] This was the new gospel it would preach, in action even more than in word.

The planned freedom march on Washington on August 28, 1963, offered the newly created Commission on Religion and Race an excuse for participation; it quickly seized it. In July it asked Protes-

---

59. *Ibid.*

60. *Ibid.*

61. "Minutes of the General Board," June 6-8, 1963, *Matthews Collection*.

62. *Ibid.*

63. *Ibid.* On July 4, 1963, Eugene Carson Blake, stated clerk of the United Presbyterian Church, USA was arrested for participating in a demonstration at a privately owned amusement park in Baltimore (*Presbyterian Journal*, July 24, 1963, p. 4).

tant and Orthodox churches nationwide to send 40,000 members to participate in the march.[64]

In December 1963 the Sixth General Assembly of the National Council of Churches, meeting in Philadelphia, organized a caravan in support of a discharge petition to force the House of Representatives to take action on pending civil rights legislation. The objective was to urge or force House members to sign the discharge petition in order to force the bill out of the House Rules Committee and onto the floor for a vote. The assembly counseled Congress to take every step necessary to secure the passage of this bill and called on all Christians nationwide to support this effort.[65]

The next day the assembly passed an additional resolution, which called on constituent denominations to take appropriate action to meet this crisis. The resolution, consisting of ten points, challenged the constituent denominations publicly to declare that their churches were open to worshippers of all races and their pulpits to ministers, otherwise qualified to perform their ministry, regardless of color. In addition, the churches should establish an interracial basis for all their various governing boards and related institutional activities. Individual congregations should even give moral and financial support to the major civil rights organizations and interdenominational groups formed to achieve racial justice.[66]

The assembly also adopted "Message to the Churches," which pressed government at all levels to guarantee to all citizens public accommodations, an open policy of participation in public education, and nondiscrimination in housing and employment.[67] By still another resolution, on December 6, the General Assembly urged that the programs of the Universal Declaration of Human Rights be more rapidly and completely achieved; the United States should take the lead in what it called the leadership of increasingly rising expectations, a phenomenon occurring among the newer nations, particularly the emerging nations of Africa.

The temper of this particular assembly was well portrayed by

64. *Facts About the Commission on Religion and Race of the National Council of Churches,* February 1965, *Matthews Collection.* This march was sponsored by ten organizations, most of which were secular and even revolutionary in nature.

65. *Triennial Report,* 1963, p. 209. This resolution was passed almost unanimously by the 840 voting delegates present.

66. *Ibid.,* pp. 209-10. Another resolution counseled the churches to withdraw their invested funds from any business that practiced racial discrimination.

67. *Ibid.,* pp. 204-16.

Bishop Reuben Mueller, president of the National Council. He employed Isaiah 53:12 to sanctify the civil rights struggle. Admitting that this passage had a real fulfillment in Jesus of Nazareth, he nevertheless felt moved to relate it equally to the Negro and the entire civil rights conflict.[68]

Through its Department of Religious Liberty the National Council sponsored the National Conference on Church and State, which was held in Columbus, Ohio, early in February 1964. One of the twelve sections of this conference dealt with issues involving civil rights agitation. When the processes of government are not adequate to offer redress for existing wrongs, the section counseled, resistance to the civil authority was a valid option for Christians. In general it was the duty of the Christian to obey the civil authority, affirmed the report, but in certain cases he might serve justice better by disobeying a particular law that was unjust. The rationale was that disobedience to civil authority in this context was intended to serve the government by moving it another step toward becoming a more just institution.[69] To sanctify this position the report went on to say that the present crisis in race relations was a struggle for human dignity that gave new urgency to the question of disobedience to civil authority, a question which previously arose over such diverse issues as conscientious refusal to bear arms, to pay taxes for purposes of war, and to salute the flag.[70]

These resolutions were essentially a summons to anarchy under the guise of Christian ethics. Remaining were basic questions that the report did not attempt to answer. Was it up to the individual Christian to decide when a law was unjust? Was a Christian to interpose his private view of justice between himself and civil authority? Did an unjust law warrant civil disobedience? Did the passage in Romans 13 support such a conclusion? Traditional Protestantism would have given a resounding no to these questions. But, it must be observed, the National Council was not really interested in offering a biblical solution to the problem. The use of "Christian conscience" in this report meant nothing more than the commitment to a vaguely defined Christian ethic shorn of any theological content.

In addition to the various formal statements on civil rights, the

68. *Ibid.*, p. 34. The blasphemy inherent in this interpretation is evident.

69. "Minutes of the General Board," February 1964, *Matthews Collection.*

70. *Ibid.*

National Council was increasingly active in lobbying for such legislation, particularly in Washington. There it maintained an office and an official lobbyist who appeared before congressional committees in behalf of projects involving the Council.

The Council also was active in the Mississippi Project. Early in 1964 it laid plans to aid the Council of Federated Organizations in recruiting over a thousand volunteers to spend summer 1964 working in the Mississippi Delta. The National Council accepted as its particular responsibility the development of summer schools—also known as Freedom Schools—through its Commission on Religion and Race, to be held at Western College in Ohio and other selected sites. In conjunction with the Lawyers Constitutional Defense Committee it arranged to send from eighty to a hundred lawyers to Mississippi as assistant prosecutors and assistant attorneys, to be available for service there.[71]

Although the public statements concerning this project implied strongly that there was great need in that area for the type of service intended, there can be little doubt that the project had quite another purpose. It is difficult not to believe that it was intended to engender racial agitation; the state of Mississippi was deemed a legitimate target for such an invasion of agitators from other parts of the country.

As preparation for the Mississippi Project or Delta Ministry, the National Council through its Commission on Religion and Race sponsored a youth ministry consultation at Nashville, Tennessee. Reportedly the young people at this conference were told that they should become involved in the demonstrations for racial equality.[72] The Delta Ministry by its very nature depended for its success on young people who were enlisted in "The Cause."

Early in 1965 the National Council urged the young people who had joined the Delta Ministry in 1964 to volunteer again for voter-registration drives in the cities of the North. In response to a call from Martin Luther King, the Council issued a call for Christians throughout the nation to join the planned civil rights march from Selma to Montgomery. Also during 1965 negotiation teams of the Commission on Religion and Race visited many Southern communities, among them Savannah and Americus, Georgia; Danville, Vir-

71. "A Statement of the Mississippi Summer Program of the Commission on Religion and Race," *Matthews Collection*.

72. U.S., Congress, House, *Congressional Record*, July 20, 1964, p. 15714. It was also reported that they should become not only involved, but "blooded."

ginia; Selma, Alabama; Wilmington and Williamston, North Carolina; Sumter, South Carolina; Canton and Hattiesburg, Mississippi.[73]

The Commission on Religion and Race was continually involved in consultations with various civil rights organizations and at times served as a coordinating agency for many of them. In this connection it also held frequent consultations with government agencies, including meetings with both the attorney general and the President.[74] The commission also acted as a watchdog of sorts over the progress of civil rights legislation through Congress and passed the information to its constituent churches through its *Legislative Bulletin*.[75]

There can be no legitimate doubt that the National Council played an important part in the continuing racial agitation. It greatly influenced congressional deliberations not only through its information services but by pressuring members who were reluctant to sponsor this kind of legislation. The areas of labor, foreign policy, and broadcasting also felt the Council's sinister influence. In a word, the Council was in the vanguard of those leading the nation down the rocky path of radicalism toward anarchy in the street and on the campuses of our colleges and universities.

That this was the case not only was admitted by Dr. Edwin Espy, the general secretary of the Council, but was for him a matter of pride, as he gleefully told the General Board meeting, in December 1965:

> It is striking to note how many of the general policies advocated by the National Council across the years have been incorporated into federal legislation. This was true during the Truman, Eisenhower and Kennedy Administrations, particularly in international policy, and it has been especially notable in domestic legislation under the Johnson Administration. This is not to suggest that the premises and motivation of church and state are to be confused or equated but the end result in legislation has been remarkably harmonious.
>
> Our Washington office has compared the statements of the General Board and the General Assembly with recent federal legislation. The parallelism has been notable in the field of civil rights, the anti-poverty program . . . technology, the conservation of natural resources, migrant labor, immigration, reform, disarmament proposals, nuclear

73. *Facts About the Commission on Religion and Race*, February 1965. This was an official statement published by the National Council.

74. *Ibid*.

75. *Ibid*.

test ban treaties, the surplus commodities program and social and economic development, federal aid to elementary and secondary education, housing and urban renewal, health and medical care . . . and numerous other fields.[76]

Espy then went on his way rejoicing that even the actions of the executive branch, by which he meant the Johnson administration, had echoed the policies advanced by the National Council. He specifically cited the administration's support of the United Nations and the opening of new cultural contacts with Soviet Russia and other Communist-dominated areas. Ecstatically he continued:

> The Supreme Court likewise has handed down numerous decisions which are in keeping with the position of the National Council. Cases in point are the civil rights rulings, the decision on legislative reapportionment and rulings on prayer and Bible reading in the public schools.
> To cite these parallels is not to explain or appraise them. Some of our constituency would feel that they constitute a reassuring sign that the National Council's position is close to what it should be, neither radical nor reactionary, since it closely parallels the position of our elected government. Others would consider our position far to the left of center. A few would see them as evidence of dangerous leanings toward communism. On the other hand, some of our constituency consider us timid, especially in international relations, for the very reason that our position is so close to that of the government. . . .[77]

Espy concluded his remarks with one note of pious assurance regarding the General Board: "I am sure that this General Board will always be guarded in its judgments by the demands of the Gospel and not by degrees of conformity or non-conformity with the position of the administration or of Congress."[78]

This report is almost unbelievable. Unbelievable that it could be written or accepted. Its attempt to reassure its readers that the Council's activity did not mean any union of church and state hardly needs refutation. The record speaks, loudly. Plainly, the Council entered into nearly every political question confronting the American

76. "Minutes of the General Board," December 2, 1965, *Matthews Collection.*

77. *Ibid.*

78. *Ibid.*

people and by its own testimony played a vital role in shaping national policy, in both the domestic and the international realms.

Laughable, though, was the comment that the position assumed by the National Council in these matters was "neither radical nor reactionary, since it closely parallels the position of our elected government." Parallelism here proved no such thing in view of the claim that such was the result of the Council's influence on the government. The record of both the Johnson administration and the National Council patently points to the fact that the policies adopted in nearly every instance were either radical or very liberal.[79]

In 1967 the Vietnam War diverted, for a time, the attention of the Council from the civil rights struggle, though the latter was by no means forgotten or even shelved. John Regier, associate general secretary of the Commission on Christian Life and Mission, reported that the commission was stressing the need for open-housing legislation for Negroes. Further, it backed the current demonstrations in Milwaukee led by Father Groppi, for "it is far better people march to express their anguish than to be caught up in the self-wounding protests of riots."[80] But Regier also reported that the Reverend Robert Kolze, Midwest director for the National Council, had been on the scene in Milwaukee for several weeks. One can only surmise to what extent he may have inspired or even aided the Groppi demonstrations.

At this same meeting of the General Board it was voted to invest ten percent of the unrestricted funds of the Council in an attack on racial injustice and urban ghettos. There was one provision: at least one hundred thousand of this amount should go for improved housing, business ventures, and credit unions for the Negroes.[81]

The board also seriously considered a consumer boycott as a means of obtaining what it called racial justice. However, the plan was sent back to the commission for further study after William Thompson, stated clerk of the United Presbyterian Church, USA, warned that serious legal dangers were involved and that the assets

79. Edwin Espy's message to the General Board is one of the frankest revelations of the machinations of the Council in American political life which this writer has found in the Council's official documents.

80. "Minutes of the General Board," September 1967, *Matthews Collection*.

81. *Ibid.*

82. In opposition to Dr. Thompson, Rev. J. Edward Carothers, executive secretary of National Missions for the Methodist church, replied, "Consumer justice cannot be exercised without consumer power."

of the National Council would be exposed to suits up to three times the amount of damages suffered by the plaintiffs in such actions.[82]

In 1968 Council president Arthur J. Fleming announced an emergency consultation to deal with the racial crisis in the offing for the nation in summer 1968. Eighty delegates responded. Fleming warned them of the real prospect of armed conflict in the United States that summer. Calling it the most serious crisis to confront the nation in the last one hundred years, he blamed it on the continued denial of equal opportunity to the Negro race.[83]

Its deliberations and attempts to meet the racial crisis make it evident that the Council was almost totally unprepared to cope with the fruits of its own liberalism. As a result, it was agreed to give financial aid to the Urban League Coalition, a lobby-action group organized with the help of Walter Reuther and Arthur Fleming; the whole staff of the National Council was to be involved. To finance this emergency action the member denominations were called upon for a donation of emergency funds, which would be used for the Urban League Coalition and other such cooperative enterprises. A special committee, including Arthur Fleming and Edwin Espy, was appointed to administer these funds and given wide discretionary power over their use.[84]

On the racial issue the National Council was a house divided. With one hand it was attempting to meet the crisis while with the other it was fanning the flames of discontent, by its pronouncements, money, and activities. It was fighting fire with combustible materials.

The year 1969 not only brought little relief from the crisis threatening the nation, but brought the problem in a new and paradoxical form directly to the attention of the National Council.[85] In January the General Board heard the report of the Committee on Social Welfare, which had been appointed by the Division of Christian Life and Mission. A curious document, to say the least, the report was hardly calculated to reduce the violence then threatening the nation. Its basic thesis was that riots in a blighted area do not introduce violence into a hitherto non-violent area; they only "make silent violence visible." The report held that some acts of violence

83. "Minutes of the General Board," September 1967.

84. To help meet the crisis the Division of Christian Education had prepared new adult Sunday school materials, which became part of the problem, certainly not its cure.

85. The Council authorized an additional $250,000 to be spent to meet the crises in addition to the $369,000 previously authorized.

were nothing more than attempts at communication.[86] Its remedy
for the situation was equally curious:

> The committee proposes the recognition that there is an ethical
> distinction to be made between the violence used by the oppressed
> and that used by the oppressor. The distinction is clear in the goals
> sought or achieved. This is not to say that ends justify means, but
> to affirm that ends and means are one; that just as means can de-
> stroy ends, ends can redeem means. Thus each use of violence is to
> be viewed on its own merits.[87]

The committee was not unaware of the danger residing in such
logic. It took pains to theologically safeguard this thoroughly pragmatic and essentially Marxian logic: "The prompting of the Holy
Spirit can lead the faithful man into darkness as well as into light."[88]
It then couples this admission with another one equally alien to the
basic philosophy underlying this document: "Violence will not bring
the Kingdom of God on earth for the Kingdom will not be fulfilled
in history." If violence will not bring the kingdom of God, then why
endorse the use of violence? Or could the endorsement have been
because the committee was seeking not the kingdom of God, but
the kingdom of Marx?

At this same meeting the General Board received an interesting
report that may have had some bearing on the report on violence.
The second report stated that the monies spent under the resolution
of the board on September 14, 1967, for ghetto community in-
vestments had not yielded the expected results. In fact, the program had been a failure. Many of the projects had folded up or
were not satisfactory as recipients under the original resolution.[89]
Can it be that this guarded endorsement of the use of violence to
obtain "racial justice" may have been inspired by the failure of the
somewhat more peaceful means mentioned in the 1967 resolution?
Nothing exists in the official records of the board to connect these
two actions, but their chronological connection does perhaps prompt
suspicion of some connection. Suspicion was strengthened by the
report of the Special Committee on Crisis in the Nation. Received
by the board at its January 1969 meeting, the report declared:

86. "Minutes of the General Board," January 1969, *Matthews Collection.*

87. *Ibid.*

88. "Minutes of the General Board," June 1969, *Matthews Collection.*

89. *Ibid.*

284

The crisis in the nation is more acute now than ever before, the relative calm of last summer notwithstanding. It is this fact which makes it necessary for the churches to organize to deal with the manifestation of white supremacy in such a way as to conquer both the symptoms and the cause.[90]

To understand, in part at least, the meaning of this statement, certain factors must be taken into account. The election of 1968 was history; victory belonged to the more conservative Republicans and defeat to the avowed liberal, even radical, Democratic candidates. The Nixon campaign had centered on the war in Vietnam and law and order at home. Domestic recommendations of the National Council would no longer receive the warm and friendly treatment about which Dr. Edwin Espy had boasted in 1965. A new day had come. With the inauguration of Richard Nixon later in January the Great Society would end. The leadership of the National Council was aware of this. Thus reliance upon friendly liberals and radicals still in Washington government posts would not offer the same assurances for success as before. New approaches must be found. "Crisis in the Nation Report" outlined the new direction the churches would take.

Although the report admitted the great importance of the Washington office in this program, its chief thrust was aimed at the churches and the efforts they must make to alleviate the crisis. They must attack the roots of the problem. Little is new in the report except the emphasis on the Council's role in the effort:

As a nation we rapidly approach the brink of armed conflict in our cities. This crisis demands unprecedented action by the churches working together. We, therefore, direct that a special action program be undertaken at once to reorder, strengthen, accelerate and fully coordinate the recourse of the churches and the National Council of Churches in the crucial struggle for justice in the nation.[91]

The meaning is too clear to be ignored. The election of what the Council thought was a conservative Republican administration had given the National Council (indirectly to be sure) a mandate to assume the burden the new administration would surrender. The quest for racial justice now belonged to the churches rather than to the government. A secularized church would to all intents and pur-

90. *Ibid.*, p. 2.
91. *Ibid.*, p. 7.

poses replace the secular government in one important sphere of domestic activity.

Another meaning exists. An election that gives "conservatism" a victory at the polls must not be allowed to hinder the liberal and radical policies endorsed by the churches of America through the National Council. But 1969 brought the National Council a rude blow from its Negro and radical allies, a blow for which it was quite unprepared.

The immediate cause of the blow was the *Manifesto to the White Christians and Jewish Synagogues in the United States of America and All Other Racist Institutions.* It was presented by James Forman at the National Black Economic Development Conference meeting in Detroit in April 1969, and adopted then.

In his address to the conference Forman, its president, used the theme that total control is the only solution to the Negro's economic problems. He emphatically rejected the idea of black capitalism and roundly denounced those militant black nationalists who jumped on the bandwagon of capitalism as the solution to their problems. Calling them pimps, black-power pimps, and fraudulent leaders, he declared that the people must be educated to understand that any Negro who advocated a perpetuation of capitalism inside the United States not only was seeking his ultimate destruction and death but was contributing to the continual exploitation of blacks around the world as well. For it was the power of the United States government, this racist, imperialist government, that was choking the life of all people everywhere.[92]

The *Manifesto* was a clarion call for revolution. Of this there can be no doubt:

> Time is short and we do not have much time and it is time we stop mincing words. Caution is fine, but no oppressed people ever gained their liberation until they were ready to fight, to use whatever means necessary, including the use of force and the power of the gun to bring down the colonizer. . . . [93]
>
> But while we talk of revolution which will be an armed confrontation and long years of sustained guerilla warfare inside this country, we must also talk of the kind of a world we want to live in. We must commit ourselves to a society where the total means of production are taken from the rich and placed into the hands of the state for the welfare of all the people. . . .

92. "Minutes of the General Board," May 1-2, 1969, *Matthews Collection,* p. 1.

93. *Ibid.,* p. 2.

286

We have an ideology. Our fight is against racism, capitalism and imperialism and we are dedicated to building a socialist society inside the United States where the total means of production and distribution are in the hands of the state, by revolutionary blacks who are concerned about the total humanity of this world.[94]

This document is a Communist statement. Its goal is world revolution, but one to be led by the Negroes of the United States. To achieve this, our government must be transferred to black control: "Racism in the U.S. is so pervasive in the mentality of the whites that only an armed, well-disciplined, black-controlled government can insure the end of racism in this country."[95]

Having then given its background, Forman then presented the *Manifesto* itself.[96] It demanded that the nation's white churches and synagogues pay reparations to America's black people in the amount of $500,000,000. This would be spent on establishing a Southern land bank, which would aid in building four major publishing houses in this country to break the white monopoly in publishing. With a capital of ten million dollars each, they were to be located in Detroit, Los Angeles, Atlanta, and New York. Four futuristic audio networks were to be established in Detroit, Cleveland, Chicago, and Washington, D.C., to provide an "alternative to the racist propaganda that fills the current television networks." Each network was also to have a capital of ten million dollars. The *Manifesto* demanded an additional ten million dollars to aid in organizing America's welfare recipients under the National Welfare Rights Organization.

An international black appeal was to be created and funded with no less than twenty million dollars. James Forman would head the appeal. This organization was to produce more capital for the establishment of cooperative business enterprises in both the United States and Africa.

The *Manifesto* also called for the founding of a black university, to be funded by a grant of $130,000,000 and located in the South.

To gain these demands the *Manifesto* requested all Negroes in America to regard themselves as members of the Black Economic Development Conference and to act in unity to help force the racist white Christian churches and Jewish synagogues to implement

94. *Ibid.*, p. 5.

95. *Ibid.*

96. *Ibid.*, pp. 7-11.

them. Part of the conference's strategy involved holding press conferences in our major cities to arouse as many black organizations as possible to the support of its demands.

Of particular importance was the willingness of this conference to use the threat of violence and violence itself as an essential part of its strategy:

> We call for the total disruption of church sponsored agencies operating anywhere in the U.S. and the world. Black workers, black women, black students, and the black unemployed are encouraged to seize the offices, telephones and printing apparatus of all the church sponsored agencies and to hold these in trusteeship until our demands are met.
>
> We call upon the delegates and members of the Black Economic Conference to stage sit-in demonstrations at selected black and white churches. . . .
>
> Such confrontations should take the form of reading the Black Manifesto instead of a sermon or passing it out to church members. The principle of self defense should be applied if attacked.
>
> On May 4, 1969 or a date thereafter, depending upon local conditions, we call upon black people to commence the disruption of racist churches and synagogues throughout the United States.[97]

But the strategy of this conference was not limited to intimidating churches. The whole community was to feel the pressure of these tactics: "We call upon all delegates to find within the white community those forces which will work under the leadership of the blacks to implement these demands by whatever means necessary." Yet in spite of this open threat to use force, the conference had the temerity to counsel white Christians and Jews "to practice patience, tolerance, understanding and non-violence as they have encouraged, advised and demanded that we as black people should do throughout our entire enforced slavery in the United States."[98]

The irony of this appeal was not quite lost upon those who drafted this document: the admonition continued: "The true test of their faith and belief in the Cross and the words of the prophets will certainly be put to a test as we seek legitimate and extremely modest reparations for our role in developing the industrial base of the western world through our slave labor. . . ."[99] In essence, however,

97. *Ibid.*, p. 9.
98. *Ibid.*
99. *Ibid.*

288

the white race was asked to accept not only this plan of reparations for past slavery, but a worldwide revolution, communistic in nature, as well: "We are so proud of our African heritage and realize completely that our struggle is not only to make revolution in the United States, but to protect our brothers and sisters in Africa and to help them rid themselves of racism, capitalism and imperialism by whatever means necessary, including armed struggle. . . ."[100]

Without doubt, here was a summons to communistic revolution. After asserting that it would demand even greater reparations from the government of the United States than it had from the churches, the conference asserted: "But to win our demands from the church, which is linked up with the United States government, we must not forget that it will ultimately be by force and power that we will win."[101]

Annexed to the *Manifesto* was a list of the slogans the framers would use to describe their cause and programs:

All Roads Must Lead to Revolution . . . Unite With Whom-Ever You Can Unite . . . Neutralize Wherever Possible . . . Fight Our Enemies Relentlessly . . . Victory to the People . . . Revolutionary Black Power . . . We Shall Win Without a Doubt.

Some of these slogans were actually used by Communists in this and other countries. Others, derived from the Communist philosophy, had particular application to the racial issue. The *Manifesto* was signed by twenty-four leaders of the conference including Renny Freeman, Howard Fuller, James Forman, and Julian Bond.

In May 1969 the Executive Committee of the General Board drafted a response to the *Manifesto*. It stated that it found itself "under Christian restraint to make every effort to understand these demands and by the Grace of God to respond in a way consistent with the Gospel of Jesus Christ."[102]

Asserting their awareness of the grave injustices done to the blacks and other minority groups by white men in the past, many of whom were members of Christian churches, the committee members asserted that "we as Christians have no right under God to refuse to listen to any demand presented to us whatever may be our own initial reaction to the form it takes." They continued:

100. *Ibid.*, p. 10.

101. *Ibid.*, p. 11.

102. "Minutes of the General Board," May 21, 1969.

But openness is not enough. There must be penitence and a readiness to make recompense. The National Council of Churches, aware of the grievances of the Black people of this nation, while rejecting the ideology of the Black Manifesto, acknowledge the Black Development Conference as a program and expression of the aspirations of black churchmen.[103]

The Executive Committee, acting under the authority of the General Board, suggested that the churches fund the five regional conferences sponsored by the National Committee of Black Churchmen. The National Council, said the committee, welcomed the commitment of many of its member denominations to use their financial and personnel resources for more aggressive action against injustice and poverty in the rural and urban slum areas of the nation. It also counseled the member churches to urge a massive governmental involvement at every level. It then added, seriously, that such an involvement would also require church school programs for the youth and adults to explain the *Manifesto*.[104]

The attitude and position of the National Council at this point were both misleading and hypocritical. The committee said it rejected the ideology of the *Manifesto*, yet it urged the Christian education agencies of the member denominations to develop study programs centering around the message of the *Manifesto*. This suggestion exposed the Council's desire to replace biblical material in Sunday schools with literature permeated with the Communist philosophy and Freudian psychology, both of which are diametrically opposed to Christianity.

The Executive Committee continued its consideration of the *Black Manifesto* (its popular designation) at its meetings on June 23, July 14, and August 29, 1969. The document constituted a serious crisis for the National Council, one which it could not ignore and which it feared. To favor the *Manifesto* virtually committed the Council to supporting the Communist philosophy; this would further antagonize countless members within the constituent churches. To reject the *Manifesto* meant that the Council was turning its back upon the program it had been pursuing throughout the greater part of its history; this would cost it the support of unnumbered liberals in the churches and the nation who had been counting on the National Council for leadership in the civil rights struggle.

103. *Ibid.*

104. It was also hoped that this educational effort would include the development of programs to relate to the militant student groups.

In his report to the General Board meeting in September 1969, Dr. Edwin Espy said:

> We have started but not completed the passage of the Red Sea. We have begun to know from experience the mind of the blacks and whites in the new mood that is abroad in the land. It is a mood that is fraught with both peril and promise.
> It calls on us to say yes to the future, but not to disown the wisdom of the past. It goes much deeper and farther than a "Response to the Black Manifesto."[105]

This delightfully vague statement characterized the thinking of the leadership at this point. Its dilemma reflected that of many of the member churches, although by September 1969 the African Methodist Episcopal Church, the African Methodist Episcopal Zion Church, and the Protestant Episcopal Church had given conditional support to the *Manifesto*.[106] The Executive Committee of the General Board recommended that the National Council assign $500,000 to be spent through the National Conference of Black Churchmen.

The *Manifesto* was not the Council's last challenge in 1969. Meeting in November in Oakland, the Conference of Black Churchmen drew up its own type of manifesto for the Detroit triennial:

> We neither believe that God is dead, white nor captive to some high rationalistic and dogmatic formulations of the Church which relates Him exclusively to the canons of the Old and New Testaments and accommodates Him to the reigning spirits of a socio-technological age. Rather, we affirm that God is Liberator in the man Jesus Christ, that His message is Freedom and that today He calls all men to be what they are in themselves, and among their own people.[107]

The message stated that in a special way God's favor rested upon the poor and the oppressed in the world of 1969, and that God had called these disadvantaged folk to be "ministering angels of His judgment and Grace as His Kingdom of Freedom and Peace would break in from the future." It then called on the white Chris-

---

105. "Minutes of the General Board," September 21, 1969.

106. Their frustration was compounded by the fact that James Forman disrupted the normal activities of the Interchurch Center at 475 Riverside Drive, New York City; from May 14 to June 17, 1969, he and his followers took over the denominational headquarters located there in an effort to reinforce their demands for reparations from the churches.

107. *Capsule* 3, no. 9: 3. (*Capsule* was edited by Edwin Espy for a limited circulation.)

tian church to be willing to submit to a radical reformation, which meant that it must become revolutionary and divest itself of all its ill-gotten wealth (gained by exploiting the oppressed).

The black churchmen's program was based on the *Black Manifesto* and equally candid: "We do not shrink from the revolutionary, anti-capitalistic implications of the Manifesto."[108] It denounced the National Council as one of the chief symbols of the white church power structure, calling it a "sorry example of institutionalized white decision-making power."

The specific demands of the black churchmen's conference were a Negro general secretary of the National Council and the selection of "Negroes in significant numbers as heads of divisions within the Council."[109] The churchmen intended also to disrupt the Council's Detroit triennial meeting if these demands were not met.

The Reverend Edwin Espy, general secretary of the National Council, penned a most interesting and revealing reply to the Conference of Black Churchmen. There was very little chance, he said, that the National Council defeat would become a joint project of the whites and blacks. He then pointed out very realistically that even if such a victory were ever achieved, it would be a defeat for the Negroes if it did not gain the support of the constituent churches. To the demand that the Council appoint a black general secretary Dr. Espy replied: "I have no intention of stepping aside as General Secretary of the General Assembly."[110]

In this important correspondence Espy made it unmistakably clear that there were definite limits to the liberal zeal for integration and that in the demand for high Council offices these limits had been transcended. The Council quite willingly counseled its member churches to appoint many blacks to responsible positions within their denominational structures, but the Council was rather unwilling to apply to itself its own advice at this point.

Espy correctly pointed out that such a victory for the Conference of Black Churchmen would also ultimately be a defeat. The member churches were not ready for such a radical change in the work of the Council. This fact emerged even more clearly in an exchange of correspondence between the leaders of the Conference of Black Churchmen and Dr. Espy in November 1969. Replying to their request that Negroes make up at least one fourth of the official nominees to the General Board's membership, to be presented at

108. *Ibid.*, p. 4.

109. *Ibid.*, p. 5.

110. *Ibid.*, p. 6; See also October 27, 1969, issue pp. 5-9.

the Council's December 1969 meeting, Dr. Espy made it crystal clear that he could not accede to this request, it being beyond his power.[111]

The real question in this running debate was the issue of integration versus the ecumenical movement. The National Council had long posed as the champion of both movements, but since 1950 they had been running on parallel tracks of thought and action. Now suddenly the Council must face the problem of merging both into one movement. Espy and the other leaders of the National Council were well aware of the dilemma this demand posed. To accede to the request from these two Negro organizations, they knew, would virtually end the National Council, at least in its present form.

The Council was confronting its greatest crisis for at least two reasons. First, the constituent churches were in no mood to integrate either the Council or their own denominational structures. The riots of the past five years had cooled the enthusiasm of many in the churches for the civil rights movement in general. Strong conservative protest against these liberal trends in the Council had arisen in several of the denominations, notably the Presbyterian Church, U.S., and the United Presbyterian Church, USA.

Second, the Communist implications of the *Black Manifesto* and the obviously radical theology of the Conference of Black Churchmen bothered many who were not necessarily opposed to the civil rights movement in general, but who would not tolerate any support of communism by the Council under any conditions. The close relationship between the two black groups on the one hand and the theological and political radicalism on the other was so apparent that the Council was forced to give way and not to yield to their demands. Thus when the ecumenical movement and the civil rights movement clashed, the Council leadership placed a higher value on its ecclesiastical goals than on racial integration.[112]

111. *Ibid.*, pp. 15-16, 17-18. This was of course technically true but the tone of the reply infers that he had no intention of even making the suggestion.

112. The Detroit triennial elected Cynthia Wedel to chair the Division of Christian Unity. Mrs. Wedel, President with her husband Canon Wedel, had long been active in the Council. She defeated her opponent by a vote of 387 to 93. Dr. Espy was re-elected general secretary by a vote of 382 to 100 over his Negro opponent. However, Bishop Frederick Jordan of the African Methodist Episcopal Church was elected vice president. The 1972 triennial elected Rev. Sterling Cary of the United Church of Christ as the first Negro president of the Council, but the power remained in the hands of the white leadership. Bishop S. G. Spotiswood of the African Methodist Episcopal Zion Church was elected chairman of the Division of Christian Unity over Bishop Alexis of the Russian Orthodox church by a vote of 357 to 87.

In spite of the fact that more Negroes had gained places of leadership by the 1969 triennial meeting, the Council and its General Board were during the next three years strangely quiet about civil rights and greater Negro participation in Council work. The events of 1969 had engendered such a crisis that some were even questioning whether the Council could survive in its present form. The division went deep, both within the Council and among its constituent churches. There was determined opposition within these churches to integration in the life of the church, but this issue was not the basic cause of the controversy. At bottom was the cozy alliance between the Black Economic Development Conference and the Conference of Black Churchmen on the one hand and the Communist philosophy on the other. In the light of the voting record of the General Board members on the issues involving the *Black Manifesto*, it would seem safe to assume that a minority was opposed to the *Manifesto* largely because of its open support of Communism. But in many of the member churches a large, vociferous majority was very much alarmed by even the qualified endorsement given to the demands of these two groups.[113]

At its June 1972 meeting the General Board took two steps, again contradictory. It named the third Sunday of January each year as Martin Luther King Sunday. Such a celebration, opined the board, would remind Christians of their need "to struggle for equity, justice and peace." But at the same time it voted to make the Delta Ministry in Mississippi an independent activity, with the understanding that funds for it would continue to be channeled through the Council.

The National Council and the Public Schools of the Nation

The involvement of the National Council with the nation's public schools was directly related to two basic issues: (1) federal aid, and (2) Bible reading and prayers.

On February 22, 1961, the General Board adopted a policy statement that aroused much controversy and forced the board to issue later clarification.[114] The statement declared, modestly, that it

113. It is exceedingly difficult to learn just what the feeling of most of the board members was on this or other issues because so few of them ever attended the meetings or voted. Most issues from 1950 on had been decided by a minority of the membership.

114. *Pronouncements of the NCC*, pp. 13. 4-1. It passed 87-1 with no abstentions.

was the duty of the nation to encourage the full development of the talents and abilities of all of its citizens. Providing general education for all required the mobilization of the best resources of our society. The conclusion to this line of reasoning was to the effect that the public schools were the one institution designed to fulfill this mission.

But these were unable to cope with the problem in many communities because of a lack of funds. The pronouncement said that new buildings must be planned and built, more teachers recruited and trained, and better methods of education perfected and applied in order to meet the educational challenge of the day. Admitting that this was a mammoth and long-term effort, the board concluded that "where there is an inability or unwillingness in any community to provide adequate educational opportunities for all children, such failure must be remedied by society as a whole."[115]

Having called for a thoroughly secularized public and even federalized system of education, the Council then went dutifully on record as stating that its belief in such a system of education arose directly out of its faith in Jesus Christ. Moreover, by asserting, as a basic Christian conviction, that the survival of our society depended ultimately upon the sovereignty of God, the Council was able to affirm its belief in the right of all parents and churches to establish and maintain a public school whose "ethics and curriculum differ from that of the community as a whole."

The Council then engaged in serious efforts to straddle the fence on this issue. Admitting that the Protestant and Orthodox churches had historically claimed the right to establish and maintain their own schools in any community where the public school was basically inimical to the Christian education of children, it nevertheless went on to say that "we believe that to encourage such a general development would be tragic in its results to the American people."[116]

The logic in all of this is wonderful to behold and impossible to understand. Having affirmed its belief in public education as absolutely necessary to the maintenance of a free society and that such a belief stemmed from certain basic Christian convictions, the Council then went on record as upholding the right of various Christian groups to maintain their own private school system in

115. *Ibid.*, p. 13. 4-1.
116. *Ibid.*

communities where the ethics were inimical to the Christian education of their children. But to encourage such a general development of schools based on Christian principles would be tragic in its results. But the encouragement of secularized public schools federally supported would not breed tragic results. The fallacies in this policy statement apparently escaped its framers, who concluded with a resounding vote of confidence in our public schools:

> We affirm our support of the public school system as an indispensable means of providing educational opportunity for all children; we urge provision of increased resources for the operation and improvement of the public schools; we declare our wholehearted support of the principle of public control of public funds.[117]

To implement this declaration of faith, the Council, through its General Board, called for federal funding for elementary and secondary public schools. However, certain conditions were attached, namely, that the funds be administered by the states, that there be no racial or other kinds of discrimination in the schools receiving the aid, and that there be an adequate safeguard against federal control of schools receiving funds.

At the same time the Council voiced strong opposition to federal, state, or local grants to nonpublic schools, and to using public funds for tuition or scholarship grants for children attending private or church-related schools.

The pronouncement of February 1961 generated a storm of controversy within some of the member denominations. In June 1961 the General Board issued a supplementary statement intended to interpret the previous pronouncement.[118] It stated that the opposition of the National Council to "grants from federal, state or local tax funds for non-public elementary and secondary schools should be understood to include special-purpose grants as well as general or across-the-board grants." The board took pains to emphasize that its stance against tax credits, tax forgiveness, and exemption from school taxes or other taxes for parents whose children attended nonpublic schools was not intended to imply either opposition to or support for making parochial school tuition tax-deductible.

The Council was again obviously on the horns of a dilemma and

---

117. *Ibid.*, p. 13. 4–2.

118. *Summary of Resolutions of the National Council of Churches, 1951-1961*, p. 7

endeavoring to please concerned parents, member churches, and its liberal constituency. The real issue was not allowed to surface in these statements. The real issue was of course the segregated school. The leadership of the National Council felt that all nonpublic schools were intended to be a shelter from integrated schools for those who could afford them. This assumption was probably correct for many private schools not supported by churches. But the Council had already gone on record as upholding the right of parents to provide the kind of education they desired for their young people. Too, the very democratic philosophy the Council espoused dictated that parents have the right to send their children even to schools that liberals deemed divisive.

The reinterpretation of June 1961 did not and could not solve this dilemma. It remained to haunt the Council throughout the rest of the decade. On the surface it seemed that the Council was acting to defend the historic principle of the separation of church and state, but its other actions make such an assumption untenable. In fact, it appeared that a real zeal for this historic principle was the motivating factor in a policy statement issued by the General Board on June 7, 1963. "The Churches and the Public Schools" asserted that although full treatment of some subjects required using the Bible as a source book, neither religion nor good education was dependent upon the Bible in a public school program.[119]

The dominant note behind this pronouncement, however, was not religion, but democracy. In fact, the statement was a strange compilation of past platitudes and contradictory positions. Such only reflected the confused thinking of that branch of liberalism that very much feared the influence of the Bible in the schools. In one breath the board could both denigrate the Bible and loftily declare, as it did in this pronouncement, that "religious ideas, beliefs and conditions are an integral part of our cultural heritage as a people," that "the public schools have an obligation to help individuals develop an intelligent understanding and appreciation of the role of religion in the lives of the people of this nation."[120] Then, following this tortuous logic, the board concluded that American public education should have the full support of Christians and Christian churches. This appeal was coupled with the insistence

119. "Minutes of the General Board," June 7, 1963, *Matthews Collection*. This was passed by a vote of 65 to 1 with one abstention. The Greek Orthodox Church of North America vigorously dissented from this pronouncement.

120. *Ibid.*

that the churches should provide intelligent appraisal and responsible criticism of the programs in public education and explore cooperative arrangements between the churches and schools so that the church's teaching on religion may be improved.

In 1964 the General Board was forced once again to consider the thorny problem of religion in the schools. Forced, partly because its pronouncement of 1963 was quite unsatisfactory to the Greek Orthodox church, which dropped hints that it might reconsider its membership in the National Council, and partly because heated public reaction had prevented direct federal aid to the nation's public schools. The Roman Catholic church had taken a determined stand against any federal aid that excluded their parochial schools on the ground that it constituted a kind of double taxation.

On June 4, 1964, the General Board issued a new policy statement, "A Protestant and Orthodox Statement Regarding Dual School Enrollment." Its purpose was to offer a new approach, one which essentially provided for systems of dual enrollment, which was defined as an administrative arrangement in "which the school time of the children was shared between the public school and the church day school."[121] Students who enrolled in church day schools could also be enrolled in nearby public schools for part of their general education. The board expressed the hope that this proposal would be a workable plan with "viable provisions for those who, for conscience' sake, maintain separate schools."

In spite of the large vote by which the statement passed, it is doubtful that those who favored the new approach really regarded it as a viable solution, except for a few. The practical aspects of the plan were too complex for it to be easily applicable. Only in large cities and towns where the schools in question were fairly close together could a workable plan be achieved.

But this practical difficulty, real as it was, did not constitute the major objection to the proposal; it rested on one dubious assumption and on another that was completely false. The assumption that some instruction in secular schools—notably in the physical and biological sciences—was superior to that offered in church-related schools, was true only in some cases and generally not in the larger towns and cities where the plan was most feasible in its practical application. The level of instruction in many of these church-related schools was much higher than that of the public

121. *Ibid.*, June 4, 1964. It was passed 103–0 with 2 abstentions.

schools in many areas of subject matter, and growing better each year.

But the proposal rested on another assumption, one totally and dangerously false; to wit: there is a neutral area of subject matter that can be safely taught in the public schools without endangering the faith of the students involved.[122]

That the General Board had another purpose in view becomes evident in its appraisal of the proposal. After paying due attention to what it felt the educational benefits would be, it then revealed its true thinking, which was that the purpose of the church-related school be nullified:

> We believe that benefits will ensue for all children if those now enrolled in separate systems have the opportunity to associate with each other through dual school enrollment. We believe that this association . . . and intermingling of the children in the school will result in a broader support for public education and will serve to unify our now partially divided communities.[123]

The purpose of the plan was thus social and not educational. It was intended to minimize the separateness and the divisiveness of the church schools and, simultaneously, to convince the parents of those children in the church-related schools that the public schools were really not so bad after all. In a word, that there was no need for church-supported institutions.

At the same time, dual enrollment was also a face-saving measure. It allowed those who were really interested in promoting various schemes of federal aid to push for this goal by disarming those who felt federal aid was basically unfair. However, it did not meet the Roman Catholic argument of double taxation. Those who sent their young people to parochial schools could still be subject to double taxation.

The practical and technical problems involved in the enrollment proposal precluded its extensive use, which fact disappointed those who sponsored it. The proposal did, however, help remove one substantial roadblock to the passage of bills providing greater federal aid to our public schools.[124]

122. For an excellent discussion of this aspect of public education in America, see R. J. Rushdoony, *The Messianic Character of American Education* (Nutley, N.J., 1963).

123. "Minutes of the General Board," June 4, 1964, *Matthews Collection.*

124. It is almost impossible to obtain statistics as to how many students entered upon dual enrollments programs over the nation.

It is admittedly exceeding difficult to assess the influence of the Council's pronouncements on the passage of bills providing federal aid for education. It is highly doubtful that they were the determining factor. Rather it would seem that "victory" resulted from the confluence of support for federal aid from various liberal and racial groups.

After victory was gained, the Council made no further pronouncements of any importance on the public school, though it continued openly to oppose the amendment allowing prayers in the schools.

The National Council and Evangelism, 1961-1972

In spite of its occasional protests of loyalty to the evangelistic task of the Christian church, the Council paid relatively little attention to evangelism, less than it paid during the preceding decade and much less than the Federal Council had given to it. Gone from the scene were the preaching crusades of the late 1930s and early 1940s. Even the work on the college and university campuses dwindled significantly.[125]

The Division of Foreign Missions was merged in 1961 with the World Council's mission arm, becoming the Division of World Missions and Evangelism of that international body. As a result, the National Council's evangelistic efforts focused on such national issues as the population explosion, urbanization of culture, secularism, depersonalization, rural slums, cultural conflict, poverty, and leisure. Solutions for these issues were sought in understanding the nature of the unity desired, the meaning of mission as over against missions, and the nature of the Christian congregation.[126]

The contents of evangelism, as outlined by the Division of Home Missions, could well be described as many programs but no Christ, much machinery but no Gospel.

Much of the work of evangelism was actually carried out by the Broadcasting and Film Commission, which had been created in 1957 and which was reorganized in 1963. The direction these efforts would henceforth take was enunciated in a 1963 pronounce-

125. The Council continued to sponsor the Faculty Christian Fellowship; it held conferences over the nation, but these had little impact on the academic community.

126. *Triennial Report*, 1963, p. 140.

ment of the commission. Specifically, the frequencies used by the television and radio stations belonged to the American people; thus "the whole public is responsible for the functioning of mass communication, and the individual Christian as citizen is impelled to exert what influence he can to have television and radio operate to the public good.[127] Since the mass media were already influencing Christian education and evangelism, the General Board insisted that if Christianity were to be a determining factor in shaping the future of mankind, Christians must not only practice their gospel of love, but proclaim it, using those means of communication to which the nation's eyes and ears are accustomed.

As an essential part of this approach to broadcasting the General Board called on the churches to take a much more direct interest in the broadcasting industry. Particularly were they to make sure that the Federal Communications Commission, operating under the act of 1934, required all licensed stations to operate "in the public interest, convenience and necessity," and that it took effective steps to ensure that each licensed station met this requirement.

In regard to religious broadcasting, the pronouncement instructed the constituent churches to conduct their own programs under the same standards of excellence and integrity they demanded of secular programming. The churches were also counseled to "cooperate closely in mass communication endeavors" in an effort "to demonstrate the wholeness of the Gospel and our oneness in Jesus Christ."[128]

The use of radio and television was to be dedicated to the ecumenical movement and the preaching of the social gospel. Said the pronouncement:

> . . . religious presentation shall never be merely inoffensive but . . . shall deal candidly with contemporary and controversial issues and concerns, bringing to bear on them the illumination, judgment and healing of the gospel . . . . mass communication by the churches should make clear to the public that the Church is concerned with all of life.[129]

127. "Minutes of the General Board," *Matthews Collection*, pp. 8. 2–1, 8. 2–3. (The pronouncement passed 55–6, no abstentions.)

128. *Ibid.*, p. 8. 2–3.

129. *Ibid.*

In this there was of course no real place for biblical evangelism, or even for that evangelism of the Federal Council before 1950.

Accordingly, the programs of the Broadcasting and Film Commission offered little in the way of sound biblical instruction. The Commission supported several television programs such as its series "Frontiers of Faith" on NBC and the "Look up and Live" series on CBS. In 1961 and part of 1962 Dr. Ralph Sockman conducted his "National Radio Pulpit" over NBC radio, which series Dr. David H. C. Read continued during 1962 and 1963. In conjunction with a number of denominations it sponsored the "Protestant Hour," which took the form of a half-hour preaching service and was heard over a large number of radio stations. In 1961 the commission commenced a new series, "Church World News," which was presented over 229 radio stations in 1963. Only "National Radio Pulpit" and "Art of Living," carried by NBC, made any pretense at evangelism and resembled the older series sponsored by the Federal Council.

By 1963 the problems of race were overshadowing other interests. At the Denver meeting in late February 1963 the General Board not surprisingly accepted a detailed report that made race the chief concern and responsibility of the Division of Home Missions. The statement contained few biblical or theological references for such a move, basing it largely on the secular concept of human rights instead.[130]

This revised concept of mission activity also colored the educational activities of the National Council. In 1962 the Commission on Higher Education sponsored the third convocation of Christian colleges at Northfield, Minnesota. Some five hundred delegates attended and considered the mission of the Christian college in the modern world. One of the results of this convocation was the emergence of the National Christian Student Federation, which combined three earlier student groups: the United Student Christian Council, the Inter-Seminary Movement, and the well-known Student Volunteer Movement. The National Council unapologetically intended to capture these three groups and mold them into a formidable student arm of the ecumenical social-action front. In 1966 the University Christian Movement succeeded the National Christian Student Federation and was promptly recognized as a related movement of the National Council of Churches.

130. The report was hatched by the recently created Policy and Strategy Committee.

Simultaneously an effort was made to take control of the Faculty Christian Fellowship for the same purpose. It was given a grant by the United Church of Christ for creating "Disciplinary Study Groups in psychology, philosophy, history, education and the physical and biological sciences in order to bring them into the ecumenical movement."[131] This faculty agency adopted the publication *Methodist Faculty Forum* as its own, to bring together its thirty-two thousand members.[132]

In 1962 the Division of Home Missions launched a series of studies on home missions under the title "Heritage and Horizons," which stressed the ecumenical nature of the church's home mission task. The same theme was stressed in Dr. Robert Spike's *Safe in Bondage,* which was deemed a provocative portrait of the contemporary home mission task and which aroused many people to new awareness of responsibility in this area of Christian activity. To further its ecumenical approach to home missions, the division also sponsored for several summers a series of interdenominational conferences.

In 1967 there was a brief revival of interest in evangelism. A flurry of evangelistic planning occurred when the General Planning and Program Committee voted that the National Council of Churches and its Canadian counterpart should jointly sponsor a mission on the 1970s. The 1967–69 period was to be used for intensive preparation. As its contribution to this evangelistic effort, such as it was, the Division of Christian Education gave birth to "Process '67," an approach to be used by the University Christian Movement to appeal to the university and college mind. This program was to utilize "Look up and Live," the CBS television series built around the issues of technology and human values. In all of this the evangelical appeal was most conspicuous by its almost total absence.

As might be expected, these various proposals fell on ears dull to such appeals. The Council therefore devoted its entire energy to the weightier secular and radical matters demanding its attention. Evangelism, being of less moment, must now bow to matters having little or nothing to do with the Lord of the harvest ripe unto reaping by the Spirit's sword.

The National Council and the Ecumenical Movement

The National Council became increasingly bold in its leadership

131. *Triennial Report,* 1963, p. 110.

132. It also supported other publications: *The Inter-Seminarian, The Mission of the Christian College in the Modern World,* and *the Protestant Stake in Higher Education.*

of the ecumenical movement after 1960, a posture consonant with the boldness it was displaying in secularizing the church. The Council had been formed to promote the ecumenical movement itself and an ecumenical influence in national affairs. Its charter and early pronouncements proclaimed its function as the voice of the churches unified in a common task. They also emphasized its role as the obedient servant of the churches. It had always disclaimed being a church or misrepresenting the thinking of its constituent denominations. Rather, its emphasis was that it was their representative voice in national affairs.

In 1963 the Department of Faith and Order Studies submitted to the 1963 triennial a working paper on the ecclesiological significance of councils of churches and of the National Council in particular.[133] The paper defined the church in terms of the doctrine of the triune God and thus declared it to be "theocentric, Christocentric and pneumatocentric." By this misuse of the doctrine of the Trinity emerged what it called a trinitarian understanding of the life of the church, and this understanding required that "the Church be seen in relation to the totality of the work of God, in the whole of creation and history. . . . "[134]

This nonbiblical view of the church was really enunciated to provide theological justification for the ecumenical movement and the involvement of the church in secular affairs: "Finally the unity of the triune God is the basis of the unity which is given to the Church and which it is called upon to embody."[135]

The purpose behind this new emphasis upon the doctrine of the church was entirely unbiblical. It was designed to create an ecclesiastical body dedicated to the social gospel and having sufficient hierarchical strength to make its voice heard in the political life of the nation. The ultimate goal was a collectivist society "democratically controlled." In a word, democratic collectivism.

The framers of the working paper were not unaware that they were on rather dangerous ground in advocating church union. They sought to save the National Council from the charge that the Council was advocating a kind of superchurch or that it was an agency of church union, while arguing that such a role was still desirable:

133. *Ibid.*, p. 7.

134. "Minutes of the General Board," January 1963, *Matthews Collection*. It was also reproduced in the *Triennial Report* for 1963, but with its own paging.

135. *Triennial Report*, 1963, p. 7.

The councils [of churches] have taken seriously—perhaps at times too seriously—that they are councils of *churches* and that they represent the churches. Councils of churches have not sought nor have they been asked or called upon to negotiate church unions. They have often been content to be agencies of cooperation—a significant role indeed. But even so they are not called to become active agents of reconciliation. They can and should show an increasing concern for feasible and Christian steps toward the larger unity of the church.[136]

Although the report defended the course of the National Council thus far, it also issued a clear call for a change of direction. No longer should it be simply the representative and the voice of the denominations in their secular concerns; rather should it now become the active agency through which church unions could take place. This plan did not fall on deaf ears. The Council leadership was only too willing to exploit such a situation and assume command in the movement for union. Indeed, the provisions of the Council's own charter called for church unity in matters of common concern. The leadership was pleased with those denominational mergers that had occurred since 1950. But these were only a step. The Consultation on Church Union, offspring of the announcement of the Blake-Pike Plan in 1960, was the leaders' cherished goal.

The general scope of the Council's future activities was given special attention by Council president Irwin Miller at the Sixth General Assembly in December 1963. He affirmed that it was definitely the duty and privilege of the Council to discern the shape of the future and help mold it according to the Council's social and economic philosophy.

> More and more it seems to me the program of the council should be aimed at discerning the shape of the future, recognizing and dealing with new evils while they are still small, seizing on new opportunities, giving direction to our time. Long range planning is the means of preserving the health and usefulness of every organization of the council. . . .
>
> If this council can resist the temptation [to freeze, to resist change] and cultivate instead a tradition of perpetual accommodation, an atmosphere wherein people welcome change and find in it an excitement otherwise lacking, then it can serve with the force which the issues require.[137]

136. *Ibid.*, p. 21.
137. *Ibid.*, p. 11.

But how was the church to bring to bear on the issues of the day the necessary force that would enable it to prove its leadership in American life? In his report to the 1963 triennial assembly, Roy G. Ross, executive secretary of the National Council, supplied the answer. There must be an ecumenical theology and ecclesiology. The old confessions and ecclesiastical structures that had served the evangelical mission of the church in the past were now inadequate for today's task:

> We now need to look at the area of our theological and ecclesiological differences and the emerging new theological insights in their bearing on the mission of the church. . . . This requires serious interconfessional research and study. . . . We are still far from showing the world that unique liberty in faith, in life, in worship and in order which is inherent in the Christian Gospel. As long as Christians remain undisturbed by their disunity in faith and order there is little hope for further significant advances in Christian unity, either through councils of churches or otherwise.[138]

Ross described further the new mission of the church:

> We find ourselves in the throes of a second Reformation, which is the ecumenical movement. It is a movement of ideas, of persons, institutions and activities. It is both theological and ecclesiological. . . . It does not insist always on organic union. Its goal is to restore the manifest unity of the church.[139]

The concept of a second Reformation underlay much of the ecumenical movement. The Reformation had served its days, but neither its theology nor its ecclesiastical structure was adequate for the second half of the twentieth century.[140]

By 1962 no doubt remained concerning the scope of the ecumenical church; it was to be broadened to include members of the Orthodox churches and, hoped the Council, even the Roman Catholic church At its February meeting the General Board approved the acceptance of an invitation from the Russian Orthodox church for a delegation of American churchmen to visit the churches of the

138. *Ibid.*, p. 24.

139. *Ibid.*, p. 26.

140. The desire to minimize the importance of the Reformation was seen in the ecumenical interpretation of Luther in the celebration of Reformation Sundays after 1950.

Soviet Union that year. The board reciprocated, extending an invitation to the churches of the Soviet Union to send a delegation to visit the churches of this country. And at its June meeting the General Board passed a resolution expressing gratification for the increasing evidence of the promise of warmer relations with the Roman Catholic church as a result of Vatican II. The exchange of visits took place as planned and occasioned a fresh barrage of criticism that the Council was entirely too friendly with communism.

A most important step was taken in December when the Membership Committee of the National Council recommended to the General Board that the Roman Catholic church be recognized as being in agreement with the preamble of the Council's constitution and that its name be added to the list of communions in such agreement.

In 1965 the General Board took another step to develop warmer relations with the Roman Catholic church. It invited the Ecumenical Commission of the National Conference of Catholic Bishops to send official observers to meetings of the General Board. The invitation, extended in June 1966, was accepted and observers have been present since that time.[141] In 1966 a joint working group was created from the Roman Catholic Commission on Ecumenical Affairs and the National Council's Committee on Ecumenical and Interreligious Affairs. The result: the appointment of the Reverend David J. Bowman of the Society of Jesus to the staff of the Faith and Order Department of the National Council.

As a result of these and other developments the General Board in June 1967 announced in triumphant tones:

> It is also safe to say there is no program activity of the National Council in which a lively contact does not already exist with the appropriate representatives or agencies of the Roman Catholic Church. In some areas these program relationships are highly developed. In practically all of them such cooperation may be expected to increase."[142]

The report of the General Board also raised the question of the cooperation of the Roman Catholic church with the World Council and gave an affirmative answer.

But the ecumenical effort was no longer simply to include Christian communions. Efforts were already under way to include Jewish

141. "Minutes of the General Board," June 1967, *Matthews Collection*, p. 8.
142. *Ibid.*, p. 9.

groups within its circle. Arthur Fleming, president of the National Council, and Archbishop John F. Dearden of Detroit, president of the National Conference of Catholic Bishops, were considering the likelihood of asking the Synagogue Council of America to join with them in a vigil for peace.

The General Board gave this new ecumenical thrust additional impetus when it sponsored a Conference on Christian Unity in Boston in May 1967. It did so through its Division of Christian Unity in conjunction with the Synagogue Council of America, and the Bishop's Commission on Ecumenical and Interreligious Affairs. The board also reported that over one half of the constituent churches of the Council were involved in conversation with National Conference of Catholic Bishops on theological issues—among them the nature of the sacraments—and related topics in the hope of reaching some common agreement in traditionally divisive areas.[143]

To further such developments the Commission on Unity published in 1967 a study paper of eighteen pages as a working guide. The approach to ecumenical involvement, said the guide, should take several forms—dialogues involving clergy and laity, participation in the work of other joint committees, the development of suitable ecumenical prayers in programs for the observance of Reformation Sunday, interdenominational (Roman Catholic and Protestant) and even interreligious (Christian and Jewish) conferences for exchanging ideas, and joint training institutions covering such common areas as marriage counseling.[144]

In his report to this June 1967 meeting of the General Board, R. H. Edwin Espy, the executive secretary of the National Council, was most enthusiastic regarding the progress of relations with the Roman church:

> I would observe again that no really new relationships have developed in recent months, rather an extension in the areas of worship, dialogue and staffing. It is with Roman Catholicism that Vatican II must have its full influence before much more may happen between Protestant, Orthodox and Roman Catholics to bring them together.[145]

After reviewing the helpful developments that had occurred since Vatican II, Espy concluded on an optimistic note: "It is my conviction that we are approaching, if not actually in, the time of the

143. *Ibid.*
144. *Ibid.*
145. *Ibid.*

American Church and the very center of that church could well be the Roman Catholic Church."[146] He admitted that there might be dangers in such a development. The resulting American church might be narrow and highly nationalistic in its outlook, claiming jurisdiction over both Rome and Geneva. He recognized that it might also be captured by a despotic political leader and used for political purposes. And doubtless, the appearance of such a church would also occasion serious splits in those established denominations whose memberships were still basically opposed to any co-operation or union with the church of Rome. But in spite of these admitted dangers, Espy felt the advantages of such a church far outweighed them.

Mrs. Cynthia Wedel, chairman of the Division of Christian Unity, perhaps summarized the thinking of the Council in her report to the General Board in December 1967. She declared; "The Roman Catholics are now asking us to join them in dialogue with unbelievers."

In January 1969 Dr. Eugene Carson Blake, long-time leader in the ecumenical movement and secretary of the World Council of Churches, called on the General Board to scale new heights of ecumenical leadership: "If you are not ecumenical enough to recognize what has happened in the Roman Catholic Church since Vatican Council II, you are not ecumenical enough."[147] Then, after cautioning the Council leaders not to give up on the Southern Baptist Convention and the Lutheran Missouri Synod as potential Council members, Blake reminded them of still other candidates for the ecumenical fold: "The whole group of Conservative Evangelicals must be made to understand that the Lord Jesus Christ is the center of the ecumenical movement and without them and their commitment Jesus Christ is obscured and crippled."[148]

But Eugene Carson Blake did not limit the ecumenical movement to these groups. With near unbounded enthusiasm for the ultimate success of his cause, he declared that there must be a place for Jewish cooperation and for men of all goodwill, whether they were religious or not.

Blake seemed not aware of the incongruity involved in his views: on the one hand that Jesus Christ was "the center of the ecumenical movement" and on the other that the movement

146. *Ibid.*
147. *Ibid.*, January 1969.
148. *Ibid.*

must have a place for Jews and for all men of goodwill, whether believers or not. Such confusion was hardly calculated to endear his cause to the Lutheran Missouri Synod, the Southern Baptist Convention, or the large group of evangelical conservatives outside the fold.

Summer 1969 brought a crisis to the ecumenical movement and endangered the goals of the Council. In his report to the General Board in September, Dr. R. H. Edwin Espy admitted that the Council had been engaged in a crisis action caused by the *Black Manifesto*; indeed, an emergency that "could well tear the council and the churches themselves apart."[149]

In its reply to the *Black Manifesto* the General Board echoed this:

> It is in this larger sense we refer to the summer that is closing as "a crossing-point" for the National Council! It has been a cross-point for the council because it has been a crossing-point for the churches, not alone because of race, but because of a maze of tumultuous issues that confront the Church and the whole of society.[150]

A vague sense that the National Council and perhaps the whole of the ecumenical movement would never be quite the same permeated the General Board and its various committees from 1969 to 1972. Espy voiced an uneasiness about the Council's future that was shared by most of its leadership:

> We have started but not completed the passage of the Red Sea. We have begun to know from experience the mind of Blacks and Whites in the new mood that is abroad in the land. It is a mood that is fraught with both perils and promises.[151]

The tone of the pronouncements and more private utterances at this point indicates clearly that the perils loomed larger than the promises. The fear of peril spurred the Council leaders to find refuge and new strength in a broadening of the Council's ecumenical base. At the 1969 Detroit triennial Espy urged that the Council issue a call for a general ecumenical council of all the churches in the nation, to find solutions for the pressing problems of the day.

And yet beneath this plea for strengthening the ecumenical movement as the proper ecclesiastical approach to the crisis threatening

149. *Ibid.*, September 11–12, 1969.

150. *Ibid.*

151. *Ibid.*

the nation, there was also the keen awareness that the ecumenical movement was being questioned and that the younger generation of Americans was growing skeptical about its need and value. Even as the *Black Manifesto* indicted the Council for being a part of the white establishment, so did white American youth, who were also in various stages of revolt against the establishment.

This was brought to the attention of the Council in the report of the Committee of Twenty to the General Board in September 1969.[152] The report said:

> Today's youth—we are speaking of persons 13 to 30 years of age— have been indelibly marked by the new world in which they have grown up. However, in spite of the fact that the majority of this generation in the United States has been reared in privileged white influences, inheriting material security and opportunity never before possible on a mass scale, it is profoundly significant that they are increasingly saying "no" to what influence and security have come to represent to them.[153]

Admitting that only a small percentage of America's youth was actively engaging in social revolution, the report nevertheless said that even the majority of our young people were giving a "growing evidence of a psychological instability to deal with well entrenched, but in their view increasingly obsolete, structures, thought patterns and life styles. . . . These young people are reflecting deeply on the meaning of our culture's value systems and are in their own way saying 'no' to much of it."[154] The committee was admitting that ecumenical institutionalism was caught up in the swelling skepticism and that young people no longer regarded it as a satisfactory answer to the problems of the day.

What then was the solution to the problem that could not be ignored or avoided? The committee supplied one: "The church must join the new generation and the issues which concern it and which face the whole society." The church must change its style, its theology, its format of worship. The ecumenical movement in general and the National Council in particular must also change and surrender some of its previous formats and approaches for the sake of the young people. The growing antagonism to the estab-

152. *Ibid.* (p. 1 of special report).
153. *Ibid.*
154. *Ibid.* (p. 4).

lishment did not exempt even this institution from the demand for change.

What then was the remedy that this Committee of Twenty recommended? Adults must work with youth, must join with this source of creative imagination and energy to conceive the new age and the new forms of the church. In short, the church must join the new generation around the issues that concern it. It even asserted that no real relationship with youth was possible outside the context of such issues. And what were these issues which must form the basis of this new relationship? The war and the draft, the increasing gap between the "haves and the have nots," institutional and personal racism, and the place and role of education. In other words, to forge a new relationship between youth and the church, the latter must become part of the revolutionary generation and no longer be the church.

The committee, however, insisted that such a departure need not mean this:

> In many ways traditional and untraditional, today's youth are religious and are seeking authentic spiritual meanings and expression in daily life. The causes they espouse are often directed toward making our common life more human, just, liberated and loving. . . .[155]

This, of course, was nothing less than a plea for an ecumenical humanism rather than an ecumenical Christianity. The new humanity envisioned was to be born not of the Holy Spirit unto obedience to the Christ of the Scriptures, but of a humanistic philosophy exemplified in the human Jesus of Nazareth.

As the 1960s drew to a close there was a growing feeling within the National Council that something was wrong with the ecumenical movement in general and with the Council in particular. This had been vaguely felt in 1964 when some changes were made in the Council's organization in the hope that these would make it a more effective instrument in the ecumenical cause. But organizational changes were not the final answer. As the decade drew to a close questions concerning the role of the Council and its place in the life of the American churches could no longer be ignored. The report of the Committee of Twenty was only one of several admissions of inadequacy.

And yet in spite of this growing bewilderment, and perhaps

155. *Ibid.*

even because of it, the Council leadership pushed for an even more inclusive unity of the churches. It intensified its effort to bring the Roman Catholic church into the Council and to establish an even closer relationship with three major Jewish groups in those areas of social and political cooperation not involving a theological confrontation.

In January 1970 Edwin Espy, general secretary of the Council, issued a statement on the Roman Catholic question that clearly outlined the goals of the Council for the next decade:

> We believe that the membership of the Roman Catholic Church in the National Council could have incalculable value for the One Ecumenical Movement both in America and throughout the world. It would say to the world that the Church is truly One.[156]

Dr. Espy argued that such a development would greatly aid in many areas of the life of the church, such as in the problem of intercommunion, intermarriage, baptism, evangelism, governmental aid to church-supported schools, and abortion and population control. He believed that the admission of the Roman Catholic church would even "strengthen the stand of the church against the crying injustices in our society, in facing together the supreme crisis of our time, the crisis of faith."

In June 1970 Dr. Espy reminded the General Board that the ecumenical commitment entailed two more elements—mission and unity: "The two are so related both theologically and operationally that it is a pity we do not have one word to cover both. . . . Perhaps the best connecting word is obedience, which invites the whole church in mission to the whole man in the whole world."[157] He then pointed out that unity and mission as obedience had been and were being used to nurture the growing collaboration between the World Council of Churches and the Roman Catholic church. He could thus argue: "The ecumenical issue is not, therefore, a side issue. It provides the basic context in which enlightened churches in our time must rediscover, rearticulate and more effectively domesticate the one Gospel of the One Lord."[158]

For Espy the conclusion of this logic was quite clear. The Council must take the lead in this creative enterprise. He even unearthed

156. "Minutes of the General Board," January 27, 1970, *Matthews Collection.*

157. *Ibid.,* June 1970.

158. *Ibid.*

an old bone: the National Council must strengthen its theological foundations for the tasks ahead. To do this it must be in contact with the most creative theological exertions: "We should be in closer alliance with the most creative expressions of the theological enterprise. It will call for more and better psychological and social analysis in the theological perspective."[159]

The "creative expressions of the theological enterprise" were of course patently humanistic and, therefore, non-Christian. Equally patent in its absence is a call to reexamine the Scriptures for further light on an ecumenical theology. Rather is light to come from sociological and psychological analysis. The theology that Espy and his fellow liberals at the helm of the ecumenical enterprise sought would not be mined from the Scriptures. Indeed, to use the word *theology* at this point is a serious misnomer. The message they had and still have in mind is the message of man to himself as interpreted by modern existentialist philosophy and behaviorist psychology and sociology.

But the dilemma appears at precisely this point. Both behaviorism and existentialism deny the biblical doctrine of man and sin because they deny the biblical doctrine of God. Thus the summons to union and unity envisioned not even the basis of the lowest possible common theological denominator, but the twin foundation of existentialism and behaviorism, both of which are antiintellectual and irrational. Such an appeal could not have been made to the Roman Catholic church in this or other countries before Vatican II. Vatican II gave nearly free rein to the forces of theological and philosophical liberalism operating in the Roman church and made it possible for the theological liberals in both Protestantism and Roman Catholicism to find common ground in their negations of basic Christian doctrines found in the ecumenical creeds of the early church, doctrines which both the Reformers and their Catholic antagonists accepted during the struggles of the sixteenth century. The ecumenical movement of 1970 was a movement that actually denied the ecumenical bonds of the church of the first five centuries and substituted a humanism that denied historic Christianity. It was ecumenism in revolt against ecumenism.

Espy continued his prescription for the future success of the National Council with some observations on how it must meet the

159. *Ibid.*

problem of the secular power structure. He called on it to make an impact on the power structure of American society—the government, marketplace, industry, universities, labor, television and radio, performing arts, theater. To accomplish this task the Council had to enlarge its base to allow a more inclusive fellowship. But even this was not sufficient. Espy pointed out that in his opinion the great weakness of the Council lay in its failure to capture the loyalty and participation of the laity, to secure this loyalty, and to penetrate the life of the local congregation.

In this Espy was quite correct. In many of the constituent denominations, the problem of securing the participation of the laity was compounded by the suspicion with which most of the laity looked on the National Council and its activities. Thus lay opposition, on the rise during the sixties, had by 1970 produced serious cleavages in several of the member denominations, even to the point of dividing asunder.

But Council leadership was undaunted by this dilemma. Early in 1971 Edwin Espy and Dr. John Coventry Smith met with the representatives of ten of the more conservative evangelical churches to explore the possibilities of closer cooperation between them and the National Council. The evangelical delegates present proposed that a consultation be held in March 1971.

Sparse indeed were the tangible results of this abortive effort to shepherd evangelicals into the ecumenical fold. However, the conviction, shared by most Council leaders, that the future of the ecumenical movement was bound up with the future of the Council produced new determination to revitalize the Council. This resulted from the growing feeling that all was not well with the Council and that it might not even be able to continue in its present form. The Detroit triennial had reinforced this feeling and caused many of its leaders to fear for its future.

This gloomy picture of the future of the Council occasioned the usual therapy for such an illness—reorganization of the institution. It never occurred to the leaders to examine the basic assumptions of the ecumenical movement. They never doubted them.

By 1971 reorganization was the first order of business for the General Board. The first steps in this direction had been taken by the Detroit triennial. A task force had been created to prepare a plan for decentralizing the Council in order to advance the cause of Roman Catholic and evangelical participation in its work. In January 1971 the task force presented to the board a model proposal, which called not for a completely new ecumenical organization, but for a national conference of churches.[160] To ensure continuity for the leadership of the ecumenical movement, the present thirty-three constituent members of the National Council would take the necessary steps to bring the national conference of churches into being as a continuation of the National Council.

The preamble of this plan was skillfully worded to present a bright picture of the health of the ecumenical movement and to give the appearance that all was well within the Council:

> Under the providence of God communions which confess Jesus Christ as Divine Lord and Saviour, in order more fully to manifest oneness in Him, do now create an inclusive agency of Christian Churches of the United States of America to show forth their unity and mission in specific ways and to bring the churches into living contact with one another for fellowship, study and cooperative action.[161]

Curiously, the model was attacked by the more liberal elements on the General Board and elsewhere. Although it did provide for greater representation of minorities on the new governing board, the model also diffused power for the sake of a broader base for the ecumenical movement. One critic charged that this Brower Task Force report had in its excessive catering to Roman Catholics and evangelicals, created a white-power model of diffusive ecumenism. The weakening of the central authority of the General Board appeared to be too great a price for the board's membership to pay for large-scale ecumenical inclusiveness. The report was rejected.

This rebuff did not discourage attempts to effect closer unity between the Roman Catholic church and the National Council. In

160. "Minutes of the General Board," January 1971, *Mathews Collection.* This model proposed a governing board, slightly larger than the General Board, that was to have greater power over the major divisions of the work of the Council. The present Executive Committee was to be replaced by an advisory committee with limited powers. Greater importance would be attached to the office of the executive secretary. To satisfy the minority groups, they would have larger representation on the governing board. Seventy-five percent of the membership of the governing board would be selected by the constituent churches and twenty-five percent would be proposed for membership by a nominating committee in turn elected by the constituent churches.

The new governing board was to have the power to establish general policies, to speak for the churches, to oversee the work of the major units (divisions and commissions) of the national conference, and to approve the budget.

161. *Ibid.*

early 1972 a joint study committee of Catholic, Orthodox, and Protestant scholars released a report recommending that the Roman church join the National Council of Churches. Nearly every argument in favor of the continuance of the National Council of Churches, or its comparable successor, was also an argument for Roman Catholic membership.[162] The committee insisted that "if the documents of Vatican II are a valid expression of what the Roman Catholic Church is and intends to be . . . Roman ecclesiological principles are in substantial accord with aims and methods of the National Council of Churches."[163]

The joint committee admitted that there might be some problems involved in the admission of the Roman church, the latter's stand on abortion being one. However, the committee, ever optimistic, believed all obstacles would be removed. It submitted a formula for Roman Catholic participation that was designed to allay Protestant fears of the danger of Roman Catholic numerical superiority and strength in the Council. Since the membership of the Roman Catholic church was forty-eight million as over against the forty million in the thirty denominations in the Council, the committee proposed that the Roman Church have not more than one third or less than one fifth of the voting strength in the council, and that no communion pay over twenty-five percent of the budget.

Agitation for reorganization of the Council continued. Finally the Dallas triennial accepted a plan of reorganization. The General Board would be succeeded by a governing board of 347 members that would meet every two years and include a larger minority representation. The 347 members would be elected by the constituent denominations according to a formula based on their membership. The delegation from each church to the governing board was to be composed according to a formula by which one half would be clergy and one half laymen, one fourth must be women, and one eighth must be youth under the age of thirty. Minorities must be represented according to their percentages of membership in these denominations.

The plan also provided for an executive committee of forty-four

162. *Ibid.*, February 8, 1972.

163. *Ibid.* The committee was under the joint chairmanship of Bishop Charles Helmsing, of the Kansas City Diocese of the Roman church, and Dr. John Coventry Smith, general secretary of the Commission on Ecumenical Missions and Relations of the United Presbyterian Church. In 1970 the Conference of Catholic Bishops had approved membership on the Council's Commission on Faith and Order, and Catholic dioceses in eleven states had joined local councils of churches.

members and program agencies of three divisions and five commissions. The three divisions would be (1) Church and Society; (2) Education and Ministry; and (3) Overseas Ministries. The five commissions would be (1) Broadcasting and Film; (2) Faith and Order; (3) Regional and Local Ecumenism; (4) Justice and Liberation Program Development and (5) Stewardship.

The Dallas triennial elected W. Sterling Cary of the United Church of Christ as its first Negro president and retained Dr. Espy as general secretary on the understanding that he would retire at the end of 1973.

Some observers believed this reorganization of the National Council would give it new vigor, a new lease on life as the symbol of the ecumenical movement in America. Others saw very little change in its basic structure and outlook.

Critics of the National Council, 1961-1972

Criticism of the National Council increased in both volume and vehemence after 1960, and its leadership found itself too often on the defensive. Criticism was not a new experience. The Federal Council had more than once been subject to vigorous attack. And from its inception the National Council had been the target of much criticism. Some of it had in fact come from its friends, who believed that it was a cumbersome bureaucracy and that because many of its policy statements and pronouncements were formulated by but a handful of men—either of the General Assembly or of the General Board—it did not always represent the constituent churches.[164]

The Council was also taken to task, even by some of its friends, for speaking on issues that were none of its concern and for harming more than helping the ecumenical cause.

But most of the criticism focused on the National Council's cozy relationship with radicalism in general and communism in particular. This became the theme of the swelling number of enemies of the Council and resulted in a new wave of hostility to it and the ecumenical movement. Sensitivity to this was evident in the deliberations of both the General Board and the General Assembly.

In his presidential address to the 1963 triennial, J. Irwin Miller, after assessing the situation, sounded a warning: "If the council is

164. *Triennial Report*, 1963, p. 3.

ever forced to rely for a major part of its basic program upon individual donors who upon whim could withdraw support, then the council would be in danger of having sold its freedom for money."[165] Miller was informing the Council that it must not become too dependent on those donors who could be and were being influenced by the ballooning criticism. It must not fashion its basic programs to meet the demands of these critics.

But neither could the Council afford to ignore all criticism. It was a treacherous path that President Miller was suggesting the Council follow. Appropriately, to this triennial he tendered further advice as to how it should meet its critics:

> No organization is beyond the need for legitimate criticism and every organization should endeavor to preserve itself responsive to such criticism. Yet, you are well aware that most of the criticism of the past few years has not come from those within the council who are personally familiar with its purposes and working and who criticize to improve and strengthen. Rather the loudest critics are often from outside the council, from persons who wish to weaken rather than strengthen and that they elect to do so by spreading misinformation and falsehood has been brought clearly to their attention. How, then, can this be a good thing? It can be a good thing . . . because it has made the National Council a subject of national debate. It has led more people to inquire seriously, "What is the National Council of Churches?"[166]

Miller was undoubtedly correct in saying that most of the criticism came from those who were outside the National Council. But he was in serious error in maintaining that they were not familiar

165. This was largely accurate. The General Board had a total possible vote of 173 divided among 273 members. A report by the Christian Social Relations Department of the Diocese of Arizona of the Protestant Episcopal Church stated that of the forty-three official pronouncements made by the General Board from 1950 to June 1961 only one was passed by the necessary eighty-seven percent majority of eighty-seven votes. The pronouncement on public funds for schools, of February 22, 1961, passed with the required majority of eighty-seven votes. However, in an official National Council statement the number of eligible votes was declared to be 171. But this same statement also asserted that a pronouncement of the General Board (as of 1961) had to be approved by at least two thirds of the board members present and had to receive the affirmative votes of at least one fourth of the total votes of the members of the General Board—see *The Record of the National Council of Churches*, rev. (1972). A similar situation existed in the General Assembly.

166. *Triennial Report*, 1963, p. 14.

with its purposes and working. They were outside the Council precisely because they were too familiar with them. And they were outside because the Council took pains to see to it that the member denominations did not elect delegates to it who were out of sympathy with the work of the Council. Its own restrictive policies created a situation in which most of the criticism had to arise outside its membership.

Miller must have been aware that these critics were not as uninformed as alleged; he admitted that even their attacks could work to advantage should the council respond to them properly. "We must therefore examine seriously those things said of us. If true, we must acknowledge them; if false, we must show them to be false."[167] He then added another note of caution as to the policy the Council should follow in dealing with those hostile to its work:

> I have never felt that we ought to attack our critics. . . . If our critics are right, they have served us. If they are wrong, they need our ministry. Why have these persons not found the cause they are seeking for in the church? Why do they live in fear, distrusting perpetually, looking under the bed? Why do they reject and attack the foundations of order in our society, the government, the courts, even the church itself?[168]

In stating that he did not believe that the Council should not attack his critics, J. Irwin Miller was hardly consistent. In his questions as to why they lived in a state of fear and were constantly looking under the bed, he was very subtly attempting to link his critics with McCarthyism. Even more inconsistent and equally ridiculous was his inference that the critics were attacking law and order and the foundations of American society. It requires a highly developed sense of humor to pay any attention to this kind of attack. Basically the critics of the Council were convinced that the Council was the enemy of law and order, the true church, and every vestige of historic Christianity.

In his last report to the Council as general secretary (he retired from this office in June 1963), Roy Ross said that the enemies of the Council were the most irresponsible in the history of the American churches in the twentieth century.[169]

167. *Ibid.*

168. *Ibid.*

169. *Ibid.*, p. 16. The whole problem of the relationship of both the Federal and National Councils to communion will be discussed in chapter eight.

Even though President Miller and Roy Ross responded to the attacks on the Council in a somewhat different way, their common concern is evident. By 1963 the entire leadership of the Council was more deeply concerned over the bitter feeling against the ecumenical movement than it either cared or dared to admit publicly. But by 1964 the leaders made no secret of their concern. Dr. R. H. Edwin Espy, successor to Roy Ross as general secretary, embarked on a new policy of a more positive defense of the Council before the general public. Reporting to the meeting of the General Board in Des Moines, Iowa, in December 1964, Dr. Espy warned that the churches of the nation "may be heading for a major struggle which has long been latent, but which is developing with vehemence," and contended that the struggles centered in a difference of understanding regarding the mission of the church in the world.[170]

Espy conceded the effectiveness of the opposition, even though, he insisted, it was fighting a false image of the Council. However, this false image was reaching millions of "victims" every week through more than seven thousand weekly hours of radio broadcasting, besides secular newspapers, public meetings, and other channels. In his analysis of the situation Espy came closer to the truth than any previous Council apologist. He clearly saw that the ultimate target of the critics was less the ecumenical movement itself than the churches "as they are now oriented and led by the present religious establishment as represented in the mainline Protestant and Orthodox communions which comprise the Council. It is the ecumenical orientation of these communions . . . that the attackers seek to destroy."[171] The Council was the focal point of the attack simply because it represented the ecumenical endeavor of these denominations in the social, political and economic areas of our national life.

Reuben Mueller, senior bishop of the Evangelical United Brethren Church and president of the National Council, at the same meeting of the General Board was even more outspoken in his attack on the Council's critics.

Mueller admitted that there were sincere and pious people who believed that the secular problems of the day were none of religion's business. He also insisted that these same people were prone to becoming secular in repeating criticisms that had been prepared and distributed by men and organizations whose religion was "pugna-

170. *Ibid.*

171. "Minutes of the General Board", December 1964, *Matthews Collection.*

cious and narrow, and whose patriotism is measured by the dollars that gullible people send them to fatten their bank accounts."[172]

But Bishop Mueller could also see some heartening aspects in this situation. He reported that all six of the member communions that had taken action in 1964 regarding the Council—the American Baptist Convention, the Methodist church, the Philadelphia Yearly Meeting of Friends, The Presbyterian Church, U.S., the Protestant Episcopal Church, and the Reformed Church in America—had overwhelmingly reaffirmed their support of the Council:

> This is cause for gratification, but it is questionable whether it reaches the heart of the problem. Is not the true issue a deeper one, namely the dissension which is being fostered, often by calculation, in parish and community life? The question is not the nature and task of the National Council, but the nature and task of the Church.[173]

There was considerable truth in this observation. But Bishop Mueller seemed not to realize that the very truth he was expressing was simultaneously an indictment of the National Council and the ecumenical movement. In admitting that the Council was a divisive factor in the life of the church in America, he was also condemning it for its divisive influence. The polarization that he clearly saw between denominations, between groups within denominations, and between the clergy and the laity in most of them, was a contradiction of the very oneness that he and his fellow liberal leaders in the National Council professed. Actually *they* were guilty of presenting a false image to the public, false because the real ecumenical goal was not true oneness in Christ according to the unchanging truth of Scripture, but oneness of ecclesiastical organization according to the latest "truths" of humanism. Liberal zeal for ecumenism did not by any means exclude a willingness to divide within churches if these divisions were along ideological lines of demarcation.

Secretary Ross advanced a long-term solution to this polarization. It contemplated training young ministers in the seminaries who would in turn train the members of local churches according to the true meaning of the ecumenical movement:

Some-time the problem we have stated may need to be discussed

172. *Ibid.* (p. 20., of report of Bishop Mueller to the board).
173. *Ibid.* (p. 21).

ecumenically in terms of the kind of preparation our seminaries are giving to our future ministers in order to help them nurture the laity in the radical nature of true commitment to Christ and His Church. All of us, clergy and laity alike, must experience an inner renewal if we are to be equal to the claim of the Gospel in a time like the present.[174]

Behind this spurious appeal for a commitment to the Gospel was the insistence on experiencing inner renewal as preparation for the outward, radical transformation of society according to the claim of a radical gospel. This in turn required a radical change in seminary training. The traditional approach to ministerial training rooted in the historic Protestant theology must give place to a new program grounded in sociology and psychology and inculcating the manipulative approaches to human nature.

At the meeting of the General Board in December 1965 Dr. Edwin Espy, the new general secretary of the Council, again raised the question of the widespread criticism of the Council. The matter was occasioned by the testimony Council representatives had given in behalf of a bill that, if passed by Congress, would have repealed section 14 (b) of the Taft-Hartley Labor Act of 1947. After admitting that these attacks were made by newspapers and important citizens of many communities, Espy went on to lament the source of such opposition to the Council:

> Most disturbing have been the organized efforts to arouse distrust of the National Council of Churches in local churches.... It is not too much to say that an articulate minority in our churches is using the National Council of Churches for changing direction of thought and witness, both theological and social, in American Protestantism. Sometimes the persons organize on denominational lines, sometimes in transdenominational groups or movements to maintain a common attack on the ecumenical outlook of official church bodies.[175]

In spite of the Council leadership's alarm over the swelling antagonism, there was no sign of any policy change. This group apparently never reckoned with the likelihood that its radical view of the

174. *Ibid.*, p. 22.

175. "Minutes of the General Board," December 1965, *Matthews Collection.* Espy cited as evidence a particular development over the last six months of 1965—the proliferation of recorded anonymous messages attacking not only the National Council, but President Eisenhower, the Supreme Court, and the United Nations as well.

nature of the Gospel and the mission of the church lay at the heart of the opposition; indeed, the Council seemed unable to relate its own increasing advocacy of radical social, economic, and political policies to the mounting volume of outspoken opposition. And so it continued, merrily oblivious, to support various policies that could only strengthen its opposition's determination to oppose the radicalism of the ecumenical program.

The Council's evaluations of its critics were inaccurate and misleading. True, extreme groups, who by no means represented the bulk of evangelical conservative thought or the mainstream of American political conservatism, were highly vocal in denouncing the work of the Council. But they were not necessarily wrong in their basic suggestions that the Council was too cuddly with radicalism and sympathetic with communism. However, the Council's defenders, like Roy Ross and Edwin Espy, failed to acknowledge that the growing body of responsible leadership, theological and political, was conducting its own attacks also at these points, whereat the Council was extremely vulnerable, and the suggestion that these critics were the victims of a false image of the Council was at best misleading.[176]

The council ofttimes seemed determined to appear before the American public in the worst light possible by continuing sympathetic to communism. In doing so it provided its critics with evidence very difficult to refute. Early in 1968 a statement prepared by David Stone of the Division of Overseas Ministries was presented to the General Board. In delivering it he said that the Department of International Affairs had great concern that Americans properly understand and interpret communism.[177] The report, however, was concerned more with presenting a favorable interpretation of communism than with educating the American people on the nature and program of this philosophy.

The report was actually a thinly veiled piece of propaganda. It stated that general educational opportunities were soaring in most Communist lands, taking pains also to point out that these entailed "a wider equality of opportunity than in many other countries." The report offered the cheery conclusion that, as a result of the expanding general education, the basis was being laid for greater cultural freedom and ultimately for all other individual liberties. The report

176. Responsible religious journals like *Christianity Today* and *Presbyterian Journal* consistently exposed the work of the Council to a rigorous criticism.

177. "Minutes of the General Board," February 1968, *Matthews Collection*.

actually insisted that the pressure of meeting material needs in Russia had helped roll back the economic tyranny that had gripped the country in 1917–18.

The optimism of this document knew no bounds. It declared that the upreach of the intellectual and spiritual needs of the Russian people was beginning to break open new cultural and religious possibilities other than those prescribed by the official philosophy.[178] This view of religious freedom in Russia was somewhat contradicted by a previous release by the Council's Information Service which admitted that it was by no means clear that the Russian government would soon respect civil liberties and civil rights. It also candidly reported that those Russian clergymen who were anti-communist often had an exceedingly difficult time, though when not centers of agitation they led a fairly peaceful existence.[179]

The *Black Manifesto* and the demands for greater representation on Council agencies by various militant Negro groups created a new crisis in public relations for the National Council. This attack from militant groups representing the philosophy of the New Left posed a different kind of problem for the Council leaders. Long accustomed to attacks from conservative groups, they knew not how to meet this onslaught. The Council's initial response to these demands was the partial reorganization undertaken by the 1972 triennial. However, the New Left attack in no way diminished the assaults from evangelicals within and without the constituent members of the Council. The sympathy the Council displayed for the *Black Manifesto* actually intensified the evangelicals' antagonism. In addition, opposition that had been smoldering just beneath the surface of the United Presbyterian Church, USA erupted, as it did to a less extent in the United Methodist Church and some Lutheran groups.

As a result, the income of the Council was sharply reduced. Denominational assemblies and conferences—many of these also in financial straits—took steps to reduce their contributions to the council. By January 1973, doubts were voiced in liberal circles concerning the National Council's continuing ability to spearhead the ecumenical movement in America. Would the reorganization of

---

178. *Ibid.* Actually this effort by the Council to influence popular thought in this country in behalf of Russia had begun in 1962 with the appearance of *Religion in Communist Dominated Areas.* From 1962 to 1967 it appeared once a month, but in 1968 it was published twice a month.

179. *Ibid.*

1972 tap new sources of strength? Or would the concessions made to the black militants further alienate those major denominations that had long been the Council's chief source of financial strength and leadership? The year 1973 offered very little information in the way of an answer to these crucial questions. The Council continued to make policy statements on many issues. But in some quarters there was a gnawing fear that somehow these statements had lost the cutting edge they once possessed.

8

The Relationship Between the Federal and National Councils and Radicalism

Since 1920 theological and political conservatives have become increasingly convinced that the ecumenical movement as represented by the Federal Council and the National Council of Churches was created to support radical political, social, and economic programs in this country. Except for its support of pacifism in the days just before World War I and its Social Creed, the Federal Council gave little evidence of radical tendencies. Indeed, in these early days it received the support of some stalwart conservatives who were under the impression that it had been founded to give a united evangelical testimony in those areas of common concern to the Protestant churches.

After 1920, however, the Federal Council began to reveal radical tendencies. Such were inherent in the Social Creed of 1908, but were more openly flaunted in the revised Social Creed of 1932. From then until it was succeeded by the National Council at the end of 1950, the Federal Council was the cause of deep concern among conservatives because of its increasingly bold stance in favor of liberal and radical causes.

This final chapter will examine the relationship between the Federal and National Councils on the one hand and the Communist party, its various affiliated movements, and radicalism in general on the other.[1] In dealing with this highly charged issue this chapter will be based only on evidence from the records of the Federal and National Councils, from their policy statements and pronouncements, from the records of the Communist and Socialist Labor parties, and from the findings of committees of Congress and other equally valid testimony, public and private.

The available evidence suggests an interesting and enduring relationship between the pronouncements of America's radical political parties and the positions of the Federal Council and the National Council on major issues. Now admittedly, a consistent relationship between the two Councils on the one hand and radicalism and communism on the other hand does not prove or even necessarily imply an organic connection between the parties (although it may strongly suggest that such a relationship did exist). But it does strongly suggest that they shared a common political, social, and economic philosophy that brought them into close cooperation in the realm of campaign politics. The requirements of the thesis of this chapter do not necessitate proving an organic relationship. All that is necessary is to demonstrate that the Federal and National Councils have in their official positions reflected the Communist-radical philosophy.

The assumption that the most dangerous radicals in this country had to be "card-carrying members" of the Communist party was a weakness of the work of Senator Joe McCarthy. Most of the influential and dangerous radical leaders in this country were not card-carrying party members. Indeed, over the past forty years many of communism's most influential salesmen have not been members of the Communist party. This fact has given an added impetus to the study of the relationship between communism as a political movement in this country and the philosophical Communists who had a

1. In dealing with this issue, this chapter will not rely on the charges of extremist groups whose zeal in opposing communism has frequently led them into questionable positions and to charge some with Communist affiliation, which could not be sustained in the light of the available evidence.

much greater influence in national affairs than their number warranted. They were not easily identified as Communists and because they were not actual members of the party, they were able to insist that they were not Communists and thus escape the charges brought against them.

It is with this category that this chapter will deal. There were relatively few card-carrying party members in the Federal and National Councils. Infiltration took place through the common bond between communism and political liberalism, which has characterized most of the leadership of the two Councils. Radical theology is nearly always the handmaid of radical politics.

An effect of this penetration is the similarity between the political and social affirmations of the Councils on the one hand and on the other the political programs of the radical parties issued for campaign purposes. At times, it seems, the similarity transmutes into identity.

The Federal Council and the Platforms of the Socialist Parties

The Federal Council was created in 1908 and issued its Social Creed the same year. Interestingly, the presidential campaign of that year offers the first meaningful basis of comparison between its social outlook and the platforms of the radical parties involved in that campaign.[2] Since the Communist party did not officially offer a platform until 1928, comparison must be confined to Socialist party and Socialist Labor party statements in that twenty-year interval.[3]

Such a comparison yields some interesting results, but they simply point to a similarity in social philosophy. The Social Creed of 1908 and subsequent affirmations by the Council's General Assembly at most points fell far short of the specific political, social, and economic planks in the platforms of these parties. True, the Federal Council echoed their demands for a shorter working day,

2. In 1908 Republican candidate William Howard Taft defeated William Jennings Bryan, the Democrat, with the aid of Theodore Roosevelt. It was a victory for conservatism over liberalism. For the complete platforms of all parties in presidential campaigns between 1908 and 1964, see Kirk Porter and Donald Bruce Johnson, *National Party Platforms, 1840-1964* (Urbana and London, 1966). All material on party platforms will be drawn from this book.

3. In 1924 the Worker's party platform was essentially communistic but the party did not admit to the name until 1928.

at least one day off from work, restrictions on the working conditions for women, and the prohibition of child labor in industry. Too, war was usually condemned in these early pronouncements, though, as we have seen, the Council wavered on this issue during our involvement in World War I.

Although the Federal Council was silent on the Marxian doctrine of the class struggle, unlike the platforms of the two radical parties, and although the Council did not call for the drastic reconstruction of American society, as these parties did, it would be misleading to imply that no relationship of any kind existed between the ecumenical interests of the day and political radicalism.

The community of interests is found in the area of theology and philosophy. The Social Creed of 1908 and the economic and political philosophy of the Socialist and Socialist Labor parties rested upon certain common assumptions; namely, man is essentially good, progress is therefore likely, and by social legislation the state can become part of the evolutionary process to produce a better humanity and society. The state through appropriate legislation can eliminate evil with the aid of a relevant education program, which must also reflect this optimistic view of human nature.

There was, then, philosophical kinship between the ecumenical movement (as represented by the Federal Council) and the socialist movement of the day, even though little formal connection existed and even though the positions struck by the Council fell far short of the radical platforms of the two parties. Some individual leaders in the Council—Harry F. Ward of the Methodist Federation for Social Action for one—who were undoubtedly in accord with the radical stance of these parties and who after 1920 would become so radical in their enthusiasm for the Soviet regime, recently enthroned in Russia, that they could see in Russian communism the Christian Gospel in its purest ethical application.[4]

Even though the position of Ward and others in the Federal Council at this time was a much more logical expression of the basic liberalism inherent in the social-gospel movement and the creed adopted in 1908, it did not then represent the majority opinion in the Council. It would take time plus the events of the 1920s for the radical impulses of the movement to take more definite shape. Ultimately it would require the Great Depression, which began in 1929, and the 1932 election of Franklin D. Roosevelt for the radical polit-

4. For the position of Harry F. Ward, see chapter one.

ical and social philosophy to achieve a position of commanding influence in the life of the Federal Council. During the war years the evidence suggests that the Council received as much criticism from pacifist religious groups (such as the Church of the Brethren) as from evangelicals at large because of its apparent retreat from its previous stand against war.

The latent radicalism of the Federal Council was identified mainly with pacifism after 1920. But because pacifism was traditionally rooted in pietism in America, it was not equated with radicalism to the same degree it was later, when it was deemed an ally of Russian communism. Many conservatives failed to grasp the logic of the pacifism that appeared after 1920; they utterly failed to comprehend what Reinhold Niebuhr clearly saw when he admitted that most of the liberals of his generation were pacifism's children. This religious pacifism shared many of liberalism's assumptions about man, the nature of his sin, and man's ability to overcome its blighting influence through a better system of education and a resulting improved human environment. Pacifism was the product of a defective theology that had more in common with secular liberalism than many religious pacifists were prepared to admit.

In general, between 1920 and 1930 the Federal Council devoted most of its interest and activity to the defense of pacifism and prohibition and did not assume a public stance on many issues, a fact which aroused the ire of conservatives. But this does not mean that the Council was not moving in the direction of a more pronounced radicalism. The greatest impetus for radicalism came from its leaders acting in other capacities rather than as leaders of the Federal Council and speaking for it.

The beginning of the depression in 1929 and the increasingly severe economic dislocations that resulted opened new vistas of action for the Council. These conditions sparked new incentive for applying the social gospel to the American economic and political scene.[5] The election of Franklin Roosevelt to the presidency in 1932 signaled various liberal and radical elements, religious and secular, that their day had come. They now had in power an administration not only quite friendly to their cause but also dependent on them for encouragement and aid as the New Dealers would set about the task

5. The socialist and Communist political parties were quick to realize that the depression had given them an opportunity to see their program realized; this was impossible during the prosperity of the previous decade.

of reordering American economic and political life to make it fit the liberal mold.

Wasting no time, the Federal Council seized the opportunities presented. In 1932 it adopted a revised social creed, which removed much of the mask that had to a great extent concealed the radical intent behind the Social Creed of 1908. The revision was the work of the biennial assembly, meeting after the election, and clearly charts the course for the Council in its social and political planning.[6]

The key to the revised creed was its plea for social planning and the control of the credit and monetary systems and the economic processes of the nation for the common good. The many references to Christian principles in this report cannot conceal the fact it was actually a call for collectivism in American life. By making the plea at this particular time it was adopting the radical positions of the various socialist and Communist parties.

The Socialist party platform in 1932 announced the breakdown of the capitalist system, cited the large numbers of the unemployed as proof of this collapse, and declared that unemployment and poverty were inevitable under the present system. The platform called for a program of public ownership of the basic industries and the socialization of the banking and credit systems of the nation.[7]

The closest parallel in specific terms was the foreign policy advocated by the Socialist Labor party in 1932. It called for the ultimate total disarmament of the United States, the recognition of Soviet Russia, and the entrance of the United States into the World Court and the League of Nations.[8]

The Socialist Labor party platform was a frank statement of the Communist philosophy. But on what measures should be taken it was far less specific than that of the Socialist party, except in the matter of calling for the complete collectivization of all the means of production and transportation.

Although the revised creed of 1932 was at some points far less specific than these platforms, it did plot the direction the Federal Council would take. The philosophy enunciated by Franklin Roosevelt in his first inaugural pledging the New Deal was all the incen-

6. *Federal Council Bulletin* 16, no. 1 (January 1933): 6-9. The revised creed also reaffirmed most of the positions adopted in 1908.

7. Porter and Johnson, *op. cit.*, pp. 351-52.

8. It is true, of course, that these provisions were not the private stock of liberalism; conservatives also shared these views. But the fact remains that by 1932 they were a vital part of the whole liberal-radical view, which looked toward the creation of a monolithic international collectivism.

tive the liberal Council leadership needed to expand this social and political philosophy into a more comprehensive system. The Democratic party under Roosevelt and the Federal Council under rejuvenated liberal leadership together drifted leftward toward the goal of democratic collectivism. The boldness of Roosevelt's leadership during those depression years emboldened the Council to come to his aid. The Council also warmly welcomed the radicalism of Henry Wallace, who by frequent reference to the Scriptures ofttimes shrouded his radical positions in a halo.

But the endorsement that the Federal Council extended to the New Deal was qualified. The New Deal was always subject to political realities and its radical nature ever tempered by what was politically possible and politically impossible. The Executive Committee made it crystal clear in 1933 that the New Deal did not go far enough. The Christian conscience, intoned the committee, can be satisfied with nothing less than substituting motives of mutual helpfulness and goodwill for that of private gain.[9]

Nothing short of democratic collectivism would fulfill the social ideals of the Federal Council. Speaking to the special meeting of the Federal Council in Washington, D.C., in December 1933, Henry Wallace forthrightly appealed to the Council to take the lead in reshaping Protestant theology in America. The Council could then take the lead in creating an ecclesiastical atmosphere favorable to the type of collectivism he envisioned for our country. Wallace correctly foresaw that in doing this the Council would in turn provide conditions under which the New Deal would be more politically effective. Here was an invitation to the American ecumenical movement to assume command in leading Americans to accept a political and economic collectivism gilded with Christian trimmings taken from the Scriptures but out of context.[10]

The Federal Council accepted the challenge. Thereafter it constantly sounded the note that true Christianity never placed the protection of property above the enrichment of life and that any government worthy of the support of the ecumenical movement must not make property rights its main reason for existence.

By 1935 the Federal Council was taking command in achieving the collectivist society. It called on the New Deal to follow its lead. The Council urged the Roosevelt administration to hearken to Christianity and the social sciences and to break through the confines of

9. *Federal Council Bulletin* 16, no. 10 (October 1933): 6.

10. *Ibid.* 17, no. 2 (February 1934): 6.

an outdated social structure in order to secure the collectivist economy. In this the Council reflected the 1932 platforms of the Socialist and Socialist Labor parties.[11] And the same year, as we have seen, Council representatives were joining the labor movement and participating in the various strikes inspired by the New Deal and the recently formed National Labor Relations Board.

In 1936 the Socialist and Socialist Labor parties reiterated their previous declarations against capitalism, charging that it encouraged war because of its alliance with militarism—a theme the Federal Council also had heralded and would continue to do. The 1936 Democratic platform applauded the accomplishments of New Deal liberalism and promised to continue and expand it during Roosevelt's second term of office. Encouraged by the double-talk of this platform and the emphatic statements of the radical parties, the Federal Council became more bold in pressing for collectivism. The Council was considerably aided in this by the popular E. Stanley Jones, whose skillful rhetoric and glowing enthusiasm concealed much of the materialistic philosophy of collectivism in the Council's pronouncements, which generally identified collectivism with the kingdom of God on earth.[12]

However, events in Europe, and America, were making it likely that neither the Federal Council nor the radical political parties would bring in this golden age of ecumenical collectivism. By 1937 war clouds hovered over Europe and Asia, and Roosevelt had run into serious trouble with Congress over his bill to enlarge the Supreme Court. Popularly known as the "Court Packing Bill," this proposal split the Democratic party into two groups. By 1938 his magic touch with Congress was largely gone. The outbreak of war in Europe in 1939 not only diverted Roosevelt's attention from domestic issues, but also raised serious problems for him on the international scene. The rise of Hitler, the Nazi persecution of the Jews, and the Munich Pact of 1938 also posed a serious problem for American pacifists. But even more disastrous for liberals and radicals in and out of the Federal Council was the Ten-Year NonAggression Pact signed by Hitler and Stalin in August 1939. This action shattered the illusion so carefully nurtured by the Communists and their fellow travelers in this country that Soviet Russia was a peace-loving nation and was as much opposed to the Nazi regime as this country.

11. *Ibid.* 18, no. 4 (April 1935): 5.
12. See chapter three, pp. 53–74.

The election of 1940 presented serious problems to the various radical groups in the nation. The Communist party, whose 1936 platform featured pacifism as the key to peace, in 1940 still insisted that this nation must keep out of the war then raging in Europe because it was an imperialist and predatory war.[13] The Communists shouted against the imperialist adventures of Wall Street and the federal government and demanded a people's peace.

The Socialist party was much less strident in denouncing the European war, though it also admitted that the defeat of Hitler would be welcomed by all antifascists.[14] The Socialist Labor party (claiming to represent true Marxism rather than Stalinism) contented itself with a statement that the war simply proved the hopeless decay of capitalism.[15]

If the war placed the secular pacifists and radicals in an uncomfortable position, its impact on the Federal Council was no less shattering. At first the Council took a strong stand against the conflict, but the horrific prospect of a Nazi triumph dampened its pacifist fervor. The fact that Russia was a party to the invasion of Poland was also a complicating factor for ecumenical liberalism, a factor not resolved until the German attack on Russia in June 1941. The Federal Council and its frequent mouthpiece, the *Christian Century*, could retreat from dogmatic pacifism to a more practical position. Now, somehow, the war would be identified with the triumph of democracy and the emergence of a Christian collectivism, which would, again somehow, approximate the kingdom of God.

This more cheery outlook concerning our involvement in World War II was first voiced by both the *Nation* and the *New Republic* early in 1942. They then indulged the affirmation that the conservatives of the prewar era must be the eventual losers in this involvement and that they should, if wisdom prevailed, accept this fact and the creation of a democratic socialist state as the inevitable result of American participation in the conflict.

The intellectual and theological agility of the Federal Council's leadership was equal to the occasion. Soon it was voicing the same hope, but with the proper theological verbiage, which naturally related the conflict to the hopeful instrumental role of realizing the kindgom of God on earth. Peace on earth was still the Council's goal. But sometimes this had to give way to a more concrete aim—

13. Porter and Johnson, *op. cit.*, pp. 376-81.

14. *Ibid.*, pp. 394-99.

15. *Ibid.*, p. 399.

the realization of the kingdom of God, which would make peace more easily realized.

The parallel in secular and religious liberal thought is obvious, but it is difficult to tell whether the willingness to abandon pacifism for this more immediate goal had its origin in the leftist political movement or in the Council. The evidence suggests that it was the product of the liberal philosophy that underlay both movements. The important fact is that it characterized both groups at about the same time. Beyond a doubt, however, is the basic kinship between the American socialist and communist movements and the ecumenical movement shepherded by the liberal leadership of the Federal Council.[16]

A close study of the various resolutions of the Federal Council and the editorial policy of the *Christian Century* reveals remarkable agreement with socialist and Communist ideology regarding opportunities offered by the war for the advancement of collectivism in America. Essentially, both camps insisted that the defeat of Hitler would be an empty victory if unaccompanied by an emerging collectivism here in the United States. War, the antithesis of the kingdom of God was to be the means of bringing this glorious society into existence. The irony of this pragmatic stance was never openly defended by the religious liberals; it was merely accepted as perhaps a necessary consequence of the rise of dictatorships in Europe.

The austerity imposed on civilians by the military necessities of the day and the resulting war psychology emboldened the Federal Council to take a more active leadership in planning the kind of peace that must emerge from the victory. In 1943 its Commission on a Just and Durable Peace issued a formula popularly known as the "Six Pillars of Peace," which enunciated the kind of victory the war must produce. The victory envisioned was strikingly close to that propounded in documents by the radical groups in this country. Basically each camp sought a victory that would enthrone interna-

16. This common bond was well expressed in the message which Franklin Roosevelt sent to Congress on March 11, 1943 urging the enactment of the Report of the National Resources Planning Board into law. This report was actually a blue print for the creation of a collectivist economy for the nation. See *Congressional Record*, Vol. 89. p. 1792. For similar sentiments echoed by Henry Wallace see *The Nation*, January 10, 1942, pp. 32-36.

The Christian Century was somehow able to deny that this report was socialistic and offered the possibility that if it were not passed by Congress, a revolution would result. March 24, 1943. pp. 350-351.

tional collectivism. The unified theme indicated intimacy between theological and secular radicalism.

During the war years the public pronouncements of the Federal Council actually predated the peace formulations of the radical political parties, as far as their platforms were concerned.[17] The Socialist party offered a formula for lasting peace that differed at no important point from that advanced by the Council. Its domestic platform, however, was more openly collectivist in its demands than the somewhat shy pronouncements tendered by the Council. But both parties looked to the establishment of a collectivist society in America under the banners of democracy.[18]

The Socialist Labor party platform was similar to that of the Socialist party except that it counseled Americans to unite with that party

> to demand the termination of the social system which dooms us to a lifelong tenure of wage slavery, with unemployment, poverty, and war as inseparable and ever recurrent features. Unite with us to establish the Socialist Brotherhood of Man, the Republic of Peace, Plenty and International Fraternity.[19]

This echoed the language of the radicals of the French Revolution and that of Marxian philosophy as well. But it also paralleled the official thinking of the Federal Council leadership.

As mentioned, after World War II the Federal Council paid more specific attention to domestic issues and became more openly radical. It was determined that the war should be used to promote the kingdom of God here. The kingdom was to be a collectivist state sponsored jointly by secular and religious groups. They would employ different language and different means to achieve their goals. But the goal was one—however much this fact might be disguised by the avowedly secular thinking of the socialists and the Communists on the one hand and the sugar-coated approach of the social-gospel advocates on the other.

Between 1945 and 1948 the intensified radicalism of the Federal

17. *Annual Report*, 1943, pp. 62-65.

18. However, the position of the Council in 1943 and 1944 paralleled that assumed by the *Nation*, the *New Republic*, and the *Christian Century*. For the platform of the Socialist party, see Porter and Johnson, *op. cit*, pp. 413-16.

19. *Ibid.*, p. 418. (The Communist party offered no platform in 1944.)

Council anticipated the platforms of the Communist and socialist parties prepared for the hectic 1948 presidential campaign. Not only did the Council fervently support the United Nations, but it also urged closer relations between the United States and Soviet Russia, declaring that the great social experiment ongoing in Russia was a major step toward bringing the kingdom of God to earth. Thus the Council pressed for closer cooperation between the Russians and the American people at the scientific, economic, cultural and religious levels.[20]

It could hardly have been accidental that cultural exchange occupied a prominent place in this statement. Cultural interaction was and remains part of the technique of international communism for penetrating non-Communist peoples with the philosophy of dialectical materialism. The policy of coexistence, then being featured by American liberals, was designed for this type of penetration. The tactics of international communism, as distinct from the policies of Soviet Russia, were tailored to take advantage of such an attitude and to infiltrate this country with Communist propaganda, even while the official Russian policy was one of friendship and peace.

We can and should argue against peaceful coexistence. It is an impossibility. The leadership of the Federal Council was aware of this. It knew a basic incompatibility existed between *historic evangelical* Christianity and Russian communism. They could not coexist here or elsewhere.

But the Council leaders who repeated the coexistence theme time and again in their official pronouncements for the Council and in their unofficial statements did not mean that communism and historic Christianity could or should. What they were saying was really quite different. They meant that their own version of Christianity— the social gospel they were peddling to the constituent churches and to the American public—could coexist with communism. And this was true, at least in this country until such time as the Communists felt they could seize power and no longer needed the American liberals. But the liberals were blind to this aspect of the Communist movement. They plunged ahead, fondly believing that by urging these policies on the American government they were vital cogs in bringing the kingdom of God to earth.

Collectivism in the guise of the kingdom of God on earth was marching to its rendezvous with the undiluted secular collectivism

20. *Biennial Report*, 1946, p. 62. The chairman of the commission drafting this report was Bishop Oxnam, whose reputation for friendship with communism was well advertised.

of the radical parties in 1948. For most liberals the presidential election of this year was the vestibule through which utopia would crash the American scene. The secular liberals agreed, even though they would not label their goal the kingdom of God.

The platforms of the radical parties in the 1948 election were specific as to the means to be used to usher in utopia. The Communist party, declaring that the Americans had a fateful decision to make as to whether the United States should follow the path of peace or war, democracy or fascism, called for the restoration of American-Soviet friendship as the key to world peace and the fulfillment of the people's hope in the United Nations.[21] It claimed to be the only true Marxist party in the country, the only party dedicated to replacing the capitalist system with socialism. And it repeated the firm conviction of its leadership that only a socialist reorganization of society would bring permanent peace and prosperity.[22]

The New Progressive party platform sought to continue the New Deal of Franklin Roosevelt. It reiterated many of the aims of his era in an attempt to revitalize the alliance between labor unions and farm organizations, an alliance Roosevelt had used so successfully from 1932 to 1938 while seeking new strength elsewhere.[23] It also called for an end to all discrimination against Negroes and for full equality for all minority groups in the country. It made a bid for Communist support by calling for economic planning on a national scale and a national welfare program. It summarized its position by insisting that this party had taken root "as the party of the common man" and that it had "arisen in response to" and drew its strength from the demands of millions of men and women for the simple democratic right to vote for candidates and a program that satisfied their needs.[24]

There was very little in this platform that the Federal Council had

21. Porter and Johnson, *op. cit.*, pp. 425-30. This platform was by far the most open statement of the Communist position to appear. It welcomed the New Progressive party led by Henry Wallace, declaring it to be an inescapable historic necessity. It also admitted supporting and even insisted that the Communist party support the progressive features of Roosevelt's policies, both domestic and foreign. It further claimed that it had helped to organize the CIO and that it had supported every democratic movement since the Communists of Lincoln's generation who fought for the Union cause during the Civil War, pp. 428-29.

22. *Ibid.*, p. 429.

23. *Ibid.*, pp. 436-47.

24. *Ibid.*, p. 447.

not espoused or could not support. The identification of the New Progressive party platform with the program of the Federal Council of Churches is important, especially in light of the fact that today it is generally admitted that Henry Wallace, whether he recognized it or not, was to a great extent a captive of the Communists, and that the latter had welcomed the appearance of the New Progressive party as a vehicle through which they could further the Communist program. True, the party platform did not openly advocate replacing the free-enterprise system with socialism. But taken as a whole, its adoption would have led the nation a long way down that path.

The similarity of political, social, and economic philosophy that existed between the New Progressive party and the Federal Council assumed even greater importance in the light of the fact that Wallace had been a liaison personage between the New Deal radicals and the radicals in the Council between 1933 and 1940. Thus Wallace could give to the New Progressive party a religious veneer. And in so doing, the New Progressive party was in a position to claim the support of many religious radicals who, for various reasons, were unwilling openly to support the Communist party.

That Wallace and his party did not receive the number of votes that he optimistically predicted should not blind us to the significance of his movement in secularizing the allegedly religious proposals of the Federal Council. His success, however limited in the 1948 campaign, greatly influenced the Council leadership, also the soon-to-be-born National Council, to become even more secular in its outlook.

In retrospect, the election campaign was important for its secularizing effect on the ecumenical movement. Its impact was to become even more pronounced on the policies of the National Council after 1950. The data indicate that the efforts to replace the Federal Council with its successor gained much strength, if not its inspiration, from the 1948 election. This campaign gave religious sanction to a thinly concealed Marxian dialecticism to a degree never before true in American political history.

The National Council in Relation to the Platforms of the Communist and Allied Parties

The defeat of the Republicans under Thomas Dewey by Harry Truman and the emergence of the New Progressive party under Henry Wallace greatly emboldened American religious liberals more openly to join forces with secular radicalism. The structure of the National Council was designed with this purpose in view. The inclusion of other ecumenical missionary and educational groups was intended to give the bolder radicalism much greater coverage in America's denominations than the older and more restricted Federal Council had been able to do. The tone of the Cleveland meeting made it evident that the National Council was to be a far more powerful voice in behalf of theological and political radicalism. And by 1952 its machinery was sufficiently perfected for use in the presidential campaign that year.

The Communist party had no platform in the 1952 campaign. However, the Progressive party provided one containing enough radicalism to satisfy the most devoted followers of Karl Marx, even though it lacked the open announcement of Communist ideology that characterized Communist literature and election platforms.[25]

Declaring that the Progressive party was the only genuine party for peace, this platform demanded an immediate end to the Korean War. It completely ignored the causes of this conflict and blamed it on the Cold War policies of Truman and John Foster Dulles. The only way to avoid future wars was to return to the Roosevelt-Willkie policy of One World. The Progressive party was dedicated to this policy.

While stopping short of blaming America for starting World War II, this campaign document indicated that we were the cause of all international tensions that followed the war. The inescapable conclusion to this line of reasoning was that Russia should be allowed to carry out its program of conquest in Asia using Red China and North Korea as its agents. The Progressives apparently were unconcerned that the resulting One World might be a Russian-dominated world.

Echoing the customary liberal and radical rhetoric, the 1952 Progressive platform informed one and all that American liberties were being destroyed by such reactionary legislation as the Taft-Hartley Labor Act of 1947 and the Smith-McCarran Act, and by McCarthyism.[26] The platform then luridly described the results of

25. *Ibid.*, pp. 487-94.

26. McCarthyism referred to the activities of Senator Joseph McCarthy in his investigation of Communist activities in the various branches of the federal government. Heinous indeed was this activity in the opinion of Communists, fellow travelers, and many liberals. While certain of McCarthy's methods are subject to rightful criticism, his work was of much greater merit than has generally been admitted or even recognized. The very fury of the assault upon him is eloquent testimony that the Communists feared his inquiry. An impartial account of the Wisconsin senator and his work is very much needed.

these, employing language which one would expect to find in a Communist document and which one later did find in many statements issued by the National Council of Churches:

> Workers, teachers, authors, actors, government employees, small businessmen and professional people are hounded, harassed, denied passports, driven from their jobs, terrorized and blacklisted for daring to express political criticism. Men and women are victimized and jailed on the unsupported testimony of stool-pigeons and paid informers or on the charges of nameless accusers brought by the FBI.[27]

To remedy this frightening situation the Progressive party offered a series of socialistic proposals. One called for a domestic social security system that would guarantee to every American a "decent standard of living." Another advocated a system of national health insurance that would guarantee "to all Americans as a matter of right and not of charity . . . adequate dental and medical care, together with a hospital and health care construction program."

Also proposed was a comprehensive farm program that would provide that the prices paid farmers would be agreed upon and set well in advance of the production season. When necessary, the market price returned to the farm should be supplemented by production payments at national expense. The purpose of this was to give the farm population a standard of living equal to that of the rest of the nation.[28]

Proposed also was the ending of all segregation in American life through such devices as a federal fair employment practices law, the abolition of the poll tax, and a new policy of federally sponsored low-rent unsegregated housing.

But the Progressive platform did not stop there. It had the audacity to call for a great national crusade to restore the full meaning of the Bill of Rights to all Americans. The deceptive and subversive intent lying behind this demand emerges when we probe the party's mind. Restoring meaning to the Bill of Rights meant repealing the Smith-McCarran Act and the more recently passed McCarran-Walter Act.[29] Furthermore, all prosecutions under these two acts were to

27. Porter and Johnson, *op. cit.*, p. 492.

28. *Ibid.*

29. The Smith Act, passed in 1940, made it a crime to advocate the forcible overthrow or destruction of any government in this country, to engage in the dissemination of revolutionary doctrines, or to belong to any party advocating such doctrines. The McCarran Act was the Internal Security Act, passed by Congress but vetoed by President Truman. The act was passed over Truman's veto, and made

be ended, and unconditional pardons and the restoration of full civil rights granted to all those convicted under the Smith Act.

To accomplish all of this, the Progressive party counseled the abolition of the House Committee on Un-American Activities and the Senate's McCarran committee on internal security. These committees were proving highly effective in uncovering the extent of Communist infiltration into government, education, industry, and the Federal Council and National Council of Churches. They were anathema to the Communists and their many fellow travelers. The effectiveness of the committees was the reason most liberals wanted them abolished.

In 1949 eleven high-ranking officials of the Communist party were tried and found guilty under the Smith Act. This decision by two lower courts (district and circuit) was upheld by the Supreme Court in 1951. The liberal elements were frenzied. The two acts became a focal point of liberal effort to remove all restrictions on Communist activities, the reason being that the acts were contrary to the Bill of Rights. With this as background, the persistent opposition of the National Council to these acts becomes significant in examining the Council's relationship to the Communist movement in America.

The Socialist party platform of 1952 is particularly interesting, both for its defense of socialism in American life and for its specific proposals. Denying that socialism would destroy democracy in the United States, the platform postulated that socialism and democracy are inseparably one. Insisting that a democratic offensive against the evils of the day was overdue, it categorically stated that only socialism could give democracy the drive it needed to win.[30] This offensive, summarized the platform, must be undertaken by the American people, who having pioneered in political democracy "must complete their democracy by taking control of their economc life."[31] Specifically, all the basic industries, public utilities, banking and credit institutions—all the economic facilities needed for the satisfaction of the primary wants of the people—must be socially owned and democratically managed.[32]

it unlawful to conspire to establish a totalitarian dictatorship in this country and barred members of Communist groups from holding any federal office or obtaining passports. It also required Communist and Communist-front organizations to register with the attorney general of the United States.

30. *Ibid.*, p. 506.

31. *Ibid.*

32. *Ibid.*

Although the social and the economic pronouncements of both Councils generally stopped short of such specific recommendations, their repeated references to democratic control of the basic economic institutions were clearly an index to the abiding desire of the Councils for a socialistic state. It is important to remember that the platforms of the Communist party also termed its proposals socialism. Thus in the phraseology of the radical parties and of the social pronouncements of the Councils a trilogy of terms was employed to describe what is basically one and the same program—collectivism. When the leaders of the Federal and National Councils were solemnly calling for economic democracy, they did not and do not mean what the average American has in mind when he uses the term. They meant, and still mean, socialism, for socialism claims to be the extension of political democracy to the economic realm. In the late 1830s Daniel Webster warned his fellow Whigs that political democracy must sooner or later occasion the demand for economic democracy. He was warning the Whig party of his day against accepting the philosophy of the Jacksonian Democrats. He saw that this political philosophy would seriously endanger the right of private property.

Webster was correct in his shrewd analysis of the radicalism of his day. The leadership of the National Council is also keenly aware of the implications of its philosophy and therefore seeks to convey it to the members of its constituent denominations in veiled language, which is, to say the least, misleading.[33]

After this interesting philosophic excursion the Socialist party platform became quite specific, at points similar to the Progressive party platform and therefore similar to pronouncements of the National Council. It called for an all-inclusive health insurance plan and a federal low-cost housing program, which also included a public supply corporation to produce the necessary materials for the program. To achieve an enforced equity of income, the tax structure should be reorganized. It stressed the repeal of the Taft-Hartley Labor Act and advocated the complete political, social, and economic equality of all races.[34]

The Socialist Labor party offered a platform in 1952 that was far

33. The author is much indebted to the late J. Howard Pew at this point. In many conversations he had with Mr. Pew, this deviousness by the Council was repeatedly asserted. In his early years J. Howard Pew was active in the laymen's work of the National Council and only gradually did he come to see what the National Council really had in mind.

34. *Ibid.*, pp. 515-16.

less specific than those of the other radical parties. It nonetheless breathed the spirit of Marx and dutifully declared the downfall of capitalism to be both certain and imminent. In so doing it maintained it was the true heir of Karl Marx and denounced the Communist party here and its counterpart in Soviet Russia.[35]

The Socialist Worker's party also appeared on the scene. It too reflected the current Communist ideology, but directed its appeal toward agricultural groups as well as industrial workers and tendered a more specific program.

The programs of these parties in 1952 differed in degree in some areas, but all were socialistic (or communistic). As such, they differed only in detail from the major emphasis of the National Council's various pronouncements from 1951 to 1956. If the policies of the Council were somewhat less openly collectivistic in their specific provisions, the philosophy behind them was essentially that of the secular radical parties. The enemies whom the National Council held in common with the radical political groups were constitutional government, the American free-enterprise system, and orthodox evangelical Christianity.

The National Council was not sufficiently organized to play a prominent role in the 1952 campaign; it was then somewhat timid in its pronouncements on the Korean War. But in 1953 courage flowered, and statements on peace negotiations and on disarmament mirrored the positions of the radical political parties in 1952. The demand for universal disarmament issued by the Fourth National Study Conference, which met in Cleveland in 1953 under the sponsorship of the Council, was also identical to the position of the Communist party. That the Council was echoing the concerns of communism is attested by the interest the *Daily Worker* took in the pronouncements of the Council's Division of Foreign Missions at a meeting in Dayton, Ohio, in December 1955. It would certainly stretch the imagination of any reader to insist that this Communist paper was interested in the foreign mission program of the National Council because of an evangelical emphasis. The Communist interest was fueled by the fact that this document was actually nothing less than a plea in behalf of a worldwide collectivistic society, in which the Division of Foreign Missions, aided by the constituent denominations, would play a prominent role. The zeal of the National Council for international collectivism was equaled only by its enthusiasm for a collectivist America.

35. *Ibid.*, pp. 517-32.

If any doubt remained that the National Council truly believed in free enterprise, it should have been removed by the publications of its *Goals of Economic Life* in 1953, the first of a six-volume series titled The Ethics of Society. This work, resulting from the cooperation of fifteen authors, was openly biased in behalf of collectivism.[36] Free enterprise could not achieve the balance between the individual and the economic group that was necessary for the most effective use of the natural and human resources of the nation. The real solution to the problem of poverty was the welfare state, for society must organize itself in such a way that production is for the elimination of poverty rather than for the accumulation of profit.

Many of the provisions in this first volume reflected the provisions, even the language, of the platforms of the Communist-affiliated parties in the 1952 campaign. The socialism and communism of the radicals had by 1953 received ecclesiastical sanction from the National Council. Little doubt exists that the ballooning political strength of collectivism during the later 1950s and the 1960s is the direct product of the close collaboration of the religious and secular agencies devoted to the remaking of American life in the image of Karl Marx and his socialist allies.

Many other examples of the cozy relationship between the National Council and the radical parties could be presented. The evidence is staggering in its amount and covers virtually every segment of national life. It was not restricted to the problems of war and peace or economic relationships on the home front, but covered the problems of labor, the public schools, Scripture reading and prayers in public class rooms, and civil rights. It is not too much to say that the Council was generally aligned with those who were enemies of the American heritage. The 1956 election campaign simply cemented these ties between the religious socialism of the Council and the avowed secular socialism of the radical parties.

In its 1956 platform the Socialist party pledged itself to building a new, more democratic society in the United States. By this was meant a society that placed human rights above property rights, that would eliminate war, racial prejudice, hunger, disease, poverty, and oppression.[37] In the next paragraph it hastily assured its readers that such a program must be achieved by democratic means. Seek-

36. Among these authors were Kenneth Boulding of the University of Michigan, John Bennett, and Reinhold Neibuhr, the last two being on the faculty of Union Theological Seminary of New York and noted for their devotion to collectivism.

37. Porter and Johnson, *op. cit.*, p. 562.

ing to remove all causes for alarm, it also insisted that socialism meant social ownership and democratic control of the means of production—not government ownership. Democratic control was not administration by the central government, but control by the people most directly affected and in the interest of all the people rather than for profit.[38] National Council pronouncements on economic issues have frequently expressed the same view. But this mild socialistic approach was not as mild as it seemed. The platform asserted that free enterprise was really the robber of the many by the few and must be ended. The platform also counseled the strengthening of the United Nations as an important step in the development of world government. In a word, the socialism of the Socialist party was a thinly disguised Marxian program.

In its 1956 platform the Socialist Labor party announced that humanity stood on the threshold of a new social order and that the wild capitalistic order was doomed. With a typical display of prescience it stated that the only alternative to social ruin was the abolition of capitalism and the establishment of socialism. But the kind of socialism being advocated, it hastened to add, had nothing in common with the bureaucratic despotism that was masquerading as socialism in Russia.[39] It counseled the kind of socialism that Karl Marx had advocated and that had been developed in America by Daniel de Leon. This kind would cleanse American society of its countless ills; such was, it modestly allowed, the cure for "every ill spawned by the Capitalist class rule."[40] The platform proffered many suggestions for accomplishing its goal. Its chief weapon was the power to tax; it urged a 100 per cent tax on all incomes over $25,000 a year.[41]

The National Council never in its public statements pressed for the complete abolition of private property or for such a heavy program of taxation. Most of its leaders, however, were not averse to these proposals.

The Socialist party platform bared the party's mind in terms that could well have appeared in a pronouncement by the National Council:

If we are to be free, we must discover new patterns for our lives.

38. *Ibid.*, pp. 565-73.

39. *Ibid.*, p. 565. Daniel de Leon founded the Socialist Labor Party in 1895 after failing to seize control of the American Federation of Labor from Samuel Gompers. De Leon was a doctrinaire Marxian.

40. *Ibid.*, p. 573.

41. *Ibid.*, p. 562.

And then we must live according to those patterns, in the midst of a hostile society, and until we have created nothing less than a new social order, a society in which the commanding value is the infinite preciousness of the human spirit of every single man, woman and child.[42]

The basic theme of this platform was the need of social, economic, and political change. The party offered America's voters "the vision of a new society, a vision that gives depth and meaning to the things that we and they (trade unionists, farmers, Negroes, liberals, lovers of peace) are doing now."[43] The Socialist goal, endorsed by the National Council again and again, was a new and truly democratic society in this country.

By 1960 the goals of the National Council of Churches and those of the Socialist party were nearly identical, and those of the Socialist Labor party differed only slightly in content. The similarity of the positions of the radical parties and of the National Council of Churches in 1960 was so striking that it is doubtful any substantial difference existed in either the goals of worldwide peace or the means of achieving it.

Also by 1960 the kingdom of God, as defined by the Council, had become a thoroughly socialized concept. Postmillennialism torn from its biblical context had become the focal point for social, political, and economic radicalism. It recalled the postmillennialism that produced abolitionism and the various reform movements of the middle decades of the nineteenth century. In sum, in 1960, as 1956, collectivism was the order of the day.[44]

The pronouncements of the National Council during and after the exceedingly close 1960 campaign followed the now familiar pattern of secular radical thought. After 1960 the question whether the National Council was influencing the radical parties or they the Council was no longer of major importance. Beginning with the Kennedy era and continuing into the Johnson administration, the more important question was the degree of influence that radicalism—religious and secular—was exerting on the federal government.

Somewhat quiescent during the Eisenhower era, this radical political, social, and economic philosophy gained new boldness as a result of the triumph of John Kennedy over Richard Nixon in the

42. *Ibid.*, p. 621.

43. *Ibid.*, p. 622.

44. The platform of the Socialist Labor party (*Ibid.*, pp. 634-40) did not differ materially from that of the Socialist party.

1960 election. Foreign and domestic policies began to conform to the demands of the left-wing political groups and the National Council far more than the American public realized.

The radicalism of the National Council grew increasingly militant after 1960. The Council continued its policy of working through Communist front groups, but its interests lay mostly in its pronouncements and public activities and toward these its energies were directed. Fittingly, Secretary Roy Ross, in his report to the 1960 triennial, insisted that the task of the church must be *mission* rather than *missions*; he interpreted this to mean that the church was to redeem the national culture rather than individual souls.[45]

Between 1960 and 1964 the Council concerned itself largely with this concept of mission at the domestic cultural level. It did not cease its vigilance over the international problems of peace and disarmament, but the conflict in Vietnam was still relatively tame. The Council leadership was, however, busy informing the Vatican that John Kennedy was a most promising candidate for political, if not ecclesiastical, sainthood. This domestic issue, in fact, demanded much (if not most) of the attention of the liberal leadership.

The Fourth National Study Conference, at Pittsburgh in 1962 and sponsored by the Division of Christian Life and Work, accepted the call to mission with enthusiasm. Its findings, published in 1963 as *The Church in a World That Won't Stand Still*, actually encouraged the churches of America to accept moral and ethical relativism as the basis for the call to mission.[46] Somewhat cryptically, it summoned the church to surrender its absolutes if the message was to be relevant to the second half of the twentieth century. This was completely consonant with the basic philosophy of the radical platforms of the 1960 campaign and was designed to make the Council and its message relevant to the radical secularists who were, it seemed, dominating nearly every segment of our national life. Change was and remained the order of the day. The Council must be willing to change both its message and its methods. Secular liberals could no longer claim that their brand of socialism was either more realistic or more comprehensive than that offered in the name of Christianity by the National Council.

In the 1964 campaign only the Socialist Labor party and the Socialist Workers party offered outright radical platforms. By 1968 the

45. See chapter seven, p. 249.

46. *A Summary of the Resolutions of the National Council of Churches, 1951-1961*, p. 6.

Democratic party had, to an astonishing degree, joined the ranks of the radicals. Much of its platform was reminiscent of those of the socialist parties. In its 1964 platform the Socialist Labor party reaffirmed its previous pronouncements, adding little that was new except for one statement, which was quickly adopted by the National Council in a somewhat different form. The platform declared: "The most luminous fact of our age is this: There is no longer any excuse for the involuntary poverty of a single member of society."[47] But one obstacle still remained before the abolition of human poverty could be achieved: "All that stands in the way of this heaven on earth, a world in which all may enjoy good housing, abundant and nourishing food, the finest clothing and the best of cultural, educational and recreational advantages, is the outmoded capitalist system."[48]

The Socialist Workers party platform was also hostile to capitalism, but more specific in its detailed proposals for ending the system. A comparison between it and the pronouncements of the National Council after 1964 reveals incredible similarity in philosophy and general goals. The virtual identity of goals was evident in a policy statement, "Christian Concern and Responsibility for Economic Life in a Rapidly Changing Technological Society."[49] Issued by the General Board in 1965, it echoed a familiar Communist refrain:

> We have pushed our machines with their mechanical minds and vast powers outward into space among the stars and inward into the secrets of matter and men, and into the fields, the factories, the mines and the market place. A world without hunger, nakedness or human beasts of burden is now a real possibility, no longer a visionary dream.[50]

Asserting that these forces and powers are of God, the General Board thus attempted to make a specific difference between its position and that of the Communists and socialists. But it went on to say that the resulting situation justified a collectivist state in this country. In fact, the traditional (Christian) right of private property must be conditioned by the right of all mankind, including future generations, to enjoy the resources and fruits of the earth.

The Council's alliance with radicalism is also evidenced in the

47. Porter and Johnson, *op. cit.*, p. 691.

48. *Ibid.*, p. 691.

49. "Minutes of the General Board," December 2-5, 1965, *Matthews Collection*.

50. *Ibid.*

strong stand it took for repeal of section 14(b) of the Taft-Hartley Labor Act. Passed by conservatives in the Truman era, the act ended some of the worst features of the Wagner Act of 1935. This latter legislation, which created the National Labor Relations Board, had placed corporations at the mercy of the monopolistic power of the big labor unions. With the help of the National Labor Relations Board, this legalized monopolistic power had been used to the detriment of employers, the public, and not infrequently, the laboring man himself.[51] In opposing the conservatives' attempt to maintain a more favorable power balance between labor and management, the National Council championed repeal and thereby sided with the radicals.

The close affinity between the Council and communism once more emerged, this time in connection with the General Board's declaration of all-out war against poverty in America. Most particularly did it emerge in the General Board's December 1966 pronouncement on poverty. The document declared that the overwhelming mass of poverty was the result of environmental (socioeconomic) dislocations and maladjustments and that the church must use recent technological discoveries to end such poverty. Social problems are environmentally caused and are in no way the consequences of human sin. The pronouncement closed with a thoroughly Marxian approach to the interpretation of history and an invitation to revolution by the poverty-stricken, whose plight was society's fault anyway. Thus society must be reconstructed to abolish poverty and the church must take part. Nowhere did this document leave any room for individual responsibility for the conditions of poverty and disease. Human sin was brushed aside as being unworthy of serious consideration.

Concurrent with its demands for reconstructing American society according to Marx, the General Board insisted that there was no longer any such movement as world communism. In this manner it sought to allay the fears of those Americans who continued to believe that communism was still what it had been and that it was the unchanging enemy of the American way of life and Christianity. By 1967 the General Board was engaged in a campaign to change this traditional American view of Russian communism and prepare the American mind for the heady business of reconstructing society. To be sure, the attention of the Council largely focused on the civil rights struggle from 1967 to the end of the decade. Nonetheless, its public utterances continued to echo the revolutionary platform

51. See footnote 28 in chapter seven.

351

demands of the radical parties. Furthermore, it regarded the nation's social upheavals as negatively preparatory to the positive toil of society-building. That is, where the demonstrators had burned, the National Council and the radicals would build.

In its 1968 platform the Socialist Labor party used the recent technology advances as justification for social revolution, in much the same way the General Board had in its 1966 pronouncement. The 1968 Socialist Workers platform was even more specific. It was the right of Afro-Americans, said the platform, to keep arms and organize themselves for self-defense from all attacks. In affirming its support of the *Black Manifesto* of 1969, the National Council used language nearly identical, and went on record as favoring revolutions of this kind. In short, the National Council endorsed in 1969 a program of revolution advocated by the Socialist Workers party the year before—a party, mind you, admittedly communistic in its philosophy and program.

By the end of the decade the National Council was knee-deep in mission, seeking the redemption of the economic, political, labor, and social spheres of life. Its redeeming activity, however, consistently entailed Communist diagnoses and solutions. The counsel of the Scripture was snubbed. As was its language. The Council's pronouncements frequently employed language almost identical to that used by the radical parties, whose kinship with communism was indisputable. The Council had all but divorced the Gospel it was supposed to espouse and advance, and had virtually become a vocal part of the radical power structure threatening the survival of America.

The National Council and its Relationship to the Communist Movement and Communist Front Organizations

The purpose of this last chapter is not, as mentioned, necessarily to offer that kind of evidence of the relationship between the National Council and communism a court of law or a congressional investigating committee would require. Which is not to say that such evidence is lacking.

The last part of this chapter will deal with other aspects of the Council's connection with communism and Communist front organizations of various kinds. However, my purpose is not to treat such an indictment in any great detail. Sufficient evidence has already been presented to prove to all but the most devout ecumenists that the Council came to accept the Marxist view of life as applied to the American scene by political parties that were and continue to be Communist in philosophy and program. This political, social, and economic orientation, common to the Council and the radical political groups is more than sufficient evidence to warrant the conclusion that the National Council for the first twenty years of its history was cooperating in programs contrary to the entire outlook of historic Christianity and contradictory of the total biblical message.

The evidence thus far presented sustains the charges hurled against the Council by its evangelical opponents.. The kernel of the charges is that the Council had subverted the true Christian Gospel by substituting dialectical materialism. The Council, moreover, has consistently applied its ersatz gospel to all manner of cultural areas, but always under the guise of applying the Christian Gospel and always on the basis that Jesus Christ is the Lord of all life.

But what about other charges heard so often? The charge, for instance, that the National Council not only has echoed radical political, economic, and social demands, but has through its various leaders and agencies played a prominent role in Communist and Communist front organizations. Is this charge merely the stock-in-trade of so-called extremists? Or does it rest on a factual basis still impervious to the sweaty exertions of the Council leadership to crack it by labeling the charge false, even libelous.[52]

Who is right, the Council or its critics? The question must be faced and answered as honestly as can be according to the available evidence. And such evidence is available. In February 1960, during the hearings on the controversial Air Force Reserve Center Training handbook, Richard Arens, staff director for the House Committee on Un-American Activities, issued a statement saying that the chairman of that committee had issued a statement to the effect that

the leadership of the National Council of Churches of Christ . . . had hundreds or at least over 100 affiliations with communist fronts and causes. Since then, we have made careful but yet incomplete checks, and it is a complete understatement. Thus far, of the leadership of the National Council of Churches of Christ in America, we have found over 100 persons in leadership capacity with either communist front records or records of service to communist causes. The aggregate affiliations of the leadership instead of being in the

52. But how can such a charge be libelous if membership in the Communist party and participation in front organizations are now legal activities?

hundreds as the Chairman first indicated is now, according to our latest count, into the thousands and we have yet to complete our check, which would certainly suggest on the authoritative sources of this committee that the statement there is infiltration of fellow-travelers in churches and education institutions is a complete understatement.[53]

The National Council criticized the document in question, and on February 17, 1960, the air force announced its withdrawal. But air force secretary Dudley Sharp defended the manual on the ground that he had no doubt that Communists had infiltrated into the churches of the nation. In his testimony before the committee on February 25 he insisted that the handbook was withdrawn, not because the charges were untrue, but because he thought it improper to name specific groups or individuals in such a manual.[54] Sharp made it crystal clear, however, that he did not find the material objectionable and that these charges were quite properly included in such a manual.

At its meeting of February 24-26 the General Board replied to the charges contained in the manual. It also authorized its officers and staff to be available to convey to the government the National Council's attitude on what appeared to be the "unconstitutional and really un-American activities of the governmental agencies."[55] The board had in mind not only the air force, but also the House Committee on Un-American Activities. In 1962 it began a vigotous campaign to abolish this committee. Fulton Lewis, Jr., the well-known conservative radio commentator, reported that he had obtained a copy of a document urging this action, and that the document was issued by the National Council Area Office and addressed to President Kennedy and all members of Congress. The document in question, "Why the HCUA Must Be Abolished," was apparently using anti-HCUA material originally issued by the New York Council of Churches whose chairman, Dr. Otto Nathan, was called a Communist by the State Department.[56]

53. U.S., Congress, House, hearings before the Committee on Un-American Activities, *Issue Presented by the Air Force Reserve Center Training Manual*, February 25, 1960, Washington, D.C., pp. 5-6. The issue arose because the air force had prepared a manual for its reserve training program that said there was evidence of Communist and antireligious activities because fellow travelers had infiltrated into the churches and educational institutions.

54. *Ibid.*, p. 3.

55. *A Summary of Resolutions of the National Council of Churches,* 1951-1961, p. 3.

56. *The Record of the National Council of Churches* (1972), p. 100.

The increasingly open opposition of the National Council to the activities of the congressional committees charged with the task of investigating Communist activities in education and the churches had the almost inevitable result of strengthening the popular conviction that the Council had something to hide. Accordingly, the intensity and frequency of the attacks on the Council increased. Accordingly, liberal religious leaders and journals rushed to its defense. But the swelling criticism could not be stayed. And the Council's continuing involvement in a variety of left-wing activities ensured as much. For only the incurably naive could regard the Council's support of these activities as happenstance or the result of ignorance.

There can be no legitimate doubt that the National Council was infiltrated by the Communists. They collaborated with fellow travelers within the Council leadership in insidious attempts to use America's churches as tools in destroying genuine Christianity and the whole American heritage of freedom. In her testimony before the subcommittee of the Senate Committee on the Judiciary— charged with investigating Communist activity in education—Bella Dodd elaborated to Senator Ferguson the basic Communist technique in infiltrating education. The witness was a former member of the Communist party; her statements can be neither set aside as mere hearsay nor successfully denied. Very carefully she explained just how the party was able to grow on a college campus:

> There are two ways of functioning. One, a communist who is an ideal-
> ist tries to take the party line into his various organizations, whatever
> club he belongs to, and tries to find others who are sympathetic to
> him or he finds where the sore spots are on the campus. . . . You
> choose an issue which you would bring up. . . . If you find two or
> three or four or five people then you attach yourself to these two or
> three or four or five people, and you begin to work on them day
> after day after day.[57]

Although Mrs. Dodd was speaking specifically about the operations of the party on college and university campuses, the basic approach was used for infiltrating into religious groups, making such modifications as might be necessary.

Of particular importance was her testimony concerning the Communist use of the "united front." "This," she said, "was always an

57. U.S., Congress, Senate hearings before the Subcommittee to Investigate the Adminstration of the Internal Security Act and Other Internal Security Laws of the Committee on the Judiciary, 82d Cong. 2d sess., September 8, 9, 10, 23, 24, 25, and October 13, 1952, pp. 14-15.

alliance with someone who didn't go all the way with the group, those who didn't believe with you in everything you believed in, but who would go along. . . ." No one formed a "united front with the Communists without being weakened because Communists form a united front when they are going to get strength anew and not when they are going to get weakened."[58]

In response to further questioning by Senator Ferguson as to why people joined the Communist party, Bella Dodd gave an illuminating reply, which applies directly to the attraction communism has had for the National Council:

> It is this desire to do the right thing that has entangled more people into the Communist movement—this desire to serve mankind, this desire to help make a better world. Those are the slogans which they [the Communists] preach, and it is only after you are in it up to your neck that you discover that this isn't what it is.[59]

Herein lies an important reason theological and social liberals in the major denominations and in the leadership of the Federal and National Councils were and are so much enamored of communism. Its emphasis upon peace, disarmament, social betterment, and human rights made it seem to them to be an ideally suited political vehicle for realizing their common aims. The Communist party and movement would be the means for bringing the social gospel to America.

Bella Dodd gave significant testimony to her own personal religious changes that brought her into the Communist party. Responding to further questioning, she admitted that she went directly from liberal, humanistic Christianity into communism and that communism requires a person to surrender his religion and substitute communism for it:

> There is no doubt that the Marxist-Leninist principles are completely materialistic and, therefore, against anything which has to do with God or religion.
>
> At different times in the history of the Communist Party, they emphasized the fact that it was possible for you to be religious and at the same time Communist. But those were the periods in which they were trying to win over large numbers of, let's say, Catholic trade unionists, Catholic workers and so forth and so on. Those were the periods which were called the periods of extending the hand of

58. bid.] p. 16.
59. Ibid., p. 25.

communism to the people in their religious groups. What you did was to say substantially this: "These men have a blind spot. They believe in God, but we Communists know that there is no God. But in order to get them to work with us, we will work with them in minimum programs."[60]

The importance of this testimony lies not so much in communism's antagonism to Christianity as in communism's approach to those who profess Christianity.[61] It sheds light on how Communist sympathizers and party members won the support of religious liberals who felt that they could work together with communism to attain goals common to both communism and the social gospel without necessarily endorsing the entire Communist program.

Despite Mrs. Dodd's testimony—and that of many more like her—religious liberals cling to their delusion about communism. More pernicious, our nation has institutionalized the delusion. Which fact is itself eloquent testimony to the innate sinfulness of the human heart—a condition the National Council deems a delusion.

The Architects of Far-Lefist Policy in the Federal and National Councils

When the Federal Council was formed in 1908, Communist strength in its leadership was small. Notwithstanding, the socialist philosophy was broadly represented; witness, for example, the popular social-gospel writings of Walter Rauschenbusch. The socialist element could only move in the direction of communism for socialist philosophy is at bottom that of communism, differing from the latter mainly in methodology.

Radicalism early had a representative in the center of the ecumenical movement. Harry F. Ward was the author of the Methodist Social Creed of 1908, for many years the executive secretary of the Methodist Federation for Social Action, and professor of Christian ethics at Union Theological Seminary in New York.

Ward's affinity with radical causes characterized virtually all of his long life. His interest in the socio-communist philosophy was

60. *Ibid.*, pp. 27-28.

61. This approach was notably worthwhile in gaining the support of those liberals who were socialists but who clung to the delusion that there was a basic difference between socialism and communism.

well developed by 1916, the year in which he wrote an introduction to a publication of the Federal Council.[62] His basic thesis in the introduction was that the social gospel had its origins in the Old Testament and that the prophets presented religion basically in social terms. The social hopes and program of the Old Testament prophets were fulfilled in Jesus whose ministry was largely concerned with social needs. Quoting Francis Peabody's *Jesus Christ and the Social Question*, Ward repeated the theme that Jesus of Nazareth was not merely a social reformer, but the first socialist.[63]

Ward's subsequent career was undergirt by the assumption that for Jesus of Nazareth the kingdom of God was a collective concept embracing the whole social life of man on earth. Since the assumptions of socialism and communism are leavened by the same lump, it was logical for Ward to come to the conclusion that communism was the logical earthly fulfillment of Christianity as regards the social and economic needs of twentieth-century man. After the Federal Council was formed Ward used his influence to sire the Commission on the Church and Social Service. To this agency belonged the task of effecting the collectivist kingdom of God in American society. The agency lives on, having survived under various names in both Councils, with this one objective still in view.

As associate secretary of the Federal Council's Commission on the Church and Social Service, Harry F. Ward was in a strategic position to further the cause of communism in the ecumenical movement. Although leaders of the Federal Council and National Council have denied that Ward had any such influence or used it for this purpose, the record seems to speak convincingly to the fact that he was an active and important member of the Communist party in America. Testimony before the House Committee on Un-American Activities during a 1953 hearing on communist activities in New York City was to the effect that Harry F. Ward had for many years been the chief architect of communist infiltration into and subversion of the field of religion, and that he had used his role as professor of social ethics at Union Theological Seminary in New York for this purpose.[64] According to the testimony of Benjamin Gitlow before this com-

62. *A Yearbook of the Church and Social Service in the United States*. Edited by the Federal Council of Churches (New York, 1916), p. 1.

63. *Ibid.*, p. 15.

64. U.S., Congress, House hearings before the Committee on Un-American Activities, 83d Cong., 1st sess., July 7, 8, 13, and 14, 1953, pp. 2075-77. The hearing was in closed session, but the testimony was made public after the Council leadership emphatically denied that communism had penetrated its membership.

mittee, the Russians used prominent American ministers as propaganda agents even in the early 1920s.

In testimony before the same committee, Manning Johnson also stated that Harry F. Ward had for many years been the chief architect of communist infiltration into and subversion of the religious field.[65] Under further questioning by Robert Kunzig, chief counsel for the committee, Johnson testified that he had known Ward personally and that Ward was then and had been a member of the Communist party during the period when Johnson himself had been a party member.[66] Leonard Patterson, also a former member of the Communist party, similarly testified that Harry Ward—along with Earl Browder, Manning Johnson, Victor Jerome, and himself—had been a member of the top policymaking group within the Communist party.[67]

This bulk of testimony about the communist affiliation of Dr. Harry F. Ward is important because of his leadership within the Methodist Federation for Social Action, an organization which he helped to found and which he led for many years. Although this federation was not organically connected with the Methodist church, it had a very close relationship with that denomination, which in turn gave the federation a place of great influence not only in that church but in the Federal and National Councils as well.

In response to questioning by Robert Kunzig, Benjamin Gitlow, Communist party candidate for vice president of the United States in 1924, stated that the communists had been highly successful in infiltrating the Methodist church. He named those involved in the conspiracy to subvert the Methodist church—Dr. Harry F. Ward, Rev. Jack McMichael (Ward's successor as executive secretary of the Methodist Federation for Social Action), Rev. Charles C. Webber, Rev. Alson J. Smith, Dr. Willard Uphaus, Margaret Forsyth, and Rev. Lee H. Ball.[68] Gitlow also stated that in his opinion the Methodist Federation for Social Action played the most important role in this subversion of the Christian churches because it served as the model for similar organizations in the various denominations and collaborated with them.[69] It is an undisputed fact that its social creed was drawn up by Dr. Harry F. Ward and served as the model

65. *Ibid.*, p. 2266.
66. *Ibid.*, p. 2169.
67. *Ibid.*, p. 2138.
68. *Ibid.*, p. 2092.
69. *Ibid.*, p. 2092.

for the Federal Council's Social Creed of 1908. It is also a matter of record that the Commission on the Church and Social Service was created by the Federal Council to implement this social creed. For this reason the various pronouncements of the Federal Council on social issues were in spirit often similar to, if not identical with, those issued by the Methodist Federation for Social Action.

But the infiltration of radical social and economic thought into the Federal and National Councils was not (and is not) dependent upon the influence of those men who entered the ecumenical crusade in its early years. Rather, the penetration of radical leaders was persistent and continual.[70] They easily saw that the ecumenical movement offered unusual opportunity for an alliance between radical theology on the one hand and radical social and political thought on the other. Thus the early initiative given by Harry F. Ward and others to this alliance has left its imprint upon the entire history of the Federal Council and has been even more visible in the work of the National Council since its formation in 1950.

The close cooperation between liberal theology and political liberalism was of course greatly aided by other than Communist party members. Some religious leaders were even more influential for radicalism simply because they were never members of the party. They could and did truthfully state as much before congressional committees. Not being a member of the Communist party apparently was no hindrance to Bishop Oxnam whose cooperation with radical causes is legend. Along with other well-known radicals, he signed a petition sponsored by the National Federation of Constitutional Liberties. This organization had been cited as subversive and communist by the attorney general of the United States in December 1947 and September 1948. In 1942 Attorney General Francis Biddle had described it as part of "the solar system of organizations having no connection with the Communist party, by which communists attempt to create sympathizers and supporters for their programs."[71] In its report of March 29, 1944, a special House committee made an even more emphatic statement on the nature of this group:"There can be no reasonable doubt that the National Federation of Con-

70. It is not the purpose of this chapter to summarize the connection of all the known radicals with the Communist movement. Such is not necessary to support the thesis that the Councils were subject to Communist penetration and that this was the cause of the radicalism they consistently demonstrated.

71. U.S., Congress, House, *Congressional Record*, September 24, 1942, p. 7687.

stitutional Liberties, regardless of its high sounding name, is one of the viciously subversive organizations of the Communist party."[72]

The evidence suggests that the influence of the Federal and National Councils has been wielded most effectively when used directly in the interest of radical causes by those who, for the most part, have never been known to be directly involved in the Communist party, but who have worked through auxiliary organizations. The career of Bishop G. Bromley Oxnam is an excellent example of this type of influence, which in his case was at work in the Methodist Episcopal Church and the Federal Council of Churches, of which he served a term as president. As a student of Harry F. Ward at the Boston University School of Theology Oxnam was greatly attracted to his social outlook. He became a dominant influence in the ecumenical movement as well as in Methodist circles, both as bishop and as a member of the Methodist Federation for Social Action (formerly Methodist Federation for Social Service).

The issue of radicalism in the churches heated up with an announcement by Congressman Harold Velde, chairman of the House Committee on Un-American Activities, that certain left-wing clergymen were to be investigated by his committee. The pressure on Oxnam became so great that he asked to be allowed to appear as a witness before the committee. In reply to questions by Robert Kunzig, counsel for the committee, Bishop Oxnam admitted his friendship for and cooperation with Harry F. Ward. He also insisted that he broke with Ward's political position in 1928.[73]

In a somewhat similar manner, the prominent Presbyterian minister Eugene Carson Blake, coauthor of the Blake-Pike Plan of 1960 for the unification of major Protestant denominations, has rushed to the support of many radical causes and spoken out against any efforts to protect this nation from communist infiltration into American institutions. He refused to clearly condemn the invasion of South Korea by the armies of North Korea and Red China. He also failed to effectively protest against the Soviet invasion of Budapest and the resultant slaughter of helpless Hungarians. In fact, it would be a chore to locate the time and place of his last opposition to

72. U.S., Congress, House, Committee on Un-American Activities, *Report*, 83d Cong., 2d sess., March 29, 1954, p. 50.

73. Edgar C. Bundy, *Collectivism in the Churches*. For a somewhat different view of Bishop Oxnam's relationship to communism, see the testimony of J. B. Matthews in Edgar Bundy, *Apostles of Deceit*, p. 227.

communist activity, and almost as difficult to find when and where he last defended theological, political, and economic conservatism. He also acquiesced in the dissolution of the Laymen's Committee of the National Council (some one hundred sixty members) when it vigorously protested against the attacks of the Council on the Bricker amendment and its increasingly radical attitude on social and economic questions.[74] As president of the National Council of Churches from 1954 to 1957, Blake became a powerful voice in the ecumenical movement in America and led it into even greener pastures of radical activity.[75]

Equally influencial in his support of radical causes has been John C. Bennett, professor of Christian ethics at Union Theological Seminary in New York and later president of that institution. Along with Methodist bishops Francis McConnell and G. Bromley Oxnam, Bennett signed a petition sponsored by the National Federation of Constitutional Liberties, which document had been twice cited by the attorney general of the United States as a Communist-front organization.

As early as 1948 Bennett had taken a strong stand for communism in his book *Christianity and Communism*. Admitting that communism has a darker side (a side which has become much darker since 1948), he hurriedly rushed to what he felt was its brighter side and insisted that dialectical materialism left room for higher spiritual and cultural values; Christianity, on the other hand, was "the most materialistic religion in the world"[76] To these distortions Bennett felt moved to add one more: Communist movements depend for leadership, he wrote—presumably with straight face—upon those who are moved by a sense of moral conviction. Incredibly, he then cited Marx and Lenin as examples of men of great moral conviction.[77] It would seem from these statements that Professor Bennett had concluded that Marxian communism was actually a more spiritual religion than Christianity.

One might protest that Professor Bennett's views of 1948 were merely a part of the postwar optimism that caused liberals to share

74. The author was fortunate in obtaining personal interviews with Mr. J. Howard Pew, who provided a great deal of insight into what was taking place in the National Council and the role played by Dr. Blake in its various radical policies.

75. For a summary of these various activities, see Edgar Bundy, *Apostles of Deceit*, pp. 101-9. Wheaton, Illinois, 1966.

76. John C. Bennett, *Christianity and Communism*, p. 24.

77. *Ibid.*, p. 25.

the belief popularized by Franklin Roosevelt that Russia was actually becoming democratized and, therefore, more friendly. Doubtless some liberals turned from this happy view of Russia as a result of the events of 1947 to 1950. But not John C. Bennett. The Fifth World Order Study Council held at Cleveland in 1958 gave him another opportunity to advance the far Leftist cause, under the guise of the ecumenical challenge of the church in the social, economic, and political life of the nation.[78]

The National Council and Radical Movements, 1958-1969

The close relationship between communism and the National Council emerges not only in the parallelism between its statements and the platform declarations of radical political parties, not only in the active involvement of many Council leaders in radical movements of various kinds, but also in the activities of the Council as an organization. The Cleveland conference of 1958 ushered in a new era for the National Council, one of corporate affiliation with radicalism.[79] Although this Cleveland conference was not the Council at work and must not be identified with the Council, it was sponsored by the Council's Department of International Affairs and convened by Dr. Edwin Espy. The Council cannot divest itself of the responsibility for the conference's findings and pronouncements.

The membership of the Cleveland conference was heavily studded with the names of those who were either leaders of the National Council or otherwise closely identified with its programs. Included on the list were such stalwart supporters of ecumenical radicalism as Dr. Benjamin Mays of Atlanta, Dr. Mordecai Johnson, Edith Greene (a member of the House of Representatives representing the Disciples of Christ), Dr. A. Dudley Ward of the Methodist church, Malcolm Calhoun of Richmond (representing the Presbyterian Church, U.S.), Dr. Theodore Gill, Dr. Frank P. Graham (formerly president of the University of North Carolina and later a United States representative to the United Nations), Dr. John A. Mackay (president of Princeton Theological Seminary), Dr. Gayroaud S. Wilmoore, Dr. Herman F. Reissig of the recently formed United Church

78. For an extended examination of the activities of all the Federal and National Council leaders and supporters involved in Communist projects, see Edgar Bundy, *Apostles of Deceit* and *Collectivism in the Churches*.

79. For an evaluation of the work of this conference see chapter six.

of Christ, and Dr. R. H. Espy, who would later become the general secretary of the National Council.[80]

In addition to these, the National Council sent a delegation consisting of its own officers or employees, including Dr. Roswell P. Barns, Dr. John C. Bennett, Rev. Harold Bosley, Dr. Fred Buschmeyer, Dr. Edwin T. Dahlberg, Ernest A. Gross, J. Quinter Miller, Dr. Frank W. Price, and Dr. Roy G. Ross. The United Church Women, a department of the National Council, sent a group of representatives, one of whom was Mrs. Sherwood Eddy, wife of a long-time leader in radical ecumenical affairs in America.

Of equal importance, not one well-known evangelical or conservative leader was present at the conference. Apparently great care had been taken to prevent any discordant voices from being heard. Communistic radicalism was to have its own day. The membership was handpicked to reflect a radical theology and political philosophy. As a further safeguard, the Department of International Affairs appointed a committee composed of twenty-three "experts" under the chairmanship of Dr. John C. Bennett. This committee was charged with the task of drawing up a "Message to the Churches." The special care exercised in selecting the membership of the conference and special committee yielded handsome dividends: among other things, an openly pro-communist message that was "as a whole unanimously approved on the floor."

The conference's accomplishments also included commending, for enlightenment, other publications to the members of the Council's constituent denominations. Some of these publications were openly communistic, notably *The Races of Mankind* by Professor Gene Weltfish of Columbia University. No mention was made that Professor Gene Weltfish was a notorious supporter of Communist front groups, and that she was released by Columbia University after appearing before the Senate Subcommittee of the Judiciary on Internal Security and taking the Fifth Amendment.[81]

The Cleveland conference also endorsed and recommended for use material published by Public Affairs Pamphlets of New York. Maxwell Stewart, the editor of this series, had been identified as a Communist by a sworn witness before the Internal Subcommittee of the United States Senate in 1951. He had also been identified

80. For a detailed discussion of the message of the Cleveland Conference of 1958, see chapter six.

81. For her evasive testimony, see U.S., Congress, Senate, Hearings Before the Subcommittee to Investigate the Adminstration of the Internal Security Act . . . , 82d Cong. 2d sess., September 8, 9, 10, 23, 24, 25, and October 13, 1952, pp. 232-41.

with *Amerasia*, a publication definitely left wing in outlook. At least six of its editors and contributors had been arrested by the Federal Bureau of Investigation on charges of conspiring under the Federal Espionage Act. Specifically, they had been charged with attempting to gain possession of official documents that had been classified as either top secret or restricted.[82]

The pronouncements of the Cleveland conference should dispel every doubt and convince even the most liberal reader that this meeting was dominated by the communist philosophy and that it intended to make the National Council the mouthpiece for advancing in America programs of social, economic, and political action that were Communist in nature and therefore hostile to the proclamation of the historic Gospel of Jesus Christ.

The willingness of the National Council leadership to make common cause with communism was evident not only in its economic and political pronouncements, but perhaps even more in its activities in the area of civil rights. The relationship between the civil rights movement and the communist movement is a matter of public record. But this fact did not lessen the enthusiasm of the Council for promoting civil rights in behalf of various minority groups and especially for the Negro. The Council leaders seemed to have little concern for the anti-Christian philosophy that imbued the thinking of many of the leaders of the movement. The climax came with the appearance of the *Black Manifesto* and the ensuing demands the extremists placed on the National Council just prior to the Detroit triennial of 1969. In its attempt to placate James Forman and other extremist leaders, the General Board in its reply accepted many of these demands, but in doing so also said it repudiated the communist philosophy that lay behind them.[83]

This was, to say the least, a paradoxical reply. How could the General Board repudiate the communist philosophy and yet accept the fruits of that philosophy: to wit, the demands of those groups that were definitely motivated by communism? This question was not answered by the General Board.

In Retrospect

From the beginnings of the Federal Council to the present, it is

82. For further insight into the nature and purpose of the Cleveland conference, see the very fine evaluation of it by Herbert Philbrick in Edgar Bundy, *Apostles of Deceit*, pp. 125-67.

83. See chapter seven, pp. 286-294.

evident that the ecumenical movement, despite its oft-repeated assertions that it was primarily interested in restoring the unity of the church for which Christ had prayed in John 17, was actually a carefully planned attack on the historic Gospel and mission of the church. Devotion to unity was a subterfuge. The unity that the ecumenical movement has been seeking is far removed from the burden of Christ's prayer in John 17. It is not a unity to be achieved by the power of the Holy Spirit on the basis of a common acceptance of and commitment to the whole counsel of God, that is the Scriptures. Rather, it is a specious ecclesiastical unity designed to make the church or churches a sociopolitical force in our national life, the better to proclaim the social gospel and create the socialistic kingdom of God on earth. Beyond a doubt, Walter Rauschenbusch, Harry F. Ward, and George Herron had this goal in view during the inceptive stages of the ecumenical movement.

If the real purpose of these ecumenical leaders was not succinctly delineated in the Social Creed of 1908 and the early pronouncements of the Federal Council, it certainly was not because they were not in essential agreement over the purposes of the Council or even the methods to be used. Rather was it because of the radical nature of the unity envisioned by these leaders. Public statements therefore must more often than not speak in guarded phrases that would neither offend nor alarm the Christian public, which was still essentially conservative in theology, and in political, social, and economic outlook.

Ecumenical radicalism was in the hands of gradualists, men who, like their allies, the Fabian socialists in England, were content to wait for the proper time to unveil their aims more fully. With the aid of increasing numbers of liberals and radicals occupying pulpits in this country, the membership of the various denominations was being prepared for the more complete revelation of the social gospel yet to come. World War I, however, intervened between the leaders of the movement and their goals. Sharp reaction against all forms of radicalism gripped the country immediately after the war, making the environment less than disposed to the preaching of radicalism on a grand scale.

The presence of some evangelicals in the higher echelons of the Federal Council also served to restrain the inclinations of the radical majority in its leadership. The role of this evangelical minority can easily be overemphasized. Seldom was it able to turn the tide away from radicalism in formal voting, but it was able to prevent the

Council from being as radical in its pronouncements and actions as it would otherwise have been.

The coming of the Great Depression of 1929 greatly weakened the voice of theological and political conservatism both within and without the Federal Council. The ensuing economic hardships prepared the way for the triumph of political and social radicalism under the banners of Franklin Roosevelt and his New Deal, and gave new strength to the theological liberals and radicals within most of the constituent denominations making up the membership of the Council. The results of these developments were the appearance of the openly radical Social Creed of 1932, and a growing alliance been the Federal Council leadership on one hand and the radical elements supporting the New Deal on the other.

The rise of Hitler and the increasing belligerency of both the German and Italian dictators revived popularity in pacifism as a way of life for America and in isolationism as the means for avoiding involvement in any conflict that might engulf Europe. Between 1933 and the advent of war in 1939, pacifism was the dominant issue in liberal thought; it served as an umbrella for other radical interests and activities.

The outbreak of the war in Europe in 1939 and the American involvement in the conflict in late 1941 posed a very real and embarrassing problem for the liberal and radical leaders, secular and religious. But by 1942 the liberals in the Federal Council had recovered sufficiently from the shock of seeing the nation at war again to realize that even the war could become an ally of their social, economic, and political radicalism. With great dexterity they combined the cause of peace with that of a political and economic collectivism; this *must* be the fruit of the war if this country were to achieve lasting peace at home as well as abroad. Thus the architects of peace led the Federal Council and the constituent denominations farther and farther down the broad road to the earthly kingdom of God as they championed a better understanding of and appreciation for communism and a closer alliance with Russia in the postwar period.

The plans for a new council, long in the making, were unveiled after the war. A new version of the Federal Council, the National Council would be geared to promote democratic collectivism more forcefully and openly. The Christian and non-Christian public of the United States would be sold democratic collectivism as the real meaning and implication of the historic Christian Gospel. In the

National Council the ecumenical movement would find a much more highly organized and apparently efficient vehicle for propagandizing in behalf of radicalism in all its forms. Indeed, for the next twenty years the National Council faithfully followed the collectivist goals outlined for it by the Cleveland conference of 1950.

The evidence of the National Council's increasingly radical stance after 1950 is so rich and abundant as to be irrefutable, even by the most stouthearted adherents of the ecumenical cause. Its open affiliation with radical causes even prompted boasting, as we have seen in Edwin Espy's report to the General Board.[84] Increasing boldness in behalf of radical movements alienated many evangelicals from the Council and caused divisions within established denominations. Threats of separation were heard. One actually occurred, within the Southern Presbyterian denominations.[85]

By 1969 the National Council found itself subject to the very radicalism it was espousing. The Council's timid response to the demands made upon it at its Detroit triennial made it clear to many observers that it was now the captive of these radicals and their allies. The ensuing reorganization, adopted in 1972, failed to allay the doubts of many of its friends that the National Council was struggling for survival and that its future as a useful vehicle of the ecumenical crusade had been imperiled by the very radicalism it had sponsored for over two decades.

84. See p. 280 for this report.

85. In 1973 some two hundred fifty churches and about 65,000 members left the Presbyterian Church, U.S. (Southern) to form the National Presbyterian Church in protest against the liberalism in that denomination and its refusal to sever its ties with the National Council. In 1974 the name was changed to the Presbyterian Church in America, by which time nearly three hundred and seventy five churches were in its fold.

𝔅𝔦𝔟𝔩𝔦𝔬𝔤𝔯𝔞𝔭𝔥𝔶

Primary Material

Federal Council of Churches

Annual Report, 1908–1950.
Biennial and Quadrennial Reports, 1912–1950.
Federal Council Bulletin, 1918–1950.
A Yearbook of the Church and Social Service in the United States. New York, 1916.

National Council of Churches

Matthews Collection, consisting of ten boxes of unpublished material containing minutes of the meetings of the General Board and the correspondence and reports of the executive secretaries. It is extremely valuable for the period after 1962 and is in the Presbyterian Historical Foundation, Montreat, North Carolina.

National Council of Churches Information Service. New York.

National Council Outlook, 1951–1959.

Policy Statements and Pronouncements of the National Council of Churches of Christ, 1951–1972.

The Record of the National Council of Churches, rev. ed. Wheaton, Ill., 1972.

Reports of the Triennial Assemblies, 1951–1972.

A Summary of Resolutions of the National Council of Churches of Christ, 1951–1961.

U.S. Government Sources

Congressional Record

House, Committee on Un-American Activities, *One Hundred Things You Should Know About Communism.* Washington, 1951.

Investigation of Communistic Activities in the New York City Area. Washington, 1951.

Hearings before the Committee on Un-American Activities, 82d Cong., 1st sess., House, July 7, 8, 13, 14, 1953.

Testimony of Bishop Bromley Oxnam. Washington, 1953.

Senate Documents

U.S., Congress, Senate, hearings before the Subcommittee to Investigate the Administration of the Internal Security Act and Other Internal Security Laws of the Committee on the Judicary, 82d Cong., 2d sess., September 8, 9, 10, 23, 24, 25, and October 13, 1952.

Abrams, Ray. *Preachers Present Arms.* New York, 1935.

Atkinson, H. A. *The Church and Industrial Peace.* Boston, 1914.

Brunner, E. S. *Christian Unity Movements in the United States.* New York, 1934.

———— and Douglas, P. *The Protestant Church: A Social Institution. New York,* 1935.

Bundy, Edgar C. *Apostles of Deceit.* Wheaton, Ill., 1966.

————. *Collectivism in the Churches.* Wheaton, Ill., 1961.

Carter, Paul. *The Decline and Revival of the Social Gospel: Social and Polit-*

ical Liberalism in American Protestant Churches, 1920-1940. Ithaca, New York, 1954.

Cauthen, Kenneth. The Impact of American Religious Liberalism. New York, 1962.

Cavert, Samuel M., American Churches in the Ecumenical Movement, 1900-1968. New York, 1968.

_____, ed. The Church and Industrial Reconstruction. New York, 1922.

_____ . Church Cooperation and Unity in America: An Historical Review. New York, 1970.

_____ . The Church Faces the World. New York, 1929.

_____ , ed. The Churches Allied for a Common Task, Report of the Third Quadrennial of the Federal Council of Churches of Christ in America, 1916–1920. New York, 1921.

Craig, Clarence Tucker. The One Church in the Light of the New Testament. Nashville, 1951.

Dasken, Arthur. "The National Council of Churches and Our Foreign Policy." Religion and Life 24 (1955).

Dombrowski, James. The Early Days of Christian Socialism in America. New York, 1936.

Faunce, W. H. P. Christian Principles Essential to a New World Order. New York, 1919.

Fey, Harold E. Ecumenical Advance: A History of the Ecumenical Movement, vol. 2, 1948–68. New York, 1969.

Goodall, Norman. The Ecumenical Movement: What It Is and What It Does, 2d ed. New York, 1963.

_____ . Ecumenical Progress: A Decade of Change in the Ecumenical Movement, 1961–1971. New York, 1972.

Gulick, Sidney L. The Christian Crusade for a Warless World. New York, 1922.

_____ . The Fight for Peace. New York, 1915.

_____ . and MacFarland, Charles S. The Church and International Relations, Report of the Commission on Peace and Arbitration, pts. 1–4. New York, 1917.

Handy, Robert T., ed. The Social Gospel in America. New York, 1966.

Hopkins, C. H. The Rise of the Social Gospel in American Protestantism. New Haven, 1946.

Horton, Walter D. Christian Theology: An Ecumenical Approach. New York, 1955.

Hutchinson, John A. We Are Not Divided: A Critical History of the Federal Council of Churches of Christ in America. New York, 1941.

Johnson, F. E. *Church and Society.* New York, 1935.

——— . *The Social Gospel and Personal Religion.* New York, 1922.

——— . *The Social Gospel Re-Examined.* New York, 1940.

——— . *The Social Work of the Churches.* New York, 1930.

Loetscher, Lefferts. *The Broadening Church, A Study of Theological Issues in the Presbyterian Church Since 1869.* Philadelphia, 1954.

Lowell, C. Stanley. *Ecumenical Mirage.* Grand Rapids, 1968.

McConnell, F. J. *Democratic Christianity.* New York, 1919.

MacFarland, C. S. *Christian Cooperation and World Redemption,* vol. 5 in Library of Christian Cooperation. New York, 1917.

——— . *The Christian Ministry and the Social Order.* New Haven, 1909.

——— , ed. *Christian Unity at Work,* 2d ed. New York, 1913.

——— . *Christian Unity in Practice and Prophecy.* New York, 1933.

——— . *Christian Unity in the Making: The First Twenty-Five Years of the Federal Council of Churches of Christ in America, 1905–1930.* New York, 1948.

——— . *The Churches of the Federal Council.* New York, 1916.

——— . *Pioneer for Peace Through Religion.* New York, 1946.

——— . *The Progress of Church Federation.* New York, 1917.

——— and Gulick, Sidney. *The Churches of Christ in the Federal Council,* vol. 1 in Library of Christian Cooperation. New York, 1917.

McNeill, J. Y. *Unitive Protestantism.* New York, 1917.

Mathews, Shailer. *Atonement and Social Process.* New York, 1930.

——— . *Christianity and Social Process.* New York, 1934.

——— . *The Church and the Changing Order.* New York, 1908.

——— . *The Faith of Modernism.* New York, 1924.

——— . *The Gospel and Modern Man.* New York, 1910.

Miller, Robert M. *American Protestanism and Social Issues, 1919–1939.* Chapel Hill, N. C., 1959.

Myers, J. *Churches in Social Action.* New York, 1935.

National Council of Churches. *Christian Faith in Action.* New York, 1951.

Porter, K. and Johnson, D. B. *National Party Platforms, 1840–1964.* Urbana and London, 1966.

Rauschenbusch, Walter. *Christianity and the Social Crisis.* New York, 1907.

——— . *Christianizing the Social Order.* New York, 1912.

_____ . *A Theology for the Social Gospel*. New York, 1917.

Roy, Ralph. *Communism and the Churches*. New York, 1960.

Sanderson, Ross W. *Church Cooperation in the United States*. Hartford, 1960.

Sanford, Elias B. *Church Federation*. New York, 1906.

_____ . *Origin and History of the Federal Council of Churches of Christ in America*. Hartford, 1916.

Singer, C. Gregg. *A Theological Interpretation of American History*. Nutley, N.J. 1964.

Slosser, G. J. *Christian Unity*. New York, 1929.

Tippy, W. M. *The Church and the Great War*. New York, 1918.

Trott, N. and Sanderson, R. *What Church People Think About Social and Economic Issues*. New York, 1937.

Ward, Harry F. Introduction to *A Yearbook of the Church and Social Service in the United States*. New York, 1916.

Index

375

McCarthy: Committee (Senate), 243, 244; "era," 244; Sen. Joseph, 244, 328
McCarthyism, 341
McConnell, Bishop Francis J., 29–31, 55, 61, 64–65, 81, 117, 362
MacFarland, Rev. Charles S., 29, 33, 34, 65, 84
Mack, Dr. S. Franklin, 232, 233
Mackay, Dr. John A., 363
Mackay, John R., 40
McMichael, Rev. Jack, 359
Manchuria, 71
Manifesto to the White Christians and Jewish Synagogues in the United States of America and All Other Racist Institutions, 286–288, 289, 290, 291, 292, 293, 294, 310, 311, 325, 352, 365
Marriage and home life, 77–79, 159, 261–264
Marshall Plan, 143, 144
Martin, Bishop William C., 191, 202, 242
Martin, Speaker Joseph, 144
Martin Luther King Sunday, 294
Marx, Karl, 135, 270, 284, 330, 335, 337, 341, 345, 346, 347, 351, 362
Marxism-Leninism, 356
Materialism, dialectical, 338, 353, 362
Mathews, Dean Shailer, 31, 35, 36, 38, 84
Maverick, Rep. Maury, 125
Mays, Dr. Benjamin, 363
Medicare, 222
Men and Religious Forward Movement, 37
Mennonite General Conference, 46, 51
Mennonites, 46
Merrill, William P., 40
"Message to the Churches," 204, 277, 364; (on Vietnam), 251, 252, 253
"Message to the Churches and Economic Life," 244
"Message to the Churches of Christ in the U.S.A.," 196, 245, 246
"Message to the Churches on World Peace," 70
"Message to the Member Churches," 238
Methodist Church, 16, 17, 30, 119, 180, 188, 322, 359, 363; General Conference, 266
Methodist Council of Bishops, 242
Methodist Episcopal Church, 361
Methodist Episcopal Church (South), 21; General Conference, 58
Methodist Faculty Forum, 303
Methodist Federation for Social Action, 84, 330, 357, 359, 360, 361
Methodist Federation for Social Service, 135, 361
Methodist Protestant Church, 117
Methodist Social Creed, 55, 357
Michigan, University of, 202
Middle East, 194, 245
Millenialism, 13
Miller, J. Irwin, 275, 305, 318–320
Miller, J. Quinter, 364
Missionary Movement of the United States and Canada, 181
Mississippi Project, 279, 294
Monroe Doctrine, 70
Moore, Bishop Arthur, 113
"Moral Aspects of Birth Control," 78

"Moral Responsibility and United States Power," 145–146
Morrison, Charles Clayton, 179
Motion pictures, criticism of, 110–111
Mueller, Bishop Reuben, 278, 321–322
Munich Pact (1938), 334
Munitions industry, investigation of, 98–100
Muste, A. J., 200
Myers, James, 109

Nathan, Dr. Otto, 354
Nation, 148, 191, 335
National Association of Radio and Television Broadcasters, Television Code of, 233
National Baptist Convention, 74
National Black Economic Development Conference, 286, 287, 288, 289, 294
National Broadcasting Company, 81–82, 232, 234, 302
National Catholic Welfare Council, 73, 274
National Christian Missions program, 115
National Christian Student Federation, 302
National CIO Community Services Committee, 207
National Commission on Marriage and the Home, 77–78
National Conference of Black Churchmen, *passim* 290–294
National Conference of Catholic Bishops, 308; Ecumenical Commission of, 307
National Conference of Church Leaders on Family Life, 160
National Conference on Church and State, 278
National Conference on Religion and Race, 274
National Conference on Social Welfare: First, 213; Second, 213
National Conference on the Church and Economic Life, Fourth, 206
National Conference on the Churches and World Peace, 102
National Council of Churches, 29, 30, 158, 162, 164, 166, 175; Anti-Poverty Task Force, 268; Boston Triennial (1954), 235–236; Broadcasting and Film Commission, 231–232, 233, 234, 300–302, 318; Brower Task Force, 316; Christian Education, Division of, 183, 228, 229, 303; Christian Higher Education, Division of, 227, 228; Christian Life and Mission, Division of, 268–269; Christian Life and Work, Division of, 183, 198, 258–259, 349; Christian Unity, Division of, 308, 309; Church and Culture, Department of, 268; Church and Economic Life, Committee on, 261; Church and Economic Life, Department of the, 202, 203, 205, 207, 218, 260–261; Church and Society, Division of, 318; Church Renewal, Department of, 268; constitution of, 182; Cooperative Curriculum Project, 228; Crisis in the Nation, Special Committee on, 284–285; criticism of, 239–247, 250, 318–326; Dallas Triennial (1972), 317–318, 325; Denver Triennial (1952), 235; Denver Triennial (1963), 264, 274, 302, 304, 318–320; departments of, 183; Detroit Triennial

Sanford, Elias B., 19, 21, 29
Schaff, Dr. Philip, 21–22
Scherer, Paul, 113, 115
Schools: dual enrollment in, 298–299; segregated, 297
Segregation: Negro, 132, 152–153, 155–156, 207–209, 210–212, 274, 342; school, 297
Selective Service System, 200
Sharp, Dudley, 354
Sherrill, Bishop Henry Knox, 181, 186, 202, 207, 236, 241, 242
Silvey, Ted, 207
"Six Pillars of Peace," 136–137, 336
Sizoo, Joseph, 115, 125
Sloan, Harold Paul, 115
Smith, Alfred E., 76
Smith, Dr. John Coventry, 315
Smith, Fred B., 38
Smith, Rev. Alson J., 359
Smith-McCarran Act, 341, 342–343
Social Creed of 1932, 71, 75, 76, 79, 82, 83, 89, 90–93, 95, 98, 107, 110, 111, 117, 124, 126, 131, 134, 152, 327, 332, 367
Social Creed of the Churches (1908), 21, 23–25, 27, 31, 49, 55–56, 60, 66, 72, 74, 79, 80, 88, 92, 177, 327, 329, 330, 332, 359, 366
"Social Ideal of the Churches, The," 65
Social legislation. See Industrial Relations
Social reform, 66–67, 93–98, 158–161
Social welfare, 206–207, 212–217, 264–273. See also Industrial relations
Socialism, 12, 25, 60–61, 67, 72, 114, 133, 135, 180, 187, 203, 220, 330, 332, 336, 337, 339, 340, 343–344, 346, 347, 349, 357, 358
Socialist Labor Party, 328, 329, 330, 332, 334, 335, 337, 344–345, 347, 348, 349, 350, 352
Socialist Party, 329, 330, 332, 334, 335, 337, 338, 343, 344, 346–348
Socialist Workers Party, 345, 349, 350, 352
Society of Jesus, 307
Sockman, Dr. Ralph, 82, 115, 181, 232, 302
Southeast Asia, 251, 252, 253, 254, 258
Southern Baptist Church, 188
Southern Baptist Convention, 181, 237, 309, 310
Southern Methodist Church, 117
Southern Presbyterian Church, 44, 50, 51, 55, 58, 59, 61, 83, 169, 368; General Assembly, 170. See also Presbyterian Church, U.S. (South)
Southern Presbyterian Journal, 188
Sovereignty, definition of, 43
Soviet Russia, 70, 109, 140, 141, 175, 190–191, 195, 200, 212, 243, 244–245, 255, 256, 270–271, 281, 307, 325, 330, 332, 334, 335, 338, 339, 341, 345, 347, 361, 363, 367; cooperation with, 140–146, 187, 192–194, 200–201, 338
Speer, Robert E., 28, 59
Spike, Dr. Robert, 303
"Spiritual Challenge of the Economic Crisis, The," 90
Stalin, Josef V., 334, 335
Stamm, Bishop Frederick K., 115
Standard, 27

Standley, Admiral, 125
Steel strike (1959–60), 205–206
Stelzle, Charles, 72
Stewart, Maxwell, 364
Stimson, Henry L., 71
Stone, David, 324
Strikes, investigation of, 72, 109
Strong, Josiah, 18
Student Volunteer Movement, 227, 302
Supreme Court, U.S., 157, 158, 161, 208, 209, 211–212, 223, 224, 269, 273, 281, 334, 343
Sweatt v. Painter, 157, 158
Swedenborgian Church, General Convention, 169
Synagogue Council of America, 274, 308
Syrian Orthodox Church, 123

Taft, Charles P., 202
Taft-Hartley Labor Act of 1947, 260, 323, 341, 344, 351
Taiwan, 254
Taxation, double, 298, 299
Taylor, Rev. Alva, 84
Templeton, Rev. Charles B., 230
Ten-Year Non-Aggression Pact, 334
Texas, University of, 157, 158
Textile Strike, The, 110
Theology, American, and transcendentalism, 12–13
Theology for the Social Gospel, A, 17
Third Internationale, 63
Thompson, William, 282
"Thy Kingdom Come," 232
Times (London), 136
Tippy, Dr. Worth M., 57, 61–62
Tito, Josip B., 199
Tittle, Ernest Fremont, 61
"To Christians of All Lands," 100–101
Totalitarianism, 101, 109, 129
Transcendentalism, 12, 13, 14
Trueblood, D. Elton, 131
Truitt, George W., 113
Truman, Harry S., 139, 142, 156, 161, 190, 208, 212, 238–239, 280, 340, 341, 351
Tucker, Henry St. George, 154

Ukrainian Orthodox Church, 168
Un-American Activities, House Committee on, 173, 200, 242, 244, 246, 343, 353, 354, 358–359, 361
Underdeveloped nations, 192, 204–205
Unemployment, 66, 107, 219–220, 332
UNESCO, 142
Union, church, 234–239
Union Theological Seminary, 135, 202, 236, 357, 358, 362
Unitarianism, 85; new type of, 12, 13
Unitarians, 56, 57, 169
United Automobile Workers, 207; Clergy Advisory Committee, 205
United Church of Canada, 123
United Church of Christ, 303, 318, 363–364; General Synod, 266

383